MOUNT MARY COLLEGE LIBRARY
Milwaukee, Wisconsin 53222

The Aesthetic Point of View

MONROE C. BEARDSLEY

The Aesthetic Point of View

Selected Essays

Edited by
MICHAEL J. WREEN
and
DONALD M. CALLEN

Cornell University Press
ITHACA AND LONDON

Copyright © 1982 by Cornell University Press

All rights reserved. Except for brief quotations in a review, this book, or parts thereof, must not be reproduced in any form without permission in writing from the publisher. For information address Cornell University Press, 124 Roberts Place, Ithaca, New York 14850.

First published 1982 by Cornell University Press.
Published in the United Kingdom by Cornell University Press Ltd., Ely House, 37 Dover Street, London W1X 4HQ.

International Standard Book Number (cloth) 0-8014-1250-1
International Standard Book Number (paper) 0-8014-9880-5
Library of Congress Catalog Card Number 82-71601
Printed in the United States of America

Librarians: Library of Congress cataloging information appears on the last page of the book.

The paper in this book is acid-free, and meets the guidelines for permanence and durability of the Committee on Production Guidelines for Book Longevity of the Council on Library Resources.

Contents

FOREWORD 7

ACKNOWLEDGMENTS 11

I. *The Aesthetic*

1. The Aesthetic Point of View 15
2. The Discrimination of Aesthetic Enjoyment 35
3. Intrinsic Value 46
4. The Aesthetic Problem of Justification 65
5. Aesthetic Experience Regained 77
6. What Is an Aesthetic Quality? 93
7. Aesthetic Welfare, Aesthetic Justice, and Educational Policy 111
8. Is Art Essentially Institutional? 125

II. *Art and Art Criticism*

9. What Are Critics For? 147
10. The Limits of Critical Interpretation 165
11. Intentions and Interpretations: A Fallacy Revived 188
12. The Generality of Critical Reasons 208
13. The Relevance of History to Art Criticism 219

III. *Creativity and Metaphor*

14. The Creation of Art 239
15. The Metaphorical Twist 263

IV. Some Persistent Issues in Aesthetics: Further Reflections

	Introduction	283
16.	Aesthetic Experience	285
17.	Redefining Art	298
18.	Critical Evaluation	316
19.	The Relevance of Reasons in Art Criticism	332
20.	Art and Its Cultural Context	352

BIBLIOGRAPHY OF WRITINGS IN AESTHETICS BY MONROE C. BEARDSLEY — 371

INDEX — 379

Foreword

IN 1958 Monroe Beardsley published his *Aesthetics: Problems in the Philosophy of Criticism*, and in the ensuing years the book has become something of a classic in the philosophy of art, having acquired almost the status of a reference work. More than any other single text, it set analytic aesthetics on its feet and made the philosophy of art a respectable area for contemporary Anglo-American philosophers to work in. But although a systematic and well-argued philosophy of art is presented in *Aesthetics*, that book, like every other in its field, constituted no last word, no final judgment in aesthetics. Objections were bound to be raised (and were raised) and needed to be answered; a number of topics would have benefited from fuller treatment; new issues were sure to arise and new concepts to be developed; advances would be made in neighboring areas of philosophy, such as the philosophy of language and the theory of value, and in neighboring disciplines, such as psychology, literary criticism, and art history. All this was duly realized by Beardsley; he has never rested content with the views developed in *Aesthetics*, but has sought to rebut or to incorporate criticism, and to comment on, to extend, or to criticize the newer ideas in or surrounding aesthetic theory. The present book, in fact, is ample testimony to his willingness to keep an open mind, to stay abreast of the latest developments in several fields, and to meet criticism honestly, by modifying or by abandoning earlier views when necessary.

The essays collected here were written at various times, for various occasions, and with various purposes in mind. A few were written in the early 1960s, several since 1980. But despite the span of time and the diversity of purpose, there is a unity to these essays and indeed to all of Beardsley's work in aesthetics. As he himself says in his Introduction to Part IV of this book, the central thread running through his work is the articulation and elaboration of a distinctly aesthetic point of view. Realizing this, we have tried to arrange the essays of the present volume accordingly.

Part I is concerned with the nature and scope of the aesthetic, and with the implications—philosophical, social, educational, and otherwise—of taking the aesthetic point of view. "The Aesthetic Point of View," the paper that opens this volume, is, in a sense, a short general introduction to the philosophy of art that is advanced and defended in the succeeding pages. Here the notion of the aesthetic point of view is explicated and its implications are explored. Other related concepts are examined or defended in later papers—aesthetic enjoyment in Essay 2, aesthetic experience in Essay 5, and aesthetic qualities in Essay 6. Value-related issues, in particular the usefulness of the concept of intrinsic value, the justification of the production and enjoyment of objects of aesthetic value, and the proper distribution of and education for aesthetic goods, are discussed in Essays 3, 4, and 7 respectively. Part I ends with "Is Art Essentially Institutional?," a critical analysis of the now very popular institutional theory of art and a bridge to Part II.

The nature of art and art criticism is the focus of Part II, with the interconnected questions of the legitimate aims, scope, and methods of criticism. Essay 11, a paper never before published, is Beardsley's first sustained treatment of the intentional fallacy since his famous joint paper with W. K. Wimsatt of 1946. Essays 12 and 13 might well be considered companion pieces, for they too are concerned with determining the proper canons of art criticism.

Metaphor and creativity are the topics discussed in Part III, which, we freely admit, is somewhat of a miscellany section. Metaphor is of particular importance, however, since its analysis, besides being of intrinsic interest, is bound to affect the theory of interpretation. And creativity, which plays a central role in some philosophies of art, is here given ample empirical study, but assigned a considerably less prominent place in the philosophy of art.

Part IV was written specially for this volume, and consists of some of Beardsley's most recent thoughts on five basic issues. Topics discussed in other essays in this volume are brought up to date in this section, in the light of developments both within and without the philosophy of art. Never one to be preoccupied with defending his own earlier views or with criticizing the views of others, Beardsley emphasizes the positive in this section, and attempts to extract what he feels is worthwhile from the views of others, to build on their and his accounts, and to make a definite contribution to the issues discussed. As for subject matter, the titles of the essays—"Aesthetic Experience," "Redefining Art," "Critical Evaluation," "The Relevance of Reasons in Art Criticism," and "Art and Its Cultural Context"—speak for themselves.

Encomiums have thus far been kept to a minimum, but if matters remained so, this Foreword would be inaccurate and somewhat less than fair. These are excellent essays, among the best that philosophy has to offer. Beardsley's writing is unusually graceful, his tone unusually inviting, his judgment unusually impartial and balanced. There are no tricks in these essays, no pretentions, no rancorous polemics, only straightforward, vigorous—and rigorous—philosophy, with the added sparkle of lively examples and an occasional dash of humor. We hope that you will enjoy these essays and find them as stimulating, and maybe even as convincing, as we do.

MICHAEL J. WREEN

Philadelphia College of Art

DONALD M. CALLEN

Bowling Green State University

Acknowledgments

FOURTEEN of the essays in this volume have been previously published: "The Aesthetic Point of View" in *Perspectives in Education, Religion, and the Arts*, ed. Howard Kiefer and Milton Munitz (Albany: SUNY Press, 1970), pp. 219–37; "The Discrimination of Aesthetic Enjoyment" in *The British Journal of Aesthetics* 3 (1963):291–300; "Intrinsic Value" in *Philosophy and Phenomenological Research* 26 (1965):1–17; "The Aesthetic Problem of Justification" in *The Journal of Aesthetic Education* 1 (1966):29–39; "Aesthetic Experience Regained" in *The Journal of Aesthetics and Art Criticism* 28 (1969):3–11; "What Is an Aesthetic Quality?" in *Theoria* 39 (1973): 50–70; "Aesthetic Welfare, Aesthetic Justice, and Educational Policy" in *The Journal of Aesthetic Education* 7 (1973):49–61; "Is Art Essentially Institutional?" in *Culture and Art*, ed. Lars Aagaard-Mogensen (Atlantic Highlands, N.J.: Humanities Press, 1976), pp. 194–209; "What Are Critics For?" in *Susquehanna University Studies* 10 (1978):239–50; "The Limits of Critical Interpretation" in *Art and Philosophy: A Symposium*, ed. Sidney Hook (New York: New York University Press, 1966), pp. 61–87, © 1966 by New York University; "The Generality of Critical Reasons" in *The Journal of Philosophy* 59 (1962):477–86; "The Relevance of History to Art Criticism" in *History as a Tool in Critical Interpretation,* ed. Thomas F. Rugh and Erin R. Silva (Provo: Brigham Young University Press, 1978), pp. 1–18; "The Creation of Art" in *The Journal of Aesthetics and Art Criticism* 23 (1965):291–304; "The Metaphorical Twist" in *Philosophy and Phenomenological Research* 22 (1962):293–307. In addition, four lines from "The Motive for Metaphor," from *The Collected Poems of Wallace Stevens*, by Wallace Stevens (New York: Alfred A. Knopf, 1955), are quoted in "The Metaphorical Twist." We are grateful to these journals and presses for permission to reprint or to quote these materials.

Special thanks are also owed to specific individuals for help in bringing this text to print. Anna May Wreen provided nigh-on impeccable typing and proofreading, and Bernhard Kendler and Barbara H. Salazar of Cornell University Press were patient and courteous beyond the call of duty. Last and greatest thanks must go to Monroe Beardsley himself, for his encouragement and aid.

M. J. W.
D. M. C.

Part I

The Aesthetic

1: *The Aesthetic Point of View*

I

THERE has been a persistent effort to discover the uniquely aesthetic component, aspect, or ingredient in whatever is or is experienced. Unlike some other philosophical quarries, the object of this chase has not proved as elusive as the snark, the Holy Grail, or Judge Crater—the hunters have returned not empty-handed, but overburdened. For they have found a rich array of candidates for the basically and essentially aesthetic:

> aesthetic experience   aesthetic objects
> aesthetic value   aesthetic concepts
> aesthetic enjoyment   aesthetic situations
> aesthetic satisfaction

Confronted with such trophies, we cannot easily doubt that there *is* something peculiarly aesthetic to be found in the world of our experience; yet its exact location and its categorial status remain in question. This is my justification for conducting yet another raid on the ineffable with the help of a different concept, one in the contemporary philosophical style.

II

When the conservationist and the attorney for Con Edison argue their conflicting cases before a state commission that is deciding whether a nuclear power plant shall be built beside the Hudson River, we can say they do not merely disagree; they regard that power plant from different points of view. When the head of the Histadrut Publishing House refused to publish the novel *Exodus* in Israel, he said: "If it is to be read as history, it is inaccurate. If it is to be read as literature, it is vulgar."¹

And Maxim Gorky reports a remark that Lenin once made to him:

> "I know nothing that is greater than [Beethoven's] *Appassionata*. I would like to listen to it every day. A marvellous, super-human music. I always say with pride—a naive pride perhaps: What miracles human beings can perform!" Then screwing his eyes [Lenin] added, smiling sadly, "But I can't listen to music too often; it affects your nerves. One wants to say stupid nice things and stroke on the head the people who can create such beauty while living in this vile hell. And now you must not stroke anyone on the head: you'll have your hands beaten off. You have to hit them on the head without mercy, though our ideal is not to use violence against anyone. Hmm, hmm,—an infernally cruel job we have."²

In each of these examples, it seems plausible to say that one of the conflicting points of view is a peculiarly aesthetic one: that of the conservationist troubled by threats to the Hudson's scenic beauty; that of the publisher who refers to reading *Exodus* "as literature"; that of Lenin, who appears to hold that we ought to adopt the political (rather than the aesthetic) point of view toward Beethoven's sonata, because of the unfortunate political consequences of adopting the aesthetic point of view.

If the notion of the aesthetic point of view can be made clear, it should be useful from the philosophical point of view. The first philosophical use is in mediating certain kinds of dispute. To

---

1. *New Republic*, January 16, 1961, p. 23. Compare Brendan Gill, in *The New Yorker*, March 5, 1966:

> It is a lot easier to recommend attendance at "The Gospel According to St. Matthew" as an act of penitential piety during the Lenten season than it is to praise the movie as a movie. Whether or not the life and death of Our Lord is the greatest story ever told, it is so far from being merely a story that we cannot deal with it in literary terms (if we could, I think we would have to begin by saying that in respect to construction and motivation it leaves much to be desired); our difficulty is enormously increased when we try to pass judgment on the story itself once it has been turned into a screenplay.

2. From Gorky's essay on Lenin, in his *Collected Works* (Moscow, 1950), 17:39–40. My colleague Olga Lang called my attention to this passage and translated it for me. Compare Gorky, *Days with Lenin* (New York, 1932), p. 52. *Time* (April 30, 1965, p. 50) reported that the Chinese Communists had forbidden the performance of Beethoven's works because they "paralyze one's revolutionary fighting will." A Chinese bacteriologist, in a letter to a Peking newspaper, wrote that after listening to Beethoven, he "began to have strange illusions about a world filled with friendly love."

understand a particular point of view, we must envision its alternatives. Unless there can be more than one point of view toward something, the concept breaks down. Consider, for example, the case of architecture. The classic criteria of Vitruvius were stated tersely by Sir Henry Wotton in these words: "Well-building hath three conditions: Commodity, Firmness, and Delight." Commodity is function: that it makes a good church or house or school. Firmness is construction: that the building holds itself up. Suppose we were comparing a number of buildings to see how well built they are, according to these "conditions." We would find some that are functionally effective, structurally sound, and visually attractive. We would find others—old worn-out buildings or new suburban shacks—that are pretty poor in each of these departments. But also we would find that the characteristics vary independently over a wide range; that some extremely solid old bank buildings have Firmness (they are knocked down at great cost) without much Commodity or Delight, that some highly delightful buildings are functionally hopeless, that some convenient bridges collapse.

Now suppose we are faced with one of these mixed structures, and invited to say whether it is a good building, or how good it is. Someone might say the bank is very well built, because it is strong; another might reply that nevertheless its ugliness and inconvenience make it a very poor building. Someone might say that the bridge couldn't have been much good if it collapsed; but another might reply that it was a most excellent bridge, while it lasted—that encomium cannot be taken from it merely because it did not last long.

Such disputes may well make us wonder—as Geoffrey Scott wonders in his book *The Architecture of Humanism*[3]—whether these "conditions" belong in the same discussion. Scott says that to lump them together is confusing: it is to "force on architecture an unreal unity of aim," since they are "incommensurable virtues." For clarity in architectural discussion, then, we might separate the three criteria, and say that they arise in connection with three different points of view—the practical, the engineering, and the aesthetic. In this way, the notion of a point of view is introduced to break up a dispute into segments that seem likely to be more manageable. Instead of asking one question—whether this is a

---

3. (New York, 1954), p. 15, where he quotes Wotton.

good building—we divide it into three. Considering the building from the aesthetic point of view, we ask whether it is a good work of architecture; from the engineering point of view, whether it is a good structure; and from the practical point of view, whether it is a good machine for living.

Thus one way of clarifying the notion of a point of view would be in terms of the notion, of being *good of a kind*.[4] We might say that to adopt the aesthetic point of view toward a building is to classify it as belonging to a species of aesthetic objects—namely, works of architecture—and then to take an interest in whether or not it is a *good* work of architecture. Of course, when an object belongs to one obvious and notable kind, and we judge it in relation to that kind, the "point of view" terminology is unnecessary. We wouldn't ordinarily speak of considering music from a musical point of view, because it wouldn't occur to us that someone might regard it from a political point of view. In the same way, it would be natural to speak of considering whiskey from a medical point of view but not of considering penicillin from a medical point of view. This shows that the "point of view" terminology is implicitly rejective: it is a device for setting aside considerations advanced by others (such as that the bridge will fall) in order to focus attention on the set of considerations that *we* wish to emphasize (such as that the sweep and soar of the bridge are a joy to behold).

The "point of view" terminology, however, is more elastic than the "good of its kind" terminology. To consider a bridge or music or sculpture as an aesthetic object is to consider it from the aesthetic point of view. But what about a mountain, a sea shell, or a tiger? These are neither musical compositions, paintings, poems, nor sculptures. A sea shell cannot be *good* sculpture if it is not sculpture at all. But evidently we can adopt the aesthetic point of view toward these things. In fact, some aesthetic athletes (or athletic aesthetes) have claimed the ability to adopt the aesthetic

---

4. In this discussion, I have been stimulated by an unpublished paper by J. O. Urmson, "Good of a Kind and Good from a Point of View," which I saw in manuscript in 1961 and which was later published as Chapter 9 of *The Emotive Theory of Ethics* (New York, 1968). I should also like to thank him for comments on an earlier version of his paper. Compare his note added to "What Makes a Situation Aesthetic?" in *Philosophy Looks at the Arts*, ed. Joseph Margolis (New York, 1962), p. 26. I also note that John Hospers has some interesting remarks on the aesthetic point of view in "The Ideal Aesthetic Observer," *British Journal of Aesthetics* 2 (1962):99–111.

point of view toward anything at all—toward *The Story of O* (this is what Elliot Fremont-Smith has called "beyond pornography"), toward a garbage dump, toward the murders of three civil-rights workers in Philadelphia, Mississippi. (This claim has been put to a severe test by some of our more far-out sculptors.) Perhaps even more remarkable is the feat recently performed by those who viewed the solemn installation of an "invisible sculpture" behind the Metropolitan Museum of Art. The installation consisted in digging a grave-size hole and filling it in again. "It is really an underground sculpture," said its conceiver, Claes Oldenburg. "I think of it as the dirt being loosened from the sides in a certain section of Central Park."[5] The city's architectural consultant, Sam Green, commented on the proceedings: "This is a conceptual work of art and is as much valid as something you can actually see. Everything is art if it is chosen by the artist to be art. You can say it is good art or bad art, but you can't say it isn't art. Just because you can't see a statue doesn't mean that it isn't there." This, of course, is but one of countless examples of the current tendency to stretch the boundaries of the concept of "art."

The second philosophical use of the notion of the aesthetic point of view is to provide a broad concept of art that might be helpful for certain purposes. We might say: "A work of art (in the broad sense) is any perceptual or intentional object that is deliberately regarded from the aesthetic point of view."[6] Here, "regarding" would have to include looking, listening, reading, and similar acts of attention, and also what I call "exhibiting"—picking up an object and placing it where it readily permits such attention, or presenting the object to persons acting as spectators.

III

What, then, is the aesthetic point of view? I propose the following: To adopt the aesthetic point of view with regard to X is to take an interest in whatever aesthetic value X may possess.

I ask myself what I am doing in adopting a particular point of view, and acting toward an object in a way that is appropriate to that point of view; and, so far as I can see, it consists in searching out a corresponding value in the object, to discover whether any

---

5. *New York Times*, October 2, 1967, p. 55.
6. Compare my "Comments" on Stanley Cavell's paper in *Art, Mind, and Religion*, ed. W. H. Capitan and D. D. Merrill (Pittsburgh, 1967), esp. pp. 107–9.

of it is present. Sometimes it is to go farther: to cash in on that value, to realize it, to avail myself of it. All this searching, seeking, and, if possible, realizing I subsume under the general phrase "taking an interest in." To listen to Beethoven's *Appassionata* with pleasure and a sense that it is "marvelous, superhuman music" is to seek—and find—aesthetic value in it. To read the novel *Exodus* "as literature," and be repelled because it is "vulgar," is (I take it) to seek aesthetic value in it but not find very much of it. And when Geoffrey Scott makes his distinction between different ways of regarding a building, and between that "constructive integrity in fact" which belongs under Firmness and that "constructive vividness in appearance" which is a source of architectural Delight, he adds that "their value in the building is of a wholly disparate kind";[7] in short, the two points of view, the engineering and the aesthetic, involve two kinds of value.

This proposed definition of "aesthetic point of view" will not, as it stands, fit all of the ordinary uses of this phrase. There is a further complication. I am thinking of a remark by John Hightower, Executive Director of the New York State Council on the Arts, about the Council's aim to "encourage some sort of aesthetic standards." He said, "There are lots of laws that unconsciously inhibit the arts. Architecture is the most dramatic example. Nobody has looked at the laws from an aesthetic point of view."[8] And I am thinking of a statement in the *Yale Alumni Magazine*[9] that the Yale City Planning Department was undertaking "a pioneering two-year research project to study highway environment from an aesthetic point of view." I suppose the attention in these cases was not on the supposed aesthetic value of the laws or of the present "highway environment," but rather on the aesthetic value that might be achieved by changes in these things. Perhaps that is why these examples speak of *"an* aesthetic point of view" rather than *"the* aesthetic point of view." And we could, if we wished,

---

7. Scott, *Architecture of Humanism*, p. 89; compare pp. 90–91, 95. In case it may be thought that architects who have the highest respect for their materials might repudiate my distinction, I quote Pier Luigi Nervi (in his Charles Eliot Norton lectures): "There does not exist, either in the past or in the present, a work of architecture which is accepted and recognized as excellent from the aesthetic point of view which is not also excellent from a technical point of view" (from *Aesthetics and Technology in Building* [Cambridge, Mass., 1965], p. 2). Though arguing that one kind of value is a necessary (but not a sufficient) condition of the other, Nervi clearly assumes that there is a distinguishable aesthetic point of view.

8. *New York Times*, April 2, 1967, p. 94.

9. December 1966, p. 20.

make use of this verbal distinction in a broadened definition: To adopt *an* aesthetic point of view with regard to X is to take an interest in whatever aesthetic value that X may possess or *that is obtainable by means of X.*

I have allowed the phrase "adopting the aesthetic point of view" to cover a variety of activities. One of them is judging: To judge X from the aesthetic point of view is to estimate the aesthetic value of X. Those who are familiar with Paul Taylor's treatment of points of view in his book *Normative Discourse* will note how the order I find in these concepts differs from the one he finds. His account applies only to judging, and is therefore too narrow to suit me. It also has, I think, another flaw. He holds that "taking a certain point of view is nothing but adopting certain canons of reasoning as the framework within which value judgments are to be justified; the canons of reasoning define the point of view. . . . We have already said that a value judgment is a moral judgment if it is made from the moral point of view."[10]

Thus we could ask of Taylor: What is an aesthetic value judgment? He would reply: It is one made from the aesthetic point of view. And which are those? They are the ones justified by appeal to certain "canons of reasoning," and more particularly the "rules of relevance." But which are the aesthetic rules of relevance? These are the rules "implicitly or explicitly followed by people" in using the aesthetic value-language—that is, in making judgments of aesthetic value. Perhaps I have misunderstood Taylor's line of thought here, but the path it seems to trace is circular. I hope to escape this trap by breaking into the chain at a different point.

I define "aesthetic point of view" in terms of "aesthetic value." And while I think this step is by no means a trivial one, it is not very enlightening unless it is accompanied by some account of aesthetic value. I don't propose to present a detailed theory on this occasion, but I shall extend my chain of definitions to a few more links, and provide some defense against suspected weaknesses. What, then, is aesthetic value? The aesthetic value of an object is the value it possesses in virtue of its capacity to provide aesthetic gratification.

There are three points about this definition that require some attention. First, it will be noted that this is not a definition of

10. Paul Taylor, *Normative Discourse* (Englewood Cliffs, N.J., 1961), p. 109.

"value." It purports to distinguish *aesthetic* value from other kinds of value in terms of a particular capacity. It says that in judging the total value of an object we must include that part of its value which is due to its capacity to provide aesthetic gratification.

The second point concerns "aesthetic gratification." My earliest version of this capacity-definition of "aesthetic value" employed the concept of aesthetic experience.[11] I am still not persuaded that this concept must be abandoned as hopeless, but it needs further elaboration in the face of criticism by George Dickie, whose relentless attack on unnecessarily multiplied entities in aesthetics has led him to skepticism about whether there is such a thing as aesthetic experience.[12] I have tried working with the concept of aesthetic enjoyment instead,[13] and that may be on the right track. For the present, I have chosen a term that I think is somewhat broader in scope, and perhaps therefore slightly less misleading.

Again, however, the term "aesthetic gratification" is not self-explanatory. It seems clear that one kind of gratification can be distinguished from another only in terms of its intentional object: that is, of the properties that the pleasure is taken *in*, or the enjoyment is enjoyment *of*. To discriminate aesthetic gratification—and consequently aesthetic value and the aesthetic point of view—we must specify what it is obtained from. I offer the following: Gratification is aesthetic when it is obtained primarily from attention to the formal unity and/or the regional qualities of a complex whole, and when its magnitude is a function of the degree of formal unity and/or the intensity of regional quality.

The defense of such a proposal would have to answer two questions. First, is there such a type of gratification? I think there is, and I think that it can be distinguished from other types of gratification, though it is often commingled with them. Second, what is the justification for calling this type of gratification "aesthetic"? The answer to this question is more complicated. Essentially, I would argue that there are certain clear-cut exemplary cases of works of art—that is, poems, plays, musical compositions, and so forth—that must be counted as works of art if any-

---

11. See my *Aesthetics: Problems in the Philosophy of Criticism* (New York, 1958), chap. 11.
12. See "Beardsley's Phantom Aesthetic Experience," *Journal of Philosophy* 62 (1965):129–36; and my "Aesthetic Experience Regained," *Journal of Aesthetics and Art Criticism* 28 (1969):3–11 (pp. 77–92 in this volume).
13. "The Discrimination of Aesthetic Enjoyment," *British Journal of Aesthetics* 3 (1963):291–300 (pp. 35–45 in this volume).

thing is. There is a type of gratification characteristically and preeminently provided by such works, and this type of gratification is the type I have distinguished above. Finally, this type of gratification (once distinguished) has a paramount claim to be denominated "aesthetic"—even though there are many other things that works of art can do to you, such as inspire you, startle you, or give you a headache.

If this line of argument can be made convincing, we find ourselves with what might be called primary *marks* of the aesthetic: it is the presence in the object of some notable degree of unity and/or the presence of some notable intensity of regional quality that indicate that the enjoyments or satisfactions it affords are aesthetic—insofar as those enjoyments or satisfactions are afforded by these properties. I shall return to these marks a little later, and show the sort of use I think can be made of them.

IV

But before we come to that, we must consider the third point about the capacity-definition of "aesthetic value"—and this is the most troublesome of them all.

The term "capacity" has been chosen with care. My view is that the aesthetic value of an object is not a function of the actual degree of gratification obtained from it. It is not an average, or the mean degree of gratification obtained from it by various perceivers. It is not a sum, or the total gratification obtained from it in the course of its existence. All these things depend in part on external considerations, including the qualifications of those who happen to resort to libraries, museums, and concerts, and the circumstances of their visits. I am thinking in terms of particular exposures to the work—a particular experience of the music, of the poem, of the painting—and of the degree of aesthetic gratification obtained on each occasion. Aesthetic value depends on the highest degree obtainable under optimal circumstances. Thus my last definition should be supplemented by another one: The amount of aesthetic value possessed by an object is a function of the degree of aesthetic gratification it is capable of providing in a particular experience of it.

My reason for holding this view is that I want to say that a critical evaluation is a judgment of aesthetic value, and it seems clear to me that estimating capacities is both the least and the most we can ask of the critical evaluator. I take it that when a literary critic, for example, judges the goodness of a poem (from the aesthetic point of view) and is prepared to back up his judgment with reasons, he must be saying something about the relationship of the poem to the experiences of actual or potential readers. The question is: What is this relationship? When a critic says that a poem is good, he is hardly ever in a position to predict the gratification that particular readers or groups of readers will receive from it. Moreover, he is usually not in a position to generalize about tendencies—to say, for instance, that readers of such-and-such propensities, preferences, or preparations will probably be delighted by the poem. If the critic has at his disposal the information required to support such statements, he is of course at liberty to say such things as: "This would have appealed to President Kennedy," or "This is an ideal Christmas gift for your friends who love mountain climbing." But when he simply says, "This is a good poem," we must interpret him as saying something weaker (though still significant) about the capacity of the work to provide a notable degree of aesthetic gratification. For *that* is a judgment he should be able to support, if he understands the poem.

The question, however, is whether the capacity-definition of "aesthetic value" is too weak, as a report of what actually happens in art criticism. I can think of three difficulties that have been or could be raised. They might be called (1) the unrecognized masterpiece problem, (2) the LSD problem, and (3) the Edgar Rice Burroughs problem. Or, to give them more abstract names, they are (1) the problem of falsification, (2) the problem of illusion, and (3) the problem of devaluation.

1. Some people are troubled by one consequence of the capacity-definition—that objects can possess aesthetic value that never has been and never will be realized: "Full many a gem of purest ray serene / The dark unfathomed caves of ocean bear." This ought not to trouble us, I think. It is no real paradox that many objects worth looking at can never be looked at. But there is another kind of aesthetic inaccessibility in the highly complicated and obscure work that no critic can find substantial value in, though it may still be there. In Balzac's short story "Le chef-d'oeuvre inconnu," the master painter works in solitude for years, striving for the perfection of his greatest work; but in his dedication and delusion he overlays the canvas with so many brush

strokes that the work is ruined. When his fellow artists finally see the painting, they are appalled by it. But how can they be sure that the painting doesn't have aesthetic value, merely because they have not found any? The capacity to provide aesthetic gratification of a high order may still be there, though they are not sharp or sensitive enough to take advantage of it.

If my proposed definition entailed that negative judgments of aesthetic value cannot even in principle be justified, then we would naturally mistrust it. But of course this consequence is not necessary. What does follow is that there is a certain asymmetry between negative and affirmative judgments, with respect to their degree of confirmation; but this is so between negative and affirmative existential statements in general. The experienced critic may have good reason in many cases not only for confessing that he finds little value in a painting, but for adding that very probably no one ever will find great value in it.

2. If aesthetic value involves a capacity, then its presence can no doubt be sufficiently attested by a single realization. What a work *does* provide, it clearly *can* provide. And if my definition simply refers to the capacity, without qualification, then it makes no difference under what conditions that realization occurs. Now take any object you like, no matter how plain or ugly—say a heap of street sweepings awaiting the return of the street cleaner. Certainly we want to say that it is lacking in aesthetic value. But suppose someone whose consciousness is rapidly expanding under the influence of LSD or some other hallucinogenic drug happens to look at this heap and it gives him exquisite aesthetic gratification. Then it has the capacity to do so, and so it has high aesthetic value. But then perhaps every visual object has high aesthetic value, and all to about the same degree—if the reports may be trusted.

I cannot speak authoritatively of the LSD experience, but I gather that when a trip is successful, the object, however humble, may glow with unwonted intensity of color and its shapes assume an unexpected order and harmony. In short, the experience is illusory. This is certainly suggested by the most recent report I have run across.[14] Dr. Lloyd A. Grumbles, a Philadelphia psychiatrist, said that while listening to Beethoven's *Eroica*, particularly the third movement, he felt simultaneously "insatiable longing and

---

14. In the *Delaware County Daily Times* (Chester, Pa.), February 10, 1967.

total gratification." Dr. Grumbles said he also looked at prints of Picasso and Renoir paintings and realized for the first time that "they were striving for the same goal." Now you *know* he was under the influence of *something*.

This example suggests a modification of the definition given earlier: The aesthetic value of X is the value that X possesses in virtue of its capacity to provide aesthetic gratification *when correctly experienced*.

3. The problem of devaluation can perhaps be regarded as a generalization of the LSD problem.[15] When I was young I was for a time an avid reader of the Martian novels of Edgar Rice Burroughs. Recently when I bought the Dover paperback edition and looked at them again, I found that I could hardly read them. Their style alone is enough to repel you, if you really pay attention to it.

The problem is this: if on Monday I enjoy a novel very much, and thus know that it has the capacity to provide gratification, then how can I ever reverse that judgment and say the novel lacks that capacity? If the judgment that the novel is a good one is a capacity-judgment, it would seem that downward reevaluations (that is, devaluations) are always false—assuming that the original higher judgment was based on direct experience. There is no problem about upward reevaluations: when I say on Tuesday that the novel is better than I thought on Monday, this means that I have discovered the novel to have a greater capacity than I had realized. But how can we explain the lowering of an aesthetic evaluation and still maintain that these evaluations are capacity-judgments?

Some cases of devaluation can no doubt be taken care of without modifying the definition of "aesthetic value." The devaluation may be due to a shift in our value grades caused by enlargement of our range of experience. I might think that *Gone with the Wind* is a great novel, because it is the best I have read, but later I might take away that encomium and give it to *War and Peace*. Or the devaluation may be due to the belated recognition that my previous satisfaction in the work was a response to extra-aesthetic features. I now realize that my earlier enjoyment of detective stories was probably caused only in small part by their literary qualities, and was much more of a game-type pleasure.

---

15. It was discussed briefly in my *Aesthetics*, pp. 534–35, but has since been called to my attention more sharply and forcefully by Thomas Regan.

But setting these cases aside, there remain cases where on perfectly sound and legitimate grounds I decide that the work, though it has provided a certain level of aesthetic gratification, is in fact not really that good. I have overestimated it. Evidently the definition of "aesthetic value" must be modified again. One thing we might do is insert a stipulation that the work be a reliable or dependable source of gratification: flukes don't count. We need not change the judgment into a straight tendency-statement. But we might insist that the enjoyment of the novel must at least be a repeatable experience. Something like this notion seems to underlie the frequent claim that our first reactions to a new work of art are not wholly to be trusted, that we should wait awhile and try it again; that we should see whether we can find at least one other person to corroborate our judgment; or that only posterity will be in a position to know whether the work is great.

I grant that all these precautions are helpful—indeed, they enable us to avoid the two sources of error mentioned a moment ago: having an inadequately formulated set of grading terms, and confusing aesthetic with nonaesthetic gratification. But I think it ought to be possible for a person, after a single experience of a work, to have excellent grounds for thinking it good and for commending it to others. And I think he would be justified in pointing out that he has found a potential source of aesthetic gratification that lies ready to be taken advantage of—even though he does not yet know how readily, how easily, how conveniently, or how frequently recourse may be had to it. Thus my escape from the difficulty is to revise the definition of "aesthetic value" again so as to stipulate that it is the value of the whole work that is in question: The aesthetic value of X is the value that X possesses in virtue of its capacity to provide aesthetic gratification *when correctly and completely experienced*.

The youth who was carried away by the adventures of Thuvia and the green men of Mars and the other denizens of that strange planet may well have gotten greater aesthetic gratification than the elderly person who returned to them after so many years. For the youth was fairly oblivious of the faults of style, and he filled in the flat characterizations with his own imagination, giving himself up unself-consciously to the dramatic events and exotic scenery. But, though he was lucky in a way, his judgment of the *whole* work was not to be trusted.

V

We saw earlier that the notion of a point of view plays a particular role in focusing or forwarding certain disputes by limiting the range of relevant considerations. We invoke the aesthetic point of view when we want to set aside certain considerations that others have advanced—as that a poem is pornographic, or that a painting is a forgery—or that (as Jacques Maritain remarks) "a splendid house without a door is not a good work of architecture."[16] But the person whose considerations are thus rejected may feel that the decision is arbitrary, and enter an appeal, in the hope that a higher philosophical tribunal will rule that the lower court erred in its exclusions. How do we know whether being pornographic or being a forgery or lacking a door is irrelevant from the aesthetic point of view? I propose this answer: A consideration about an object is relevant to the aesthetic point of view if and only if it is a fact about the object that affects the degree to which the marks of aesthetic gratification (formal unity and intensity of regional quality) are present in the object.

Thus: Is the fact that a painting is a forgery relevant to a judgment of it from the aesthetic point of view? No, because it has no bearing on its form or quality. Is the fact that a painting is a seascape relevant? Sometimes. It is when the subject contributes to or detracts from its degree of unity or its qualitative intensity. Is the biography of the composer relevant? According to a writer in *The Music Review*, "it is a well-known fact that knowledge of the circumstances surrounding the composition of a work enhances the audience's appreciation. . . . It is because of this that programme notes, radio comments, and music appreciation courses are in such demand. To secure such knowledge is one of the important tasks of musical research."[17] Now, I'm not sure that this "well-known fact" is really a fact, but let us assume that it is. Does it follow that information about the circumstances of composition is relevant to consideration of the work from an aesthetic point of view? We can imagine this sort of thing:

> It was a cold rainy day in Vienna, and Schubert was down to his last crust of bread. As he looked about his dingy garret, listening to the rain that beat down, he reflected that he could not even afford

---

16. *L'intuition créatrice dans l'art et dans la poésie* (Paris, 1966), p. 53.
17. Hans Tischler, "The Aesthetic Experience," *Music Review* 17 (1956):200.

to feed his mice. He recalled a sad poem by Goethe, and suddenly a melody sprang into his head. He seized an old piece of paper and began to write feverishly. Thus was "Death and the Maiden" born.

Now even if everyone, or nearly everyone, who reads this program note finds that it increases his appreciation of the song, a condition of appreciation is not necessarily a condition of value. From this information—say, that it was raining—nothing can be inferred about the specifically aesthetic character of the song. (It is relevant, of course, that the words and music match each other in certain ways; however, we know that not by biographical investigation but by listening to the song itself.)

Here is one more example. In a very interesting article, "On the Aesthetic Attitude in Romanesque Art," Meyer Schapiro has argued:

> Contrary to the general belief that in the Middle Ages the work of art was considered mainly as a vehicle of religious teaching or as a piece of craftsmanship serving a useful end, and that beauty of form and color was no object of contemplation in itself, these texts abound in aesthetic judgments and in statements about the qualities and structure of the work. They speak of the fascination of the image, its marvelous likeness to physical reality, and the artist's wonderful skill, often in complete abstraction from the content of the object of art.[18]

Schapiro is inquiring whether medieval people were capable of taking the aesthetic point of view in some independence of the religious and technological points of view. He studies various texts in which aesthetic objects are described and praised, to elicit the grounds on which this admiration is based, and to discover whether these grounds are relevant to the aesthetic point of view. Form and color, for example, are clearly relevant, and so to praise a work for its form or color is to adopt the aesthetic point of view. And I should think the same can be said for "the fascination of the image"—by which Schapiro refers to the extraordinary interest in the grotesque figures freely carved by the stonecutters in Romanesque buildings. These centaurs, chimeras, two-headed animals, creatures with feet and the tail of a serpent, and so forth, are the images deplored by St. Bernard with an ambivalence like that in Lenin's remark about Beethoven: "In the cloister, under the eyes of the brethren who read there, what profit is

18. In *Art and Thought*, ed. K. Bharatha Iyer (London, 1947), p. 138. I thank my colleague John Williams for calling my attention to this essay.

there in those ridiculous monsters, in that marvelous and deformed beauty, in that beautiful deformity?"[19]

But what of Schapiro's other points—the image's "marvelous likeness to physical reality, and the artist's wonderful skill"? If a person admires skill in depiction, he is certainly not taking a religious point of view—but is he taking the aesthetic point of view? I should think not. No doubt when he notices the accuracy of depiction, reflects on the skill required to achieve it, and thus admires the artist, he may be placed in a more favorable psychological posture toward the work itself. But this contributes to the conditions of the experience; it does not enter into the experience directly, as does the perception of form and color, or the recognition of the represented objects as saints or serpents. So I would say that the fact that the medieval writer admired the skill in depiction is *not* evidence that he took the aesthetic point of view, though it is evidence that he took *an* aesthetic point of view, since skill was involved in the production of the work.

VI

There is one final problem that may be worth raising and commenting on briefly, although it is not at all clear to me how the problem should even be formulated. It concerns the justification of adopting the aesthetic point of view and its potential conflicts with other points of view. On the one hand, it is interesting to note that much effort has been spent (especially during recent decades) in getting people to adopt the aesthetic point of view much more firmly and continuously than has been common in our country. The conservationists are trying to arouse us to concern for the preservation of natural beauties, instead of automatically assuming that they have a lower priority than any other interest that happens to come up—such as installing power lines or slaughtering deer or advertising beer. And those who are concerned with "education of the eye," or "visual education," are always developing new methods of teaching the theory and practice of good design, with the aim of producing people who are aware of the growing hideousness of our cities and towns, and who are troubled enough to work for changes.

But the effort to broaden the adoption of the aesthetic point

---

19. Ibid., p. 133.

of view sometimes takes another form. According to its leading theoretician, the "Camp sensibility" is characterized by the great range of material to which it can respond: "Camp is the consistently aesthetic experience of the world," writes Susan Sontag. "It incarnates a victory of style over content, of aesthetics over morality, or irony over tragedy."[20]

Here is an extreme consequence of trying to increase the amount of aesthetic value of which we can take advantage. But it also gives rise to an interesting problem, which might be called "the dilemma of aesthetic education." The problem is pointed up by a cartoon I saw not long ago (by David Gerard), showing the proprietor of a junkyard named "Sam's Salvage" standing by a huge pile of junked cars and saying to two other men: "Whattya mean it's an ugly eyesore? If I'd paid Picasso to pile it up, you'd call it a work of art."

The central task of aesthetic education, as traditionally conceived, is the improvement of taste, involving the development of two dispositions: (1) the capacity to obtain aesthetic gratification from increasingly subtle and complex aesthetic objects that are characterized by various forms of unity—in short, the response to beauty in one main sense—and (2) an increasing dependence on objects beautiful in this way (having harmony, order, balance, proportion) as sources of aesthetic satisfaction. It is this impulse that is behind the usual concept of "beautification"—shielding the highways from junkyards and billboards, and providing more trees and flowers and grass. As long as the individual's aesthetic development in this sense is accompanied by increasing access to beautiful sights and sounds, it is all to the good. His taste improves; his aesthetic pleasures are keener; and when he encounters avoidable ugliness, he may be moved to eliminate it by labor or by law. On the other hand, suppose he finds that his environment grows uglier as the economy progresses, and that the ugliness becomes harder to escape. Second, suppose he comes to enjoy another kind of aesthetic value, one that derives from intensity of regional quality more than formal fitness. And third, suppose he comes to realize that his aesthetic gratification is affected by the demands he makes on an object—especially because the intensity of its regional qualities partly depends on its symbolic import. For example, the plain ordinary object may be seen

---

20. Susan Sontag, "Notes on Camp," *Partisan Review* 31 (1964):526.

as a kind of symbol, and become expressive (that is, assume a noteworthy quality) if the individual attends to it in a way that invites these features to emerge. Suddenly, a whole new field of aesthetic gratification opens up. Trivial objects, the accidental, the neglected, the meretricious and vulgar, all take on new excitement. The automobile graveyard and the weed-filled garden are seen to have their own wild and grotesque expressiveness as well as symbolic import. The kewpie doll, the Christmas card, the Tiffany lampshade can be enjoyed aesthetically, not for their beauty but for their bizarre qualities and their implicit reflection of social attitudes. This is a way of transfiguring reality, and though not everything can be transfigured, perhaps, it turns out that much can.

What I mean by the dilemma of aesthetic education is this: that we are torn between conflicting ways of redirecting taste. One is the way of love of beauty, which is limited in its range of enjoyment but is reformist by implication, since it seeks a world that conforms to its ideal. The other is the way of aestheticizing everything—of taking the aesthetic point of view wherever possible—which widens enjoyment but is defeatist, since instead of eliminating the junkyard and the slum, it tries to see them as expressive and symbolic. The conflict here is analogous to that between the social gospel and personal salvation in some of our churches—though no doubt its consequences are not equally momentous. I don't suppose this dilemma is ultimately unresolvable, though I cannot consider it further at the moment. I point it out as one of the implications of the tendency (which I have been briefly exploring) to extend the aesthetic point of view as widely as possible.

But there is another weighty tradition opposed to this expansion. Lenin and St. Bernard stand witness to the possibility that there may be situations in which it is morally objectionable to adopt the aesthetic point of view. A man who had escaped from Auschwitz commented on Rolf Hochmuth's play: "*The Deputy* should not be considered as a historical work or even as a work of art, but as a moral lesson."[21] Perhaps he only meant that looking for historical truth or artistic merit in *The Deputy* is a waste of time. But he may also have meant that there is something blameworthy in contemplating those terrible events from a purely historical or purely aesthetic point of view. Renata Adler, reporting

---

21. *New York Times*, May 4, 1966.

in *The New Yorker*[22] on the New Politics Convention that took place in Chicago on Labor Day weekend, 1967, listed various types of self-styled revolutionaries who attended, including "the aesthetic-analogy revolutionaries, who discussed riots as though they were folk songs or pieces of local theatre, subject to appraisal in literary terms ('authentic,' 'beautiful')." That is carrying the aesthetic point of view pretty far.

This possibility has not gone unnoticed by imaginative writers, notably Henry James and Henrik Ibsen.[23] The tragedy of Mrs. Gereth, in *The Spoils of Poynton*, is that of a woman who could not escape the aesthetic point of view. She had a "passion for the exquisite" that made her prone "to be rendered unhappy by the presence of the dreadful [and] she was condemned to wince whenever she turned." In fact, the things that troubled her most —and she encountered them everywhere, but nowhere in more abundance than in the country house known as Waterbath—were just the campy items featured by Miss Sontag: "trumpery ornament and scrapbook art, with strange excrescences and bunchy draperies, with gimcracks that might have been keepsakes for maid-servants [and even] a souvenir from some centennial or other Exhibition." The tragedy of the sculptor Professor Rubek in *When We Dead Awaken* is that he so ably aestheticized the woman who loved him and who was his model that she was not a person to him. As she says, "The work of art first—then the human being." It may even be—and I say this with the utmost hesitation, since I have no wish to sink in these muddy waters—that this is the theme of Antonioni's film *Blow-up*: the emptiness that comes from utter absorption in an aesthetic point of view of a photographer to whom every person and every event seems to represent only the possibility of a new photographic image. In that respect, Antonioni's photographer is certainly worse than Professor Rubek.

The mere confrontation of these two vague and general social philosophies of art will not, of course, take us very far toward understanding the possibilities and the limitations of the aesthetic point of view. I leave matters unresolved, with questions hanging in the air. Whatever resolution we ultimately find, however, will surely incorporate two observations that may serve as a pair of conclusions.

22. September 23, 1967.
23. I set aside the verse by W. H. Auden called "The Aesthetic Point of View."

First, there are occasions on which it would be wrong to adopt the aesthetic point of view, because there is a conflict of values and the values that are in peril are, in that particular case, clearly higher. Once in a while you see a striking photograph or film sequence in which someone is (for example) lying in the street after an accident, in need of immediate attention. And it is a shock to think suddenly that the photographer must have been on hand. I don't want to argue the ethics of news photography, but if someone, out of the highest aesthetic motives, withheld first aid to a bleeding accident victim in order to record the scene, with careful attention to lighting and camera speed, then it is doubtful that that picture could be so splendid a work of art as to justify neglecting so stringent a moral obligation.

The second conclusion is that there is nothing—no object or event—that is per se wrong to consider from the aesthetic point of view. This, I think, is part of the truth in the art-for-art's-sake doctrine. To adopt the aesthetic point of view is simply to seek out a source of value. And it can never be a moral error to realize value—barring conflict with other values. Some people seem to fear that a serious and persistent aesthetic interest will become an enervating hyperaestheticism, a paralysis of will like that reported in advanced cases of psychedelic dependence. But the objects of aesthetic interest—such as harmonious design, good proportions, intense expressiveness—are not drugs, but part of the breath of life. Their cumulative effect is increased sensitization, fuller awareness, a closer touch with the environment and concern for what it is and might be. It seems to me very doubtful that we could have too much of these good things, or that they have inherent defects that prevent them from being an integral part of a good life.

2: *The Discrimination of Aesthetic Enjoyment*

I

EVERY branch of philosophy cherishes its classic fallacies, partly as a dire warning to the neophyte, partly out of a repressed but lingering fear that the celebrated inference may be valid after all—as has sometimes turned out to be the case. One of the famous scandals of aesthetics concerns "significant form"— the circular route by which Clive Bell first introduced this term into aesthetic discourse. As is well known, Bell began by saying that there is a unique "aesthetic emotion," and set as the main task of aesthetics the isolation of "some quality common and peculiar to all the objects that provoke it."[1] This quality he then named "significant form," which he defined thus: "These relations and combinations of lines and colors, these aesthetically moving forms, I call Significant Form."[2] It is easy enough to fit this pair of remarks into a logical circle, since he gives no other description of aesthetic emotion. What is it that we get from art? Aesthetic emotion. What is aesthetic emotion? It is what is produced by significant form. What is significant form? It consists of those combinations of lines and colors that produce aesthetic emotion. Bell has often been scolded for this logical lapse.[3] If we wish the statement "Aesthetic emotion is produced by significant form" to be synthetic, we must of course define each term independently of the other. If (like Bell) we wish to make the statement definitive of one of its terms, then the other must be defined independently of it. And if we start with aesthetic emotion, on the quasi-naturalistic premise that the value of aesthetic objects

1. *Art* (New York, 1948), p. 17.
2. Ibid., pp. 17–18.
3. See C. J. Ducasse, *The Philosophy of Art* (New York, 1929), pp. 307–14.

is a function of the psychological responses they evoke, then it seems we must (unlike Bell) explain how aesthetic emotion is to be discriminated from other emotion, without referring to significant form.

Bell's dilemma is helpful because he was too enthusiastic and philosophically naive to try to disguise it. But it is one that is confronted, in some form or other, by any quasi-naturalistic account of aesthetic value. For the distinction between aesthetic and other values seems to require the discrimination of a peculiarly aesthetic manner of affecting people acceptably. There is some difference of opinion about the proper choice of a genus. We can speak of "aesthetic pleasure," but "pleasure" strikes some people as too restricted, at least in its connotations. We can speak (like J. O. Urmson)[4] of "aesthetic satisfaction," but "satisfaction" perhaps suggests too strongly an antecedent interest or desire. I shall choose "enjoyment," and hope that it makes reasonable sense to speak of "aesthetic enjoyment," or of "enjoying something aesthetically." Some will reject this locution: after we have been deeply moved, have passed through the emotionally shattering experience of a great tragic drama, would we say that we had "enjoyed" it? I agree that the term is inadequate, if that is all we have to say; but I do not think it is incorrect, for anyone who stays through the whole play without any ulterior aim, such as winning a bet—who is kept in his seat by the play itself—is enjoying what he is experiencing (he is taking a kind of pleasure in it), however profound and stirring his enjoyment may be, compared to other sorts.

II

Let us begin with a brief look at some illuminating passages from Samuel Johnson, Aristotle, and Edmund Burke, in whose writings we can discern three distinct responses to the dilemma, which, like any such animal, may be seized by either horn or avoided by evasive action.

Johnson supposes that it is the function of poetry to produce pleasure, and relies on this supposition at crucial points in his criticism. For example, there is his defense of the digressions at

---

4. See "What Makes a Situation Aesthetic?," *Proceedings of the Aristotelian Society*, suppl. vol. 31 (1957):75–92.

the beginning of the third, seventh, and ninth books of *Paradise Lost*: "Perhaps no passages are more frequently or more attentively read than those extrinsick paragraphs; and, since the end of poetry is pleasure, that cannot be unpoetical with which all are pleased."[5]

What this says is that all pleasure is poetical pleasure; what is meant, no doubt, is that all pleasure derivable from poetry is poetical pleasure. A similar notion is implicit in Johnson's remark about *Henry IV*, Parts I and II, that "perhaps no author has ever in two plays afforded so much delight,"[6] and in his General Observations on *King Lear*, where he dissents from the *Spectator*, which had censured Nahum Tate's revision of the play, giving it a happy ending: "Since all reasonable beings naturally love justice, I cannot easily be persuaded that the observation of justice makes a play worse; or that, if other excellencies are equal, the audience will not always rise better pleased from the final triumph of persecuted virtue."[7]

In these remarks Johnson refuses to make any distinction between a specifically aesthetic pleasure and the kind of (moral?) pleasure we take in seeing justice done. Pleasure can readily be identified without any reference to poetry, and poetry (though not *good* poetry) without any reference to pleasure, so there is no dilemma for him. But these arguments strike us queerly, precisely because no distinction is admitted. When we ask whether Nahum Tate's *King Lear* is better or worse than Shakespeare's, it seems quite irrelevant to be told that his version gives us the added pleasure of seeing Lear back on the throne and all the good people suitably married. Tate's *King Lear* might, of course, be disparaged on Johnson's general hedonistic grounds by the argument that in providing this pleasure the play loses other and greater ones, so that it comes out short in the account ("other excellencies" are not equal). But that seems insufficient—we want to say that to be a better play Tate's *King Lear* would have to

---

5. *Lives of the English Poets*, ed. G. B. Hill (London, 1905), 1:175.
6. See *Samuel Johnson on Shakespeare*, ed. W. K. Wimsatt, Jr. (1960), p. 88; cf. Robert W. Daniel, "Johnson on Literary Texture," *Studies in Honor of John C. Hodges and Alwin Thaler* (Knoxville, Tenn., 1961).
7. Wimsatt, *Samuel Johnson on Shakespeare*, pp. 97–98. The *Spectator* had said (No. 40; April 16, 1711): "*King Lear* is an admirable tragedy . . . as Shakespeare wrote it; but as it is reformed according to the chimerical notion of poetical justice, in my humble opinion it has lost half its beauty." (I confess to some chagrin at finding the term "beauty" applied to this work!)

provide a greater quantity of specifically *aesthetic* pleasure, and that the satisfaction of our moral sensibilities cannot be weighed in the same scale.

I think we must reject Johnson's methodological procedure, because unless we can discriminate aesthetic enjoyment from other sorts, we cannot have a category of specifically critical evaluation at all.

The logic of Aristotle's method is less easy to discern, but some clues to a possible approach can be found in the *Poetics*. "We should not require from tragedy every kind of pleasure," he remarks forthrightly, "but only its own peculiar kind."[8] He says the same in Chapter 26, and in Chapter 23, where he is discussing epic poetry, which shares the same end as tragic drama. What is this kind of pleasure—the *oikeia hedone* of tragedy? Aristotle's answer is quite brief: "the tragic poet must aim to produce by his imitation the kind of pleasure which results from fear and pity."[9] Since it seems that fear and pity cannot be identified except as responses to certain kinds of situation, Aristotle has implicitly defined the "proper pleasure" of tragedy—let us call it the tragic pleasure—as the sort of pleasure felt in seeing tragic events. If we take into account Aristotle's discussion (Chapter 4) of the origins of poetry (we enjoy, he says, imitation and also melody and rhythm), we can sharpen this definition: tragic pleasure is the sort of pleasure felt in seeing the harmonious imitation of tragic (pitiful and fearful) events.

Aristotle's procedure avoids circularity, so long as no concept of aesthetic value or critical judgment is introduced. But then it has awkward consequences. It seems a little odd to say that the function of tragedy is to produce tragic pleasure. When we speak of the function of the spleen, or of a gear, we mean its unique or special ability to produce results that can be defined and detected independently of any knowledge of the spleen or gear itself. But apparently the function of tragedy is to produce, by being watched, a pleasure that can be described only as the pleasure of watching tragedy.

A highly instructive analytical method is employed by Edmund Burke in his *Philosophical Enquiry into the Origin of Our Ideas of the Sublime and Beautiful* (1757). Exactly like Bell, he is looking for

8. *Poetics*, trans. G. M. A. Grube (New York, 1958), chap. 14, p. 27.
9. Ibid.

those properties in sensible objects that are capable of producing certain desirable feelings, of which he distinguishes two main aesthetic ones, the feeling of the beautiful and the feeling of the sublime. He realizes that the inquiry runs into trouble unless the feelings can be described independently of their sensory correlatives. But consider first beauty, defined as

> that quality or those qualities in bodies by which they cause love, or some passion similar to it. . . . I likewise distinguish love, by which I mean that satisfaction which arises to the mind upon contemplating anything beautiful, of whatsoever nature it may be, from desire or lust; which is an energy of the mind, that hurries us on to the possession of certain objects, that do not affect us as they are beautiful, but by means altogether different.[10]

At first glance, here is Bell's scandal almost exactly. Beauty is what produces love; love is what beauty produces. But this is not quite the situation. The first definition (of beauty) Burke means to keep—so that he can then go on to inquire what qualities of objects beauty consists of—but notice how he phrases it. Beauty is what causes "love, or some passion similar to it." The reference to beauty in the sentence distinguishing love from desire is supposed to be nonessential, merely clarificatory; and the logic of the matter is this. Begin with the feeling of being attracted to a woman as an individual (not as a member of a species); abstract from this the ingredient of sexual desire, and what you have left is a certain feeling ("love"). The beauty of a woman (as distinct from her desirability) is what enables her to arouse this feeling; her visible qualities and any qualities, wherever found, that arouse the same or a similar feeling are then (by definition) constituents of beauty.

This analysis is at least not circular, for it does not need to refer to the beauty qualities in order to define the relevant feeling of (aesthetic) love. The serious question here is whether Burke has succeeded in isolating, identifying, and sufficiently characterizing a feeling that is in fact the feeling evoked by those objects that are widely agreed to be beautiful. And it seems doubtful that he has.

His treatment of the sublime is parallel in structure, but teaches a different lesson. The passion to be discriminated in this case (whose cause will then be defined to be the sublime) is

---

10. *Enquiry*, ed. J. T. Boulton (New York, 1958), p. 91. I want to thank Jerome Stolnitz for some very helpful corrections of my interpretation of Burke.

astonishment; and astonishment is that state of the soul, in which all its motions are suspended, with some degree of horror. In this case the mind is so entirely filled with its object, that it cannot entertain any other, nor by consequence reason on that object which employs it. Hence arises the great power of the sublime. . . .[11] Whatever is in any sort terrible, or is conversant about terrible objects, or operates in a manner analogous to terror, is a source of the sublime.[12]

As before, the method is first to characterize "astonishment" as the emotion we feel when we are faced by something fearful to a high degree, but are at the same time protected from it, so that we know we are safe. The consequent mixed feeling of being freed from pain, together with the feeling of being absorbed and filled with the sense of the terrible, is the delight of astonishment, and whatever qualities produce this feeling, or some feeling close to it, are (by definition) constituents of the sublime.

Burke is more successful in telling us what the sublime feels like than he is in discussing beauty, and it may seem at first as though here, at least, he has been successful in avoiding the circularity. Yet this success depends, just as it did in Aristotle, on defining the feeling in terms of the quality perceived: astonishment is what we feel when we see an object that is terrible, or looks terrible, or is associated with what is terrible. But Burke introduces another procedure that is interesting and instructive. We are of course not surprised, after this account, to discover that more terrible objects are more sublime, but he goes on to argue that vastness and power and obscurity in the terrible increase the intensity of astonishment because they increase the terribleness. Thus the properties of visible objects seem to be connected in two very different ways with the feeling of the sublime, some of them by definition and some contingently. Burke does not make this distinction very explicit or emphatic, but it contains an important truth.

III

How do we go about discriminating aesthetic enjoyment from other kinds? Presumably we must first identify a certain *source* of enjoyment, and isolate those properties of it that are productive

---

11. Ibid., p. 57.
12. Ibid., p. 39.

of that enjoyment. That these features are, as such, enjoyable has, of course, to be shown; and then there may be some debate about the propriety of labeling this enjoyment "aesthetic." The procedure recommended by J. O. Urmson, in the paper referred to above, is interesting. He argues that "aesthetic satisfaction" is distinguished from moral, economic, personal, and intellectual satisfactions, by "the explanation or grounds of the satisfaction" (p. 79). He rejects the proposed differentia of "a special emotion or a special emotional tinge" (p. 81)—including the physiological responses (gooseflesh and tears) of A. E. Housman.

> To judge a thing aesthetically good or first-rate is not to call it good in a sense different from that in which we call a thing morally good, but to judge it in the light of a different sub-set of criteria. . . . We may recognize an aesthetic reaction by its being due to features of the thing contemplated that are relevant criteria of the aesthetic judgement, and the aesthetic judgement is one founded on a special sub-set of the criteria of value of a certain sort of thing. [P. 83]

Thus Urmson discriminates the "aesthetic reaction" (of which "aesthetic satisfaction" must be the positive type) by appeal to "aesthetic judgment"—it is a reaction to those properties that are relevant to judgment. And he distinguishes the properties relevant to judgment as those that are criteria of a certain kind of value (which may as well be called "aesthetic value"). But these two proposals are in imminent peril of circularity, since there appears to be no way of characterizing the criteria of aesthetic value other than to say that they are the properties that supply aesthetic satisfaction. Surely the satisfaction is primary here; the value, and hence the judgment of value, depend on it.

Actually, Urmson's procedure tacitly acknowledges this, for he looks about for the most general and elementary situations in which a satisfaction that can reasonably be called aesthetic is available. Here a certain arbitrariness appears. Urmson begins with enjoyable smells, and though this particular satisfaction is no doubt akin to that of art, the inclusion of smell satisfaction among aesthetic satisfactions has been regarded with suspicion by some aestheticians. But there is no need to bog down in terminology; I recommend a narrower sense of "aesthetic," but am willing to pick a narrower term instead, if need be. Suppose we characterize aesthetic enjoyment as the kind of enjoyment we obtain from the apprehension of a qualitatively diverse segment of the phenomenal field, insofar as the discriminable parts are unified into something of a whole that has a character (that is, regional qualities) of its own. No doubt many questions can be raised about this proposal; at the moment, I am interested in exploring its logical consequences.

Suppose we set down the following definitory statements:

1. *Aesthetic enjoyment* is (by definition) the kind of enjoyment we obtain from the apprehension of a qualitatively diverse segment of the phenomenal field, insofar as the discriminable parts are unified into something of a whole that has a character (that is, regional qualities) of its own.
2. *Aesthetic value* is (by definition) the capacity to provide, under suitable conditions, aesthetic enjoyment.
3. *Positive critical criteria* are (by definition) properties that are grounds of aesthetic value.

From propositions 2 and 3 it follows that:

4. Positive critical criteria are (analytically) properties that help or enable an object to provide aesthetic enjoyment.

And from propositions 1 and 4 it follows that those features of an object that are mentioned in the very definition of aesthetic enjoyment—unity, complexity, and intensity—will necessarily be positive critical criteria. Thus when someone asserts that one work of art has greater aesthetic value than another, and gives as his reason that it is more unified, there is a certain lack of surprisingness in this little argument, since it amounts to saying that the work has a greater capacity to provide aesthetic enjoyment because it has more of a property the enjoyment of which is (by definition) aesthetic. Yet it is not utterly trivial, since the work might have been better in other ways—for example, because it unified a greater collection of elements or because it had a more intense regional quality.

There is no circularity, then, in defining aesthetic value in terms of aesthetic enjoyment, and defining aesthetic enjoyment in terms of the properties enjoyed. But this set of definitions does have an interesting consequence, for it divides positive critical criteria—those properties that can be cited as grounds of aesthetic value (or artistic goodness)—into two sets. When we cite those properties that are involved in the definition of "aesthetic enjoyment," we are giving the sort of "safe" answer that Socrates describes in the *Phaedo*: "the safe course is to tell myself or anybody else that beautiful things are beautiful because of the beautiful itself."[13] Naturally, if aesthetic enjoyment is (in part) the enjoyment of unity, unity is a ground of aesthetic value, and greater unity (other things being equal) a ground of greater aesthetic value. But when the critic cites properties that are not involved in the definition of "aesthetic enjoyment"—such as that a modulation is too abrupt, or not abrupt enough—he is giving a more interesting answer, because a synthetic connection has to be established to make the reason relevant (it must be argued that the too abrupt modulation mars the unity of the music, or that the insufficiently abrupt modulation weakens its dramatic intensity, or some other quality).

This distinction between the safe and the risky critical criteria may offer an explanation of an intuitive difference that has been felt by some recent writers. For example, Dorothy Walsh[14] has distinguished between "reasons" and "norms" in critical judgment. The norms she lists[15] are unity, complexity, and "generative powers" (the parts "interact with one another to generate emergent regional qualities"). The norms, in her view, are not themselves reasons but "regulative principles guiding choice in the selection of reasons" (p. 392); that is, the statement "X is more unified" does not, for her, constitute an answer to the question, "Why is X better than Y?" but it (or one of the other norms) will be operative, even if not mentioned, whenever answers *are* given to the question. Norms "are, methodologically, ultimate. Accordingly, they must recommend themselves on their own merits; they must be and seem plausible simply as such. To have this plausibility, they must be general *to the point of obviousness*" (p. 391).

Professor Walsh does not, so far as I can see, justify her claim that unity, complexity, and intensity of regional qualities are obviously the correct norms of the critic; evidently she thinks it is not seriously deniable. But in the light of my previous argument, a justification might be given. Since these three Primary Critical Criteria enter into the very definition of the enjoyment that is in view, we might say, they do have a sort of obviousness. So, one might say, to cite a Primary Criterion is not so much to give a

13. *Phaedo*, trans. R. Hackforth (Cambridge, Eng., 1955), p. 134.
14. "Critical Reasons," *Philosophical Review* 69 (1960):386–93.
15. Corresponding to what I have called General Canons (*Aesthetics: Problems in the Philosophy of Criticism* [New York, 1958], pp. 465–69) and Primary Criteria ("On the Generality of Critical Reasons," *Journal of Philosophy* 59 [1962]:477–86).

reason as to indicate the area in which a reason can be given—to classify criteria as unifying, complexifying, intensifying. The distinction between the Primary and Secondary Criteria would then be somewhat like that between rules of inference and premises in critical argument.

Nevertheless, I don't think this analysis is quite correct. Critics quite often (and sensibly) cite unity as a reason. They may say: "It hangs together better"; "It is better organized"; "It seems to have more of a shape" (actual examples are not hard to find). We can sometimes sense the unity, or the lack of it, in a work even before we discover by analysis which detailed features are responsible. Unity is itself a regional, or gestalt, quality, and it has its perceptual conditions. The question is: *Why* does unity function as a guide to our selection of specific reasons for justifying a particular judgment? The answer, I think, is that it so functions because the specific criteria are properties which, in this particular work, tend to promote or inhibit unity. Professor Walsh says something close to this (p. 393). If there is anything strange about citing unity or lack of it as a critical reason, it is only that this remark would be quite general, and not very informative unless it were pursued further, and also perhaps not very surprising, since one work of art can be better than another only by surpassing it in at least one of the three primary respects.

More recently, Morris Weitz[16] has asserted that not all the reasons that critics give to validate their judgments require vindication in turn. After a survey of discussions by four Shakespearian critics, he says:

> It seems to me, as I read critical evaluations of Shakespeare's dramas, that at least some of the reasons offered in support of the praise of the drama are good reasons, hence validate the praise, not because further reasons for them can be given, but simply because they employ certain criteria—certain P's—about which the question "But what have these to do with dramatic greatness?" cannot be intelligibly asked since no answer to it can be given. [P. 436]

There are two remarkable omissions in Weitz's argument. In the first place, he gives no general characterization of those "logically unchallengeable" (p. 437) reasons, by which they are to be distinguished from the challengeable ones. He just asserts there are some reasons (his examples are Johnson's "Because they rep-

---

16. "Reasons in Criticism," *Journal of Aesthetics and Art Criticism* 20 (1962):429–37.

resent general nature" and Coleridge's "Because they are true to nature") for which it is "appropriate and legitimate" (p. 436) to ask a vindication, though he does not think that these reasons have actually been vindicated. On the other hand, Pope's reason ("Because the characters are individuals, various and consistent") and Coleridge's reason ("Because the puns in *Hamlet* intensify the passions and move the action of the drama") "can stand alone," and need not be further justified (p. 436).

In the second place, Weitz gives no argument, so far as I can make out, to show that some reasons are unchallengeable. He says that when a critic (such as Coleridge) employs unity as a criterion of evaluation, it makes no sense to ask why unity is a good thing in a drama rather than disunity, "for what could be a further reason for the reason, 'Because they are unified,' offered in support of the praise of Shakespeare's dramas?" (p. 437). This is a bit surprising, when we recall that Aristotle did not hesitate to answer precisely this question (*mutatis mutandis*), when he remarked of the epic that "it must have a beginning, a middle, and an end, in order that the whole narrative may attain the unity of a living organism and provide its own peculiar kind of pleasure."[17] That is, unity is a good thing because it enables the drama to produce its special enjoyment. I don't think Aristotle was giving an unintelligible or useless answer to the question, but, as I have said, it is in a way obvious. It always makes sense to ask of *any* critical reason why it is relevant—why that particular property counts for or against the aesthetic value of a work. Yet there is this much truth in Weitz's distinction, that some of the critic's criteria cannot sensibly be challenged by someone who knows the nature of the relevant kind of value. Anyone who understands that aesthetic enjoyment is (among other things) a relishing of highly organized wholes does not need to ask why unity is a positive critical criterion, though he might need to ask whether, and why, the puns in *Hamlet* are merits or defects.

In short, it is philosophically interesting (if true) that some critical criteria (the Primary Criteria) are established by the initial discrimination of aesthetic enjoyment, and consequently are of aesthetic value; but what makes criticism an interesting and adventurous business is that the Secondary Criteria are connected with aesthetic enjoyment in a synthetic and contingent way.

17. *Poetics*, chap. 23, p. 49.

3: *Intrinsic Value*

I

MANY philosophers apparently still accept the proposition that there is such a thing as intrinsic value, that is, that some part of the value of some things (objects, events, or states of affairs) is intrinsic. John Dewey's attack seems not to have dislodged this proposition, for today it is seldom questioned. I propose to press the attack again, in terms that owe a great deal to Dewey, as I understand him.

The predicates (1) ". . . has intrinsic value," (2) ". . . is intrinsically valuable," and (3) ". . . is intrinsically desirable" will be used interchangeably—not for the sake of elegant variation, but because each permits idiomatic constructions that bring out different features of what I take to be the same concept. "Desirable" associates with "to desire," which will be convenient to have available at a later stage of the argument. (No doubt "valuable" and "to value" are similarly related, but the latter is not free from the suggestion of reflective appraisal.) On the other hand, the noun "value" is useful because we can speak of "a value" and "a kind of value." "Value" lends itself more readily than "desirability" to such adjectival qualifications as "cognitive value" and "moral value."

Two phrases are the most often used in defining "intrinsic value": "for its own sake" and "in itself." Their meanings are close but not identical, and the second seems more satisfactory than the first.

We might say that something is intrinsically valuable, in some degree, if it is valuable for its own sake, and that if it has value for the sake of something else, then its intrinsic value, if any, is that which would remain if that other-regarding value were subtracted. One inconvenience of this definition can be brought out as follows: A sheet of postage stamps has been misprinted—the central figure, say, is inverted. The stamps derive part of their value from their rarity. Is one of these stamps valuable, in part, for its own sake? Well, its value is not for the sake of anything else—if we speak of its philatelic value, not its market value. But is this value then intrinsic? It seems strange to say this when it can be taken away, without altering the stamp at all, simply by having the U.S. Postal Service print a few hundred million more copies. Since its rarity is a relational property, there is a sense in which the rare stamp is valuable not for the sake of anything else, either. It might be replied that, even if the issue becomes plentiful, the philatelic value of each individual stamp is not destroyed, but only reduced; rarity cannot transform an object with no value into one with value; it can only increase certain sorts of value in things that already have some degree of it. Still, that part of the stamp's philatelic value that is supplied by rarity seems to be neither intrinsic nor extrinsic, if these terms are defined as "for its own sake" and "for the sake of something else" respectively.

The second definition of "intrinsic value" is that proposed by G. E. Moore in his paper "The Conception of Intrinsic Value." Suppose we can distinguish between the internal and external properties of a thing, that is, between (1) its qualities and inner relations and (2) its relations to other things. Then the value that depends on a thing's internal properties alone is its intrinsic value; the value that depends (wholly or partly) on a thing's external properties is its extrinsic value. The intrinsically good thing is "good in itself." Moore states the definition this way: "To say that a kind of value is 'intrinsic' means merely that the question whether a thing possesses it, and in what degree it possesses it, depends solely on the intrinsic nature of the thing in question."[1]

It is this definition of intrinsic value that leads to Moore's thought experiment in *Principia Ethica*. To decide the question "What things have intrinsic value?," he says, "it is necessary to consider what things are such that, if they existed *by themselves,* in absolute isolation, we should yet judge their existence to be good."[2] If the intrinsic value of a thing is independent of its relationship to anything else, it cannot be destroyed by the removal of every-

---

1. *Philosophical Studies* (London, 1922), p. 260.
2. *Principia Ethica* (Cambridge, Eng., 1903), p. 187; compare *Ethics* (London, 1947), pp. 42, 101.

thing else. Moore holds that only by applying this test can we sort out intrinsic from extrinsic value with clarity and confidence.

Some puzzles in Moore's definition of "intrinsic nature" have been further discussed by him and by others.[3] One difficulty is to explain how intrinsic goodness can be a property dependent solely on the intrinsic properties of things without itself being an intrinsic property—this explanation is needed to fix the status of goodness as a "nonnatural property." Another is to decide whether dispositional properties are to be called internal or external, and to dispose of a certain element of arbitrariness or conventionality in the classification of some properties as dispositional. In the case of the most self-contained and self-sufficient of the valuable objects we are acquainted with—that is, works of art—the internal–external distinction has an immediate appeal. Thus we tell people to listen to the music "itself" and pay no attention to anything outside it, such as objects it might suggest or the biography of the composer. And the so-called Formalist has been known to assert that the (aesthetic) value of a painting depends on internal properties alone (lines, shapes, and colors) and owes nothing to its representational relationship to the world outside it. But even if these notions are regarded as acceptable, serious questions can be raised about the sharpness and decisiveness of the internal–external distinction.

And it is no doubt for this reason, as well as for others, that most contemporary value theorists have concluded that if anything is intrinsically valuable it is not an external object, but an experience or psychological state. At best, the work of art can be said to have only "inherent value" (in C. I. Lewis's terminology) if exposure to it can result in an aesthetically enjoyable experience. The distinction between internal and external properties seems clearer in regard to experiences. Of course, intentionality—a reference to other states of mind or to the external world—must be taken as internal to the experience itself; but neither an ostensible memory of a past pleasure nor the expectation of a future one is causally dependent on the occurrence of those pleasures, and so, theoretically at least, we can conceive any short stretch of conscious life apart from its antecedents and consequents. And apparently we can ask whether it has intrinsic value.

3. See C. D. Broad, "G. E. Moore's Latest Published Views on Ethics," *Mind* 70 (1961):435–57.

I take it that to say that something is valuable is to say that it deserves to be valued; and to say that something is desirable is to say that it is worthy of being desired. Now when we add "intrinsically" to, say, "desirable," how does it fit into the definiens? Does "X is intrinsically desirable" mean (1) "X is intrinsically worthy of being desired" (that is, by definition, "X is worthy of being desired on account of its internal properties alone")? Or does it mean (2) "X is worthy of being intrinsically desired" (that is, by definition, "X is worthy of being desired on account of its internal properties alone")? I have puzzled over the relationship between these two expressions, and find that I can understand the former only in terms of the latter. For if X's desirability depends on its internal properties alone, then these properties must be the ones that ought to be, or deserve to be, desired; and what ought to be the case is that X is desired on account of these internal properties.

Thus in order to attach a sense to "intrinsically desirable" we must first attach a sense to "intrinsically desired." And there is, I think, no trouble about this. For there is an evident psychological distinction between desiring something on account of its internal properties alone and desiring it on account of its relationships to other things. The distinction is not easy to apply, because in most of our desires, care for the thing itself and concern for what will come of it are thoroughly mixed. But we can pretty well fix the extremes: at the one end, the candy that the child in the grocery store wants and screams for and evidently would count the world well lost for; at the other end, the pieces of string and bits of cellophane that we instantly discard once we have secured the goods they serve to wrap. And we can use Moore's test with some success to make the psychological distinction, by asking a person, for example, to think what he would choose to do if he had only a short time on earth, with limitless resources and no obligations to others. The child no doubt would gorge himself on candy, but nobody would pore over chewing-gum wrappers.

So I would like to allow, and exploit, the term "to desire intrinsically." But of course it does not follow automatically that because we can attach "intrinsically" to "desire," we can therefore attach it to "desirable." There are obviously other adverbs that go with "desired," but not with "desirable" (for example, "eagerly," "strongly," and "widely"). An argument must be made out to show that things can be intrinsically desirable as well as intrinsically desired.

II

The question, then, is this: What good reasons are there, if any, for believing that there is such a thing as intrinsic value? Since this proposition is seldom considered to be in need of elaborate proof, formal arguments are difficult to collect. I can discover only three such arguments: (1) an argument from definition, (2) a dialectical demonstration, and (3) an attempt at empirical confirmation.

1. *The argument from definition.* In the view of some thinkers, the existence of intrinsic value can be simply shown in this way: Some extrinsic value is instrumental value, which is defined as follows: "X has instrumental value" means "X is conducive to something that has intrinsic value." (Call this Definition A.) I have selected the loose term "conducive to" in order to avoid some distinctions that we do not need at present. Thus if Y is an end to which X is a means, or a whole of which X is a necessary part, then X is conducive to such intrinsic value as Y possesses. Obviously, if we accept Definition A, we are as committed to the existence of intrinsic value as we are to the existence of instrumental value—however long the chain of conduciveness may be.

But must we accept this definition? In order for Y to confer its value on X when X is conducive to Y, it is certain that Y must have some value to confer, but whether that value is intrinsic or instrumental does not matter as far as X is concerned. So the following alternative definition should be acceptable: "X has instrumental value" means "X is conducive to something that has value." (Call this Definition B.)

The arguer from definition rejects Definition B. It is all right if the key term in the definiens, "value," can be defined by itself, without reference to intrinsic value. But the word "value," he might contend, is necessarily an ellipsis; it cannot stand by itself. Up to this point I have been speaking as though value is a genus with two species, so that value can be defined first and then divided by Moore's test. And it is true that in describing that test, Moore speaks as though we could first know that an object has a certain total value before going on to discover how much of that total is intrinsic and how much extrinsic. But this, according to the arguer from definition, is all misleading. The terms "extrinsic value" and "intrinsic value," despite the noun they share, do not name coordinate species of a genus, but designate two very different concepts, one of which is derivative from the other.[4] And Moore's own way of speaking agrees with this interpretation, on occasion. For example, he speaks as though the phrase "good as a means" (i.e., having instrumental value) is synonymous with the phrase "a means to good" (i.e., conducing to intrinsic value).[5] Being good as a means is not a way of being good—the instrumentally valuable thing is not a valuable instrument, strictly speaking, but an instrument of value. And similarly, "To have value merely as a part is equivalent to having no value at all, but merely being a part of that which has it."[6] This line of thought would issue in the rejection of my Definition B. For it seems to show that instrumental value can be defined only in terms of intrinsic value; so that the existence of the former automatically entails the existence of the latter.

Nevertheless, it seems to me that the word "value" does have a meaning by itself, and does mark out a genus. We can sensibly ascribe value as such to things, and this is even more clearly true of "desirable" and "worth having."[7] The terms "good as a means" and "good as an end in itself," if they may be taken as synonymous with "instrumental good" and "intrinsic good," suggest that the distinction is between two *grounds* of goodness, not two *senses*. This is the position assumed by Moore in his *Ethics* when he asserts that "saying a thing is intrinsically good . . . means it would be a good thing that the thing in question should exist, even if it existed *quite alone*, without any further accompaniments or effects whatever."[8] For here "intrinsically good" is defined by means of "a good thing." If this is a correct procedure, Definition B is acceptable, and the argument from definition fails.

2. *The dialectical demonstration* is closely connected with the argument from definition, but deserves exhibition on its own. I think of it as logically parallel to the First Cause argument for the existence of God. "Instrumentally valuable" is a relational con-

---

4. "Intrinsic" and "extrinsic," in the convenient terminology of Austin Duncan-Jones, would then be "sense-discriminating" rather than "concept-modifying" adjectives (see "Intrinsic Value: Some Comments on the Work of G. E. Moore," *Philosophy* 33 [1958]:240–73, esp. 261–62).
5. *Principia Ethica*, p. 24.
6. Ibid., p. 35.
7. See Duncan-Jones "Intrinsic Value," pp. 257–58.
8. *Ethics*, p. 42.

cept—X borrows its value from Y, or Y confers its value on X. If the value Y confers is itself instrumental, so that it is merely passed along from Z, then where does Z get its value? In the last analysis, something must (according to this argument) possess its value in itself, or nothing can get any value.[9] So the existence of any instrumental value proves the existence of some intrinsic value, just as the occurrence of any event is said to prove the existence of a First Cause.

To align the demonstration of intrinsic value with the venerable First Cause argument may lend it prestige but may also suggest its faults. As Kant showed, the First Cause argument projects a certain kind of ideal explanation that cannot be completed if the causal series has no beginning term. That is, if to explain an event, X, requires not only that we assign its cause, W, but that we assign an *explained* cause, then the ideal explanation of X would involve the explanation of all its causal antecedents; and if these antecedents have no first term, no such explanation can be given. Similarly, the dialectical demonstration of intrinsic value projects a certain kind of ideal justification that cannot be completed if the series of means and ends has no last term. That is, if to justify ascribing a value to X requires not only that we show it is a means to Y, but also that we justify ascribing a value to Y, and if there is no stopping point, no such ideal justification can be given. But ordinary justification, like ordinary causal explanation, involves no such infinite regress.

The dialectical demonstration cannot be a pure formal demonstration, for, unless the argument from definition is valid, it cannot be proved strictly self-contradictory to assert the existence of instrumental value but deny the existence of intrinsic value. The demonstration must rather be thought of as applying to our *knowledge* of value. Premise 1: We know, or have good reason to believe, that some things are instrumentally valuable. Premise 2: We could not know this unless we knew some things to be intrinsically valuable. Conclusion: We know some things to be intrinsically valuable. Now, Premise 1 seems to me clearly true. But the conclusion seems to me quite clearly false. The paradoxical feature of our value knowledge is just that we have a good deal of sound knowledge about instrumental values but are in consider-

---

9. Compare Hume's argument that "something must be desirable on its own account" (*Inquiry Concerning the Principles of Morals* [New York, 1957], p. 111).

able doubt about intrinsic values. Philosophers have disputed, and still dispute, about whether pleasure is an intrinsic value, and if so, whether it is the only intrinsic value; and it is significant that as ordinary people we have not had to wait upon the settlement of these issues before discovering a great many valuable things nearer to hand. We must have some way of knowing that in many concrete situations it is better for a person to be healthy than sick without knowing whether that is because it is intrinsically best for him to maximize his net positive hedonic quality, or realize his potentialities, or cultivate a good will, or whatever.

The apparent hopelessness of resolving problems about instrumental value without knowing antecedently what, if anything, intrinsic value may be can be cleared away, I believe, if we go back to the concrete contexts of value problems.[10] When we are in the position of having to decide what is valuable, or more valuable, we are in Dewey's "problematic situation," and such a situation is one in which certain ends are in grave doubt and others are (on that occasion) taken as temporarily fixed. If the value of everything in the situation were in question at once, nothing could be decided at all, and indeed no problem could even be conceived; only in terms of certain tentatively held values can we decide, or even ask, whether other things are valuable or not. There must be a basis on which it is reasonable for us to pick out salient elements in the situation and assign them probable values without transforming the task of assignment into another problematic situation, thus endlessly postponing a decision. A state of affairs such as good health, for example, has retained its eligibility through earlier problems and experiences; its value has survived them, in the sense that up to this point health does not seem to have interfered with our pursuits, but a lack of it from time to time has not only contributed to the rise of difficult problems, but limited our capacity to resolve them. We need not suppose that health is an intrinsic good, or that it is always good, or even that we are necessarily right in taking it to be good on the present occasion; but we do have rational justification for supposing that it has positive value that ought to be taken into consideration now.

This is the merest sketch of a way of looking at the problem of

10. Here I want to acknowledge my debt to Sidney Hook's essay "The Desirable and Emotive in Dewey's Ethics," in his collection *John Dewey: Philosopher of Science and Freedom* (New York, 1950).

evaluation. The gist of it is that reasonable decisions about instrumental values do not presuppose or wait upon previous reasonable decisions about intrinsic values (even if such decisions were possible, which I shall argue in the next section they are not). So there is no infinite regress in a purely instrumentalist theory of value.

3. *The empirical confirmation.* Some writers on the theory of value have not relied on either of the a priori forms of argument that I have just considered, but have held that the existence of intrinsic value is attested by direct experience. One of the most carefully considered theories is that of C. I. Lewis. He distinguishes three kinds of value predication, of which the basic kind is the "expressive statement," having a form like "This is good," where "this" refers to immediate presentations in experience.[11] Expressive statements report "value-apprehensions" or "direct findings of value-quality in what is presented,"[12] and are therefore incorrigible.[13]

> It will hardly be denied that there is what may be called "apparent value" or "felt goodness," as there is seen redness or heard shrillness. And while the intent to formulate just this apparent value-quality of what is given, without implication of anything further, encounters linguistic difficulties, surely it will not be denied that there are such immediate experiences of good and bad to be formulated.[14]

It is this immediate value quality that Lewis calls intrinsic value, and that imports intrinsic value into those experiences that possess it. To it all forms of value judgment are ultimately anchored. And because it is only in experiences that we are directly acquainted with such qualities, only experiences can, strictly speaking, have intrinsic value. When an object enables us to "realize" intrinsic value in experience, by being directly presented to us, the object has "inherent value," which is a form of extrinsic value.[15] "The goodness of a good *object* is a potentiality for the realization of goodness in experience."[16] "We have suggested—and intend to abide by—a distinction between intrinsic and extrinsic values by reference to the question, 'Is that which is valued, valued *for its own sake* or for the sake of something else?'"[17]

11. *An Analysis of Knowledge and Valuation* (La Salle, Ill., 1946), p. 374.
12. Ibid., p. 365.
13. Ibid., p. 375.
14. Ibid., pp. 374–75.
15. Ibid., pp. 386–87, 391.
16. Ibid., p. 389.
17. Ibid., p. 385.

What is most surprising in Lewis's characterization of this value quality is the way he employs alternately and indifferently the two expressions that other philosophers have been at such pains to keep distinct: "valuable in itself" and "valued in itself." There are passages in which Lewis seems to suggest that being valuable and being valued may not be the same thing, since one of them may be evidence of the other. "Such appellations as these—'liked' or 'disliked,' 'wanted' or 'unwanted,' 'good' or 'bad,' as addressed to the directly presented—are better indices of the immediately valuable or disvaluable than others."[18] Here being liked is an *index* of being intrinsically valuable, hence not identical to it (though the force of this distinction is certainly much blunted by putting "good" and "bad" in with "liked" and "disliked"). And later he says, in the antecedent of a concessive conditional, that "liking and disliking are decisive of immediate value,"[19] again as though there might be an evidential relationship between being immediately liked and being intrinsically valuable. But in Lewis's prevailing usage, "valuable" is simply reduced to "liked" or "likable," and "per se desirable" means only "per se desired." The normative element in "value" is completely lost sight of.

It is intrinsic desiredness that Lewis substitutes for intrinsic desirability. Thus he speaks of "the likeability and dislikeability of things; their directly gratifying quality or the opposite,"[20] and says that "value–disvalue is that mode or aspect of the given or the contemplated to which desire and aversion are addressed."[21] These remarks suggest that when he speaks of "desirability" he means only likability, and when he speaks of "finding value-qualities" he means only finding something that excites desire or aversion. But in that case, Lewis has not really shown that the existence of intrinsic desirability (in the usual sense) is confirmed in immediate experience.[22]

Charles A. Baylis[23] explicates "intrinsic good" as what is "worthy of existence entirely apart from any extrinsic value it may have"

18. Ibid., p. 404.
19. Ibid., p. 410.
20. Ibid., p. 418.
21. Ibid., p. 403.
22. Compare Duncan-Jones, "Intrinsic Value": "I do not think that worth-havingness is more or less the same as pleasantness or enjoyableness" (p. 266), because "worth having" involves an element of "deliberation." And compare John Dewey: "To pass from immediacy of enjoyment to something called 'intrinsic value' is a leap for which there is no ground" (*Theory of Valuation*, International Encyclopedia of Unified Science, vol. 2, no. 4 [Chicago, 1939], p. 41).
23. "Grading, Values, and Choice," *Mind* 67 (1958):485–501.

(an interesting example of reversing the order of definitions proposed in the argument from definition above). And he explicates "worthy of existence" by saying "that anything which has this characteristic ought, *ceteris paribus*, to exist rather than not, that it would be better for it to exist, and that anyone who can bring it into being ought to do so unless there is something preferable he can do instead."[24] Like W. D. Ross, in short, he makes "intrinsic value" entail a conditional "ought" sentence, a prima facie obligation. He then goes on to say that "the best initial evidence . . . we could have" for ascribing intrinsic value to something

> is that we find ourselves *prizing* things of that kind, i.e. liking, approving, desiring, preferring, and commending them, for their own qualities (rather than because of their relations to other valuable things) in circumstances where to the best of our searching knowledge we are making no mistake in our cognition of them. Such evidence gives us an initial probability that what we thus prize is intrinsically good.[25]

Since Baylis agrees with Lewis that only experiences can be intrinsically good, his position contrasts interestingly with Lewis's on the question of our knowledge of intrinsic value. For Lewis, the desiring of a mental state while it is occurring (i.e., the enjoyment of it) is conclusive evidence of its desirability. For Baylis, it is only "initial evidence," the probative force of which is then to be increased "by making repeated examinations of things of the same kind under circumstances which vary just enough to guard against the kinds of cognitive error which might occur."[26]

It seems to me that Baylis gives two completely unrelated accounts of intrinsic value, and only makes them seem the same by passing so swiftly from one to the other. Up to the middle of his paper, all characterizations of intrinsic value are in terms of such words as "worthy," "better," and "ought"—and it clearly retains its normative character. But when he comes to his thesis that particular well-conducted prizings constitute *evidence* for intrinsic value, a quite different characterization takes over. "The attribution of intrinsic goodness to an experience is like the attribution of an ideally defined, but not actually observable, physical property, e.g., weighing precisely one pound, to an object."[27] Weighing

24. Ibid., p. 494.
25. Ibid., pp. 494–95.
26. Ibid., p. 495.
27. Ibid., p. 497.

exactly one pound is explicated in terms of being equal in weight to a standard pound; and the latter turns out to be a complicated conditional about what would happen under ideal weighing conditions (not all of which, he admits, can be specified). Thus "X weighs exactly one pound" means (approximately) "X would be found to be one pound in weight by an Ideal Weigher, under Ideal Conditions, with an Ideal Scale, etc., etc." And similarly, "X has intrinsic value" turns out to be equivalent to a complex conditional to the effect that X would be prized by an ideal observer, defined by all the necessary accoutrements and qualifications of such an individual.[28]

I do not propose to take up the ideal observer theory here, or related proposals for defining intrinsic value, such as have been very carefully worked out by Roderick Firth and Richard Brandt.[29] Yet I hesitate to set aside so important a position without more careful consideration. Essentially, my view of it can be put in the form of a dilemma. When "X has intrinsic value" is defined in terms of the attitude or desires or satisfactions of an ideal observer, the specified characteristics of the ideal observer either do or do not include any normative concepts. If the ideal observer is defined wholly in nonnormative terms, as one who is omniscient, impartial, and so forth, then (1) statements about the ideal observer can be confirmed by reports of my own prizings, under controlled conditions, but (2) it will remain an open question, in Moore's sense, whether the ideal observer actually desires what is desirable; and from the statement that something is desired by the ideal observer, nothing follows about what deserves to exist or to be done. On the other hand, if normative terms are smuggled into the definition of the ideal observer—so that he is defined in effect as one who knows intrinsic value when he sees it—then (1) it does follow that I ought to desire, as far as I can, what the ideal observer desires, but (2) statements about the desires of the ideal observer can no longer be empirical hypotheses, and cannot be confirmed or given initial probability by reports of any actual desirings or prizings; from the statement that a certain

---

28. Ibid., p. 499.
29. See Firth, "Ethical Absolutism and the Ideal Observer," *Philosophy and Phenomenological Research* 12 (March 1952):317–45; Firth and Brandt, "The Definition of an 'Ideal Observer' Theory in Ethics," *Philosophy and Phenomenological Research* 15 (March 1955):407–23; Richard Henson, "On Being Ideal," *Philosophical Review* 65 (1956):389–400; and Richard Brandt, *Ethical Theory* (Englewood Cliffs, N.J., 1959), chap. 10.

musical experience is found prizeworthy by an ideal observer, no predictions can be derived about my prizings or disprizings.

I conclude that the existence of intrinsically valuable things, including mental states, cannot be made certain by direct experience or probable by inductive inference from direct experience.

It is interesting, by the way, that Paul Taylor, in his recent book, rejects the argument from definition, and holds that "a world where all values were extrinsic, the value of one thing depending on the value of another whose value in turn depends on the value of something else, *ad infinitum*," is not logically impossible, or even unimaginable.[30] In his view, it is an empirical fact about our world that all extrinsic values ultimately do go back to intrinsic ones. But it seems to me that Taylor, for all his care, mixes the desirable and the desired as Lewis and Baylis do. Thus, in describing the "world in which instrumental and contributive values did *not* depend on intrinsic value," he says that in such a world "no one would do anything for its own sake, simply because he found personal enjoyment in it. It would be a world of 'practical people' who knew how to get things done but had no reason for getting one thing done rather than another."[31] But this is a caricature of a world in which all values are extrinsic. For, in the first place, the question whether people "do anything for its own sake" is not at all the question whether there is intrinsic value; the world without intrinsic value (that is, our world) is a world in which people may often do something for its own sake, and may experience many enjoyments, but they cannot *justify* doing something for its own sake by simple appeal to enjoyment. And in the second place, a world in which all values are instrumental would be precisely a world in which every correct value judgment could be supported by a reason, and so there would always be a "reason for getting one thing done rather than another."

III

I now turn from the arguments for the thesis that there exists at least one thing with intrinsic value to my argument against this thesis. It is that the concept of intrinsic value is inapplicable—that even if something has intrinsic value, we could not know it, and

---

30. *Normative Discourse* (New York, 1961), p. 26.
31. Ibid., p. 32.

therefore that it can play no role in ethical or aesthetic reasoning.

Richard Brandt has remarked that "X is desirable" means the same as "Desiring X is justified."[32] What "desirable" adds to "desired" is this claim to justifiability. But the only way this claim can be made good is by considering X in the wider context of other things, in relation to a segment of a life or of many lives. Thus the term "intrinsic desirability" pulls in two directions: the noun tells us to look farther afield, the adjective tells us to pay no attention to anything but X itself.

This implicit contradiction in the concept of intrinsic value can, in theory, be removed on one epistemological assumption. If we could detect the presence of intrinsic value by immediate intuition—in the way Moore claimed to know that the satisfactions of personal relationships and of artistic beauty are the highest intrinsic values available to human beings[33]—then we would not require reasons in order to know it. If we ask why the experience of a good painting has intrinsic value, the answer will be "It contains [or is characterized by] aesthetic enjoyment."[34] And if we then ask why aesthetic enjoyment is intrinsically valuable, we have reached an end. For no further reasons can be given, so long as we are confined, in answering, to the experience itself. We can only say that it is self-evident to some cognitive faculty that is equipped to grasp the self-evidence of such truths as this. I cannot honestly appeal to such intuitive apprehensions of intrinsic value when I do not possess them myself. But I can fairly question whether others are mistaken in thinking that they possess them. The familiar arguments against ethical intuitionism will not be reviewed in detail here. Since intuition is a last resort as a way of resolving the problems of value theory, it is fatal that ethical intuitions conflict; that criteria cannot be given for distinguishing correct from incorrect ones; and that the alleged analogies with other types of a priori knowledge (mathematical, for example) break down. It can never be a necessary truth that any particular instance of aesthetic enjoyment is desirable, since later experience may reveal that it was not in fact desirable at all; therefore it can never be a necessary truth that any particular instance of aesthetic

32. *Ethical Theory*, p. 302.
33. *Principia Ethica*, p. 188.
34. Supposing there is such a special sort of enjoyment; see my paper "The Discrimination of Aesthetic Enjoyment," *British Journal of Aesthetics* 3 (1963):291–300; pp. 35–45 of this volume.

enjoyment is *intrinsically* desirable; therefore no *general* or *universal* proposition about the connection of aesthetic enjoyment and intrinsic value can be necessary; and therefore, there is no necessary truth about the intrinsic value of aesthetic enjoyment to be grasped by intuition.

Brandt gives an excellent example for discussion:

> Consider a child who is swinging, in a rapturous state of enjoyment. We shall probably think that being in this state of mind (and perhaps body) is worthwhile for itself alone. To be in a state of rapturous enjoyment of the experience of swinging is for one's state of mind to have an intrinsic property, on account of which the child's experience is desirable. So we shall say that the child's experience is of intrinsic worth.[35]

Now, how could one justify the assertions that this experience is (a) intrinsically desirable and (b) desirable? If intrinsic desirability is in question, we can only say, "It is an experience containing the rapturous enjoyment of swinging." But it would be odd if we were content to accept this as a sufficient reason for saying that the experience is intrinsically desirable when we would not accept it as a sufficient reason for saying that the experience is desirable. For to support the latter statement, we would need at least to say that in the first place the swinging doesn't do the child any harm (it is an innocent pleasure) and that there is nothing else more important for him to be doing at this time. Otherwise we should not say that this particular experience of swinging is desirable at all. But as soon as we bring in these considerations, making the desirability of this experience depend in part on the lack of unwanted consequences and on the comparison of this action with other possible actions, then the desirability we have defended is no longer intrinsic, but extrinsic.

When we call a thing desirable, it seems to me, we claim to place it in a larger perspective; we suggest that alternatives have been considered, and the desirable thing selected with a view to its implications and connections. And this is the trouble with Moore's test, and all such artificial desert-island ethical models. Let us suppose the child has only a few minutes to live, because the world is about to come to an end, and he is rapturously swinging; and suppose anything else you like, to close off other alternatives. He wants to swing, he is ecstatic about it. Of course we

---

35. *Ethical Theory*, p. 303.

are not going to call him in to do his homework, or worry about his catching cold. Suppose we narrow his opportunities to two, swinging and doing some unpleasant alternative, like washing the dishes. We are asked to choose which he shall do, and we say, "Let him swing!" Are we then conceding that the enjoyment of swinging has intrinsic value? I do not think so.

It is essential to distinguish between two propositions about this one-minute-to-live version of Moore's test: (1) There is no reason for the child not to swing on this occasion, if he wants to and enjoys it. (2) There is reason to say that the child's swinging enjoyment on this occasion is intrinsically desirable. The situation we have artificially set up is designed to make the first proposition true. But this is a very different proposition from the second, which is what the example is supposed to prove.

What can be shown by the swinging example is that we can imagine cases in which there could be nothing to make a particular experience undesirable—neither intrinsic nor extrinsic reasons. But once we deliberately set aside all extrinsic factors, there is nothing to argue about, either for or against. No reason can be given why the child should not swing if he wishes, and since he does not need a reason for doing what he already wants to do, reasons do not come into the picture at all. In normal everyday life, with its continuities and connections, the fact that he desires to swing would raise the question of its desirability—but it would not settle that question, of course. It would also assign the burden of proof. When the child expresses or evinces the desire to swing, the next question is whether any reasons can be given against the satisfaction of this desire (of course, if such reasons are given against it, it will then be in order to see whether reasons can be given *for* it). What makes the artificial situation artificial is just that it rules out any possible reasons against swinging, and so prevents any real problem from arising. I accept the spirit (though not every word) of a remark by William James, which is quoted with approval by William Frankena in his book on ethics: "Take any demand, however slight, which any creature, however weak, may make. Ought it not, for its own sole sake, to be satisfied? If not, prove why not?"[36] If not, why not? That is exactly what I mean by the burden of proof.

36. *Essays in Pragmatism* (New York 1948), p. 73; see William Frankena, *Ethics* (Englewood Cliffs, N.J., 1963), p. 38.

And I think that this concept of the burden of proof is very important in many problems. We say that in a criminal trial the burden of proof lies upon the prosecution. An a prioristic philosopher might express the situation this way: "In criminal trials, there is an antecedent probability that the accused is innocent." Then the question would arise in the philosophy of law: How can that antecedent probability of innocence be established? And hopeless problems would appear. Is it a pragmatic postulate? Is it self-evident? Is it intuited by a special sense of justice? Is it deducible from theological premises about the nature of man? But all these questions would be beside the point. And I think the same thing holds for intrinsic value. The child wants to swing. It is a mistake to say that this fact gives initial probability to the proposition that the pleasure of swinging has intrinsic value. And it is a mistake to say that the pleasure he gets in swinging *justifies* the act of swinging. Say rather that his wanting to swing raises the question whether it would be justified for him to swing, but as long as no reason can be given *against* it, the swinging does not require any justification.

The value judgment "This act of swinging is desirable" is best thought of as an answer to a question, a solution of a problem. But as long as the child wants to swing and in the nature of the case there can be no objection, there is no problem to be solved. To say that "beauty is its own excuse for being" is to say that beauty *needs* no excuse for being.

The artificial dead-end situation dreamed up according to Moore's instructions is essentially misleading. But some real-life situations may seem to approximate it. There are occasions when we want to say such things as "You'll find Mammoth Cave well worth seeing in itself," or "Go ahead and eat the ice cream cone; it's tasty," or "Forget business. Relax. Just have a good time." Borrowing a Deweyan term, let us call these "consummatory judgments"—they point out that something can be enjoyed for its own sake, they locate sources and occasions of intrinsic enjoyment in food, art, and so on. They do not seem to be judgments of extrinsic value: they are hedged about in such a way as apparently to recommend a course of action without considering consequences at all. Are they, then, really judgments of intrinsic value?

I think this inference would be mistaken. Consummatory judgments are better interpreted not as value judgments but as statements to the effect that no judgment is required, because there is no conflict of values, no occasion for deliberation and choice. "Go ahead and swing" surely has to be based on a preliminary survey of the situation: the rope looks safe, the child's stomach is not easily upset, there is no homework in the offing, there are no visiting children who should have the first turn on the swing, and so on. Once we know these facts, we can adopt a vacation point of view, and when the child asks politely, or simply starts running toward the swing, we say, "Go ahead." This is not a judgment of intrinsic value at all, but a kind of *nihil obstat*. If some contrary reason loomed, we would have to stop and think, and decide. Consummatory judgments are then judgments of a metalinguistic order. "No reason why you shouldn't if you want to" is the basic formula.

In closing, I should like to pay my respects to John Dewey once more. I am always frustrated in reading Dewey, trying to separate the enormously good points from the confusing ones. Much of Dewey's famous attack on intrinsic value is really concerned with something else, namely, ends-in-themselves (as opposed to ends-in-view). What he exposes over and over again is the danger of fixing on goals without reasonable regard to their means and consequences, and he is convinced that the belief in intrinsic value fosters this fixation, with its attendant train of ills: fanaticism, utopianism, opportunism, and the rest. But of course it does not logically follow that if there are intrinsically valuable things, then there are necessarily ends-in-themselves. The world might be full of things that have intrinsic value, but whose intrinsic value is always outweighed by harmful effects. This would be the opposite of F. H. Bradley's description of Leibniz's universe, when he said it was the best of all possible worlds but everything in it was a necessary evil. The means might be delightful but the ends always awry. It is only in Moore's artificial isolation that a thing with intrinsic value would necessarily be an end, and a great part of Dewey's concern should have been allayed by assurance that from the fact that a thing would be an end in isolation it does not follow that it would be an end in the context of human life. Nevertheless, I believe Dewey was also right in rejecting intrinsic value, and that this part of his theory has important ethical and social consequences, too. To connect the desirable and the desired, to connect values with human needs and wishes, is indeed the task of a naturalistic theory of value. But to make this connection prematurely, through an identification of intrinsic value with immediate enjoyment, encourages a dangerously one-sided approach to human problems. For then desires, which provide the data and conditions of value problems, and set some of the limits within which solutions are to be found, are taken as something more final than they really are, rather than as states of affairs that may themselves have to be transformed. And reasoning about values may become too exclusively a matter of balancing interests and finding ways to satisfy existing and conflicting wants, rather than an inquiry into their conditions in the natural and social environment. When we recognize the essential relatedness of all value, we are on the way to recognizing that in the deepest and most poignant conflicts in ourselves or in our society, it is often desires themselves that must be transformed if lives are to be freed and fulfilled.

4: *The Aesthetic Problem of Justification*

I

THERE is one question that, I suppose, can be asked of anything: What good is it? This may be called the "justification question," for what it invites is a good reason why the thing in question should exist: why it is worthy of existence and deserves to be preserved.

If I am right, works of art are no more exempt than other objects from the justification question. In one way or another, and with more or less definiteness and precision, critics and aestheticians have asked this question about art for a long time. But quite recently there have been social developments that perhaps make the question a bit more insistent or urgent: for example, the vast increase in the scope of our system of higher education has helped make us self-conscious about what in the world we are actually achieving in our colleges and universities, including our courses in the arts; the undertaking of vast city-planning and highway-building activities has forced tougher decisions about the real worth (in any terms) of attention to aesthetic aspects of our natural and artificial environments; the leisure explosion has enormously increased the demand for aesthetic experiences while at the same time threatening to submerge them under the general category of entertainment or antiboredom devices.

At the same time, the justification question has become harder and harder to answer, as our conception of art and our philosophical reflections on art have developed over the past century. Not being able to accept a transcendental or Transcendentalist view of abstract and absolute Beauty, we can no longer address a painting or a poem as Emerson addresses the Rhodora, confident

> that if eyes were made for seeing
> Then Beauty is its own excuse for being.

We have lost confidence in the long-accepted moral answer to the justification question: in uplift, nobilification, and the strengthening of character. And a great many of us have come to have serious reservations about a cognitive or intellectual answer: that the arts as such provide us with a special form of knowledge or insight into reality.

Here, I take it (speaking very broadly), is where the aesthetic justification problem stands today: we are still asking, but we seem to have prohibitively high standards of answering.

In this paper I am not able to propose a new answer, but I hope to help in obtaining one. It seems to me that part of what stands in the way is unclarity and even confusion about what we are trying to do; and it is a peculiarly philosophical business to provide conceptual clarification that might put us a step nearer to the goal, by bringing out better what sort of further inquiry is called for if we are to reach it. First, then, I shall introduce some distinctions that seem to me essential in this matter; and second, I shall comment on some types of answer to the justification problem.

II

When we ask about a particular work of art what good it is, the critic's answer (if positive) generally has a certain pattern. He begins by saying what goodness it *has*: that it is a good painting or a good poem. He may go on—and indeed has some obligation to go on, if pressed—and give us reasons for this appraisal. But we are not concerned with reasons here, only with the nature of the judgment itself. To ascribe to the poem the kind of goodness peculiarly associated with poems, or to ascribe to the painting the kind of goodness peculiarly associated with paintings, is to claim the presence in the work of a certain sort of value, which is often called "aesthetic value." A good poem or painting is one that has a substantial degree of aesthetic value—a type of value that is presumably discriminable from other types and discussable as such.

It is possible to hold that the recognition or discovery of aesthetic value in the poem or painting provides the whole answer to the justification problem. For if someone asks, "What good is X?" and we reply (truthfully) that X has aesthetic value, should he not be satisfied? Suppose he is not satisfied, but goes a step further to ask: "What good is aesthetic value?" or "What is aesthetic value good for?" Then, according to one theory of value, the proper reply is that aesthetic value is an intrinsic value, so the question "What for?" does not arise.

This seems to be the theory (if we interpret "beauty" as aesthetic value) that the speaker holds in Emerson's poem—though the contradiction between the two quoted lines is a hint about the difficulties of maintaining any such theory. The speaker's problem is why the Rhodora's "charm is wasted on the earth and sky"—that is, what good its beauty is when no one is there to enjoy it. His proposed solution is that the value of the Rhodora (as a visual object) is its own excuse for being. Fair enough. But why does he preface this thesis with the words "if eyes were made for seeing"? Surely this clause implies that it is not the Rhodora's beauty that is its own excuse for being, but the experience of *seeing* that beauty that is its own excuse for occurring.

The word "excuse" is extravagant in these contexts, of course, since even if it were homely, the Rhodora would have done nothing for which an excuse is required. But let us try to restate the situation more exactly, with the help of a technical term. Let us assume for the moment that we understand what it means to say that an object has value—is valuable or desirable. Insofar as its value belongs to it independently of its relationship to any other object (including, in this case, persons)—insofar, that is, as it is desirable for its own sake, rather than for the sake of anything else with which it is connected—its value is said to be *intrinsic*. And whatever portion of its value is not intrinsic is then said to be *extrinsic*.

Now most philosophers hold that at least some value must be intrinsic, though they then part on various questions that immediately arise: What things are intrinsically valuable? How do we know that a thing has intrinsic value? How many distinct kinds of intrinsic value are there? One *could* claim that the aesthetic value of the Rhodora (considered as a design of colors and shapes) has nothing to do with the fact that it can be seen and enjoyed.

In fact the theological point of Emerson's poem requires this position, since he doesn't want to say that only the Rhodora here encountered is worthy of existing, but that all Rhodoras are. But this view, by its very nature, is hard to defend. If the aesthetic value of the unseen Rhodora has no connection with actual or possible experiences, how could we ever know, or prove, that it is there?

A sensible modification of the Emersonian position, suggested in the first of the two quoted lines, is to locate the intrinsic value in the experience rather than in the object that occasions it. Thus we might speak of a certain kind of enjoyment as "aesthetic enjoyment"—however that may be analyzed.[1] Then the aesthetic value of an object would consist in its capacity to provide that kind of enjoyment (if we assume that the enjoyment is worth having). I don't mean that the sentence "This flower has aesthetic value" has the same meaning as the sentence "This flower has the capacity to provide aesthetic enjoyment"; the former is a value judgment, the latter is not. What the former adds to the latter is subject to philosophical dispute; at the very least, I should say, it adds the implication, or presupposition, that aesthetic enjoyment itself is desirable.

The clearest way I can think of to talk about aesthetic value, then, is this: The object has certain properties (colors and shapes). On account of these properties, it is capable of arousing a certain complex of sensations and feelings. On the assumption that this resulting experience is valuable, we can say that this capacity is a kind of value: aesthetic value. The presence of this value in the object does not, of course, depend on its actually being experienced—even if no one ever sees the Rhodora, it still retains its *capacity* to provide aesthetic enjoyment, if a suitable occasion should arise. So in that sense the Rhodora's value is independent of anyone's experience of it. But at the same time its value is not unconnected with actual or possible experiences, for its value is in fact defined in terms of such experiences. So conceived, aesthetic value is not intrinsic value, but consists in instrumentality to aesthetic enjoyment.

As I have indicated, the next logical proposal would then be to say that while the Rhodora has only instrumental (aesthetic) value, the experience it provides has intrinsic value: is worth having for its own sake, independently of its relationship to any other experiences. This is the position that would be taken by many philosophers, though not all. Everyone will grant that we often *desire*

---

1. See "The Discrimination of Aesthetic Enjoyment," *British Journal of Aesthetics* 3 (1963):291–300; pp. 35–45 of this volume.

such experiences in and for themselves, apart from any further experiences to which they lead. One generally takes the subway to the concert in order to hear the music, rather than being willing to put up with the music for the sake of the subway ride. The difficulty arises when we try to give a convincing philosophical proof that aesthetic enjoyment is good in itself; indeed, I don't think any such proof has been or can be given.[2]

If there is no such thing as intrinsic value, or even if it simply cannot be shown that aesthetic enjoyment has intrinsic value, the justification question begins to look somewhat less tractable. It would be fine if we could stop with the enjoyable experience itself, and say that *that* is its own excuse for being (or occurring), and there the matter ends. But the step from "enjoyable" to "justifiably enjoyed"—from "can be enjoyed" to "is worthy of being enjoyed"—is a big one; the logical gap is quite distinct, and not to be glossed over. The fact that you like to listen to music is important; by itself, however, it does not settle the question whether music is worth listening to.

What is required, then, is an answer to the further question: "What good is aesthetic enjoyment?" or, if you prefer, "Why should we cultivate aesthetic experience?" Obviously, we hope not to get drawn into an endless series of questions, for then the final answer to the justification question will elude us forever. But if we can push the inquiry far enough to connect aesthetic evaluation with other and already acknowledged forms of value, then we will have provided an adequate provisional justification of art—will have given at least one good reason (if anyone should ask) why artists should be encouraged to create, why a study of the arts should be an essential part of our school and college curricula. For example, if someone can show that a certain sort of music not only is aesthetically enjoyable, but also has a beneficial effect on manic-depressives, then we have connected the music's value as music with another generally accepted value, mental health.

Now it is this kind of example that is likely to irritate the true lover of the arts. "You're talking about usefulness," he may retort, "but art glories in its uselessness. You distort the whole situation when you expect art to serve these practical purposes, as

---

2. See "Intrinsic Value," *Philosophy and Phenomenological Research* 26 (1965):1–17; pp. 46–64 of this volume.

though a painting were a pair of shoes, a poem a piece of advertising copy, and a musical composition a safer substitute for tranquillizers and hallucinogens. Art has no purpose beyond itself. It's good for nothing. That's what's good about it. Art for Art!"

I think we can clear up the misunderstanding here if we are careful about the claims we want to make. The trouble with my mental-health example is that it makes the work of art a direct means to an effect that is only contingently, or tangentially, related to the work itself: first, in that the effect is produced only by a selection of works of art (only by some pieces of music), rather than by art as such; and second, in that the effect is unrelated to the aesthetic value of works of art (since the music that is most effective with the manic-depressive is not the greatest music). To use a work of art in this way, then, seems like a misuse of it, or at least a deviant application of it. The *Winged Victory* could no doubt serve as ballast in an underloaded aircraft—but it would be absurd to call that a justification of it, a good reason for creating it.

The trouble with the mental-health justification, then, is not that it justifies aesthetic experience by pointing to a more distant desirable effect, but that the effect it points to is a side effect, so to speak. The capacity to produce this effect is an *incidental value* of the work. But suppose there is another kind of effect, or set of effects, that is more directly dependent on the work of art *qua* work of art—that satisfies two conditions: first, it is produced by means of, or via, aesthetic enjoyment, and therefore it is produced to some degree (however small) by all good works of art; second, the degree to which it is produced is correlated (at least roughly) with the aesthetic value of the work, so that, on the whole and generally speaking, the better the work of art, the greater the effect it is capable of producing. Then the capacity to produce this sort of (desirable) effect is an *inherent value* of the work.

The dispute, then, between the serious-minded person who asks for a justification of art and the indignant defender of Art for Art is often both heated and darkened by confusion between intrinsic value and inherent value. And when this distinction is clarified, the dispute can often be cooled and lighted. The defender of Art for Art may be thinking that the only way to counter defenses of art that are based on incidental values is to insist that art has intrinsic value; but this is to escape one error by another.

What he or she should only, but firmly, insist on is that the existence of works of art is justified in terms of their inherent value; this is enough to claim for art, enough to give it uniqueness and autonomy, without cutting it off completely from all the other human interests and goods.

III

It is enough to justify art in terms of its inherent value. But is it too much to ask? That is the question we now have to face. And to turn from fairly definite and manageable philosophical abstractions to what can only be called psychological speculation is to leave security for uncertainty.

What reason do we have for thinking that it is desirable for people to experience aesthetic enjoyment—and to develop whatever capacity they may have for this enjoyment? I could put the question more bluntly—"What good is art, after all?"—except that this wording might again inflame the true lover of art. Our purpose here is not to ask an unfair, illegitimate, and deprecatory question about art, but only to ask what inherent value it has, if any—and this question is one that anyone should be willing to ask and try to answer.

The kinds of answer that have been tried might be classified in a preliminary way according to their degree of depth or ambitiousness. (1) There are those that appeal to episodic psychological effects: the claim is that particular aesthetic experiences are valuable because they produce short-term adjustments within the psyche. Aristotle's theory of catharsis, at least as it has sometimes been interpreted, may be a theory of this sort; a modern psychologist might talk in terms of temporary relief of tensions, or a feeling of elation, heightened power and control, or a sense of harmony. But since the value of these resulting psychological states (assuming that they do characteristically occur) can itself be questioned, persistent inquiry would lead to a further theory in the second group.

(2) There are those answers that appeal to particular psychological capacities or faculties: the claim is that repeated aesthetic enjoyments have a tendency to develop or strengthen or sharpen or refine one of these capacities. Under this heading, the key notions are those of (a) feeling and/or emotion, (b) imagination, and (c) perception. For example, Aldous Huxley has argued for

the importance of "training perception," and though he thinks that special techniques, such as those that have been experimented with at Ohio State, are very effective in this regard, he also thinks that extensive and intensive experience with the (nonverbal) arts will help.[3] This would be a defense of the 2c type.

Again, of course, the justification question can be pressed: What is the point of extending these capacities? And this may lead to those further (3) answers that try to relate the experience of art to effects on the whole personality structure. Huxley himself does this in his essay. The Confucian aesthetic, with its claim that music and poetry can bring about harmony within the individual and within society, provides a type 3 justification.[4]

In order to see the possibilities of a theory of the inherent value of art, as well as the difficulties in formulating a clear theory and obtaining empirical evidence to support it, let us consider Donald Arnstine's interesting and stimulating discussion.[5] It belongs in the 2a category but has implications for 3 as well.

Arnstine's position is that the inherent value of art consists in its capacity, when fully and properly experienced, to "educate the emotions," and thereby develop "emotional maturity," which in turn will not only have value to the individual, but help to perpetuate a democratic society (see pp. 46, 51). We must first see what is involved in emotional education. Arnstine's first statement is puzzling: "Normally, then, we think and we feel, and either may be done well or badly" (p. 45). A person can surely think badly, but it is odd to say that he feels badly (just as it is odd to say that he sneezes badly). What Arnstine means is that a person's emotional response to a given situation may be more or less appropriate to it. It may be controlled by the wrong cues in the situation, or inadequately controlled by the right cues. So the

---

3. See "Human Potentialities," in *Control of the Mind*, ed. Seymour M. Farber and Roger H. L. Wilson (New York, 1961), esp. pp. 68–70. Compare Jerome Bruner, *Toward a Theory of Instruction* (Cambridge, Mass., 1966), p. 34.

4. See Siu-chi Huang, "Musical Art in Early Confucian Philosophy," *Philosophy East and West* 13 (1963):49–59. It is interesting to read that the Mohist philosopher Mo Tzu (465?–385? B.C.) "was so anxiously concerned with the economic welfare of the people that he severely criticized the Confucian theory of music as dangerous. . . . Music (he held) is of no practical value and produces no material benefits to society" (pp. 51–52).

5. Donald Arnstine, "Shaping the Emotions: The Sources of Standards for Aesthetic Education," *Journal of Aesthetic Education* 1 (1966):45–69. Compare Rosemary Hebden, in the symposium "Theoretical Problems of Art Education," *British Journal of Aesthetics* 6 (1966):40–45.

person remains indifferent in witnessing an act of wanton cruelty, or reacts oversentimentally to an event that is mildly pathetic (see pp. 46–47). Emotional maturity, then, consists in a tendency to make appropriate emotional responses to situations—to feel in the right way toward or about them.

Now, I agree that there is such a thing as appropriate or fitting emotional response, and that it is possible to miss it, either by falling short (as with a cold-blooded person) or by overdoing it (as with a sentimental person) or by missing the cues and thus being led to respond in a way appropriate to a quite different situation. I don't think it's easy to specify the criteria of appropriateness, and in fact it may be that we have here a complicated normative concept that is bound up with a number of other important concepts. (If to respond appropriately is to respond as one *ought* to respond, then this judgment is an ethical judgment, and has to be supported by ethical arguments that the response is right or obligatory.) But let us set aside the difficulty of knowing what emotion is appropriate to what situation, and consider what would be involved in educating for appropriate responses.

Why should we believe that frequent intensive exposure to works of art will in fact increase a person's tendency to respond with appropriate emotions to life situations? Such a question has two aspects: we can ask what evidence there is that this outcome does actually occur; and we can try to theorize plausibly about psychological mechanisms that could operate to make it occur. As far as the experimental evidence goes, we are, of course, still at the earliest stage. It would be difficult to detect lasting increases in appropriateness of response in subjects who have, let us say, undergone a course in music or poetry, and to show that the increase is probably attributable to the course. And the nonexperimental evidence, not surprisingly, is far from unambiguous; we do not know that composers, opera singers, painters, playwrights, and actors are typically above average in the appropriateness of their emotional responses to life situations.

When we consider the more indirect line of inquiry, we can find plausible proposals, but they are surely not yet in a state to warrant confident acceptance. For example, Arnstine suggests that works of art may encourage emotional maturity "through the heightening and refinement of sensitivity to the emotional qualities of experience" (p. 51). Now this does seem a reasonable claim to make for literature, at least. In a lyric poem, precisely what happens is the response of a speaker to a situation that confronts him: anything from a revolution to a certain chilliness in his beloved. And since an understanding reading of much lyric poetry (and, *mutatis mutandis,* of novels and plays) would require one to make subtle discriminations among qualities of situations and qualities of emotional responses to them, it would seem reasonable to expect that such experiences can refine one's sensitivity to nuances of human experience. (But we don't *know* this until we have more solid psychological information.)

Many claims, however, might be made for literature[6]—which after all deals directly with human predicaments and human emotions—that it would be harder to make for nonverbal works of art. Still, something might be said. Consider music. Music moves us, it is true; but music doesn't arouse emotions in us—not, it seems to me, in a straightforward sense of the term. We may read a lyric poem in which the speaker is angry about a wrong that has been done to him or to another, and we may contemplate his anger as an object of aesthetic interest. We may also participate in it, and feel something of it ourselves, while we read the poem. We may listen to a passage of music that can fairly (if metaphorically) be described as angry; we simply hear that quality in the music. To use the classical formulation of Carroll C. Pratt, it sounds the way an angry person feels. But since there is nothing in the music, or referred to by the music, for us to be angry *at,* we do not share this emotion ourselves at all; the music doesn't make us angry, it simply presents the quality of angriness. Since there is no situation to be responded to in the music, we can hardly learn from it a lesson in appropriate response. Our emotions are not involved at all; therefore, they cannot be "shaped" or molded by the music.

Yet, on the other hand, it might be claimed that the experience of contemplating the phenomenally objective emotion-like quality of musical angriness, just like the experience of contemplating the phenomenally subjective experience of anger itself, could sharpen our perception of that quality which is common to both perceived (metaphorical) angriness and felt anger and refine our sensitivity to differences among various shades and degrees and nuances of that quality. So perhaps, after all, music—and, in a similar way nonrepresentational works of visual art—may make an indirect

---

6. See "The Humanities and Human Understanding," in *The Humanities and the Understanding of Reality* (Lexington, Ky., 1966).

contribution to emotional maturity, as Arnstine seems to hold. But if this is what makes music inherently valuable, the justification seems somewhat slight: musical experience is a rather roundabout way of producing emotional maturity; certainly literature would be more direct and efficient.

What this suggests to me is that our question about the inherent value of the arts in general may be too rigid and demanding. It may be that there are several relevant values, each inherent in one or more of the arts, even though there is little that can be hoped for across the board. And especially it may be that the verbal and the nonverbal arts are to be justified in very different ways. Many years ago John Dewey wrote, in an article in the *Journal of the Barnes Foundation*:

> For to make of paintings an educational means is to assert that the genuine intelligent realization of pictures is not only an integration of the specialized factors found in the paintings as such, but is such a deep and abiding experience of the nature of fully harmonized experience as sets a standard or forms a habit for all other experiences. In other words, paintings when taken out of their specialized niche are the basis of an educational experience which counteracts the disrupting tendencies of the hard-and-fast specializations, compartmental divisions and rigid segregations which so confuse and nullify our present life.[7]

Again, this is speculation. But it is (I would say) interesting and challenging speculation, and it suggests lines of empirical inquiry that still await serious and sustained pursuit. That the integrated painting, as a work of art, "sets a standard," or serves as a model, of what experience can be when its strands are made harmonious, when ends-in-view and means-at-hand are seen in relation to one another, when divisions and segregations are overcome, without being erased and lost—this is something we can learn by ordinary study. But that it also "forms a habit for all other experiences," by leading the percipient to acquire a taste for integration that carries over into his life and helps to shape his works and days—this is what we need inquiry to be assured of.

But note two limitations in this statement of an inherent value of art. The first is that the claim may not even be valid for paintings in general. Contemporary painters who have explored the maximum intensification of regional qualities—of autumnal grav-

---

7. "Affective Thought in Logic and Painting," in *Art and Education*, 3d ed. (Merion, Pa., 1954), p. 104.

ity or springtime freshness—have sometimes had to be content with a comparatively low degree of integration in the formal design. Yet they have produced some fine paintings. So we may have to conclude that there are two distinct inherent values here: the capacity to be a model of (and perhaps an influence on) psychic integration, and the capacity to produce a lasting sense of heightened awareness of the perceptual qualities about us. And it may be that paintings whose aesthetic value is largely dependent on their unity specialize in one sort of inherent value, and paintings whose aesthetic value is largely dependent on the intensity of their regional qualities specialize in another sort of inherent value. (Many great paintings of course do both; and it may be that any painting that is very good must do both to some degree.)

The second limitation of Dewey's statement is that even if it is true of all or much good painting, it may not apply to literature—at least in quite the same sense or degree. Does a good lyric poem or a good novel always provide us with "a deep and abiding experience of the nature of fully harmonized experience"? No doubt it may, if it is the sort of literary work whose aesthetic value is largely a function of its careful design and style. But I should think that many literary works of a high order cannot claim very much inherent value of the sort Dewey speaks of, though they may have considerable inherent value of the sort that Arnstine describes.

One thing we can be sure of, and that is that psychological inquiry in the not too distant future will tell us a good deal more than we know now about the types of inherent value that are to be found in works of art of various sorts. Meanwhile, we ought to become as clear as possible about what we are looking for. And while we must take care not to overestimate our present knowledge about the inherent values of art, we may reasonably consider that we have enough on hand to justify a strong hunch that these values are very great.

5: *Aesthetic Experience Regained*

I

THIS is not the ideal historical moment for discoursing on aesthetic theory. That ought to be done with quietness and patience. But a quiet voice is all too easily drowned out by the cries of anguish and of anger we hear around us, and patience is a virtue that only those who live in a less terrified society can afford to cultivate. Even hardened aestheticians (an obvious oxymoron) may suffer from doubts that beauty or significant form is what the world needs most right now, when quite different goods—intelligence and charity, for instance—are more likely to restore our sense of community and stop us from creating a society whose answer to all problems, aesthetic and otherwise, will be violent repression. When so many of us in this troubled land do not seem to care very much even for one another, much less for the ravaged nature and crumbling cities our descendants will inherit, the aesthetic point of view becomes difficult to sustain. It may even seem absurd.

But though it would be more than human never to feel such doubts, it would be less than human to succumb to them. If all rational reflection on the domain of art must be indefinitely postponed, we have already lost our struggle and reduced the chances that others can win theirs later. It is not as though we were shutting our eyes to reality by resolving to continue our aesthetic dialogue, but rather that we refuse to let certain important things be lost sight of.

It is in this spirit that I address you now. I draw some comfort—which it is yours to share—from the nature of my mission. I have cast myself in the role of do-gooder. Not quite as much of a do-gooder as my title suggests, of course: it's not salvation that I have to offer, but something more like hot soup. Call it a conceptual rescue operation—an attempt to rehabilitate or maybe even rejuvenate a concept that has played an important role in twentieth-century aesthetics, but has lost its respectability in sophisticated circles and is in peril of its very life.

II

It would be interesting to know who first used the term "aesthetic experience" with intent to mark out a kind of experience that is obtainable from some of the works of nature and some of the technological works of man, but is characteristically and preeminently afforded by works of art. Interest in the typical effects—both immediate and delayed—of music and tragic drama goes back, of course, a long way in the history of aesthetics. And the emergence of a quasi-scientific psychology in the eighteenth century gave much impetus to this empirical inquiry. But these earlier students preferred narrower—some would say better—terms to describe the effects they were particularly interested in, whether, like Aristotle, they welcomed these effects or, like Plato, viewed them with alarm. They spoke of feeding and watering the passions (in Jowett's poetic version), of catharsis (to be sure), of instruction and delight, transport, pleasure, or peculiar operations of the transcendental faculties of understanding. But the concept of a kind of *experience* must be much more recent.

Whatever its origin, this concept undoubtedly achieved its fullest development and its richest application in the aesthetic theory of John Dewey. I think it is largely to his work that we owe the extensive adoption of the term by contemporary aestheticians, even though not all of us, of course, accept everything that Dewey said about aesthetic experience. Most of us, indeed, have—I think fortunately—refused to follow some of the more cryptic passages in *Art as Experience* where Dewey proposes to identify the work of art with an experience. It has become usual to talk about the experience, or an experience, *of* a work of art as something distinct from the work that is the object of, and in, the experience. In any case, it has been very widely accepted that there is such a thing as aesthetic experience, describable in its own terms and distinguishable, at least by the practiced introspecter, from other sorts of experience.

It may be that scholarly status seeking or academic social climbing has had some part in promoting the term "aesthetic experience." The spread—and to my mind, the beneficent spread—of progressive education, with its early-Deweyan involvement with "interactions" and "transactions" and "doings and undergoings," had numerous consequences. On one educational level it popularized such expressions as "experiencing pictures" and "the musical experience." On a more elevated level, some aestheticians may have felt that if other university departments were to have their things, such as "the religious experience" and "political man," then we ought to stake out a comparable segment of life as our own concern. Even if we found it no easy task to teach people how to tell when they were having an aesthetic experience, we were confident that to be in this glorious state is not the same as feeling tipsy or merely comfortable.

Our confidence, after all, was sustained by some phenomenological evidence. It seemed obvious that musical, literary, dramatic, plastic, and other such experiences do have something rather special about them. And though they are not exact substitutes for each other, they seem to go together: the experience of listening to a song has more in common with the experience of looking at a piece of sculpture than it does, say, with that of walking in a picket line or driving down the Schuylkill Expressway. So perhaps it was a bit "non sequiturish" for W. E. Kennick to say, in his famous iconoclastic essay: "To put it dogmatically, there is no such thing as *the* Aesthetic Experience; different sorts of experiences are properly referred to as aesthetic."[1] I grant the differences; however, they leave open the question what there is about the different experiences that makes it "proper" to call them aesthetic.

Moreover, the concept of aesthetic experience provides a convenient and—to me—persuasive analysis of artistic goodness. Here lies, I think, its greatest philosophical significance. Those of us who are committed to a naturalistic metaphysical position, whatever our differences may be, will seek the ground of artistic goodness, as of all other forms of goodness, in the import of things for human welfare. Not that to be good is simply to have effects on human beings, but that to be good is to have the poten-

---

1. "Does Traditional Aesthetics Rest on a Mistake?," *Mind* 17 (1958): 323. Compare Marshall Cohen, "Aesthetic Essence," in *Philosophy in America*, ed. Max Black (Ithaca, N. Y., 1965): "There is no reason to believe any property essential to aesthetic experience or certainly, to believe that such a property distinguishes aesthetic from, say, 'practical,' or intellectual experience" (pp. 116–17).

tiality for such effects, assuming that the effects are desirable. And since works of art are typically destitute of any power to affect other objects, in the way a fork-lift truck or a stick of dynamite can, they must be classed among the consumer goods, rather than the production goods, of this world. Setting aside transcendent beauties or ineffable intuitions, the only ground that seems to be left for attributing goodness to works of art is the sort of experience they have it in them to provide. This is the use to be made of them. If artistic goodness is that sort of goodness that an object possesses in virtue of its capacity to provide aesthetic experience (which is here assumed to be desirable), then there can be no artistic goodness unless there can be aesthetic experiences.

I cannot, of course, deny that we could frame other naturalistic definitions of "artistic goodness" that dispense with the term "aesthetic experience" in favor, say, of "aesthetic satisfaction." These alternatives, which are several, have been partly, though by no means fully, explored.[2] The difficulty common to those I know of—not perhaps an insuperable difficulty—is that of distinguishing between the relevant kind of satisfaction and other kinds. To know "what makes a situation aesthetic," in J. O. Urmson's well-known words, we must first know what makes a *satisfaction* aesthetic, and that seems to depend entirely on the kind of properties that you take satisfaction in. But an experience is larger than a satisfaction, and more independently describable. Perhaps, then, we can distinguish an aesthetic experience from a nonaesthetic one in terms of its own internal properties, and thus decide whether or not an experience is aesthetic without having first to know whether or not the *object* of (and in) the experience has the properties that permit aesthetic experiences.

Despite the good uses it can undoubtedly be put to, if it will do the job, the notion of aesthetic experience is surely a queer one. There is first the difficulty in talking intelligibly about experiences as such. Dewey applies the most extravagant predicates to experiences, some of them metaphorically far out; for example, "slack and discursive" and "having no holes, mechanical junctions, and dead centers."[3] Some of these expressions may be taken meton-

2. See, for example, J. O. Urmson, "What Makes a Situation Aesthetic?," *Proceedings of the Aristotelian Society* 31 suppl. (1957): 75–92; M. C. Beardsley, "The Discrimination of Aesthetic Enjoyment," pp. 35–45 of this volume.

3. For further examples see my essay "Aesthetic Theory and Educational Theory," in *Aesthetic Concepts and Education*, ed. Ralph A. Smith (Urbana, Ill., 1970).

ymically as applied to the objects of the experience. Some cannot. An experience can have a certain duration; so much is clear. But what else can correctly be said about it? This is one puzzle. But even if we are allowed to apply some predicates to experiences, it may also be questioned whether they will be rich enough and exact enough to afford a reasonably clear distinction between aesthetic experiences and other kinds. That is the second puzzle.

And now another aesthetic iconoclast has come upon this scene to challenge the entire concept. In his provocative essay of some years ago,[4] George Dickie directed his attack against "the causal conception of aesthetic experience" in general, and certain typical forms of it in particular. His critique is both sharp and forceful, and his arguments should move us all—either to give an adequate defense of aesthetic experience or to learn to do without it. It is this challenge that I take up now.

III

What does it mean to say that someone is having an aesthetic experience? Strangely enough, in all the literature on aesthetic experience, I cannot find a direct and concise answer to this question. In fact, when I make the attempt, I realize that it is by no means easy to give a satisfactory answer. What is worse, I have the uneasy feeling that my own answer has latent flaws, the ruthless examination of which might lead to just the consequence this whole essay is aimed to ward off: namely, the abandonment of the concept of aesthetic experience. But we shall see.

I propose to say that a person is having an aesthetic experience during a particular stretch of time if and only if the greater part of his mental activity during that time is united and made pleasurable by being tied to the form and qualities of a sensuously presented or imaginatively intended object on which his primary attention is concentrated.

The structure of aesthetic experience, then, might be sketched in the following way. As someone listens to a piece of music, say, or watches a motion picture, he attends to various features of a phenomenally objective field: to sounds, pictures, and so forth.

---

4. George Dickie, "Beardsley's Phantom Aesthetic Experience," *The Journal of Philosophy* 62 (1965): 129–36; compare my *Aesthetics: Problems in the Philosophy of Criticism* (New York, 1958), pp. 527–30, 552–54. I wish to thank Dickie for his helpful critical comments on the present paper.

At the same time, he is aware of various phenomenally subjective events: his expectations are aroused and he feels satisfactions when they are fulfilled, or he has sympathy-like or anger-like emotions toward the events that occur in the film. We can describe the phenomenally objective qualities and forms: these are the properties of the work of art that appear in the experience. We can describe the phenomenally subjective feelings and emotions: they may be said to be "evoked by" or to be "responses to" the work of art, and in this special sense these *affects* can be said to be caused by the objective features. The experience, as such, consists of both objective and affective elements, and, indeed, of all the elements of awareness that occur in the perceiver during the time of exposure to the work of art, except those elements that are unconnected with that work of art (e.g., traffic noises or sudden thoughts of unpaid bills).

Now, it is agreed that some interesting things can be said about the work of art as experienced: that it may be more or less unified—that is, that it may be more or less coherent and more or less complete in itself. The difficulty is in my second assumption: that we can also apply these terms (and similar ones) to the experience as such. If that second application makes sense—if it is intelligible to speak of "experience" as having coherence and completeness, and not merely of "works of art" as having these properties—then it becomes possible to hold (as I have held) that the unity of an aesthetic experience is "due to," is "determined by," the unity of the work of art that it is the experience of. This would be a synthetic, empirical statement. But it is just this statement that Dickie rejects, because, according to him, the term "unified" cannot intelligibly be applied to experiences.

This philosophical mistake is described by Dickie as a simple, though serious, confusion. The word *experience* is a very convenient catch-all term that we use on many occasions when we do not need to describe what went on very definitely. But Dickie suggests that it must always be able to be cashed in: "'It was a great experience' simply means 'It (the game) was thrilling' or 'It (the play) was exciting or moving,' and so forth. 'It was an experience that I shall never forget' simply means 'I shall always remember the game (painting, play, or whatever)' and so on." And so "the harmless expression 'the experience of unity,' which is used as a general way of referring to the seeing of the unified design, the hearing of the sound pattern, and so on, is somehow inverted and becomes 'the unity of experience.'"[5]

"Somehow" is not really the right word here; Dickie, in fact, attributes this error in Dewey to the lingering malign influence of German idealism, which made such expressions as "the unity of experience" seem to mean something. As his examples show, Dickie thinks that statements about aesthetic experiences, to make sense, must be regarded as shorthand expressions either for (1) the work of art as perceived (the music was unified) or for (2) the affects evoked by the work (one was thrilled or moved). From this he concludes that *no* terms (including the crucial critical terms that interest us here) apply intelligibly and irreducibly to experiences as such. Let us, for convenience, call this Dickie's experience thesis, that is, the thesis that the terms "unified," "coherent," and "complete" do not apply to aesthetic experiences as such. If it is correct, then we cannot, of course, use any of these concepts as criteria to distinguish aesthetic experiences from other sorts of experience.

Dickie also holds that we cannot intelligibly apply the terms "unified," "coherent," and "complete" to the phenomenally *subjective* features of the experience as such. Let us call this Dickie's affect thesis. Dickie, of course, does not deny that such affects occur in our encounters with works of art: we are, he says, thrilled and moved. But he does not think it makes sense to talk about the unity of sequences of such affects.

The relation between the two theses seems to me to be this: given a certain natural assumption, the experience thesis entails the affect thesis. Thus, suppose the affect thesis is false, and there are sequences of affects that are unified. Then it is possible for someone to perceive a unified piece of music and at the same time feel a unified sequence of affects. But if each of these sequences (of sounds and of affects) could be unified, they could also be so related as to be united with each other (this is my assumption), and in that case the experience as a whole would be unified. Hence the experience thesis would be false.

But though the falsity of the affect thesis implies the falsity of the experience thesis (if we make that one assumption), the *truth* of the affect thesis does not imply the *truth* of the experience

---

5. Dickie, "Beardsley's Phantom Aesthetic Experience," p. 135.

thesis. For even if Dickie is right in thinking that it does not make sense to speak of sequences of affects as "unified," it may still make sense to speak of *experiences* (made up of both affects and phenomenally objective qualities) as "unified." And whether it does make sense is just what we wish to know.

IV

Let us first consider Dickie's treatment of the concept of *coherence*. My position, briefly, is (1) that (for example) a musical composition, as heard, may be a highly coherent phenomenal object and (2) that the experience that involves close continued attention to the music may also be highly coherent, when the affective elements of the experience are under the control, so to speak, of the perceptual elements. A coherent experience is something more than an "experience of coherence"—though what makes an (aesthetic) experience coherent is that it is, in part, an experience of something coherent. In describing coherence of experience (relying, obviously, on John Dewey), I wrote that "one thing leads to another; continuity of development, without gaps or dead spaces, a sense of overall providential pattern of guidance, an orderly cumulation of energy toward a climax, are present to an unusual degree."[6] Dickie's comment is this: "Note that everything referred to here is a perceptual characteristic (what Beardsley calls 'the phenomenally objective presentation in experience') and not an effect of the perceived characteristics. Thus no ground is furnished for concluding that experiences can be unified in the sense of being coherent."[7]

On the contrary, it seems to me that some of these expressions apply not only to phenomenally objective fields. A feeling, for example, may vary in intensity over a certain stretch of time, and it may change by gentle degrees or abruptly; or it may be interrupted by quite opposed or irrelevant feelings; it may fluctuate in a random way, at the mercy of shifts in the phenomenally objective field, or it may begin as one feeling among many and slowly spread over the whole field of awareness. It seems to me that the terms "continuity" and "discontinuity" apply quite clearly to such

---

6. *Aesthetics*, p. 528.
7. Dickie, "Beardsley's Phantom Aesthetic Experience," p. 131; compare p. 133.

sequences, and continuity makes for coherence, in affects as well as in objects.

In order to quiet the suspicion that this way of talking is due to philosophers' habitual high-handedness with plain language, let me appeal to the authority of a psychologist. In his studies of what he calls "peak-experiences"—among them experiences of works of art—Maslow has discriminated and generalized various characteristics of these experiences. He says, for example: "The person in the peak-experiences feels more integrated (unified, whole, all-of-a-piece) than at other times. . . . He is now most free of blocks, inhibitions, cautions, fears, doubts, controls, reservations, self-criticisms, brakes. . . . This is both a subjective and an objective phenomenon, and could be described further in both ways."[8] The phenomenology of this matter is no doubt very difficult to be clear about. But if it is true that the person in aesthetic experience feels a high degree of "integration" (which I construe as a kind of coherence), then it would seem that there is in fact an integration of his feelings: they feel closely related to each other, as though they belong with each other and to each other.

I turn now to Dickie's treatment of the concept of *completeness*. And, again, my position is (1) that a musical composition (for example) can be highly complete, in the sense of finishing what it starts and thus being sufficient unto itself, and (2) that a complete musical composition can help to provide an *experience* that is complete. But the experience of completeness (of the music) is only part of what constitutes the completeness of the experience (as a whole).

In my earlier treatment, I tried to describe two forms of completeness, or two patterns of experience that (it seemed to me) are highly complete. One of these was a "balance" or "equilibrium" of impulses or tendencies (say, the confrontation of opposed feelings about the same object). Dickie's critical analysis of this line of thought is devastating; he shows that I was thoroughly mistaken about it. The second pattern of experience, however, was the pattern of expectation and fulfillment. Again the phenomenology is elusive and subtle. It is agreed that a musical passage, for example, may arouse the expectation that certain other musical events are to follow (this is the kind of experience that is so fully

---

8. Abraham H. Maslow, *Toward a Psychology of Being* (Princeton, N. J., 1962), pp. 98, 101.

studied by Leonard Meyer in his *Emotion and Meaning in Music*). It is also agreed that the promised events, when at last they occur, may fulfill the expectation and thus end the condition of suspense. This kind of thing is what I cited as a paradigm case of completeness. I said that music has (phenomenally objective) completeness, and the experience as a whole also has completeness. But Dickie objects: "Now when an expectancy is satisfied a process is completed; i.e., over with; but is the process (the expectation and the satisfaction) complete in the sense of being unified?"[9] When the expected actually occurs, a gestalt has been completed: we have, says Dickie, the experience of a completion. This sense of finality may pervade both the objective and the affective parts of the whole field of awareness. But (he argues) the "experience of completion" is something that occurs at the end of the experience of the music (or of some well-defined part of it); so it cannot provide the further and quite distinct concept of the *completeness of the experience*.

But this is just the nature of an experience, considered as such: that its character is partly given by its end. When the gestalt completes itself, we now think of the whole experience as building to that end; the (musical) significance of much that we have heard is now at last revealed, and the recollection of our earlier expectations and the way the music played with them takes on a new intensity in the light of what is now happening, in the final moments. It is in something like this sense, I think, that the experience as such takes on the character of completeness. And I think this is what Maslow has in mind when he writes: "All peak-experiences may be fruitfully understood as completions-of-the-act in David M. Levy's sense, or as the Gestalt psychologists' closure, or on the paradigm of the Reichian type of complete orgasm, or as total discharge, catharsis, culmination, climax, consummation, emptying, or finishing."[10]

V

This defense of aesthetic experience is far from being a whole brief; it mainly replies to certain key points in the indictment. The most fundamental point of all is Dickie's allegation that *unity* and

9. Dickie, "Beardsley's Phantom Aesthetic Experience," p. 133.
10. Ibid. p. 104.

its family of related terms do not even apply, strictly speaking. If that point can be rebutted, then we face the possibility that unity, while indeed a property of aesthetic experiences, is no more special to them than to any other experiences. This is the view, for example, of Marshall Cohen: "Surely, the experience of riding a crowded subway, or of being badly beaten, has at least as great a degree of unity as (and is more surely pervaded by a single individualizing quality than) the experience of hearing many a sonata or symphonic suite, or of reading many a picaresque novel or chronicle play."[11]

This is the sort of example that contemporary critics of "aesthetic essences" are likely to toss out, like sausages to wolves chasing a Siberian sleigh, to keep the philosophic reader occupied while the argument rushes headlong on. The business about the "single individualizing quality" alludes, of course, to one of Dewey's more dubious statements about the unity of *an experience.* But apart from that, does the experience of riding a crowded subway really have unity, or is it a mass of jarringly diverse and confused impressions, without dramatic structure or formal development? Even in a "chronicle play" the appearances and disappearances of important characters are far more interrelated than the arrival and departure of subway straphangers. (I must add that I checked this impression only last week while riding on the Broadway–7th Avenue subway.)

These brief remarks are only the beginning of an argument to show that, contrary to Marshall Cohen, our experiences of works of art, and especially our experiences of good works of art, are in fact generally of a high order of unity—of coherence and completeness—compared with most daily experiences. But even if I had time I would hesitate to present such an argument here: the point seems to me somewhat elementary, once we establish the propriety of discussing the question at all.

There is one further question that I think we should look into, however, because it grows so directly out of the line of thought we have been following. I said awhile back that perhaps the main philosophic use to be made of the concept of aesthetic experience is in giving a satisfactory analysis of artistic goodness. But there remains the problem of artistic *betterness.* To attribute artistic goodness to an object is, I claim, to attribute to it the capacity to

---

11. Cohen, "Aesthetic Essence," p. 119.

provide a certain desirable kind of experience. What, then, does it mean to say that one object is artistically better than another?

What we must look for, I suppose, is a dimension along which we can compare aesthetic experiences—call it the dimension of D-ness—so that we can say, justifiably, that it is X's capacity to provide aesthetic experiences with greater D-ness that gives it greater artistic goodness than Y has. Unless we can identify, and exhibit, such a dimension—whether simple or compound—we cannot claim to have provided a value theory adequate to the requirements of critical judgment.

So far as I can see, there is only one tenable answer: that D-ness is amount of pleasure. Other hedonistic terms may be preferable, at least in certain contexts where misunderstanding lurks: enjoyment, satisfaction, gratification, or delight. But the main thing to note is that the pleasure here involved is aesthetic pleasure, that is, that kind of pleasure that is found in aesthetic experience. The view I propose, then, is that X is artistically better than Y if X is capable of providing a more pleasurable aesthetic experience than any that Y is capable of providing.

I realize that up to this point my discussion may have suggested a rather dry and solemn view of aesthetic experiences. I have not spoken, for example, of those delightful characteristics of Maslow's "peak-experiences": the sense of liberation, the joy of play, elation, fullness of power. Letting the term "pleasure" cover all such positive affective states, it seems to me plain that aesthetic experience is pleasurable, and indeed, essentially so. If the fabled businessman dragged to the opera by his wife does not enjoy himself, that is a reliable indication that he is not having an aesthetic experience—though, of course, the fact that his wife *does* enjoy herself does not show she *is* having one.

My proposed account of artistic betterness, then, presupposes that aesthetic experience is always pleasurable. But this has been denied, for example, by Marshall Cohen: "But, as we may question whether beauty is, indeed, the essential property of art, we may question whether pleasure, which aestheticians have normally supposed to be characteristic of its apprehension, is, truly, an essential feature of aesthetic experience."[12] At this moment,

---

12. Ibid, p. 118. There are some good remarks about the pleasure of aesthetic experience in Pepita Haezrahi, *The Contemplative Activity* (New York, 1956), esp. p. 43.

beauty is not in question (fortunately), but pleasure is. Cohen's climatic example is that "the muzzles of the battleship *Potemkin*, pointed at the audience, are positively menacing." This is another one of those sacrificial sausages, though not meaty enough to detain us long. It is not the battleship *Potemkin* that confronts us when we go to a motion picture theater to see the Eisenstein film, but merely a picture of it. And this picture does not in any way menace us, but instead it offers us the *quality* of menace—a quality that we deeply enjoy in its dramatic context. If we recall Burke's or Kant's or Schopenhauer's account of the sublime, it becomes obvious enough that examples like this do not in any way show that aesthetic experience can be unpleasurable.

VI

The more unsettling objection to the hedonistic account of aesthetic experience comes from a very different source: the current avant-garde, including both practical and theoretical wings. The "new aesthetic" of contemporary art escapes (according to these thinkers) the bounds of mere hedonism. The dimension of D-ness is not to be sought in pleasure, but in blowing the mind. It does not matter what sort of reaction a work of art evokes in us; the important thing is that it evoke *some* reaction, and as intense a reaction as possible. There is, for example, the psychedelic school of turning us on without drugs—one of the current impresarios of total environmental assaults (acid rock, strobe lights, incense, and multiscreen viewing) explains: "We try to vaporize the mind by bombing the senses." The more far-out sculptures and dramatic events are praised by avant-garde critics because they are so startling, terrifying, irritating, disgusting, shocking—or even stupefyingly boring. Never mind that boredom is no Maslow-type peak experience: at least it is a feeling. If Walter Kerr or Clive Barnes walks out of the play, or objects to its nonsensicalness, then the play is a success: it has provoked the very objection that was intended; it has wakened the conventional playgoer, if only for a moment, from his spiritual torpor. To turn away is to pay tribute to the "theater of cruelty" or the "living theater" that frees us from "bourgeois repressions"—like wearing clothes. When someone produces a film that makes everyone in the audience sick to his stomach, it may be hailed as supreme cinematic art.

This reactionist position is, then, that intensity of feeling is the dimension of *D*-ness, the ground of artistic betterness. It follows that newness is a prime requisite for really good art, since shocks wear off in time; this is why, in fact, avant-garde writers seldom talk about the goodness of works of art but much about novelty and originality. The first box of dirt brought into the Metropolitan Museum as natural art is a surprise; the second is just more dirt; to save this little artistic movement from exhaustion you then have to fill the whole museum with dirt, or throw it at the visitors.

My object is not to dismiss these ideas with ridicule, for their existence presses upon us some basic aesthetic questions. Why not broaden our concept of aesthetic experience and its dimension of comparative value so that we can include all of these activities, so long as something is really happening? First let us distinguish. The fact is that being bored (or being beaten up or shot at by battleships) is a very different sort of experience from the experience of reading Wallace Stevens or watching the Pennsylvania Ballet Company perform. And whatever may be the hunger that is satisfied by ear-splitting noises, it is not the hunger that draws us to the compositions of Beethoven or Bartók. Many contemporary experiments are, of course, attempts to open up new qualities and forms, new sources of aesthetic experience. Others are really an abandonment of anything we can recognize as aesthetic objectives, in favor of something else. Perhaps there is a need for these forms of sensuous masochism, artificially induced insanity, desperate lunges toward interpersonal contact on the most primitive levels. Such questions must be left to the deep social prophets and the gurus—among whom I am not to be numbered. But it is up to us to study these contemporary developments—more openly, sympathetically, and thoroughly than we have done so far—and to point out similarities and differences. When the experience is largely painful, when it consists more in blowing the mind than in revitalizing it, when it involves no exercise of discrimination and control, we must frankly say that what it provides is not much of an *aesthetic* experience, however intense it may be. And so its goodness, if it has any, cannot strictly be artistic goodness.

You see that my attempt at a conceptual rescue operation turns out to be even more substantial—it is not only the term "aesthetic experience" whose future I am trying to ensure, but even aesthetic experience itself. It seems on the face of it ridiculous to fear that a society, or a large part of it, could lose its understanding and desire for the kind of satisfaction that works of art afford. But there are times when a large part of the population, including its elected and unelected officials, seems to lose its grasp of what free scientific inquiry is all about or what is really at stake in such enterprises as universities and churches. Similarly, under present social and economic conditions, we may forget that there is a kind of gratification that is something more than gags or shocks or kicks.

We can hardly be too often reminded (if I may paraphrase a splendid sentence from John Stuart Mill) that there have been serious creative artists between whom and the aesthetic authorities of their times there took place some memorable collisions. An eternal problem of philosophy—how to cope conceptually with change—is perhaps most acute in aesthetics, where the phenomena ultimately to be understood are in a constant and necessary flux. We must somehow achieve that most difficult intellectual stance which keeps us open to everything that may have worth or the seeds of worth, yet without relinquishing all distinctions that give order to our thought.

It may be that we are now living through a revolution comparable to the broadening of aesthetic appreciation from beauty to the sublime a few centuries ago. If so, then along with a willingness to extend our concept of art—keeping it an "open concept"—must go a willingness to extend our concept of aesthetic experience, assimilating whatever happens to us when we confront these novel works. Or perhaps we should let the concept of art expand freely—applying it to any sort of object that is made to be given our undivided attention—but at the same time keep our concept of aesthetic experience rather restricted: then we would accept the consequence that some contemporary artists are not concerned to provide aesthetic experience, either because they have a need to share their own boredom or because they sincerely believe that beauty and significant form are no longer good for modern man. I am inclined, though without rigid conviction, to describe what is happening in this second way—though I do not accept its premises. No doubt other sorts of experience are important besides aesthetic experience. But if we concede the right of the artist to evoke them, we ought, by the same token, to insist that aesthetic experience is important, too—and we ought to do what can be done by such abstract labors as ours to ensure that aesthetic experience does not disappear amidst the troubles that now try our civilization.

6: *What Is an Aesthetic Quality?*

I

How do aesthetic qualities differ (generically) from nonaesthetic qualities? In putting my question this way, I assume what I defend elsewhere,[1] that there are such things as aesthetic qualities (*A* qualities), and that aesthetic attributions (e.g., "*H*'s recent sculptures have an air of ominousness") are best construed as attributing such qualities to objects.

It is remarkable how much disagreement there is about the distinguishing features of *A* qualities and how much agreement there is about particular cases. (But this sort of remarkableness is not unfamiliar to philosophers.) It seems that merely by giving a handful of examples—a method on which there has been a certain amount of reliance—one can teach a standard use of "*A* quality" and achieve a considerable degree of unanimity in the classification of other examples.

Not that this unanimity, at least among aestheticians, is complete. There are divergences when it comes to drawing the line between what I would call "objective" and "affective" *A* attributions. In "The play is engaging," is engagingness an *A* quality or a disposition of the work to produce certain effects? How about funniness, shockingness, distressingness, triteness (the last two were among Frank Sibley's original examples)? Dorothy Walsh says that "trivial" and "tiresome" are affective terms.[2] In some, perhaps in typical contexts, all of these terms are used affectively, but they can also be used to attribute phenomenally objective

---

I would like to thank John Fisher and Alan Tormey for their helpful comments on this essay.
  1. "The Descriptivist Account of Aesthetic Attributions," *Revue Internationale de Philosophie* 28 (1974): 336–52.
  2. "Aesthetic Descriptions," *British Journal of Aesthetics* 10 (July 1970): 246.

qualities. No doubt it would be convenient to have clearer criteria for distinguishing affective from objective uses, but that problem need not detain us now, for it would universally be conceded, I think, that when such words are used to attribute qualities to objects, the qualities they attribute are *A* qualities.

Another problem is more troublesome, though it has not been much discussed. Are all *A* qualities "regional qualities," in the weak sense of that term?[3] Sibley said that the *A* qualities he had in mind are "roughly" a subclass of regional qualities, thus suggesting that there may be exceptions.[4] Isabel Hungerland and K. Mitchells say without argument that a particular color can be cheerful and that its cheerfulness is an *A* quality, although it is not, of course, a regional quality.[5] But it doesn't seem to me that a particular homogeneous color patch, considered by itself, can really be cheerful, though of course a complex color design can be cheerful. We do say that someone is dressed in "gay colors" or "somber colors," but such a judgment does not entail that particular color patches have these qualities—only that their color tones contribute toward the gaiety or somberness of the whole. The design is gay or somber—or lively or garish—chiefly on account of the colors. We speak of "garish colors," too, but we do not suppose that a particular color can be garish. A particular color can be warm or cool, but are these *A* qualities? I think we must mean something different by "warm" when we call a color warm and when we call a visual design warm.

What about the timbre of a single note played on a French horn or an English horn or a saxophone? This can't be a regional quality; can it be an *A* quality? We do describe such timbres in poetic ways, as piercing, blasting, biting, harsh, smooth, clear, murky. If these qualities are classified as *A* qualities, many—very many—*A* qualities turn out not to be regional qualities; if they are not so classified, how do we draw a line? There is no apparent consen-

---

3. This is the sense ("A regional quality is a quality that a complex has as a result of the relation between its parts") suggested by Robert Mathers and George Dickie ("The Definition of 'Regional Quality,'" *Journal of Philosophy* 60 (1963): 465–67), who were properly critical of the stronger sense adopted in my *Aesthetics* (New York, 1958), p. 83.
4. "Aesthetic and Nonaesthetic," *Philosophical Review* 74 (1965): 155.
5. Isabel Hungerland, "Once Again, Aesthetic and Non-Aesthetic," *Journal of Aesthetics and Art Criticism* 26 (Spring 1968): 285; K. Mitchells, "Aesthetic Perception and Aesthetic Qualities," *Proceedings of the Aristotelian Society* 67 (1967): 57; compare p. 60n.

sus on this question. But one thing we may expect from a defensible characterization of *A* qualities is a decision about the status of timbre terms.

Another problem is the converse of the previous one: are all regional qualities *A* qualities? Mitchells say that not all "structural *gestalt* qualities" are aesthetic qualities; but this is expanded to mean that "structural *gestalt* qualities as long as they are perceived in a neutral manner for the purpose of factual object recognition lack aesthetic ambience"—a thesis we shall return to shortly.[6] The dominant compositional pattern of a painting (e.g., the pyramidal organization of masses or its consistent three-point perspective) would presumably be a "structural *gestalt*." This kind of property (like the sonata-allegro form in music) can usefully be distinguished from the other kind of regional quality, such as gracefulness or somberness. But if we count structural gestalts among regional qualities, then some regional qualities are presumably not aesthetic qualities. When we say that a passage of music has a definite tonality, that a poem is in duple meter, that a painting is synthetic cubism, we are attributing regional qualities, but not aesthetic qualities. Or should these, too, be considered aesthetic qualities? Again, it might be convenient to have a reasoned answer.

II

When linguistic intuitions about the applicability of a descriptive predicate largely coincide, the simplest hypothesis is that the rule of application is phenomenological. Certainly there are some ways in which *A* qualities generally or often differ from nonaesthetic qualities (*NA* qualities). They seem to have (in Humean language) less "force and vivacity" than *NA* qualities. In an interesting and perceptive discussion of what he calls "objective feelings," Otto Baensch has written that "with all the force they might develop, they still lack the sensory vitality and materiality of sense-impressions, that inner weightiness which is a part of even the most delicate colors and the most ephemeral odors."[7] This distinction is difficult to fix: certainly *A* qualities can sometimes thrust them-

---

6. "Aesthetic Perception," p. 57. "Gestalt quality" is synonymous with "holistic quality" for Mitchells; see p. 60n.
7. "Art and Feeling," in *Reflections on Art*, ed. Susanne K. Langer (Baltimore, 1958), p. 12; reprinted from *Logos* 12 (1923–24): 1–28.

selves forcefully on our attention, even before we have consciously noted the *NA* qualities on which they depend. But there is also a sense in which *A* qualities appear as less firmly anchored to the object. The painting or the music is somber, and the somberness is fused with its *NA* qualities; but it is a little as though the painting or the music has put on, or is showing forth, the quality, rather than simply possessing it. The mood of a landscape, says Baensch, "surrounds, fills and permeates it like the light that illuminates it, or the odor it exhales."[8] But all this seems to me to be another way of describing regional qualities, which are bound to have a slightly disembodied air in comparison with local qualities. So we have not made a phenomenological distinction *among* regional qualities between the *A* qualities and the *NA* qualities; much less have we justified Baensch's view that some regional qualities are "non-sensory qualities."

III

If the distinction between *A* qualities and *NA* qualities is not phenomenological, perhaps it is epistemological: perhaps it lies in the way in which *A* qualities are known or in the manner of our acquaintance with them. This proposal has appeared in a variety of forms, some of them rather strange. Sibley made it clear from the beginning, I would say, that on his view *A* qualities are perceived—are seen or heard—and he said this quite explicitly later on: "People have to *see* the grace or unity of a work, *hear* the plaintiveness or frenzy in the music, *notice* the gaudiness of a color scheme, *feel* the power of a novel, its mood, or its uncertainty of tone."[9] (I take it that "feel" is used here for the apprehension of a phenomenologically objective quality of an intentional object— the world of the novel, as presented through the text.) Unfortunately, Sibley led up to the sentence just quoted by saying, "It is of importance to note first that, broadly speaking, aesthetics deals with a kind of perception," and this remark, although it doesn't seem to me (in context) misleading, has encouraged others to talk about "kinds of perception" or "modes of perception" in a way that sets the perception of *A* qualities quite apart from the perception of redness or loudness or the basic events of a novel.

8. Ibid., p. 11.
9. "Aesthetic and Nonaesthetic," p. 137.

But although Sibley never thought of himself as falling back on a special kind of "intuition" or an "inner sense" (despite some interesting parallels between his argument and that of Francis Hutcheson), much less "nonnatural properties," he did believe that something more is involved in seeing that something is "graceful, dainty, or garish" than in seeing that something is "large, circular, green, slow, or monosyllabic."[10] That something is *taste*.

The term "taste," in this connection, has been echoed uncritically by some writers, but quite as often taken exception to. Some of the uneasiness about it might be eased by bearing in mind the observation of one of Sibley's defenders that the term "need not denote a distinct faculty of perception; it could just as well denote a special achievement in the employment of the familiar faculties."[11] My objection is that (as I believe) it cannot be independently explicated. When Sibley later came to restate and clarify the distinction he had in mind all along (though not all of his readers and critics grasped it) between two main senses of "taste," he said that in one sense it is "an ability to recognize aesthetic merit"—this is the sense he was *not* concerned with—and in the other sense it is "an ability to discern the aesthetic qualities of things."[12] This is an excellent way of defining "taste" in the relevant sense, but of course if we adopt this definition, we cannot define "aesthetic quality" as "quality discerned by taste." To discover whether someone has taste (in this sense), we naturally try to discover whether he can perceive the balance of a complex design, the special lilt that one performance of a musical phrase has but another lacks, the charm of a delicate vase. Of course it does not take much taste to see the balance of a simple bold design or to hear the cheerfulness of a highly cheerful melody; but this is no doubt a different degree of the same ability. (And "ability" need mean no more here than it does when we say that some people have the ability to distinguish close hues in the green-blue area or the orange-red area, while others—being slightly color-blind—do not.) However, to decide whether or not a particular perceived

---

10. Ibid., p. 135.
11. J. F. Logan, "More on Aesthetic Concepts," *Journal of Aesthetics and Art Criticism* 25 (Summer 1967): 405, in reply to R. David Broiles, "Frank Sibley's Aesthetic Concepts," *Journal of Aesthetics and Art Criticism* 23 (Winter 1964): 219–25.
12. Comment on an essay by Eva Schaper, *British Journal of Aesthetics* 6 (1966): 68.

quality is an *A* quality, we would not inquire whether its perception requires the exercise of or exhibits taste.

The coordinate terms used by Sibley to clarify the nature of this special ability do not serve very well, it seems to me. I would say that it requires perceptual sensitivity to distinguish close shades of colors and subtle variations in the dynamics of music, or to notice differences between two slightly different ovals or harmonic progressions—and these are all *NA* qualities. If it is a special *sort* of sensitivity that is in question, I don't see how it could be specified noncircularly. Certainly we can call someone "perceptive" not only if he notices balance and gracefulness, but if he notices that in a painting the palette is limited in certain ways or that a musical work contains a bass clarinet or a pentatonic melody—while, on the other hand, if he reports that the shapes in a late Van Gogh seem to him tortured and tense, and that the finale of Beethoven's D minor symphony is powerful, I don't think we would want to say that he is "perceptive."

Similar reflections have no doubt occurred to others, and indeed few have accepted the appeal to taste (in this sense) as a basis for distinguishing *A* qualities from *NA* qualities. But Sibley's phrase "a kind of perception" has been tempting. Mitchells, for example, takes off from Sibley with this remark: "Sibley's designation of certain features of a work of art as non-aesthetic because they can be noticed without special aesthetic perceptivity, takes no account of the possibility that such features may acquire an aesthetic character when perceived by an aesthetically sensitive observer."[13] An "aesthetic observer," according to Mitchells, sees blues and greens in a different way from a "non-aesthetic observer": not as "neutral," but as cool and tranquil. He sees pastel colors as soft and mild, curves "not just as indifferent lines of a certain geometrical definition" but as gentle or finely drawn. Thus, on this view, there are two modes of perception, which give different views of the object, so the difference between the two sets of qualities is basically a difference between the two modes of perception that reveal them.[14] How, then, are the two modes of perception themselves distinguished? It turns out that "aesthetic perception and non-aesthetic perception differ inasmuch as they aim at different targets and reveal thereby a differ-

---

13. Mitchells, "Aesthetic Perception," p. 53.
14. Ibid., p. 54.

ent aspect of perceptual reality."[15] But if the two modes of perception are distinguished by their "targets," the aesthetic mode of perception is simply the perception of A qualities. In the last analysis, no distinction has really been provided.

The question whether there is a special aesthetic mode of perception has figured in a debate between Virgil Aldrich and George Dickie. In his book, as in his earlier essay,[16] Aldrich distinguished an "aesthetic mode of perception" (which he calls "prehension"), in which a "material thing" is "realized" as an "aesthetic object."[17] But if we try to distinguish A qualities from NA qualities by stipulating that an A quality is one that is prehended (rather than "observed"), we again become entangled in circularity.

> Take for example a dark city and a pale western sky at dusk, meeting at the sky line. In the purely prehensive or aesthetic view of this, the light sky area just above the jagged sky line protrudes toward the point of view. The sky is closer to the viewer than are the dark areas of buildings. . . . Thus prehension is, if you like, an "impressionistic" way of looking, but still a mode of perception, with the impressions objectively animating the material things—there to be prehended.[18]

That is Aldrich's way of telling us what he means by "prehension": evidently prehension is to be identified in terms of what it receives or obtains (not only A qualities, but also representational "aspects"). Aldrich's later example of his "impressionistic way of looking" is that if one fixes one's eye on a distant point while attending to illuminated falling snowflakes, one can see them as comet-shaped.[19] I think Dickie is quite right in replying that this capacity to attend to peripheral parts of one's visual field while not focusing on them does not establish anything that ought to be "contrasted with an ordinary mode of perceiving."[20]

Of course, if there are A qualities (and especially if they are regional qualities), there will be some differences in the way they are perceived. Say you are looking sharply at a wood a hundred

15. Ibid., p. 57.
16. "Picture Space," *Philosophical Review* 67 (1958): 342–52.
17. *Philosophy of Art* (Englewood Cliffs, N. J., 1963), pp. 7, 8, 21.
18. Ibid., p. 22.
19. "Back to Aesthetic Experience," *Journal of Aesthetics and Art Criticism* 24 (Spring 1966): 368–69.
20. "Attitude and Object: Aldrich on the Aesthetic," *Journal of Aesthetics and Art Criticism* 25 (Fall 1966): 90; Compare Joseph Margolis, *Language of Art and Art Criticism* (Detroit, 1965), p. 27.

yards or so in the distance, scanning openings between trees for the sight of someone who is to appear; then suddenly you begin to widen the lens (so to speak), forget the trees and take in the woods as a whole, becoming aware of its bunchiness, bushiness, heaviness, stateliness, or ominousness. To perceive such *A* qualities, you have to apply a more diffuse attention, to let yourself go to a certain extent, to surrender yourself to what is given rather than trying to force the visual field to disgorge the desired or predicted datum. In this way of seeing there is a relaxation, an absence of strain, but also a kind of visual fulfillment, an escape from impoverishment, as one takes in a variety of qualities, instead of concentrating on certain "relevant" ones and trying to exclude others. There is an enjoyment, almost an exhilaration, in the exercise of the pure unfettered *power* of seeing as seeing is freed from subservience to a practical end. All this, or something close to it, I take to be characteristic of *A*-quality perception, and it is this that is the "something more" that it requires, beyond what it takes to see reds and hear loudness; but it is a "something less," too, because it is seeing that is more autonomous than the seeing that is directed toward an expected figure emerging from a wood, a clock dial, an X-ray picture of a lung, or a photograph in the rogue's gallery. Aldrich's allusion to Hume's phrase "carelessness and inattention"[21] is suggestive, but not really apt here, for there is (I believe) no loss or diminution of attention in the switch from localized seeing to regional seeing—or in the switch from following one voice in counterpoint to hearing several voices simultaneously—but a widening of the scope of attention.

Regional perception[22] is possible for anyone who can perceive at all, though where the region is comparatively large and complex and the *A* quality subtle and delicately poised, regional perception can be a difficult feat. But (again) to test whether someone can perform this feat, we can only try him out on *A* qualities that we know of; it would be putting things backward to define an *A* quality as one that is perceived this way.

IV

A possibility worth considering is that the distinction between *A* qualities and *NA* qualities is a *semantic* one: an *A* quality is

21. "Back to Aesthetic Experience," p. 368.
22. C. L. Stevenson uses the term "synoptic attention" in "The 'Analysis' of a Work of Art," *Philosophical Review* 67 (1958): 35.

(roughly) a quality whose possession by an object involves a reference by that object to something else. Such a proposal could be worked out along lines laid down some time ago (similarly, though not identically) by Charles Morris and Susanne Langer: an *A* quality would be a quality in virtue of which an object is an "iconic sign" or "presentational symbol." But recent work by Nelson Goodman suggests a more rigorous and potentially more fruitful way of working out the proposal; let us see what can be done with that.[23]

When a predicate (or "label") applies to an object, the object possesses that label—or the corresponding property (though Goodman much prefers to eschew all talk of properties and to stick to the language of objects and their labels). "(Is) scented" applies to a bar of toilet soap; the soap has the property of scentedness. When the bar is sent through the mail to "Occupant, 1916 Delancey St.", accompanied by promotional material extolling the glories of Ecstasy Soap and urging the recipient to try it forthwith, we can say that this bar of soap is offered as a *sample* of Ecstasy Soap. And in that case, two kinds of reference—inverses of each other—are present in the situation: the predicate "(is) scented Ecstasy Soap" *denotes* this bar, among others, and the bar *exemplifies* the property of being scented Ecstasy Soap. Exemplification (in Goodman's technical language) is possession plus reference.

The predicate "(is) scented soap" applies literally to the bar, but other predicates might apply to it metaphorically: "(is) fresh" or "(is) overripe." And insofar as it is offered as a sample, the bar of soap might be said to exemplify these properties as well—which is to say, on Goodman's analysis, that it *expresses* them. Expression, he argues, is metaphorical exemplification.

A problem about Goodman's analysis is that not all of the qualities that aestheticians have wished to include under expression are named by words in metaphorical senses: gracefulness, elegance, garishness, for example. But for our purpose, which is to find (if possible) a distinguishing mark of being an *A* quality, we could take part of Goodman's analysis and try using it in our own way: a quality of an object is an *A* quality if and only if the object exemplifies it (i.e., possesses it and refers to it).

Perhaps this formulation makes explicit the linguistic intuition that guides us in distinguishing *A* qualities from *NA* qualities. We note that a piece of music has a tonality and that a poem is in

---

23. See Nelson Goodman, *Languages of Art* (Indianapolis, 1968), chap. 2.

duple meter, and that is all; but when we perceive that the music has an air of tranquillity or that the poem is flowing, we take these objects as samples of the class of things having those qualities—as referring to tranquillity and flowingness. For tranquillity is basically, or initially, a character of a state of mind; and flowingness is a general character of all sorts of physical movement. They are features of the world, and if we see the work of art as containing and presenting for our inspection some aspect of the world, we are ascribing to it a capacity to refer beyond itself. This is fundamental to art, according to a general view such as Goodman's. If a work of art is, as he holds, essentially a compound character in a symbol system, and if "symbolization . . . is to be judged fundamentally by how well it serves the cognitive purpose," then "aesthetic excellence" is simply good symbolic functioning when it occurs in an object that "qualifies as aesthetic."[24] The distinction between A qualities and NA qualities is a distinction between those aspects of the work that enter directly into its symbolic functioning and those that are merely auxiliary.

All this is most interesting, and may be true. The theory can certainly be applied with profit to one artistic phenomenon: the way in which persons, objects, and events acquire symbolic status (and, correspondingly, thematic weight) in literary works. The daffodils in Wordsworth (to take the simplest and humblest example) are gay and jocund; they dance in the breeze. But they are also an exemplification of that innocent and unaffected and uninhibited gaity; they are a literary symbol.

The question remains, however, whether the theory is true of such things as works of music and sculpture. We know how the bar of soap became a sample; it was offered as such. Even here there is a difficulty. For the bar of soap was offered as a sample of fresh things (so the promotional materials tell us); but, though in fact it has a heavy, excessively sweet, and somewhat sickening odor, it was *not* offered as a sample of overripe things. So perhaps, after all, we are not allowed to say that it exemplifies that quality. And is a passage of tranquil music offered (by composer, by performer, by conductor, by impresario) as a sample of tranquil things? I don't know of any solid arguments against that claim, but I don't know of any solid arguments that would support it, either. Finally, it is hard to see how the semantic defini-

24. Ibid., pp. 258, 259.

tion of *A* qualities would cope with the qualities of nature. A woody glen can be tranquil, too; and Wordsworth's daffodils were "tossing their heads in sprightly dance"; but nature is not a "character in a symbol system," even if a string quartet is.

V

The alternative that remains is to say that the distinguishing feature of *A* qualities is their intimate connection with normative critical judgments—or more explicitly (though still tentatively and roughly) that an *A* quality of an object is an aesthetically valuable quality of that object. On this proposal, what guides our linguistic intuition in classifying a given quality as an *A* quality is the implicit recognition that it could be cited in a reason supporting a judgment (affirmative or negative) of aesthetic value.

This proposal is vaguely foreshadowed in the views of Mitchells and Walsh already discussed, and in a remark of Hungerland's that *NA* qualities could not serve as "relevant reasons" for an "aesthetic rating."[25] It has been explicitly set forth by Marcia Freedman, who says (using the term "B-predicate" instead of "*A* quality") that "B-predicates are bad (excellent, poor, fair)-making characteristics. "B-utterances are not themselves evaluations or value judgments, however; but they tend toward or imply value-judgments. . . . The value-tending feature of B-predicates, I would argue, is not just an incidental and acquired feature, but is *the* distinguishing or defining feature of them."[26] Gracefulness, tranquillity, dynamic power, clumsiness, and luridness count (or count directly) as grounds of aesthetic judgement in a way in which *NA* qualities do not: that is the proposed distinction.

To see whether it can be sustained, we must formulate it more carefully. First, as Freedman notes, the proposal is not to regard *A* predicates (using this term, as I do, to refer to the words) as themselves normative, but as having a logical relevance to normative judgments. There is room for a good deal of dispute on this point, no doubt: various aestheticians from time to time have declared that such words as "unified" and "graceful," in the context of criticism, are normative, and that to say "This work is

---

25. "The Logic of Aesthetic Concepts," *Proceedings and Addresses of the American Philosophical Association* 36 (1962–63): 43.
26. "The Myth of the Aesthetic Predicate," *Journal of Aesthetics and Art Criticism* 26 (Fall 1968): 52.

unified and graceful" is to utter a value judgment. The criteria of normativeness remain unsettled, and in the absence of established criteria the question at hand cannot be fully disposed of. We can say a number of things about the normative suggestiveness, or normative implications, of such a statement as "This work is unified and graceful." It presents (if true) a reason that stands ready to lend support to a judgment of aesthetic value ("This work is a good one"), if anyone wishes to make such a judgment. Unlike some aestheticians, particularly those associated with the phenomenological school, I do not want to say that unity and gracefulness are "values," but rather that they are (aesthetically) valuable, that they contribute aesthetic value to the objects that have them. (For convenience, let us call them "value-grounding qualities," or *VG* qualities, using this term for qualities that affect aesthetic value either positively or negatively.)

That *A* predicates are not "pure" normative terms is shown, I think, by the fact that their application neither requires nor accepts the support of reasons. There are reasons why an object has such a quality, but these are not reasons for believing or accepting the allegation that an object has such a quality (its presence has to be perceived).[27] A value judgment, such as "This work is a good one," does permit and even invite reasons for accepting it. It might be the case, however, that "unified" and "graceful" have a mixed character, as "honest," "courageous," and "modest" are sometimes said to have: that "This work is unified and graceful" both describes the work and evaluates it. Perhaps it is impossible to make a clear distinction between predicates that designate grounds of value and predicates that designate value, when the context of judgment is widely understood and well established. If a certain disposition to behavior, for example, comes to be accounted a virtue, then any name of that disposition to behavior may acquire normative character, so to say "*X* is courageous" or "*X* is thrifty" is already to praise *X*, not merely to offer a (partial) justification for praising *X*. If unity always counts toward an affirmative critical evaluation, it can easily come to be taken (by an elision of argument) as itself conveying that evaluation.

Yet the distinction is worth preserving, I think. There is a difference between what "unified" and "graceful" *mean* as predicates of objects and what their application *suggests* in the way of poten-

---

27. See my "Descriptivist Account of Aesthetic Qualities."

tial value judgments to those who know that these are *VG* qualities. Goodness is not entailed by "unity" or "gracefulness," and hence is not part of their meaning; the connection is contingent, I think, even though it has a certain constancy. If we know that a cake has been assembled according to a certain recipe, that the prescribed ingredients were used and no others, and that it was baked at the required termperature, we can infer that it is almost certainly a good cake. If we inform someone that these directions have been followed, we may make his mouth water. But it is he who has drawn the inference and hazarded the judgment of value, and his leap to a conclusion, however natural, predictable, or desirable, does not convert our original set of statements into a value judgment. Much less could it make the statement "The cake was baked at 400°," taken by itself, a value judgment. In the same way, "This is unified" and "This is graceful" remain descriptions, whatever they may be taken to suggest about possibly justified evaluations.

Two lines of questioning may be thought to undermine this proposal for distinguishing *A* qualities. The first objection would be that it makes no distinction at all, since in appropriate contexts, any quality could be cited as a perfectly good reason for a judgment of aesthetic value. Aldrich remarks that of two prints we might say that one is worse than the other because it is "too dark."[28] He adds that "This is too dark" is also an "evaluative judgment." But suppose we were to restate it as "It is very dark." Could that be a reason? Not, I think, without further explanation. And that further explanation might take some such form as "It is so dark that the dynamic contrast between the hues is lost." Now we have something that can be a reason, but notice how it has become one: the *NA* quality is hitched to an *A* quality. It may be, therefore, that we need to reformulate our proposal: a quality is an *A* quality if it can independently be cited as a ground of aesthetic value (i.e., if it counts without the help of any other quality).

If the proposed definition of "*A* quality" is not too broad, as the first objection suggests, then perhaps it is too narrow, as a second objection suggests. It would be generally agreed that some *A* qualities, at least, are citable in reasons supporting affirmative (or high) aesthetic evaluations, and some in reasons supporting nega-

---

28. *Philosophy of Art*, p. 99.

tive (or extremely low) aesthetic evaluations: the work is bad or poor because it is clumsy, garish, anemic, whatever. But are there neutral *A* qualities—*A* qualities that don't count either way at all? What about such predicates as "languid," "calm," "swaggering," "grotesque"? But it doesn't seem to me that these words are really neutral. There is something puzzling about them, but it is, I think, their variability of sense, or their vagueness, rather than their neutrality. "Grotesque" covers so many different qualities that one kind of grotesqueness in a work may be a good thing in it, while another kind of grotesqueness may be a bad thing. So with "languid": the languidness of a passage from Debussy may be much more valuable (musically) than the languidness of a passage from a Liszt tone poem. Thus the proposed definition does not seem too narrow: anything that I have seen called an *A* quality can be subsumed under it.

This proposal has another advantage, I think (though I'm not so sure about this): that it helps answer one of the questions posed at the start of this essay, namely, the question whether all *A* qualities are regional qualities. To give a reason in support of a judgment of a work—or of any object, considered from the aesthetic point of view—you have to cite a quality of that object or of some part of it. The shapes and colors, or notes and silences, that make it up are not, in this sense, parts, but elements or basic ingredients. Their qualities enter as texture, as infrastructure, but not strictly as characters of the work *qua* work. It is an *A* quality of the musical work that it is somber, that it has a somber opening section, that it opens with a somber melody, or even that its first note gives its opening a portentous air; but it is not an *A* quality of the work that its first note is harsh or piercing. If *A* qualities are to serve for evaluations, they must be regional qualities; the local qualities, though basic, enter only insofar as the regional qualities depend on them.

VI

I am inclined to accept the "value-grounding" definition of "*A* quality." It probably marks the most significant distinction that the discussions of *A* qualities (with their various examples and proposed criteria) have been moving toward, or at least circling about. But to accept it is, of course, to be confronted at once with another large problem: how to explain why certain qualities, but not others, *can* be cited in reasons supporting judgments of aesthetic value. Although I have tried before to come to grips with this problem,[29] I believe that it is far from being solved. No more than a hint of a solution is offered here.

One answer to this question might be that VG qualities are just those qualities whose possession involves some kind of reference; in this way the semantic account of A qualities would be reinstated, not directly, as a definition, but indirectly (and perhaps more plausibly). If a work of art is properly regarded as a character in a symbol system, then those features of it that function referentially would presumably be those that count when it comes to judging the work in terms of its fundamental nature. This view has genuine merits. It might explain the vagueness and uncertainty of the line dividing A qualities from NA qualities, since there may be no NA quality that couldn't, in some context or circumstances, take on the character of a symbol—tonality, for example, could be used as a symbol of cultural stability or religious faith. It might explain why some A qualities are positive and some negative, since characters in symbol systems do not always play their role well, but have their infirmities—the garishness of a visual design or the raucousness of music might be connected with certain sorts of communicative failure.

This line of thought seems to me worth exploring further, although some of the difficulties noted earlier in the semantic definition of "A-quality" would turn up again. And they might be fatal. But suppose we eliminate the referential element from Goodman's concept of expression; then he has identified the following class of qualities:

Group 1   (G qualities): named by terms imported metaphorically from other realms of discourse.

This is "metaphorical possession." Note that Group 1 would include the somberness of music or visual design and (unless restricted to regional qualities) the harshness of a single note and the warmth of a color tone; it would exclude such technically named qualities as tonality and meter, and it *may* exclude such frequently cited A qualities as grace and garishness.

A subclass of Group 1 is

Group 2   (HG qualities): qualities named by terms imported metaphorically from the realm of human traits and actions.

---

29. See *The Possibility of Criticism* (Detroit, 1970), chap. 4.

This group would exclude, for example, terms that literally apply to physical movement and are used metaphorically of music ("soaring," "floating," "sinking").

A closely related concept has recently been introduced and analyzed by Alan Tormey: "Expressive properties are those properties of art works (or natural objects) whose names also designate intentional states of persons. Thus 'tenderness,' 'sadness,' 'anguish,' and 'nostalgia' may denote expressive properties of art works because they also denote states of persons that are intentional, and thus expressible in the fullest and clearest sense."[30]

Tormey's semantic terminology may lend itself to misinterpretation. He is *not* proposing to mark out his set of predicates in the following way: "A predicate P designates an expressive property of an artwork (or other object) if and only if P denotes (truly applies to) intentional states of persons." This proposal would lead to unacceptable consequences. Since mental states (and processes) can be intense and sluggish, can reach a crescendo, can even be (metaphorically) allegro or presto, it would follow that the sluggishness of a stream is an expressive property and that being allegro is an expressive property of music.

Tormey's proposal, I believe, is that "a predicate P designates an expressive property of an artwork (or other object) if and only if to apply P to a person is to ascribe to that person an intentional state." Thus we have:

Group 3 (T qualities): Tormey's expressive properties.

Group 3 is in certain respects broader than Group 1 (since it is not limited to metaphorical terms) and in other respects narrower than Group 1 (since it is limited to qualities assimilated verbally to intentional states of persons).

This proposal is not without a difficulty. A chair can be moved; to say that a person is moved is to ascribe to that person an intentional state; yet being moved is not an expressive property of the chair. Similarly, switches are turned off, soup is stirred, pails are upset, sculptures have been cast down. It is not plain how best to escape these unfortunate consequences. One way is to reintroduce the concept of metaphor—and assume the burden of resolving its attendant problems. In the unacceptable examples, the predicate is applied literally to the object and metaphorically

---

30. *The Concept of Expression* (Princeton, N. J., 1971), p. 128.

to the person (though sometimes in a rather strained and remote sense). We might qualify Tormey's proposal by stipulating that P must apply literally (i.e., nonmetaphorically) to persons, though it may apply metaphorically to a work of art (or other object).

If the group of T qualities can be marked out reasonably well, it constitutes (as Tormey recognizes) a subclass of the group of A qualities. And it may be a subclass worth noting and distinguishing by its own name. Yet it suggests a way of being extended. Why should we limit our attention to qualities that works of art (or other objects) share with intentional states? Persons have other qualities. The graceful vase or sculptural construction has a quality we also find, and admire, in human movement and speech; the elegance or dignity or stateliness of music resembles the qualities we would be attributing to persons in applying these words to them. So, though grace and dignity are not T qualities, we can place them in a larger group:[31]

> Group 4 (H qualities): Human qualities—that is, qualities similar to qualities found in persons, including their intentional states, their demeanor, and their behavior.

This group includes HG qualities. It also includes some qualities designated by physical metaphors. When physical predicates, applied metaphorically to persons—"soaring spirits," "floating on air," "sinking into despair"—designate qualities that can also be perceived in works of art (and other objects), then the qualities they designate are H qualities; for example, the soaring, floating, and sinking of music.

No doubt this line of thought has an air of prestidigitation, and it remains to be seen whether it will hold up when it is worked out more fully and more carefully. The conclusion it seems to lead to is that the A qualities of a thing are its H qualities. There is surely an approximate identity of these two classes, but the thesis of their exact identity might be challenged. If we look back at Sibley's original examples of A qualities,[32] we find some "formal" qualities that may not be H qualities at all: being tightly knit, balance, unity—to which we could reasonably add coherence, completeness, complexity, simplicity, order, disorder. Perhaps all

---

31. See my *Aesthetics*, pp. 328ff.
32. "Aesthetic Concepts," *Philosophical Review* 68 (1959); I cite the somewhat revised version in *Philosophy Looks at the Arts*, ed. Joseph Margolis (New York, 1962), pp. 63–65.

of these terms can be applied, in some contexts and in some sense, to human beings—for example, thoughts and feelings can be coherent, as well as visual and musical designs. But the similarity is fairly abstract, and we may prefer to handle these qualities in a different fashion. We could say that they are indeed *not* H qualities, but their being A qualities (i.e., VG qualities) can be explained; that is, we can show why they count for or against aesthetic value judgments of the objects in which they are present.

With this qualification, then, the question remains whether those A qualities that are H qualities (that is, the vast majority of them) are A qualities *because* they are H qualities. Here we venture, but only hesitantly and momentarily, on a puzzling line of thought. But perhaps, in the end, it should not be too difficult to understand why H qualities are eminently suitable to play a special value-grounding role in our consideration of an object from the aesthetic point of view. They are naturally *interesting* to us; we can attend to them for a time; we can work up feelings about them. They touch us where we live. The more firmly and fully they are held up for our contemplation, the more clearly and distinctly they are articulated, the more abundantly and yet purely they are displayed, the more reason we have for the aesthetic judgment we make.

7: Aesthetic Welfare, Aesthetic Justice, and Educational Policy

I

THE concept of aesthetic welfare, if it can be framed clearly and concretely, ought to be useful in our thinking about some broad and fundamental problems. It could identify a distinguishable area of concern as a subject of public policy, in terms of which a basic educational goal might be defined. It could contribute to our understanding of what is involved in some difficult political choices and help to make these choices more rational.[1]

One way of framing this concept is to begin by noting that our experience from one stretch of time to another may vary considerably in the degree to which it is marked by aesthetic quality—that is, in its aesthetic level. By "aesthetic quality" I mean the kind of pleasure or sense of satisfaction and fulfillment that comes from awareness of the way elements of experience interrelate in order to bring about the formation of complex unities that are marked by emergent regional qualities. I do not extend the aesthetic dimension of experience to include sheer sensuous agreeableness or local pleasure; but neither do I claim that the lines of demarcation are sharp. Still, I would say that, in designing a public transportation system, a concern for harmonious color combinations and good proportions is aesthetic, but a concern for quiet operation and comfortable seats is not.

The aesthetic level of experience ranges from the neighborhood of zero to utter absorption, such as is likely to occur only in the presence of great works of art or rare natural settings. The level is

---

1. Compare an earlier essay, "Aesthetic Welfare," *Journal of Aesthetic Education* 4 (October 1970): 9–20; also in the *Proceedings* of the VII International Congress of Aesthetics, Uppsala, 1968.

dependent on what is available in one's surroundings, for the surroundings are the occasion for aesthetically qualified experience and provide the ingredients for it. It is also dependent on the will of the experiencer, who may choose to ignore what is around him, or to attend only fitfully and selectively.[2] We can nevertheless speak of the *capacity* of objects, situations, events, and so forth (including, of course, literary works of art and the intentional worlds they project) to raise the aesthetic level of experience significantly when they are encouraged to do so. This capacity is what I take to be aesthetic value—with the important qualification that to say that an object has aesthetic value is, I hold, to say not only that it has the capacity to raise the aesthetic level of experience significantly, but also that to do so is itself desirable. Judgments of aesthetic value are, in one aspect, estimates of a particular capacity, but they are not reducible to empirical estimates, for they have an ineradicable normative character.

That it can be not only enjoyable but also desirable for experience to have a high aesthetic level is a proposition I shall have to assume without argument here. I do not say that this is the only feature of experience that makes it worth having, and I do not deny that it is incompatible with other desirable features and so must often be sacrificed for their attainment. But when a rise in the aesthetic level of experience occurs without loss of other desirable qualities, experience always becomes more desirable. And that a person's experience in general has recurrent aesthetic quality and sometimes reaches high aesthetic levels is (I claim) a necessary element in a good life.

The concept of aesthetic value, framed in the terms I propose, presents philosophical problems that I shall have to pass by here. It may even be that the whole attempt to discriminate a particular species of value—that sort of value characteristically and preeminently possessed by works of art—is misguided. But unless we make some distinctions among species of value, or kinds of good, I don't see how our value-seeking or value-realizing enterprises can hope to be conducted very reasonably or effectively. Difficult though it is to distinguish a peculiarly aesthetic value from others with which it is intertwined, I do not think the task has been shown to be hopeless or useless. Moreover, there are

2. Olgerts Puravs, among others, has emphasized the importance of the individual's "imaginative activity" in the aesthetic encounter. See "Cultural Values, Environment, and the Imagination," *Arts in Society* 9 (Spring–Summer 1972): 54–60.

good reasons to believe that aesthetic value, as a distinct sort, must be one of the general and fundamental categories of value.

II

Considering a particular society and its "habitat," to borrow a term from A. E. Parr,[3] we can form the concept of the totality of objects (using this term broadly) that belong to that habitat and that possess discernible aesthetic value. They may include natural objects and scenes, articles of use and decoration, and what in some narrower sense are marked off as works of art; they may even include the people themselves, insofar as they are part of each other's environment. This totality of aesthetically valuable objects I call the *aesthetic wealth* of that society.

It may be questioned whether we have here a logically acceptable sort of totality. We can't really count objects as such, but only kinds of objects. Yet objects that are identified by members of a society as individual things will be objects of some kind—stones, trees, hats, beards, songs, dances, or whatever. And within each category we can, in principle, separate the objects that have aesthetic value from those that lack it. Or am I mistaken about this? I think, offhand, of a lot of things that I would unreflectingly discard from the aesthetic pile: many stones, many buildings, most pigeons, ordinary shoes, old soiled raincoats, and so on. I do not say that nothing could be done with these objects by an artist who set out determinedly to transform them into works of art, but I think that as they stand, in their natural setting, they are for all practical purposes devoid of aesthetic value. Perhaps I am being too hasty; an extremely sensitive and imaginative aesthete, trying very hard, might discern something in the old soiled raincoat—some bit of color harmony or of visual rhythm—that would raise the aesthetic level of his experience, even though the rest of us are blind to it. I doubt that this is true for every object. But suppose I am mistaken: then everything in the habitat must be listed in an inventory of the society's aesthetic wealth, though some things may add so little to the total as to fall under an aesthetic *de minimis* principle.

Wealth is a potentiality; welfare is its actualization. The *aesthetic welfare* of a society at a given time consists of all the aesthetic

---

3. "The Happy Habitat," *Journal of Aesthetic Education* 6 (July 1972): 25–38.

levels of the experience of members of the society at a given time. The concept is more useful when it is framed with respect to a period of time; we then speak of the aesthetic welfare as of a particular day or year. A day on which one has heard a fine performance of Beethoven's D-Minor symphony, or on which one has spent a number of hours exploring a beautiful lake in the mountains, may be said to involve greater aesthetic welfare than a day spent, say, in a subway and in a noisy, cluttered office. The problems of comparison are formidable, and may be thought insurmountable. There is no great difficulty in one person's comparing one stretch of his experience with another—he can tell, if he possesses the concept, when the aesthetic level has risen or declined. But does it make sense to sum these levels over a day or a year, to average them, to compare averages interpersonally? If we cannot make sense of these procedures, the concept of aesthetic welfare will remain too amorphous to be manageable, and we shall have to dispense with it. There is no doubt a kind of sense we cannot make until we provide something operationally equivalent to a thermometer, which would enable us to assign numbers to aesthetic levels, even though such magnitudes would be no more extensional and additive than are degrees Fahrenheit. Such a prospect would alarm some of us who are concerned with the arts, but I don't see that it would necessarily do any harm, and I don't see that it would be in principle impossible. Meanwhile, we speak of aesthetic levels as we would of the weather and the climate if we had no thermometers, and we say many things worth saying.

The distinction between wealth and welfare is important to bear in mind, especially in relation to social decisions. Consider, for example, the notorious "deaccessioning," as they call it, that has been done in recent years by the trustees of the Metropolitan Museum of Art in New York. Certainly it is up to these trustees to decide when parts of the collection should be sold in order to acquire other works that would increase the total value of the collection—remember, this includes pedagogical value as well as aesthetic value. Moreover, they evidently recognize a duty to preserve the aesthetic wealth of their society, which in this case may justifiably be thought of as a world society. So they find a buyer who will presumably take care of the paintings they have parted with. But I believe they have also a duty (which they apparently do not acknowledge) to preserve the welfare of their society. This would require them to sell only to other museums or institutions that can make the paintings publicly accessible. Selling them to a wealthy buyer to lock up in his vaults or in his private gallery is diminishing aesthetic welfare considerably. The transaction is particularly distressing because the deaccessioning can provide an opportunity to increase aesthetic welfare, if the paintings are spread around where they are most needed. The Metropolitan's clientele may not miss one or two Corots or Constables, but there are many struggling art museums whose visitors would be brightened considerably by having them in the vicinity.

III

There is something else that the Metropolitan's trustees could have promoted by selling their deaccessioned paintings to smaller art museums—a fairer distribution of aesthetic welfare, or what might be called *aesthetic justice*. I even think that, as custodians of quasi-public works of art, they had a duty to respect this ethical demand. Current movements to take Shakespeare into parks and music into inner-city streets, like the older movement to place sculpture on central-city sites, reflect a recognition of this obligation, though a pitifully small proportion of our social resources has so far been put into such projects. It may be that, as Francis T. Villemain has recently argued, the United States has achieved a state of "aesthetic affluence."[4] But, like other kinds of affluence we boast, it seems to allow enormous deprivation at the lower end of the scale.

One may question the propriety of dividing distributive justice in general—which applies to all kinds of value or welfare—into distinct species. Why not simply aim at justice per se? But suppose a society succeeded reasonably well in achieving a fair distribution of goods; if they were distributed very one-sidedly (with one person having excellent health but no access to works of art, another having plenty of food but treatment that constantly undermines his self-respect),[5] I think we would have to say that the society fell short of the highest justice. Where we can carve out an

---

4. "Aesthetic Education in Social Perspective," *Journal of Aesthetic Education* 4 (April 1970): 18.

5. The importance of this primary good, self-respect, has been especially emphasized by John Rawls in *A Theory of Justice* (Cambridge, Mass., 1971).

identifiable kind of welfare and legitimately consider it basic, we ought to insist that distributive justice be applied within that category as well as across the board.

The problem with justice is to formulate an acceptable criterion, or set of philosophically defensible principles, such that we can say that a society is just to the degree that it lives up to those principles. This profoundly difficult and complex task may be even a little more difficult for aesthetic justice than for other types. We certainly cannot legitimately aim at ensuring equal distribution of aesthetic welfare, since the capacity for aesthetic experience (i.e., for experience with a notable degree of aesthetic quality) is not itself evenly distributed, nor is the motivation to seek it out. We could equalize aesthetic welfare only at a very low level. We can at best frame a principle of equal opportunity (which is not without its own problems), insisting that deviations from it be themselves justifiable in terms of the promotion of aesthetic welfare or greater justice. (For example, why should all those Rembrandts be concentrated in New York, or all those Renoirs in the Barnes Foundation at Merion, Pennsylvania?) Something like the equal opportunity principle must be what the framers of Article 27 of the Universal Declaration of Human Rights had in mind when they stipulated that "everyone has the right freely to participate in the cultural life of the community, to enjoy the arts and to share in scientific advancement and its benefits."[6] This is something we may well remind ourselves of from time to time.

But the second section of that same article raises one of the hard questions about making a serious effort to attain aesthetic justice: "Everyone has the right to the protection of the moral and material interests resulting from any scientific, literary, or artistic production of which he is the author."

The first principle, of equal opportunity, invites us to regard the artistic talents of gifted members of our society as natural resources, to be exploited for the general good. But the second principle is what Kenneth J. Arrow, in a critical discussion of John Rawls's *Theory of Justice*, has called the "productivity principle": "that an individual is entitled to what he creates."[7] Of course,

---

6. I quote from A. I. Melden, ed., *Human Rights* (Belmont, Calif., 1970), p. 148.
7. "Some Ordinalist-Utilitarian Notes on Rawls's Theory of Justice," *Journal of Philosophy* 70 (May 10, 1973): 248.

these principles are reconcilable, and each contains some ethical truth. I merely point out that there is a problem.

Even if we agree that the concepts of aesthetic welfare and aesthetic justice can be framed satisfactorily, and that an increase in both of them is highly desirable, we may still have doubts about the usefulness of these concepts as a practical guide for public policy. Aesthetic welfare seems at once difficult and dangerous to subject to social control.

It is difficult for various reasons. For example, today I was walking down a street in Philadelphia after a rain, and I came across a small puddle with a beautiful patch of oil on it. Here is a bit of accidental aesthetic wealth that is difficult to inventory and no doubt short-lived. I don't know how many other people noticed and enjoyed that oil slick, and finding out would hardly be worth the cost. Evidently a certain amount of aesthetic welfare would elude the planners and their computers, even if the existing Rembrandts were all carefully catalogued and the forgeries clearly separated from the authentic works. But this is not a fatal difficulty; rough estimates will serve for these marginal items. Changes of taste are more troublesome for a planner. I mean by "a taste" a capacity to derive aesthetic experience from objects of a certain kind (say, from Matisses but not from Braques). A policy of trying to maximize and equalize opportunities for aesthetic welfare will of course aim at variety, recognizing that there are many tastes and that tastes can change. But suppose it is decided that, in view of the great interest in hard-edge abstractionism and the Gospel of St. Matthew set to rock music, the production of such works should be encouraged. It may turn out next season that hard-edge abstractionism has lost out to conceptual art, and that the crowds are avoiding such productions as *Godspell* and *Jesus Christ Superstar*. Such considerations show the limits of aesthetic planning; it is just as well to emphasize them, since the last thing we need is a government that decides what kind of art is to be produced.

This is the danger of official aesthetic policy—that is, government efforts to promote aesthetic welfare and justice. The tendency of national administrations in our time to think of everything in terms of "national security," and to think of national security in terms of minimizing criticisms of what they do, does not inspire confidence that a United States government deeply involved in supporting the creation and exhibition of works of art would keep its hands off suspected political or even aesthetic ideologies. (The cancellation of plans to open the Kennedy Center film festival with the Costa-Gavras film *State of Siege* is a case in point.) But nothing can be accomplished without risks, and little that is worthwhile, it seems, can be accomplished these days without great risks. Without a National Foundation for the Arts, the importance of aesthetic welfare and justice, and the need to find them a place among the heavily competing social goals, might be wholly lost sight of in official Washington.

So, on the whole, and recognizing the need for various forms of vigilance, I would place among the legitimate objects of public policy the promotion of aesthetic welfare and justice. It must be done in ways that open up, rather than circumscribe, the freedom of artistic expression (by which I mean here only the creation of expressive objects)—which may perhaps be said, by an extension of the First Amendment guarantees of freedom of speech and of the press, to be a constitutional right. It must be done not by directing that our surroundings shall be altered or supplemented in some specific way, but by releasing creative energies to find their own ways to add to freely accessible aesthetic wealth. It must be done with a constant and lively awareness that fine works of art (though we are not concerned solely with them) are unlikely to be produced according to official formulas, and more often than not carry within themselves aesthetic values that do not meet already felt needs or trigger stock responses, but which will be best understood and enjoyed by citizens of the future. Municipal art commissions, with the power to veto designs for new buildings, have sinned most often in this respect, perhaps—in their fear of artistic experimentation and novelty, not only in their commitment to what is commercially acceptable.

Conflicts must inevitably arise between the aesthetic demands and other goods that cannot be accommodated with them in a given situation (as, for example, the need for more school classroom space, the desire to make an apartment building secure against burglars, the demand for a good return on real estate investments). I know of no defensible universal principle that will tell us simply in all such cases how much weight must be given to the requirements of aesthetic vis-à-vis other values. A minimal requirement is that there be a kind of due process in the proceedings, ensuring that aesthetic considerations are at least taken into account. This requirement might include a provision that the decision-making group include at least some members who, without being committed to a narrow range of tastes, are able to make sensible aesthetic judgments. Minimal standards of aesthetic quality need not rule out the strange or seemingly bizarre; still they would save us from many buildings now going up in Philadelphia, for example, that have nothing at all in the way of proportions, surface texture, rhythmic order, or expressiveness to commend them. Such buildings are not the result of a conflict of tastes, with one side winning the struggle for power; they simply show that nobody really cared much about how the thing would look.

IV

Educational or instructional institutions must play a central role in any undertaking to carry out a public policy of promoting aesthetic welfare and justice. It follows from the nature of these concepts that we can distinguish two fundamentally different educational functions in this role. One is to promote *aesthetic opportunity*: the number and/or quality of available objects with aesthetic value. The other is to promote *aesthetic capability*: the number and/or the ability of persons to take advantage of the opportunities presented.

The phrase "available objects with aesthetic value" refers to the society's accessible aesthetic wealth, to that part of its aesthetic wealth that is, so to speak, in the public domain. The first of the two educational functions itself divides into two subordinate functions, one having to do with the production of aesthetic wealth and the other having to do with its distribution.

The first subfunction is to train more and better makers of objects with aesthetic value. This is most basic of all, for even in a society that has inherited great aesthetic wealth, the vitality of its aesthetic life and the vigor of general participation in it will depend on the continuing creation of new sources of aesthetic experience. Under this first subfunction, a further distinction has to be made from an educational point of view. The function of academies of the arts, or of universities serving as academies, is to train professional makers of art objects: those who will devote themselves wholly or primarily to this task, and who may accordingly be expected to create the most satisfactory works. But it is also an important educational task (if we wish to promote aesthetic welfare) to develop powers of aesthetic-value creation wherever they may be found. Amateurs may add to the aesthetically valuable objects in the world by growing plants or beards, arranging flowers or hair, designing or assembling clothes, and so forth. Such activities become significant to the aesthetic economy when they are widely engaged in.

The second subfunction is to train more and better *aesthetic auxiliaries*—people who, along with professional artistic creators, belong to the "artworld," as Arthur Danto has named it.[8] Their task is to help make works of art accessible by arranging the conditions under which they are most likely to be widely enjoyed: by scheduling dramatic performances and museum exhibitions, publishing poetry, copying scores, restoring damaged paintings, helping sculptors get commissions, and so forth. The class of occupations comprised under this facilitating or enabling role is extremely varied. Indeed, I'm not sure exactly how to draw its boundaries; the compositor who sets type for a novel, the agent who sells the manuscript of a short story to a magazine, and the plumber who repairs the heating equipment in the art museum also make their contributions, no doubt. But at some point the contribution becomes separated from aesthetic experience by so many causal stages that we can no doubt exclude it from that set of interconnected roles which make up the institution of the artworld. What is common to those roles is that their performance requires some capacity to have relevant aesthetic experience and some understanding of how aesthetic experience is brought about. (If the museum curator moves the plumber's handiwork to an exhibition gallery and gives it an appropriate label, it enters the artworld—at least according to some philosophers—but I don't know that that makes the plumber an artist.)

We might even envision a broadening role for the aesthetic adviser, so to speak, who is professionally qualified to help institutions with their problems relating to aesthetic welfare and justice. Many institutions now have their health advisers (nurses, public health authorities they can consult) and legal advisers (attorneys on retainer). In time we may see the emergence of ethical advisers for businesses, governmental agencies, and other

---

8. See "The Artworld," *Journal of Philosophy* 61 (October 15, 1964): 571–84; and the discussion by George Dickie, *Aesthetics: An Introduction* (Indianapolis, 1971), pp. 101ff.

sorts of institutions—persons whose sensitivity to moral implications and wise judgment of rights and duties may be sought out when tricky questions of moral conflict arise. I must confess, however, that current trends in both business and government make this proposal laughably utopian. Similarly, as the best department stores now employ persons with some aesthetic expertise in arranging window displays, and as law offices hire interior decorators to plan their decor (though many of these professional decorators are aesthetic quacks), so we might envision a general practice of consulting those who can tell institutions something helpful about the aesthetic aspects of their activities, products, or physical settings.

Of course we would also have to be aware of the danger of letting such advisers become more than consultants. Just as the ethical adviser would not take moral responsibility away from the official who asks his advice, but only try to help him see aspects, implications, and distinctions that have been overlooked (for example, certain infringements of civil liberties), so aesthetic advisers could not be allowed to become a guild or academy that sets standards of taste and restricts aesthetic competition. This has happened with certain organizations of architects and sculptors, even in our own time. The solution to the problem of aesthetic quackery is not licensing by some department of the state government that requires everyone to pass an official art appreciation test before being allowed to accept a fee for giving aesthetic advice. Still, some tastes are better than others. Some people are able to discern aesthetic values that others miss, or to derive high levels of aesthetic experience from what others can but feebly apprehend. Unless more of this ability gets worked effectively into the decision making that leads to the production of so much of our manmade or man-unmade environment, it does not seem likely that actual aesthetic opportunity will be substantially increased, no matter how many string quartets are composed by Elliott Carter—and I mention his works precisely because they have in fact added more than most to our aesthetic wealth, though it may be some time before large numbers of music lovers will be capable of enjoying them fully.

If we put together all the various careers that might fall wholly or partly under the role of promoting aesthetic opportunity or aesthetic capability, we have a diverse group. No less diverse is the set of educational processes involved in preparing people for such careers. But there is a kind of unity here, nevertheless, a central direction in which the activities participate. Ralph Smith's proposed concept of "cultural services" seems to include them nicely, and helps us see ways in which they belong together.[9] But I'd like to throw out for discussion a suggestion about the relationship among these concepts which may supplement that proposed by Ralph Smith.

I can't help thinking of the cultural aspect or dimension of a society as including a cognitive as well as an aesthetic component. I'm not thinking of knowledge in a purely formal sense, as one might speak of the number of true propositions stored in our libraries or the memory banks of our computers. I'm thinking of understanding, in a way that includes scientific and historical understanding as well as less clearly defined cognitive states and achievements, such as we might more naturally call insight, grasp, or even wisdom. Part of what marks a society as having a high culture, or as being rich in culture, or as giving a high priority to cultural matters, is the state of its cognitive activities as well as its aesthetic activities.

We can distinguish between aesthetic and cognitive interests or values well enough for many purposes, but we often cannot separate the aesthetic from the cognitive, or promote the former without promoting the latter. Part of the educational task in increasing the aesthetic capability of our students is indeed largely independent of their state of knowledge. We want to help them develop greater sensitivity of perception, as in hearing the subtle differences in the way two pianists play a particular passage; we want them to acquire the habit of noticing relationships, for example, the way touches of a certain hue turn up on various parts of a painting; we want them to release their feelings to respond to the lines in a poem. These abilities do not seem to involve cognitive processes, or at least very elaborate ones. But to grasp fully the iconological meaning of a painting, the student may have to study social and religious history; to see the difference between early and late stages of a Rembrandt print, he may have to learn something about the technical process of etching; to grasp the richness and complexity of some works of art, he will have to learn the

9. I am referring to his (as yet unpublished) essay, "Cultural Services and Educational Policy: Recommendations for Educational Research"; see "Cultural Services, Aesthetic Welfare, and Educational Research," *Studies in Art Education* 16 (1975): 5–11.

"symbol systems" (using this term in the way Nelson Goodman uses it to make this point)[10] involved in their referential dimension or in their production: systems of representation, conventional gestures in dance or film, musical notation, and so forth. So a great deal of cognitive activity, of articulate learning and abstract thought, may be indispensable for aesthetic growth. I think this fact helps to support the usefulness of the concept of "cultural services," in which there is a collaboration of aesthetic and cognitive elements.

Considering the importance of aesthetic welfare and the diverse ways in which educational processes can contribute to it, and especially considering the economic weakness of the artworld compared to the great complexes of power in our society, a heavy responsibility for aesthetic welfare falls on educational institutions. Indeed, I believe that promoting aesthetic welfare and justice should be one of the highest aims of such institutions. Here it is tempting to talk in grand terms that may be hard to cash in on specific points. I would consider the fostering of rationality in the broadest sense—that is, developing powers of creative and critical thought—to be the foremost educational goal. Not far behind we should probably place ethical development, taken in an adequately fundamental sense, in which it is kept distinct from indoctrination in conventionally approved rules of conduct, but involves concern for others, the perception of ethically significant differences in human actions, judiciousness in judging the stringency of moral obligation, and a serious effort to work out and live up to a personal but defensible scale of values. Not far behind the ethical I would place the promotion of aesthetic welfare, including both the long-range welfare of the student himself and his powers to promote the aesthetic welfare of others.

I don't know whether there are developmental stages of aesthetic growth analogous to those stages that Lawrence Kohlberg, following Piaget, has pointed out in ethical development—though Michael J. Parsons has made some interesting progress in articulating three stages of aesthetic development toward maturity.[11] If

10. See *Languages of Art* (Indianapolis, 1968).
11. See Michael J. Parsons, "A Suggestion Concerning the Development of Aesthetic Experience in Children," *Journal of Aesthetics and Art Criticism* 34 (Spring 1976): 305–14; Parsons, Marilyn Johnston, and Robert Durham, "Developmental Stages in Children's Aesthetic Responses," *Journal of Aesthetic Education* 12 (1978): 83–104.

there are underlying similar patterns in cognitive growth, ethical growth, and aesthetic growth, they may help to show a basic unity in the whole educational enterprise, though, as we know, one or another of these capabilities often develops faster than another or is blocked at an early stage while others continue to develop. Since we can make the distinctions and observe differential rates, each must be given attention on its own account. What I am arguing for, in the end, is just that if there is such a thing as aesthetic welfare, and such a thing as aesthetic justice, and if they are important parts of a life and of a society worthy of human persons, then aesthetic development must be of very serious concern at all stages of the educational process.

8: *Is Art Essentially Institutional?*

I

THAT those processes and products we broadly call "art" are often inextricably involved and intertwined in social institutions has long been known. It was noted by Plato, in the *Laws* (II. 656 E), where the Athenian Stranger praises Egypt as a land in which music and dancing and visual art were sternly guarded against unsettling innovations by force of law: "And you will find that their works of art are painted or moulded in the same forms which they had ten thousand years ago; this is literally true and no exaggeration."[1] The researches of modern sociologists, and especially of Marxist social thinkers,[2] have added much to our understanding of the social conditions and consequences of art activities. And anthropologists have shown how pervasively among the varieties of human society such activities have themselves been institutionalized, either on their own or as segments of religious and other systems. Our awareness of these connections is inevitably intensified by the unprecedented proliferation of satellite and service occupations in our time—for example, those connected with publishers, art galleries, museums, art commissions, city-planning offices, and educational institutions.[3]

But however extended, this institutional implication of art is not in itself a matter for philosophical debate, since it may be considered as merely contingent. What I aim to clarify here, and to discuss briefly, is a somewhat more significant and challenging thesis: that art is not just contingently, but *essentially* institutional.

---

1. *The Dialogues of Plato*, trans. B. Jowett (New York, 1937), 2:435.
2. S. Morawski, "Art and Society," in *Inquiries into the Fundamentals of Aesthetics* (Cambridge, Mass., 1974).
3. See the papers given at R. Smith's Illinois conference "The Arts and Career Education" and published in *Journal of Aesthetic Education* 7 (1973).

II

It seems desirable—especially for the (hoped-for) benefit of those who are properly suspicious of all essentialist theses, whether affirmed or denied—to begin with a plea for some care in framing a concept of *social institution*. A *social practice* is a kind of recurrent action or activity that is governed or guided by rules and that is recognized by a social group as acceptable because it serves the needs, or at least satisfies the desires, of some members of the group. Some practices may be said to be *institutionalized* in that they are combined with others to form something like a system, and are carried on by what may be called institutions, in the token sense of this term. An *institution token* (General Motors, the Unitarian-Universalist Society) is a collective entity (with, it may be, changing membership) that is individuated by sets of persistent practices (such as manufacturing cars or holding regular meetings at which certain ceremonies are performed) and by some continuity of what may, in a broad sense, be called sovereignty, that is, the authority to maintain or alter practices. We may also speak of institution types (such as the institution of marriage or a legal institution). And particular social practices (such as suttee or divorce or the debut) that are institutionalized, in that they are associated with certain institution tokens, are also commonly called institutions.

In a highly amusing account of her attempt to prove the universality of *Hamlet* by recounting its plot to her friends among the Tiv, Laura Bohannon remarks that "storytelling is a skilled art among them; their standards are high, and the audiences critical—and vocal in their criticism."[4] Though the storytelling was not organized and ritualized like the ceremonials it replaced when the season of swampiness suspended them, there was a controlling sense of the sort of occasion on which the activity was appropriate, and evidently there were standards of storytelling and of storytelling criticism. So we may, in the broader sense, refer to storytelling among the Tiv as an institution type.

But merely because an action is an action of a certain sort by virtue of some social convention (including those conventions, if they are properly so called, that govern the use of language in

---

4. "Shakespeare in the Bush," in *Theme and Form*, ed. M. C. Beardsley, R. W. Daniel, and G. Leggett, 4th ed. (Englewood Cliffs, N. J., 1975), p. 234.

communication), that is no basis for designating the action itself as institutional. Waving good-bye has (in our culture) a conventional basis, but it is no part of an institution. Similarly, if Nelson Goodman is right in holding that a work of art is a character or class of characters in a symbol system, it does not necessarily follow (in my usage, which I commend to others) that all such characters are institutional objects. Moreover, when we speak of an activity as institutional, it is not enough that the description we give of it be one that has been institutionally instituted. For example, a state legislature may be prevailed on to pass the sort of law now sought by transplant surgeons and define "death" as the cessation of brain activity (thus protecting the surgeon against criminal charges if he artificially keeps the heart pumping blood to various organs until he can remove them for transplant). The definition of "death" would thus be decided by an institution. But that does not make death an institutional fact, so to speak.

I suppose here that it is possible and useful to distinguish between those actions (and objects) that are essentially institutional, in the sense I expect to clarify shortly, and those that are not.

Jones's depositing his paycheck in his checking account is clearly institutional. The act could not be performed unless there existed some employing concern and some bank. On the other hand, Smith's hiding his gems behind a brick in his chimney is just as clearly noninstitutional, even if his act is performed with a similar motive. True, the chimney may have been built by a construction company, whose activities were *causally* requisite to Smith's action; but its connection with that action is not, as some would say, *conceptual*. In performing his action, Smith had no truck with, made no necessary use of, any institution.

The question before us (which may now be more fully revealed) is how this distinction applies to *artistic* activity, the act of creating a work of art. The Romantic era left us a picture of the artist, still alive in our minds, that reminds us much more of Smith than of Jones. Withdrawn into his ivory tower, shunning all contact with the business, governmental, educational, and other institutions of his society—or perhaps just hidden in his lonely bohemian garret—he works away on his canvas, carves his stone, polishes the rhymes and meters of his precious lyric. Later, of course, he may decide to compromise with reality, to sell, publish, exhibit, or whatever. But until he does so (according to this account) his action is not institutional, nor is what he produces. I have presented the account in somewhat overcolored terms, no doubt; and perhaps I should stress that it is something that I take quite seriously. Of course we cannot deny that the Romantic artist may be supplied electricity by an institution, that his paper or canvas has to be manufactured, that his very thoughts will be (in the word of Jowett-Plato) to some extent "moulded" by his acquired language and previous acculturation. But that is all beside the point, which is (on this account) that he can make a work of art, and validate it as such, by his own free originative power. And it is this claim that has in recent years been explicitly challenged by those who hold that art is (in my words) essentially institutional.

To clarify this term and thesis, we may first draw upon some ideas once suggested by Elizabeth Anscombe, in a brief discussion of what she called "institutional facts."

> For the statement that I owe the grocer does not contain a description of our institutions, any more than the statement that I gave someone a shilling contains a description of the institution of money and of the currency of this country. On the other hand, it requires these or very similar institutions as background in order so much as to be the *kind* of statement that it is.[5]

I prefer to put the matter as follows:

> 1.1 If the existence of some institution is included among the truth conditions of "*A* is an artwork," then artworks are essentially institutional objects.

Notice that I have stated only a *sufficient* condition here, in order to leave room for a second proposal.

I think we may allow a weaker condition for something's being an institutional object, though I can't formulate it very precisely. Suppose we are considering objects of a certain kind, K, and a property, P, that is characteristic of or normal in objects of that kind. By that I mean that objects of kind K always have P, unless some special and aberrant conditions interfere; that P is a significant and prominent feature of Ks, and is therefore one of the more telling criteria for being a K. Now suppose that among the truth conditions for the statement "This K has P" is the existence of some institution; then Ks are institutional objects, in this extended sense.

> 1.2 If the existence of some institution is included among the truth conditions of "This artwork as property P," where P is a

---

5. "On Brute Facts," *Analysis* 18 (1958): 6.

normal property of artworks, then artworks are essentially institutional objects.

The application of condition 1.2 to specific properties may not be very easy or decisive, though some cases are fairly clear. In a society with an official censorship, such as ancient Egypt or Soviet Russia, every work of art may have to carry the tacit imprimatur of a censor; and since the censor's office is an institution, or part of an institution, the need for official approval makes artworks institutional objects in that society. But of course it does not make artworks in general into institutional objects—as would happen if, for example, in every society the law required that all artists be licensed or employed by the government. On the other side, someone might hold that all artworks, or at least all those worthy of notice, have artistic form, however simple. Then form would be a normal property of artworks. But that would not make them institutional objects, since the truth of "This artwork has form" does not seem to presuppose any institutional facts.

A more debatable case in between these two clear-cut ones is that of genre. And it helps to bring out the way in which disputes about whether art is essentially institutional on the second condition will often turn on the question whether a certain property is in fact normal for artworks. Someone might argue, first, that works of art normally belong to some genre or other, and second, that belonging to a genre is an institutional property, since "A belongs to a genre" has the existence of some institution as a truth condition. Consider the second claim first. Now if it is to hold, a genre has to be taken as something more than a mere class or kind. No doubt works of art can always be placed in some category along with other works: they are, say, unrhymed poems, watercolors, works for the piano. But these are not genres. Consider *elegiac poem*, and the following argument: To describe a particular poem as an elegy is to place it in a certain historical or traditional relationship to a body of other poems. The writing of elegies has often been guided by a concept of elegy as a genre, with certain conventions (though this is of course by no means true of all poems that their authors have called elegies—Rilke's *Duino Elegies*, for instance). Then it may be correct to say that elegy writing is a social practice within a certain literary tradition, and that a society that recognizes that practice contains the institution of elegy writing. A poet could then conceivably write an elegy without knowing he was doing so, being ignorant of the existence of the genre; but it could not *be* an elegy unless the practice existed.

This argument might be a dubious extension of the term "institution"—if, as I have suggested, we try to preserve a distinction between institutionalized and noninstitutionalized practices. If everybody brushes his teeth, that is a general practice; but this does not make teeth brushing an institution. The difference between teeth brushing and, say, the burial of the dead is that the latter practice is associated with various other practices, religious and civil, which give it an institutional character. Still, one could argue that poetic genres (in neoclassical periods) form a loose system: there are epics, comedies, tragedies, pastorals, odes, sonnets, and so forth. And the practice of composing in each of these genres is an institution in virtue of its association with the practices of the others.

The first claim, however, does not seem to hold. While any work of art can be classified, many works of art do not belong to a genre—if we take genre in a sense strong enough to make the practice of composing in a genre an institution. Even if a poet is writing in blank verse, and knows it, and understands the techniques involved, he is not necessarily being guided by the sense of any preexistent poetic form. The same is true of the painter and composer. At certain periods, genres may exercise a strong influence; at others, no more than a weak one. In any case, it seems that the property of belonging to a genre is by no means a normal feature of artworks, and therefore cannot serve as a ground for saying that artworks are essentially institutional.

Are there stronger grounds, then, for justifying this thesis? I distinguish three sorts of ground that have been advanced in recent years. Though a good deal has been said of each, and much more could probably be said, I shall be concerned only to sketch them and comment briefly. My aim is not to diminish the importance of all these lines of thought, which have brought various kinds of illumination, but only to cast doubt on the thesis that art is essentially institutional.

III

The most direct version of the institutional thesis, making use of condition 1.1 above, is that the property of being an artwork is "conferred" on objects in an institutional way. (I state the conferring view vaguely at the start, so as to leave some refinements open.) To be adequate as an account of art, such a view must present answers to at least these questions:

2.1 On what is the conferring done?
2.2 What is conferred?
2.3 Who does the conferring?
2.4 What constitutes conferring?

It is George Dickie, of course, who has offered the most carefully worked-out and impressive version of the conferring view, and I shall comment on his version shortly. But I begin by glancing at the version offered independently by T. J. Diffey.[6] Those objects on which the property of being an artwork is conferred are, according to Diffey, those already identifiable as "say a novel or as a play" (p. 151). The range of acceptable presupposed predicates is not specified, so this is not much of an answer to question 2.1. We are not told what sorts of object are excluded, if any. Diffey's answer to question 2.2 is that what is conferred is a "status"—"the status of something as a work of art" (p. 146). Diffey does not explain why being a work of art (but not being a novel or a painting) is a status; it seems to have something to do with being, say, a good novel or a good painting, but discussion of this connection is deliberately set aside (p. 154). Moreover, to explain why something is a work of art by saying that the status of being a work of art has been conferred upon it is not really to tell us much about what sort of thing being a work of art is. So I don't think we have here an adequate answer to question 2.2.

Diffey does discuss question 2.3 in some detail, and in the course of that discussion proposes an interesting distinction. First he says that "this status is conferred by the judgment of the public" (p 147), drawing the consequence that "until a work has been submitted to the public it cannot have the status of a work of art" (p. 147). Thus "A is an artwork" expresses an "institutional fact," in Anscombe's sense (p. 147). Now the public is, of course, not an institution, so we may well ask how institutions come into this picture. One way is hinted at, another spelled out more explicitly. The term "submitting" might be given an institutional interpretation—Diffey suggests, for example, that a painting's "public exhibition" (p. 147) is necessary (though not sufficient) for

---

6. "The Republic of Art," *British Journal of Aesthetics* 9 (1969): 145–56.

it to qualify as an artwork. If we insist that public exhibition involves recourse to some institution such as an art museum, then "*A* is an artwork" (where *A* is a painting) would have as a truth-condition that "*A* has been shown in an institution." But it's not clear that Diffey means to go this far; perhaps just hanging up the painting on a sidewalk would be sufficient. The second, and more promising, argument is that the public includes a subpublic—the "republic of art," which is what really has the authority to confer artwork status. The problem is to decide "who are the members of this republic" (p. 150). It contains "anyone involved with the arts whether as creator, performer, spectator or critic of novels, plays, paintings, music, poetry, etc." (p. 105), plus others admitted by the original "self-elected" members. If, as Diffey says, the original group qualify as members of the art republic by setting themselves up as writers, painters, spectators, critics, and so forth, a curious presupposition seems to emerge. Setting oneself up as a plumber, philosopher, or pawnbroker is apparently not enough to qualify; how, then, does one know whether one's chosen occupation or activity is the right one? I can only suggest that in marking out the range of art-status-conferrable kinds of object, Diffey is tacitly making use of some such criterion as "object of a kind such that it is at least potentially an artwork." Without such a criterion, I do not see how the classes of eligible entities are bounded; but with such a criterion, the whole analysis would become circular.

I have passed over the claim that most troubles me: that nothing is a work of art until it has actually been submitted to a public. To me this claim is astonishing; but it helps to bring out, by contrast, the (at least) quasi-Romantic view of art that I cling to. Surely what Monet and Manet and Cézanne created were works of art even before they were exhibited to (and recognized and acknowledged as such by) the artistic establishment. Of course "artwork" has, as Diffey remarks, a "revisable denotation" (p. 149); it is obvious that from time to time it has been applied to different things. But this does not entail that what makes something an artwork is being so called—even by a self-elected or self-elected-elected body of art republicans. No doubt one task of the aestheticians is to explain how something is a work of art even before it is generally or officially designated as such; but this is just the problem of defining "art," and any analysis that eliminates this problem seems to me to have a prima facie unacceptability.

Dickie's analysis is a good deal more illuminating.[7] It may even turn out to be right. But I'm still not quite convinced, and I offer a few comments—which, however, touch only on some points in his complex argument, and therefore are far from doing it justice.

Dickie answers question 2.1 very explicitly: the subject of the artwork-property conferring is an artifact, an object made what it is by a human being. (I pass over his further extension of the class of artifacts; without that extension, the class is at least reasonably well delimited.) More precisely, it is not on the artifact as such, but on some set of its aspects, that the conferring is done. Dickie's answer to questions 2.2 and 3.3 are again explicit and significant: "A work of art in the classificatory sense is (1) an artifact (2) a set of the aspects of which has had conferred upon it the status of candidate for appreciation by some person or persons acting on behalf of a certain social institution (the artworld)" (p. 34). What is conferred is the property of being a candidate for appreciation. The second key term here, "appreciation," I do not pause to query: others have suggested that it is too broad to select the class of artworks unless it is qualified by some such adjective as "aesthetic," but it is, of course, a fundamental and tenaciously defended tenet of Dickie's aesthetic theory that no such distinction can intelligibly be made. I do find, however, that "candidacy" is less fully explained than I think desirable for Dickie's purpose. A candidate for appreciation cannot be merely something that is potentially appreciable; such a property, I suppose, stands in no need of being conferred by anyone. A candidate for office is presumably not merely someone eligible for that office, but someone who has taken some preparatory steps toward obtaining it, or who has been given some initial endorsement for the job. His hat is in the ring; he is running. What sort of preparation or endorsement is contained in the assignment of candidacy for appreciation, then? The figurative term suggests that something cannot be appreciated until it has been declared a candidate for appreciation, but surely nothing in the way of an imprimatur is required. A mountain could be appreciated without having been declared such a candidate. Perhaps the difference lies in the mountain's never having been intended for appreciation, or in the absence of any declaration that it *is to be* appreciated (unless someone puts

---

7. See the chapter titled "What Is Art?" in *Art and the Aesthetic* (Ithaca, N. Y., 1974), pp. 19–52. Compare R. J. Sclafani, "Art as a Social Institution," the *Journal of Aesthetics and Art Criticism* 32 (1973): 111–14; W. L. Blizek, "An Institutional Theory of Art," *British Journal of Aesthetics* 14 (1974): 142–50.

up a sign saying "Scenic Mt. Washington" at a point where the view is especially appealing—and then the sign might make the mountain a candidate for appreciation).

Dickie's answer to question 2.2 evidently is closely connected with his answers to 2.3 and 2.4. By whom is the candidacy status conferred? By an agent or agents of the "artworld"—"a bundle of systems: theater, painting, sculpture, literature, music, and so on, each of which furnishes an institutional background for the conferring of the status on objects within its domain" (p. 33). "When I call the artworld an institution," says Dickie, "I am saying that it is an established practice" (p. 31)—not that there are necessarily institution tokens corresponding to all these labels (such as the Mystery Writers of America or Ford's Theatre), but that sculpturing, writing poems, composing music, and so on are social practices.

One point that gives me trouble is the concept of "acting on behalf of." I understand what it is for the president of the university, acting on behalf of his institution (or the Board of Trustees) to award the status of being a doctor of philosophy (as in Dickie's example, p. 34). What he acts on behalf of, essentially, is an institution token, such as Temple University. But the artworld is not made up of institution tokens—it's not *that* well organized. Yet if we then switch, as Dickie does, to the broader sense of "institution," and include general (artistic?) practices, does it make sense to speak of acting on behalf of a *practice*? Status-awarding authority can center in an institution token, but practices, as such, seem to lack the requisite source of authority. Perhaps the artworld, as Dickie conceives it, could not confer status.

Dickie's argument, as he has recognized, is in some peril of circularity: artworks are what are given the cachet of the artworld; the artworld consists of people who have something to do with artworks. Nor does he try Diffey's mode of escape. Instead, he accepts the charge, but claims that his circle is large enough to make the process interesting and informative nevertheless (pp. 43–44). I'm afraid I haven't been able to suppress my disappointment at this outcome: I can't help thinking that if artworks are ultimately defined in terms of themselves, some important piece of the truth must not have been encompassed in the circle.

For further light we must turn to Dickie's answer to question 2.4. Artistic conferring is not very clear-cut, Dickie concedes (p. 35). Hanging the painting in a gallery or putting on the play or reviewing it is a conferring act; moreover, if any single member of the artworld "*treat[s] an artifact as a candidate for appreciation*" (p. 38), he acts on behalf of the artworld, and the artifact becomes art. Now if conferring can be done by mere treating (say, by looking at the painting in the hope of seeing something worthwhile in it), and if the artworld is a society in which there are no Indians, only chiefs, it would seem that Dickie's definition is broad and generous enough to suit anyone. Yet even so, it may be too narrow.

I propose a dilemma. Imagine a busy businessman or financier who has hitherto had no time for poetry (though he may recall reading poems in high school), and who sits down in middle years, under an odd compulsion, and writes his first poem. He also appreciates it—very much. Is it an artwork? Not, presumably, until he can confer the proper status on behalf of the artworld; but he is not yet a member of (at least that segment of) the artworld, since he has not yet composed (or, I am supposing, recently even read) a literary work of art. He cannot represent the artworld until his poem is accredited an artwork. Then does the poem become an artwork only after he shows it to some poet, critic, or constant reader of poetry who can perform the act of conferral? To say yes, it seems to me, is as linguistically disturbing as Diffey's requirement of public exhibition; to say no is to breach the definition proposed by Dickie.

IV

In our search for theories that may imply the essential institutionality of art, we may turn now to two thinkers who have inquired into the ontological status of artworks and whose conclusions at least point in this direction, since they locate artworks as elements in a larger social, historical, or cultural context.

Dickie's key term, "artworld," was borrowed, as he remarks (see p. 29), from the first of three highly original and provocative essays by Arthur Danto[8]—though with a shift of reference from a class of paintings to a class of people.[9] The subtleties of Danto's

8. "The Artworld," *Journal of Philosophy* 6 (1964): 571–84; "Artworks and Real Things," *Theoria* 39 (1973): 1–17; "The Transfiguration of the Commonplace," *The Journal of Aesthetics and Art Criticism* 33 (1974): 138–48.
9. Note Danto's usage.

thought cannot be explored here, but some features of his position require consideration.

Danto's original argument can be summarized in two propositions. He first introduces a new sense of "is," the "is of artistic identification"—the sense in which we point to a painting by Gilbert Stuart and say, "That is George Washington" ("Artworld," pp. 576–77). I borrow from Latin to mark this "is" by "est."

> 3.1 For it to be true that A is an artwork, there must be an X such that A (or some of A) est X.
>
> 3.2 For it to be true that A est X, there must exist an enabling theory of art.

The concept of artistic identification seems to come down to some kind of representation or reference, and in a later version of the argument is supplanted by a concept of "aboutness"—"which something acquires when it is construed as an artwork."[10] It is aboutness, according to Danto, that keeps a "space" open between the artwork and reality, and prevents the work from collapsing into a real thing—though it seems to me that there must be other ways of doing this, as in the case of music, since I am not yet convinced that all works of art must be about something.

Proposition 3.2, however, is the relevant one here. Danto expresses it—or expresses the conclusion implicit in the pairing of premises 3.1 and 3.2—in thought-provoking ways. We can easily grant that "these days one might not be aware he was on artistic terrain without an artistic theory to tell him so." But Danto goes on to say, "And part of the reason for this lies in the fact that [that] terrain is constituted artistic in virtue of artistic theories, so that one use of theories . . . consists in making art possible."[11]

On this view, then, it is a truth condition of "A is an artwork" that there exists a theory of art that provides a rationale for saying that "A is an artwork"—and the theory is not just a condition of *knowing* that A is an artwork. This claim is a form of what might broadly be called "social and cultural contextualism," but does it make art essentially institutional? That hinges on some questions to which Danto has not yet given answers, though it is much to be hoped that he will.[12] What sort of thing is an "artistic

---

10. Danto, "Transfiguration of the Commonplace," p. 146.
11. Danto, "Artworld," p. 572.
12. Some of these questions have been well raised by R. J. Sclafani in "Artworks, Art Theory, and the Artworld," *Theoria* 39 (1973): 18–35.

theory," in this context? Danto tells us something about this, but much is left to our guesswork. Presumably it will be, or include, a principle according to which Warhol's *Brillo Box* is an artwork—but the principle is left unformulated. What does it mean to say that the theory exists? That it is accepted (believed, promulgated) by the artist? the art dealer? a segment of the art establishment? If we insist on a good deal here, the existence of some institution will begin to emerge as a truth condition of "*A* is an artwork." But the stronger the claim, the more doubtful it may become—or at least, the more in need of elaborate defense.

It is crucial to our understanding of what kind of predicate "is an artwork" is, according to Danto, that we realize that of two indiscernible objects, one may be an artwork, the other not; and that a particular object may become an artwork at a certain time, though it was no such thing before. Thus "artwork" is not a descriptive, but an ascriptive, term.[13] We can think of artworks, as we think of persons (he suggests),

> in terms of privileges, exemptions, rights, and the like. Thus artworks, which happen to contain neckties, are entitled to hang in museums, in a way in which neckties indiscernible from the former are not. . . . A necktie which is an artwork differs from one which is not like a person differs from a body: metaphysically, it takes two sets of predicates amazingly similar to the P- and M-predicates which *persons* take on a well-known theory of P. F. Strawson's.[14]

Now, if "artwork" is really ascriptive, one might say, then "*A* is an artwork" does not *have* truth conditions, so art cannot be, by my definition, essentially institutional. Yet in a not very extended sense it might still be. There are two ways. First, if what is ascribed is a privilege or entitlement of some sort, and the nature of this privilege can be spelled out only with reference to institutions, then the existence of an institution will be a success condition of the ascription "*A* is an artwork." Thus Danto suggests that to say a painting is an artwork is to "entitle" it to hang in a museum or art gallery (though the question remains: *Who* is entitled to award this entitlement?). If we build such institution types as the concert hall, publishing, and drama criticism into the act of artistic entitlement, art can reasonably be said to be essentially institutional, even if in fact not all paintings are pur-

---

13. Danto, "Artworks and Real Things," p. 11.
14. Ibid., p. 12.

chased by museums or even hung. For to be an artwork would be to be eligible for institutional treatment.

Second, Danto notes that an ascriptive predicate carries along with it certain defeating conditions that may prevent it from being applied in certain cases. For example, following Danto's example, one might build into the concept of artwork that if the necktie has been painted by a child, then even if it is indistinguishable from a Picasso-painted necktie, it may not be called an artwork. But in explaining the exclusion of the child, and in laying down general rules of defeasibility, one might have to bring in, once again, institutions—the child is not an established artist, in the sense that he has never sold a painting, so his work is ineligible to be art. If selling is an institutional action, and is required as a condition of artwork-status ascription, then such ascriptions are institutional.

I believe that in the long run ascriptivism will fare no better in aesthetics than it has in ethics, or does (in my judgment) in the theory of persons—though I recognize that the ascriptivity of "is a person" can be persuasively defended. The success conditions, when they are worked out with care, are hard to keep from turning into what look suspiciously like truth conditions of nonascriptive propositions. "It is analytically true," says Danto, "that artworks can only be *by* artists."[15] That reads more like a truth condition for "*A* is an artwork" than like a rule governing the proper ascription of artwork status. But is Danto right here? Not, I think, if he means that no one is in a position to create an artwork unless he is already an artist; I would think one gets to be an artist by producing some artworks, not the other way around. Danto suggests that we assign artist status to the artist and art status to his work at the same time, and adds that we are not allowed to do this in the case of "douaniers, children, chimpanzees, counterfeiters"[16]—or, I suppose, businessmen who set themselves up as amateur poets, as in my example above. I make no plea for douaniers and chimpanzees, but children and amateur poets seem to me to be in a different category; I do not see why they cannot even in principle create artworks, even though they lack the union card. That's like saying that if someone fixes the leaking faucet, it isn't really fixed unless he is a registered plumber.

15. Ibid., p. 14.
16. Ibid.

Joseph Margolis has also made interesting use of an analogy between artworks and persons: both are "culturally emergent entities" that are "embodied" in physical entities, with which they are not identical.[17] He also relies on another analogy, that with human actions: "A man raises his arm to signal; the action has that Intentional property. Apart from human society there is no such action, no more than a movement of the arm; within the conventions of a culture the actions may be seen as such, embodied in the arm's movement" (pp. 192–93). It will help us to come to grips with Margolis' ontology of art if we pause to consider the analogue with some care.

In this passage, Margolis writes as though only two descriptions were involved, though in fact there are three, even in the passage itself:

4.1 The man's arm's moving.
4.2 The man's raising his arm.
4.3 The man's signaling.

Phrase 4.1 is, as Margolis says, analyzable in merely physical terms; it is the description of an event. Phrase 4.3 describes an action, and indeed one that can be performed only in a social group that has adopted a certain convention, according to which raising one's arm under certain circumstances counts as signaling. Note that the convention states a relationship between 4.2 and 4.3, not between 4.1 and 4.3. What is the relationship, then, among these three descriptions? On my view, they all describe the same event, some properties of which are specified in 4.1, other properties in 4.2 and 4.3. The signaling is just the arm's moving through the agency of the man and in a certain social setting. There is no need to talk of "embodiment," any more than there would be to say, for example, that the world chess champion is embodied in such-and-such an organism: the world chess champion *is* that organism, but considered in one of its social aspects.

Recognizing the identity of 4.1, 4.2, and 4.3 does away, then, with a term that at best is far from clear. "The 'is' of embodiment," as Margolis calls it (p. 194), introduces complications that are best avoided if they are unnecessary. It has not been proved, I

---

17. "Works of Art Are Physically Embodied and Culturally Emergent Entities," *British Journal of Aesthetics* (1974): 188; Compare *Knowledge and Existence* (New York, 1973), p. 246.

think, that the arm movement *cannot* be the same event as the signaling; it occurs at the same time and place.[18] It is not unintelligible to say that the movement is, in the sense of constituting or amounting to, a signaling. Moreover, recognizing this identity also enables us to avoid the error of saying that apart from human society there is no such action, no more than the movement of the arm. Granted that apart from human society there is no such act as signaling, surely there may be such an act as raising one's arm—*that* is not dependent on society or culture.

Turning now to artworks, we can summarize Margolis' position: The artwork known as the Pietà is embodied in a physically identifiable block of marble in the Vatican; it is not identical with the block of marble, but emergent from it. "*Qua* embodied, a work of art must possess properties other than those ascribed to the physical object in which it is embodied, though it may be said to possess (where relevant) the properties of that physical object as well." As a cultural object it will "exhibit culturally significant properties that cannot be ascribed to the merely physical objects in which [it is] embodied." Margolis' argument against saying that the block of marble simply *is* the Pietà is that blocks of marble cannot intelligibly be said to have expressive properties such as the Pietà has—just as "stones cannot properly be said to feel anger" (p. 189). If it is not merely false but "inappropriate" to say, "This stone is angry," it does not follow that it makes no sense to say, "This physical organism is angry" or "This block of marble is serene." Indeed, Margolis later says that when "confronted with a physical object of a suitable sort, I will identify and make reference to a work of art that I take to be embodied in it" (p. 191)—and I confess I do not understand what would make the physical object one "of a suitable sort" for such an attribution unless it has certain formal and/or expressive properties.

When we ask whether Margolis' view of artworks makes them essentially institutional, the answer is not wholly explicit. He speaks of tradition rather than institutions. But it is not clear how much is to be packed into that concept. "But to locate or specify something *as* a work of art thus embodied requires as well reference to the artistic and appreciative traditions of a given culture. . . . Only relative to some cultural tradition . . . can anything be

---

18. For a defense of my view, see "Actions and Events: the Problem of Individuation," *American Philosophical Quarterly* 12 (1975): 263–76.

identified as a work of art" (p. 190). "Reference" is all very well, but it does not tell us just what we must look for in the tradition in determining whether a particular physical object embodies a work of art. Consider the first examples of op art, and the predicament of the artist and his agent. As yet there was no tradition of op art, except in the sense in which the college is said to have put up a sign reading "Beginning Oct. 1 it will be a tradition that only seniors can walk on the grass." Is there even now anything that could be called a "cultural tradition" that makes art of *Brillo Box*—or that excludes it from the artworld? We understand the convention by which arm raising can become signaling; but it is much less easy to understand (without more help than we are given) the convention by which Brillo-box imitating becomes artwork creating, if indeed that transformation is secured by a convention. For, after all, it is not a convention, but a certain intention, that makes an arm movement an arm raising. I think that Margolis' arguments—important and illuminating as they are—have not eliminated the possibility that it is also a certain intention that sometimes makes the act of making a physical object into the act of creating an artwork.

I shall not attempt to pursue this suggestion further here, but I think there is something in it. Suppose it is true, as Ina Loewenberg has argued, that "something is a work of art if it was intentionally made as such by someone who intends it to be taken as such by observers."[19] No doubt this argument needs some gap filling, but it points up a basic contrast between a view like Danto's or Margolis' and what I called the quasi-romantic view. For according to this description, art creating is always in one way like arm raising (4.2), even if it may also often be at the same time rather like signaling (4.3).

V

It would be useful and relevant to pursue another line of argument for the essential institutionality of art that would rely on my condition 1.2 and launch itself from some important aesthetic developments in recent years. Though I shall not undertake to discuss this argument (or potential argument) here, I cannot resist

19. "Intention: The Speaker and the Artist," *British Journal of Aesthetics* 15 (1975): 45.

alluding to it briefly. We may easily agree, I believe, that the possession of aesthetic qualities (in Frank Sibley's sense) is normal to artworks. If, therefore, the possession of such qualities could be shown to depend directly on the existence of an institution, art would be essentially institutional by 1.2.

I do not know of anyone who has actually worked out this argument, but I discern at least the germ of it in E. H. Gombrich's challenging treatment of expression in art.[20] He argues that "we cannot judge expression without an awareness of the choice situation, without a knowledge of the organon."[21] That is, in his example, whether the Mondrian *Broadway Boogie-Woogie* has the aesthetic quality of, say, jazziness depends on (1) the range of patterns (i.e., other signs) we understand to be within the painter's repertoire and (2) the range of musical qualities that we understand to be available. There is much more to Gombrich's subtle account than this, of course, but my purpose is only to point out that *if* the very presence of aesthetic qualities in artworks depends on the existence of a social framework of conventional sign contrasts (the "organon"), and *if* these conventions define an institutionalized practice, *then* art is essentially institutional, by condition 1.2.

Something similar might be said of Kendall Walton's argument for what he calls "categories of art," whose "standard features" make possible those deviations that (he holds) give artworks their determinate aesthetic qualities.[22] He argues that (some) facts about the origins of works of art have an *essential* role in criticism, that aesthetic judgments rest on them in an absolutely fundamental way (p. 337).

Suppose—going beyond Walton—one were to argue that an artwork's being in (or being properly assigned to) a particular category is necessary not only for it to have the aesthetic quality it has, but for it to have any aesthetic quality at all. And suppose that the assignment of category depends on existing or historical conventions that define institutionalized practices. Then this would amount to an argument for the essentially institutional character of art.

20. See *Art and Illusion*, 2d ed. (Princeton, N. J., 1969), chap. 11; "Expression and Communication," *Meditations on a Hobby Horse*, 2d ed. (London and New York, 1971).
21. Gombrich, *Art and Illusion*, p. 376.
22. See "Categories of Art," *Philosophical Review* 79 (1970): 334–67.

As I have tried to suggest, I think of the issue of art's essential institutionality as involving very basic issues in the philosophy of art, and as having significant implications. For there is another form of essentialism that has sustained the main tradition of Western aesthetics and has continuously claimed for art a special cultural status. This is the assumption that there is a function that is essential to human culture, that appears in some guise in any society that has a culture, and that works of art fulfill, or at least aspire or purport to fulfill. The search for this essential cultural function, the wish to discriminate and describe it, has motivated some of the best (and maybe some of the most unfortunate) ideas of disparate aesthetic schools. But the enterprise itself has been taken to be of central philosophical importance. This essentialism was rejected by the followers of Wittgenstein, who said that we may but trace the family resemblances among objects labeled artworks among speakers of ordinary language, and perhaps list some of the criteria that are sometimes used in assigning the label. The institutional theory of art grows out of this movement, it seems to me; it, too, rejects the question "What is art?" in its traditional form, and proposes to substitute the question "Which objects have been assigned the label 'artwork' by the artworld of such-and-such a society?" That's certainly an askable question, but it is no adequate substitute. For when we know what things are or are not called "art" by artistic establishments, we still do not know whether there are basic and pervasive human needs that it is the peculiar role of art to serve.

Part II
Art and Art Criticism

9: *What Are Critics For?*

I

WHEN Socrates, in Plato's *Republic*, more in sorrow than in anger, banished the poets from his ideal commonwealth, he did not say what was to be done with the critics of poetry. Perhaps he classified them with philosophers and mathematicians, and hence as potential purveyors of knowledge, or at least true opinion, rather than of illusion and moral weakness. Or perhaps he simply assumed that when the poets left town the critics would tag along—just as, no doubt, the Pied Piper of Hamlin assumed that when he lured the rats away, they would take their fleas with them.

We seem to have hit upon an unsettling figure of speech, and I have no intention of pressing it any further. Even if we cannot deny that one of these social roles, or enterprises, is parasitic upon the other—the criticism of art upon art itself—the question remains open whether the form of parasitism is harmful, beneficial, or innocuous to the host. Or, since we are dealing not with biological fixities but with human arrangements that we may be able to alter if we try, the question is how and in what ways the criticism of art can be made most beneficial—not only to the arts on which it feeds, or preys, but to the whole cultural ecology within which artist and critic play their parts.

II

From one point of view, which I shall now develop a little way, the criticism of art appears as a most natural, indeed inevitable and indispensable, activity. To begin with a touch of metaphysics (on which I do not plan to linger), we have human existence as characterized essentially by the constant need to choose among courses of action, and hence to develop preferences for certain kinds of action over certain other kinds. "To live," remarks Nietzsche in one of his scornful blasts against the Stoics, "—is not that just preferring, being unjust, being limited, endeavoring to be different?"[1]—in contrast, that is, with the cold *indifference* of Nature, which the Stoics would have us follow. Except for a few rather general ones, preferences, of course, have to be learned. And since, under the restrictions imposed by most environments, they come into continual conflict with each other, they have to be unlearned, too—that is, corrected in the light of experience. Thus we get reflective, more or less intelligent preference, as John Dewey has taught us; and this is evaluation. We not only want X more than we want Y, but we judge X to be better than Y. To judge is to claim some rational basis for the preference expressed. And to make judgments of particular items in the world around us, rather than of general *kinds* of items, is, I take it, to criticize. So we are inevitably critics of one thing or another, just insofar as we form and reform our preferences in a way that is to some degree rational—that is, rests on intelligent reflection.

I need not dwell on other branches of the animal kingdom; it is perhaps too fanciful to speak of a cow as a grass critic when she seeks out a certain pasture because of what she has learned from past experience. Maybe the rat in the maze can be called a pathway critic—at least he acquires a certain expertise—but I don't think we can call the Pied Piper's rats music critics just because they were charmed by his melodies. Our concern is with humankind, and on this conscious level of symbolic activity, we can distinguish so many kinds of criticism that we must sort them out into general categories. So, for example, there is moral criticism—assessing the rightness or wrongness, praiseworthiness or blameworthiness of actions.[2] There is political criticism, economic criticism, medical criticism, environmental criticism. And there is aesthetic criticism, judging items that come to our attention in terms of their aesthetic goodness or badness.

Among these items there happen to be, of course, most notably works of art. I suppose that even if human beings had never made any artworks at all (and I'm not yet ready to regard the products of other species as artworks), there could be aesthetic

1. *Beyond Good and Evil*, Aphorism 9. From *The Philosophy of Nietzsche*, trans. Helen Zimmern (New York, 1927).
2. I borrow this concept from Elizabeth L. Beardsley.

criticism. Perhaps it would never have been developed without the stimulus of art—or perhaps art would never have developed without the previous activity of aesthetic criticism, directed toward flowers, crystals, moths, seashells, snakeskins, clouds. In any case, aesthetic criticism, when directed to art works, is art criticism. And thus we see, from this point of view, how inevitable art criticism is: it arises simply because as soon as artworks come into being and attract our notice and require to be dealt with, they have to be criticized like everything else—since we must choose (among them, and between them and other things), and hence must try to form rational preferences.

So far what I have sketched makes us all critics, will-nilly—in fact, all art critics, unless we can manage to avoid any commerce with artworks. This broad usage has the merit of reminding us of the continuity between what book reviewers and architecture professors do and what the rest of us do, at least from time to time—without getting paid for it, but that's because (the theory is) we don't do it as well. Still, we also need the concept of an art critic in a narrower sense, as one who makes criticism his occupation: one whose function is not merely to criticize but to help others make their criticisms. I take this to be the important distinction here, the mark of professional status. Two distinctions, in fact, are to be kept in mind, but kept distinct. The first one is a matter of degree: criticism, as I have outlined it, may be done better or worse—and I hope you'll bear with me if I simply postulate this point, without undertaking the systematic defense it requires. What I have in mind is that, since critical judgments (whether of landscape paintings or airlines or flu vaccination programs) implicitly claim to be supportable by reasons, some may be supported by better reasons than others; and thus there can be more capable judges and less capable judges of these matters. One could, of course, draw an arbitrary line marking some rough level of qualification or authority and call anyone above that line a critic, in the professional sense. But I think it clearer to introduce the second distinction: between those who criticize only in the course of making their own decisions about what items to elect and what to forgo, and those who set themselves up, or are set up by others, to make public judgments for the purpose of guiding the choices of others who are less qualified than they, perhaps by the lack of talent or time. These are the critics, in the stricter sense.

From this first point of view, then, we get a comparatively clear and focused picture of the art critic as professional rather than amateur judge: when we want to know whether one artwork is better than another, or how much better it is, he is the one to ask. And if this reminds you of other appeals to normative authority, you have the essential idea. Some people know—or are more likely to know—what's the best treatment of a disease; others know how best to bargain with the D.A. for a plea to a lesser criminal offense; and if we want to know which are the best microwave ovens, electric hair dryers, or house paints, we go to the pages of *Consumer Reports* for its ratings. What we have sketched, then, may not inappropriately be called the *Consumers' Union model of (professional) criticism*.

Note that on this model, the critic (like the specialist in *Consumer Reports*) would not make your decisions for you; he would not tell you what artwork to choose, because that would depend on various other considerations involving values that he has no authority to speak on: money, morality, health, safety, marital concord, and so forth. But he could tell you that one bank building is (or would be) a substantially better work of architecture than another—and the abler the critic, the more reliable the judgment. And this information—if we can speak of value judgments as conveying information—would be one thing to take into account in deciding what to buy, or build, or just go and see. Thus on the CU model, the critic's primary obligation is to the consumer of art—the audience, the viewer, the reader, the listener. His service is a public service; he tells us, as best he can, what we need to know to make intelligent choices about works of art.

It can be said on behalf of the CU model, I believe, that it fits pretty well what some well-known critics actually are doing, at least a good part of the time. For example, I read two reviews of the re-remake of *A Star Is Born*: a highly critical one by Pauline Kael in *The New Yorker* and a really scathing one by John Simon in *New York*.[3] The main thrust of both is to present overall evaluations of the aesthetic worth of the film—backed up, of course, by detailed analyses of selected sequences, shots, and even frames.

3. *New Yorker*, January 10, 1977, pp. 89–94; *New York*, January 10, 1977, pp. 56–57.

III

The CU model of criticism is rather neat—perhaps too neat to fit the facts. We must now entertain some objections to it, and consider how serious they may be.

First objection: that artworks have no definite function, like tools and compounded chemicals, so there is no sense to the notion of judging how well they perform a function. A can opener, it will be conceded, is supposed to open a can, and we can judge how well it does so. But what is a sonnet supposed to do? This puts the objection starkly, but I suppose misleadingly. For, first, we need not compare a sonnet with so specialized a tool: take instead a university student center, which may be designed to serve various needs, though no doubt in some order of importance. Nor need we consider a sonnet merely as a sonnet; it is a literary work, and literary works in general might have some identifiable function, or group of functions, not utterly incomparable with that of student centers. Still, the sense of disparity may linger. So it may be strongly urged that artworks are not means, that a poem—to rewrite Archibald MacLeish but at the same time paraphrase W. H. Auden—must not do, but be, and that the very mode of speech in which readers are referred to as "consumers" of poems, rather than as "users" of them, gives the game away. True, in his notes to the Westminster recording of Handel's *Messiah*, Edward Tatnall Canby describes this oratorio as "perhaps the most durable piece of fine musical hardware in common use today"—but this idiom is rare.

Second objection: that a critic cannot escape the responsibility of concern for the accessibility of the artworks he speaks about. The writer in *Consumer Reports* does not care—indeed, he *must* not care—whether you buy a microwave oven, or which one you buy. He simply presents his ratings. But a drama critic, it will be said, ought to care about the theater as an institution, and wish it to flourish. So he is obliged to give advice that goes beyond the CU model—as when he may say, "This is a great picture, but if you can't stand the sight of blood, stay away," or "Those who are addicted to the sound of Barbra Streisand's voice will no doubt enjoy this film, despite its lack of discernible merit." Or to take a subtler example, here is Benjamin DeMott discussing the last volume of Anthony Powell's long work, *A Dance to the Music of Time*:

> I'm an admirer of Anthony Powell's judgments, which places me, among Powelldolators, a shade far out. His less eccentric fans usually hail him for wit and characters, beings whose names chime on from book to book. . . . Also much esteemed by fans is this author's way with social history—which is, I admit, utterly painless. . . . But, as I say, the delight of *A Dance* runs deepest for me in the author's stream of judgment—or in what might be called his standards.[4]

Here DeMott seems not so much to be noting and praising these features of the novels as pointing out what readers of different sorts (including himself) will like—a very different matter, logically speaking, from evaluation.

It may be a serious oversimplification to think that there is just one thing the critic is supposed to do. Shouldn't he be trying to get the right consumers and the right artworks together, calling special attention to emerging talent among black playwrights, encouraging young architects to form cooperatives with community groups, raising aesthetic consciousness in general, and urging the National Endowment for the Humanities to put more of its funds into dance companies?

Third objection: that critics have a unique task of interpretation, which has no counterpart in the CU model. The writer in *Consumer Reports* is not required to explain how microwave ovens work; but a critic must often explain what's really going on in a new musical composition, what is meant by a new play, what a painter is implicitly saying in his new concatenation of images. If artworks, or at least many or most of them, are in some way to be regarded as characters in symbol systems (and this "if" is subject to much current discussion), then they have to be understood: the signs or symbols have to be grasped and the semantical rules of the system have to be applied. Here is surely a significant, even indispensable, role for the critic, in enabling the receivers of artworks to interpret them correctly.

Fourth objection: that in our commerce with artworks there is, after all, an overwhelmingly significant element that is totally lacking in our commerce with technological objects, namely, the sense of a relationship to another person, the artist. This objection, as I understand it, need not rest on any biographical considerations: it is that even in the simplest melody, whose origin is lost in the recesses of musicological history, or in the most min-

---

4. *Atlantic*, April 1976, p. 108.

imal of minimalist sculptures, a human voice is speaking to us, so there is at least a rudimentary form of communication. Certainly critics often talk this way. To cite one example, Donald Henahan in *The New York Times*, a propos of George Crumb's composition "Makrokosmos III": "Like many a significant artist, Mr. Crumb seems obsessed with one highly personal vision, which in work after work he attempts to express. This latest piece, like so many of his others, is suffused with infinite loneliness, time-suspending contemplations and mysterious hints of apocalyptic wonders."[5] Nothing like this can be said about hair dryers and housepaints. To reduce a work not just made but *created* by another person to a mere consumer item, like something in a grocery or hardware store, is to degrade it—on this view—and to lose touch with what is most precious about art, its humanness. Some philosophers have recently stressed the analogy between artworks and persons and have suggested that something like the same approach is appropriate to both.[6]

Besides being in trouble on such general principles as these, the CU model of criticism is especially questionable under current conditions of the arts. Even if it may once have applied reasonably well to traditional forms of art, we may think it no model at all for the critic of today to follow.

Some of these difficulties arise from the nature of certain avant-garde developments. First of all, to apply the model we need some sort of object to apply it to, but sometimes it is not at all clear that we *have* an object, or what, if anything, *is* the artwork. To point up this difficulty, let me remind you of a few examples. There is, of course, the old notorious piano work of John Cage, 4'33": the pianist sits down at the piano for that length of time, then goes away. Is this good or bad? Is *what* good or bad? What are we talking about? We could say that the pianist performed a negative action: he refrained from playing anything. And we can add, if we want to be mean, that this was a good thing, considering the sounds he might have been producing if he *had* been playing. But that doesn't seem to be the point. We could commend his posture and poise, but then we would be treating the

5. *New York Times*, January 11, 1975, p. 15.
6. See, for example, Joseph Margolis, "Works of Art as Physically Embodied and Culturally Emergent Entities," *British Journal of Aesthetics* 14 (1974): 187–96; reprinted in *Culture and Art*, ed. Lars Aagaard-Mogensen (Atlantic Highlands, N.J., 1976).

action as a minimal dramatic performance. We can say that by not striking the piano keys, after making us expect to hear something, he has made us acutely aware of the audience sounds around us, however hushed; and this sequence of sounds is, then, the composition he performs. Well, if *that* is the artwork to be judged, perhaps we *can* judge it to be more or less worth hearing—though Cage himself would have no truck with such comparisons.

Or consider the conceptual artist who tacks up on the gallery wall a list of what he has eaten for breakfast during the past month—or who merely writes that what he calls his "piece" consists of all the words uttered on westbound transcontinental United Airline flights last July 4. Is the piece good or bad? This question is a bit hard to get hold of. What *is* the piece? We may think of that month of breakfasts, all those sunny-side-up eggs laid end to end: a bit nauseating, perhaps? Well, at least we are reacting; if that's the piece, then it is getting through to us. But clearly there are problems in applying the CU model here—though I do not say insoluble ones. We characteristically formulate our judgments of artworks in such terms as "this is a good poem" or "that was an awful movie." When we try to speak of conceptual artworks in such a way, we are frustrated: what is the class of things to which this particular item belongs, and of which it is so good or so poor an instance? A month of breakfasts is a good—what?

Other difficulties in applying the CU model to the present artistic scene arise from the peculiar stresses imposed on that scene by the way our economic system functions. In all spheres of life, the tremendous pressures toward larger scale mass production and technological prepackaging constantly make it more expensive and hence desperately difficult to maintain activities designed to create works of art (or anything else) of the highest quality. This is vividly though indirectly shown in a book by Lehman Engel, *The Critics*, which examines at some length the writings of a score or more theater critics. What troubles Engel most is their vast power, as he sees it, to close a show—especially those who write for the daily press in New York City. He stops short of saying that theater critics should write only nice things about shows and plays, if they don't want to destroy the very institution that feeds them. But in the first paragraph of his book he writes: "Like it or not, the critic has a responsibility to the theater without which he would not be a reviewer. It would therefore seem important . . . that he keep in mind his obligation to make certain that what he has to say inflicts the least damage possible on the theater."[7] I'm sure this was not meant to sound like presidents of the 1960s deploring people who lacked enthusiasm for the Vietnam War. But if critics are caught in a situation in which to praise or dispraise an artwork is not only a critical but somehow an economic and perhaps even a political act, they can hardly be expected to hew single-mindedly to the task of judging aesthetic goodness.

Thus out of these and other reflections has emerged a second point of view with respect to the proper role of the critic, especially in contemporary society. From this point of view, the critic's primary obligation is not to the consumer, but to the producer— that is, to the artist and, indirectly, to the art itself as a form of enterprise involving many artists, present and future. The critic is the handmaiden of the work, preparing the way for it when necessary, helping it find a fit audience, breaking down barriers of custom and habit, encouraging novelty and exploration. His central tasks are analysis and exegesis: that is, he is to help us see the underlying structure and texture of the artwork, when we have not yet been able to grasp it; and he is to help clear up our puzzlement about the meaning or meanings of the work. Without, I hope, too much prejudice to this point of view, we may call it *the press agent (or PA) model of criticism*. (I don't suggest "PR," because I assume that it is no mere image we are dealing with.)

To raise the question, by the way, whether the critic's primary obligation is to the artist or to the artist's (potential) audience is not to deny that the critic's ultimate obligation may be to his whole society. The two views here contrasted are similar to the view that the doctor's primary obligation is to his patient, the lawyer's to his client, the priest's or minister's to his parishioner. The assumption is that a system that recognizes such networks of primary obligations will be one in which all will benefit the most. This assumption can, of course, be challenged, as it is (in the case of art criticism, but not only in that case) by many Marxist thinkers.

A corollary that is sometimes drawn from the PA model is that value judgments are out. The attitude that the PA critic wants most to cultivate in his readers is a mixture of openness to the new, sympathy, toleration of the bizarre, willingness to surrender to the object (or event); and perhaps such an attitude cannot

---

7. Lehman Engel, *The Critics* (New York, 1976), p. xiii.

coexist with the evaluative disposition. To judge is always in some respect to compare; to judge X good is always to open up a complementary category, or range of categories, ready to receive the Ys and Zs that may be judged less than good. To appreciate, on the other hand (if one may co-opt a tarnished old term for the exposition of a more swinging theory), is to take things as they come, in a wholly receptive frame of mind. Thus one does not ask whether John Cage's *4'33"* is better or worse than a later imitative work by someone else who publicly refrains from playing the violin for four minutes and thirty-three seconds. What would be the point? Perhaps on the PA model, which makes originality or at least novelty, the supreme mark of artistic distinction, the later imitation would be of no interest, because the thing has already been done. Or we could envision a whole series of minimalist musical compositions, each replete with its own surprising, fresh, fascinating audience noises—and all from the hands of an acknowledged modern master.

IV

I do not know that you can find either of my models exhibited in a pure form. Like all models, they are more or less ideal constructs, designed also to suggest ways of making fact conform better to normative theory. I have set up the models so that they can be opposed to one another, though I left the last step of the PA model optional. When we think back over the reflections that led to the PA model, we notice that they lead in various directions, and by no means add up to a tidy and conclusive refutation or proof. Since it's high time I began to show my own hand more plainly, I had perhaps best state a few of my own conclusions about these models and offer reasons in direct support of them. Blunt statements to begin with may provide welcome relief from my roundabout exposition thus far:

1. The last step in the development of the PA model (that is, the rejection of critical evaluation) must not be taken.
2. Without that last, egregious step, the PA model is substantially consistent with the CU model.
3. The PA model calls attention to important but secondary roles of the art critic.
4. The CU model remains essentially correct as an account of art

criticism, capturing its primary character, on which its other features depend.

To begin with, we must acknowledge, I think, that the PA model opens up a number of important critical activities that are not provided for in the CU model. Certainly a critic ought to be generous in his sympathies (which is not to allow him mere spinelessness), and ever on the alert to encourage budding talent and help it make its way in the world. To do so, he may have to master some of the arts of the PR person, or circus barker, by which he prepares the general public for what might otherwise baffle or distress or even shock them. And in this way he is true to the art he serves, whichever it may be, keeping an attentive finger on its pulse and seeking ways of improving its health. Like Socrates with the poets whom he was always fondly quoting, the critic should be pained to condemn, mixing pity with his anger when he finds that artists themselves have not been true to their own art.

More central and basic are the two ways in which the critic increases understanding, according to the PA model: what I have called analysis and exegesis. Not all artworks call for explanation, but some that are radically strange, extremely complex, or just cast in unfamiliar idiom can benefit from critical commentary. Analysis provides explanation of how the work fits together and projects its notable qualities; thus the film critic tells us that the breathless pace of a film is due to the quick cutting and the prevalence of short shots. Exegesis provides explanation of what the work means, in a broad sense of this term; thus the dance critic tells us that a certain modern dance features movements that symbolize aspects of the presentation of the self in everyday life, as described by Erving Goffman. I take it that some people are better than others at seeing these patterns and meanings in artworks, and among those who can see them, some are better than others at explaining them. So, on the PA model, the critic, in the professional sense, is one who does not merely understand difficult artworks but undertakes the task of helping others understand them. Moreover, many of the same skills are plainly requisite for both the competent judge (on the CU model) and the competent interpreter (on the PA model).

There are no doubt still other tasks for the critic, not encompassed in either of our models so far. Not that he must always perform them. Consider a characteristic act of the artist or his lieutenants: we may call it the act of *issuing* the artwork, that is, presenting it to a public or potential public. I use this term, perhaps a bit awkwardly, to include publishing, exhibiting, showing, performing, placing in a public space, and so on. The act of issuing is a social act, most obviously when it is done in accordance with some existing practice and under the aegis of a social institution, such as an art gallery or a municipal art commission. Such an act has two aspects, which may interest the critic.

First, it is an artistic act: the work issued now belongs to the history of art, or of its art, and we can inquire into its significance, if any, for that history: for example, does it mark the emergence or perhaps the exhaustion of a style? This is a question for the art historian, of course; but there is no rule that says a critic cannot be a historian, and some perspective on art history must surely be indispensable to him.

Second, the act of issuing an artwork may be an act of saying something about the society in which the act is performed. For example, to place in front of the Physical Education School at Temple University a sculpture depicting a partly clothed male athlete holding aloft an unclothed female athlete is to accept, implicitly, an asymmetrical view of the sexes, at least as far as physical education is concerned. According to the Marxists, *every* issued artwork makes an implicit social statement (a sculpture in which the two figures were on the same level would presumably be affirming the equality of the sexes). I am not prepared to go that far, but the question is too large for this occasion. At any rate, many acts of issuing are certainly acts of saying, and it is always in order for the critic to note, or at least to offer his interpretation of, what is said. The trouble is that such interpretations are often rather speculative and subjective, so we can't always put much stock in them; still, I don't think they are nonsensical and I don't see why they can't at least sometimes be testable, true, and apt. For example, some time ago Paul Goldberger wrote a piece about what he called the "stage-set," "make-believe" architecture in Southern California, land of Disneyland, San Simeon, and the Madonna Inn in San Luis Obispo, in which all 109 rooms are decorated differently. He remarked on the way this architecture appropriates all forms:

> The style of the time and the style of the place thus becomes all styles. Each mood, each period, is there for the asking. One is less

a servant of history than a commander of it; in this, perhaps, is the essence of the California dream. . . . As California amplifies and expands so many American social characteristics, so it does with its architecture, breaking still more free of academic rules and precedents and becoming much more frankly hedonistic.[8]

Thus according to Goldberger, to erect these polyglot buildings and groups of buildings is to say that California culture has triumphed over the limitations of history and also that any kind of building is all right if it gives you pleasure.

Here, then, are various other duties with which we may burden the critic—or, if you prefer, opportunities that we may permit him to seize. What is important to note next is that none of them is logically incompatible with the CU model. In order to be capable of explaining artworks, of placing them historically, and of reading their social messages, the critic does not have to renounce the right to judge—or excuse himself from the obligation to judge. So in these respects, the PA model simply adds to the CU model by remarking other things for the critic to do, if he has the interest, the ability, and (of course) the space (for many of the deficiencies in art criticism today are due in part to the cramped conditions imposed on the critic, who is seldom given enough room to develop his ideas and illustrate and defend them). Nor, I think, is it impossible for friendliness toward new art and insistence on standards to exist together in one mind: just because one is concerned to distinguish the better from the worse, one is not prevented from being eagerly on the lookout for the better, in however novel a form it may appear. True, at one and the same moment the attitude of critical evaluation and the attitude of relaxed enjoyment will often conflict: one who gets carried away by a film is not likely to be counting how many seconds the shots last or how many times the camera angle shifts in a sequence. But of course we do not ask the psychologically impossible of critics. And it is possible for a skilled film observer with a trained memory to respond emotionally to a film while noting facts for later consideration in an analytical and exegetical frame of mind. Or he can see the movie twice.

We call one who makes judgments a judge, for short. But when we call the critic a judge we do not, of course, mean to apply a third model of criticism, so dear to earlier periods: *the judicial model of criticism*. The artwork or the artist is not brought before a

---

8. *New York Times*, September 7, 1975.

court on charges of criminal offense (except, unfortunately, in obscenity cases), or to answer a civil complaint that the film-theater patron or book buyer has been defrauded. A judge in such a process no doubt should be as cold as possible. But I take it that the judicial model of criticism is quite dead today, and that there is little demand for its exhumation.

I haven't found any really good reason why critics ought to refrain from making value judgments—even if there are occasions, such as when John Cage's pianist is refraining from playing the piano, on which value judgments may appear to be pointless. One good forbearance perhaps deserves another, although we must not push that too far, for certainly there are many cases of forbearance that are justly subject to *moral* criticism, even if not to aesthetic criticism. In any case, the critical practices subsumed in the PA model are surely important and legitimate. But what I want now to claim is that they are secondary practices, for they presuppose and depend on the more basic function of evaluation that is central to the CU model.

My line of argument here can be briefly sketched. Granted that the critic is to promote artworks, to help them become appreciated, and that he is to support his art so that other artworks will be forthcoming. But of course he is not to make people like every artwork—appreciation is not indiscriminate liking, any more than refined taste is indiscriminate loathing. Before he starts to puff, he must decide whether the work is worth the effort; and if he encourages the art of painting, it is not because that will produce more paintings, but because that will produce more *good* paintings. This is what makes him a sort of press agent, rather than a public relations person, for in PR no prior value judgments are necessary. Granted, again, that the critic is to give us analysis and exegesis; but he must first judge that the work deserves to be explained and interpreted, because it has value that ought to be more widely enjoyed. And in fact much of his analysis and exegesis comes into play so that he can give us his reasons why a work is good, or why it is seriously flawed—in either case, the analysis and exegesis support a value judgment, which gives point to them.

I concede that the case for the primacy of the evaluative function is much less decisive when it comes to reading the social significance of the work, if it has one. This has been a source of some confusion in our time, I believe. Some artworks, or quasi-artworks, including those notorious ones issued some time ago by Marcel Duchamp, have been big with implicit statements, about art and other things, though not notably rich in aesthetic value—unless we say that their aesthetic value consists just in their saying something. But that may be questionable. To erect a huge, impressive, lavishly decorated city hall in the very center of Philadelphia was to say that civic government is important and deserves our respect. To surround it later with overbearing office buildings was to say that civic government does not deserve that much respect, after all. But I don't think this latter statement makes the office buildings good works of architecture. (If my example seems too fanciful, at least I'm not going as far as Paul Valéry, who divided buildings into those that say nothing, those that speak, and those that sing.)

v

If the CU model articulates the core of criticism, it also provides us with a standard for assessing the critic's work. I don't wish to misrepresent either the risks or the reliability of the critical enterprise, especially as conducted under current social and artistic circumstances. Yet it does seem to me that we ought to hold the critic to his central tasks, whatever else it may please him to do, and let him know when he lets us down. So, by way of coda to the argument so far, I shall say a little about the main ways in which criticism can go astray, as I see it. I have three sorts of failure in mind.

First, the critic may fail to keep his eye on the object to be judged, allowing himself to be distracted into irrelevant and trivial matters. This error we may call *diversion*. The PA model tempts to it, but the CU model reminds us that the name of the game is to make a judgment of that X, whatever it may be, that has been nominated for consideration. The critic, of course, is not forbidden to talk about other things as well, though I think there is a point beyond which chatter about peripheral matters becomes overly self-indulgent. What he must not do is palm off talk about other things under the pretense of talking about the artwork. It is all too easy, for example, to mix remarks about the play with remarks about the playwright, or remarks about the painting with remarks about the painter, so that the focus becomes blurred and the truth and relevance of the remarks uncertain. It is equally easy, at least for some critics, to confound remarks about artworks with remarks about themselves; the personal pronoun intrudes distractingly when you think you are going to be told something interesting about the architecture of the new art museum or the choreography of the new ballet. I do not mean that critics should never refer to themselves. A critic who says, "I thought the play was extremely funny," may be using the personal pronoun innocuously; we can translate his statement readily enough into a statement about the play itself. But a critic who says, "My ten-year-old daughter and I were equally delighted by the goings-on," gives us a bit of autobiography from which we can extract hardly any information about the play.

Second, the critic may describe the artwork, but fail to reach a judgment of it. This error we may call *defection*, or dereliction of critical duty. Now, when I speak of judging, I do not limit it to explicit overall appraisals of the work. If a critic feels able to say of the work as a whole that it is good, or poor, or great, or detestable, then he should do so. More often, and more usefully, perhaps, he will be interested to point out what is good about the work, and what less good—what it has going for it, so to speak, that is capable of yielding aesthetic satisfaction. Such discriminating and restricted value judgments are much to be prized, and are surely very common; because of their caution, they are likely to be more reliable than the grosser and more global ones. It is not even necessary on all occasions for value judgments to be explicitly formulated: a critic who points out several admirable features of a play, and finds no serious fault, can convey in the rhetoric of his exposition and in the tone of his words an implicit and highly favorable judgment.

Third, the critic may make a judgment but fail to support it by reasons. This error we may call *dogmatism*: though seldom blatant, it turns up in some degree from time to time. I say "in some degree" because this third critical failure is not as simple as I may so far have suggested. To pronounce a value judgment and refrain from giving any reasons at all may fairly be called "dogmatism," I think—in the untechnical sense of that word. To judge an artwork very bad and give but a few scattered instances in support is not quite so dogmatic, but is dogmatic in some degree, I would say, since the judgment goes so far beyond the reasons offered. It is stretching the word somewhat to make it encompass a third possibility: the case where the critic gives reasons, but highly inadequate reasons for his judgment. Perhaps in the usual sense he cannot be called dogmatic if he *thinks* he is giving good reasons, logically deluded though he may be. But insofar as his judgment rests, at least in part, on assertions that are quite irrelevant to the judgment and do not make it reasonable, to that extent the judgment may be classified as dogmatic.

My rather abstract account of the three forms of critical failure needs to be pointed up by examples. And I can cite you bad examples of criticism—or rather, good examples of bad criticism. To do so runs the risk of invidiousness, but never mind: I'll take the risk. You will understand that I am not attacking these critics (whom I respect) in a general way, but noting a few sample lapses that I think are instructive, or at least provocative.

Here is Alan Rich on a revival of *The Night of the Iguana*: "One learns from neither actor anything of [Tennessee] Williams' state of mind in creating the play, senses none of the melancholy tragedy that underlies the desperation that haunts these people as we meet them in the play."[9] Note the mid-sentence shift. That *Iguana* has a tragic quality which this cast failed to project is a fact (or may be a fact) about the play and about the performance of the play—both objects to be judged. But what is the bearing of Williams' "state of mind in creating the play"? That's a diversion here. How could we expect the actors to tell us anything about the playwright's state of mind—would they have to ask him? And suppose they don't tell us—is that really a fault in their performances?

Here is John Simon on the film *Network*:

> What makes *Network* such a repulsive movie, though, is its combination of nasty-mindedness and hypocrisy. The shallow jibes aimed at television, even if they contain a good measure of truth, are top-heavy with leaden sarcasm, and rather unseemly coming from the commercial produce of a movie industry hardly in the position to cast stones at TV. There is no vileness attributed to television here of which the movies have not shown themselves capable.[10]

Isn't this a strange argument? The point of it is that *Network* is a bad movie, partly because it is hypocritical, in that it attacks television for certain evils without attacking the film industry for the same evils. Is hypocrisy a good reason for condemning an art-

---

9. *New York*, January 10, 1977, p. 63.
10. *New York*, November 22, 1976, p. 91.

work? Does it make the work bad? This may be a legitimate moral criticism of the producers, but it is hardly a legitimate aesthetic criticism of the film.

Here is Max Kozloff on a show of abstract paintings by Kenneth Noland:

> Aside from the intimations of landscape in Noland's multiple horizons, he has also not been able to avoid effects similar to prism refractions, so that even if he puts blue below and red on top, as in "Graded Exposure," there are illustrational aspects to the present works. These would not be disturbing if it could be demonstrated that they were intentional. Rather I think of them as merely unfortunate by-products of Noland's new way of arranging things. A more serious objection resides in the linear functioning of the narrow stripes in what is essentially a chromatic context.[11]

The sharp insight of the second objection contrasts with the strange logic of the first one: surely the question is whether the "illustrational aspects" are in fact at odds with the painterly design, not whether the painter intended them. Even if they are not "by-products," they may still be "unfortunate." But perhaps the word "demonstrated" is supposed to avoid (or disguise) this difficulty: it is not the artist's intention that would be demonstrated, but the internal congruity of the artwork.

I could regale you with more examples, but my aim is not to put down critics, whose job is already hard enough as it is, and whose sensitivity and insight I cannot begin to match myself. Rather, I wanted to show how the CU model helps the critic by articulating the structure of his task and gently admonishing him when he occasionally neglects it. We must not ask too much of the critic, as perhaps we are sometimes inclined to do, when we demand profound and wide-ranging reflections on the rifts and warps in modern culture. But we must not ask too little of him, either, for there is something he can tell us, when he is doing his job well—namely, where high aesthetic quality, in all its endlessly varying forms, is to be found. And this is something we want—or should want—to know.

11. *Nation*, December 18, 1976, p. 668.

10: *The Limits of Critical Interpretation*

I

WHAT interpretation encompasses, in the context of the present discussion, will be plainer as we go on, but no doubt some initial effort should be made to fix this overworked term. I am talking about interpreting works of art (not scores or scripts)—one of the main things a critic or teacher does with them. Definition: to interpret is verbally to unfold or disclose meaning (either sense or reference).

The scheme I am operating with can be outlined this way:

I. Description
  1. The painting includes a mauve elliptical area.
  2. The sections of the music are balanced.
  3. The sculpture has a quality of barely contained frenzy.

II. Interpretation
  1. The painting represents a Conestoga wagon.
  2. The metaphor connotes helpless and merciless desire.
  3. The object in the literary work symbolizes the separateness of human beings.
  4. The object in the painting symbolizes the depersonalization of modern man.
  5. The (nonrepresentational) visual design denotes madness.
  6. The music refers to the (composer's?) fear of death.

Parts of the discussion below will have to be adjusted if we differ about the exact line between I and II or about the location of some of the examples. Charles Stevenson, in his famous paper,[1] would have placed statements I.2 and I.3 under "Interpretation," because he would hold that they, like the examples under II, are

---

1. "Interpretation and Evaluation in Aesthetics," in *Philosophical Analysis*, ed. Max Black (Ithaca, 1950), pp. 342–48, 358.

subject to a certain irremediable sort of dispute. W. E. Kennick[2] would have placed II.1 under "Description"; that is because he equates description roughly with statements about what is "obvious" in the work. In my earlier treatment of these problems,[3] I would have put II.2 under "Description" as analyzing the texture of the poem, considered as a composition of meanings—and I was pleased by my distinction among interpretation, elucidation, and explication. I haven't altogether abandoned my earlier classifications. But the six types of statement exemplified above have all, quite frequently, been called "interpretations," and I am willing to consider them as such on this occasion. Moreover, their similarities and differences, and even more the order in which they are listed, will prove to be instructive later.

The problem before us has to do with the nature and validity of critical interpretation statements. And certain points that are to be stressed can most sharply be brought out, I think, if we begin with what might seem to be something of a digression. I would like to contrast, in a broad fashion, two general ways of viewing art—two attempts, we might say, at monolithic theories. It will appear that they bear more than a casual resemblance to theories that have actually been held and defended, though representing them somewhat crudely. What will help us most is to look carefully for the seams in these theories, to note the points at which a certain strain and artifice are required to keep them in one piece.

II

The first theory is one that takes art—*all* art—as inherently semantic. According to this theory, it is the very nature of a work of art to point beyond itself to something else; the work is always, in a broad sense, a sign or symbol of something; it copies, or imitates, or represents, or expresses. Of course we must distinguish among all these different concepts. But those who hold this theory are after a concept more abstract than any of them. And perhaps I will be excused if I make the term "significance" do. According to the significance theory, then, all works of art have a meaning, in this exceedingly broad sense, and therefore all works require to

2. Ed., *Art and Philosophy* (New York, 1964), p. 498.
3. *Aesthetics: Problems in the Philosophy of Criticism* (New York, 1958), pp. 130, 242, 402–3.

be interpreted—or at least are capable of being interpreted (though what the work means may often be too obvious to mention).

The significance theory, in its various forms, has been supported by many studies of particular works and particular arts—studies that have, incidentally, contributed much to our knowledge of them. But I want to sketch a generalized argument for this theory in order to see how persuasive it can be made.

Consider first literature—surely the most favorable case. Whatever else a poem may be, it is at the very least a series of sentences in a natural language. And what is a sentence (even a one-word sentence) if it is not *about* something? The sounds a poem makes may seem to please us in themselves, but their full force comes only with the support they give the sense; and a senseless poem is a contradiction in terms.

It may be possible to take issue with this, though I think not for long. The strings of more or less random words or nonsense syllables or even mere letters set down by Dada writers should not trouble us. I do not think we have to be counted as enemies of art if we refuse to call these productions poems, or as dull in spirit if we fail to find much of aesthetic interest in them. But suppose the Dada poet defends his nonsense syllables. What might he say? "My poem is not intelligible in the ordinary sense, for it is not an ordinary poem. It has not been grasped by the critics, because they are looking for familiar elements of poetry and are bogged down in the traditional stereotypes. By breaking away from the limitations of English syntax and word construction, I demonstrate the freedom of the creative artist, who has the boldness and imagination to be different. So if I had been a little more conventional, I could have called my poem 'Freedom,' instead of 'No. 97.' "

It turns out that the poem *is* about something, after all, namely freedom—however obscure it seems to those who lack the skeleton key. Though ostensibly about nothing, it speaks (on a deeper level) of the poet's freedom to talk about nothing if he wants to.[4] I don't say that the defense is a good one; my point is that if he *makes* a defense at all (which he may be too proud to do), then it looks as if his defense would have to consist in showing that the

---

4. G. S. Fraser has come pretty close to this in his argument on behalf of the "coherence within incoherence" of Pound's *Cantos* in *Ezra Pound* (Edinburgh and London, 1960), p. 77: "What the *Cantos* in the end are 'about' is the isolated artist, and his struggle through an *idea* of tradition and community, towards sanity."

poem does indeed signify something, as the significance theory declares.

After that, we shall not be surprised to find that the theory can be made to cover many other unlikely cases as well. Probably the next easiest is the painting or sculpture that is plainly and thoroughly representational. Let's say there is a statue on the campus, its pedestal reading "Elihu Yale (1649–1721)." Certainly in a fairly clear sense this statue calls attention to Elihu Yale; it aims to preserve in the minds of living men the memory of this person, whom it represents and (I suppose) resembles. But now what if the name and dates were effaced—by time or by undergraduates—so that we had no verbal clue to the identity of its prototype? Would it then no longer refer to anyone? There is still the resemblance, to be sure. If it was not carved or molded from the life, it was probably copied from a contemporary portrait; and if we could dig up the portrait for comparison, we would have our clue. The statue doesn't have to be *named* Elihu Yale to represent him.

Let us make things harder, and suppose that the face, too, has been so worn away that it no longer much resembles either the man himself or any existing portrait of him. *Now* shall we say that it has lost its reference? Well, still there is its bulk and location. We would recognize it as a statue of a man. And to make him larger than life, and place him on a pedestal in the middle of the campus, where he serves no apparent utilitarian purpose (where, indeed, people have to walk around him to get where they are going)—doesn't all this implicitly claim that he is *somebody*, at least, a worthy man, even if we don't know on what account he is worthy, or what he is worthy of? So even if the statue no longer refers to Elihu Yale, it may signify *worthiness* in general, and to any other qualities we find depicted on that countenance, such as dignity, scholarly pride, strength of character.

Let us carry the matter further. Let us do as perhaps some archaeologist may in fact one day do: cart the partially ruined sculpture off to a museum, making way for someone more memorable, such as the late president of the university or its most eminent fund raiser. Standing (or sitting) there in the art museum, shorn of name, individual features, and campus context, is the statue still a bearer of meaning? Yes, the significationist will say, for it still represents a man, and a man of a certain sort—a strong or weak man, a rough or kindly man, a reflective or impulsive man. Now suppose the statue is slowly melted down. As long as its recognizable resemblance to the human form remains, however abstract it may be, it still speaks to our human condition and about our human nature. Toward the final stages of melting, we may be able to say of it nothing more than that it is (1) vaguely humanoid, (2) droopy or humble or dejected. Still it depicts sorrowing humanity. And when, finally, we can no longer even say that—when we can say no more than that it is brown, bronze, and rounded—then we no longer have a piece of sculpture, no longer a work of art. We have a lump. We are back to the material.

In this way the significationist makes out his case for the view that even nonrepresentational paintings and sculpture are, in a broad sense, meaningful—they don't just sit there; they have relevance to the deep concerns of man, his needs and aspirations; there is more in them than meets the eye. And once we have made out this case for purely formal art, there is no great difficulty in extending it to music. There is, of course, no difficulty at all about music that comes with words, or about music in which we can hear birds twittering. But take the most austerely formal music you can find, the most remote (at first glance) from all apparent interest in birds. Still, the significationist would say, it has a reference. Consider a familiar example: the first six notes of "The Star-Spangled Banner," in B-flat—as usually written, to make what accommodation it can to the limits of the ordinary human voice. Forget the words, and the voice of Lucy Monroe. Consider the notes only as a sequence of events in time. Something is happening—how shall we describe it? The melody dives down abruptly from fifth to tonic, by way of the third, and then with great determination and decisiveness climbs through the third and fifth to the octave. The downward plunge, as we see it in retrospect, while we are on the way up, was like a catching of breath, a stepping back to leap better, and this preparation makes the rise to the octave all the more emphatic. It is not aggressive, since the phrase ends at the octave, at home; it is an assertion of right, a resolution not to be dispossessed—like free men standing guard before their loved homes, or a flag waving amidst the smoke. There is nothing perfunctory or hesitant or languid about this little bit of musical action—it is at the opposite extreme, for example, from the opening bars of Wagner's *Tristan*. It has a quality of self-assurance, strength of will, defiance.

Stop right there, says the significationist, and you have it. For quite apart from its patriotic lyrics and official status as national anthem (and even if it lost these, the way Elihu Yale was imagined to lose his name and lineaments), the melody would still breathe these human qualities of will and strength. And it is capable of reminding the listener who really hears (or better, the hearer who really listens) that such qualities exist: it displays them, and shows them off admiringly, you might say. Thus music, too, without external aid, may have external reference. We need not give examples from architecture, the dance, and so on—we can see how the significance theory would deal with them. The strength of the argument lies in the continuity of cases. It seems that no one can deny that literary works are significant, but then by easy and apparently inescapable extensions of the method of analysis, representational works of fine art, then nonrepresentational works, and finally music turn out to exhibit something of the same sort of significance—though of course more subtle and perhaps more difficult to put your finger on and describe as you go down the list. The heart of the argument is this challenge: if you admit that there is signification at one end (in *Paradise Lost*, which surely refers to the creation of the world and man) and deny that there is signification at the other (say, in Bach's two-part inventions), where and with what excuses do you draw the line?

III

The second general theory of art relies on the same argument from continuity. But it begins at the other end and works in the opposite direction.

Let us consider again a simple strain of melody. We can agree that the first six-note phrase of "The Star-Spangled Banner" has the qualities of vigor and forcefulness. But why must we go on to say that it *refers* to vigor and forcefulness as qualities existing in man and in man's behavior? It is perfectly all right to say:

1. The music *is* vigorous and forceful.

It is also all right to say:

2. The music's vigor and forcefulness *resemble* the vigor and forcefulness of human beings and human actions.

It is in fact this resemblance—vague and fleeting as it sometimes is—that justifies us in transferring these terms from human beings, where they literally apply, to music, where they apply only metaphorically. This little snatch of melody certainly acts as if it knows where it is going and is determined to get there; there is no nonsense about it, and no subtlety either. Its motion is something like that of a man making a decisive gesture, or uttering a few short words of definite commitment to a cause, or rising to show where he stands on an issue. One could say a lot more about this, but that's enough to convey the general idea—if you don't find it too fanciful. The music *is* vigorous; its vigor is *similar* to human vigor. But that is still not the same as saying what the significance theory says:

3. The music signifies (means, expresses, represents, indicates, communicates) vigor.

From our second point of view, then, the music is not a sign of anything at all, but simply an object, or event, in its own right, with its own shape and qualities. Its parts are purely musical happenings: upward and downward movements, speedings and slowings, swellings and fadings. They fit together and make something of a whole precisely because, far from pointing beyond the music to something else, like the dots and dashes of a Morse transmitter, they actually point to what is coming next in the musical process itself. When we hear the first sudden descent of "The Star-Spangled Banner," we do not ask what sort of human trait it is starting to imitate, but rather we find ourselves expecting (indeed, demanding) that it will turn in its course to rise again—though we are somewhat surprised to have it rise so far and so fast. This following of the music's course with intentness, with absorption, and with interest just in what is going on there, rather than anything else, is exactly *the* musical experience. Music essentially is a moving pattern of rhythmic and/or tonal happenings that permits this absorbed attention; and good music is music that rewards it. We might call this the immanence theory of music.

As with music, so with nonrepresentational visual designs, including the freest products of the abstract expressionists, insofar as they can truly be called designs at all. Here the relationships holding the work together and making the wholeness of it are a web of contrasts and similarities, tensions and oppositions, tendencies toward motion or rest, repulsions and attractions of kindred or jarring shapes, colors, and lines. Think of the painting—or the abstract sculpture—in this way and see it as it really is, says the immanentist. And if you note also, as you should, that the design has vigor and force, as some designs undoubtedly do, then remember that these belong to the design, which is quite content merely to hang together and show off its qualities, and has no desire to direct our attention elsewhere; in fact, it wants all our attention on itself.

Now imagine we are able to reverse the process by which we gradually melted down the statue of Elihu Yale into a more and more abstract design until it became a formless (though, of course, not a shapeless) lump of metal. First we see the lump stretch itself into a more complicated form with certain vague qualities: of humility, contrition, or perhaps of power and drive. It doesn't *suggest* these qualities; it *has* them. A little later, as this form becomes more and more articulated, it begins to resemble a human being, and later a man—not any man in particular yet, but some man, any man. At that point, we say, it becomes representational. And as it individualizes itself more and more, it comes at some point to resemble Elihu Yale in particular (or his portrait, anyway) so closely as to allow us to say that it is a statue of him—not of *a* man, but of *this* man.

How could an immanentist deny that at this point we have reference to the world? Elihu Yale was a historical person who existed before his statue did. But perhaps there is a way around this. Of course, we cannot dispute the fact that there is a resemblance between the statue and the man, and this resemblance justifies us, if we wish, in carving his name on the pedestal and setting him up on the campus *in memoriam*. The statue can be *used* to refer, by being named and exhibited, especially in a suitable location. But let us consider the statue as a statue—in the fine arts museum. Then what have we got before us? We have shapes and forms, well or ill put together. Some of the shapes are round, some oval or angular; some of them happen to be eye shapes, finger shapes, leg shapes, and that's a perfectly fair way to describe them. But we have here two different modes of expression:

1. This part of the statue is an eye shape.
2. This part of the statue represents an eye.

The significationist moves without hesitation from 1 to 2—just as he moved from "resembling" to "referring" in music. But this is a distinction the immanentist is inclined to draw with firmness. What is the justification, he asks, for jumping from one to the other? Of course there is such a thing as representation—the photograph with "Khrushchev" printed under it. Certainly, with its caption, the photograph represents Khrushchev. Statues, too, may have labels, but the labels are not part of them as statues: and the statue itself, the work of art, is not a representation of anything, but simply (or complexly) a form. So the immanentist would maintain.

Does this seem too paradoxical? Then what difficulties will this philosopher face when he moves one step further along, and arrives at literature? The nonsense poem, made up of odd syllables, gives him no trouble, of course. He merely calls attention to a distinction that ought not to evoke a protest from any of us, though it could easily be overlooked by a mad Dada poet. It is surely one thing to *act* freely, and another thing to *refer* to freedom. If a person pretends to fall downstairs, as in a charade, you can say that his act (for he is acting) signifies *falling downstairs*; but if he really falls downstairs, then he is not referring to it, he's doing it. So even if the nonsense "poem" is the product of freedom, that doesn't make it a poem *about* freedom.

But after all there *are* poems about freedom (though not as many as one might expect). Byron's sonnet to Chillon is one: and surely, therefore, in literature we have works of art that are inherently and inescapably significant.

But at this point we are called upon to examine more closely this concept of signifying. We may say that the name "Khrushchev" signifies Khrushchev. But what about the name "Oliver Twist"? There is evidently one important sense, after all, in which novels and poems don't signify anything, but rather create and manipulate their own entities, which are purely imaginary. Some of these entities have names; some of them, like the lads who are hanged or killed in war in A. E. Housman's poems, are nameless. Of course you may say that lads have often enough been killed, and that's what Housman's poems are about. But the specific lads he talks about are not the real ones.

> The night my father got me,
> His mind was not on me. . . .

Who is the "me" in this poem? Not Housman, of course, for the speaker is hanged, whereas Housman died of heart disease. The speaker is not an actual, news-story criminal at all. And even when a poem or a novel happens to contain the names of genuine historical characters, such as Mary Queen of Scots, there is only a pretense of history, not history itself—as we acknowledge in granting the writer the license to change dates and events if he can make his work more interesting that way.

Even if we concede, however, that a poem may contain only fictional characters and events, there remains a question about the abstractions it also deals with: freedom, faith, mutability, the chanciness of life—in short, its subjects and themes. The chanciness of life is surely a feature of the world, and a poem that speaks of it speaks therefore, the significationist would say, about the world. But what is this "speaking of," in the case of poetry? A man who says the sky will be sunny tomorrow is speaking of something, namely tomorrow's sky; and he is saying something about it. But the ideas that turn up in poems, the immanentist holds, are not handled this way. They do not purport to be predictions of future events, or laws of nature or of man. The poet uses them in a different fashion. He is interested in them, all right, vitally and passionately. But he is interested in their qualities—their grandeur or pettiness as ideas, their sweep and maggificence, their subtlety or ridiculousness, their connection or lack of connection with other ideas entertained by someone at the same time. He uses ideas the way he uses visual and auditory images, sounds and smells—the way a novelist uses his characters—that is, to build a complex pattern or design that will be somewhat of a whole, yet full of action and tension. He is like a child playing store who happens to get hold of real money to play with, or a sculptor who steals automobile parts from a stockroom in order to make an abstract sculpture of them.

This is the way some critics think of literature: when the poet speaks of freedom, he is only trying to give the *feel* of it—to show what it would be like to love freedom of a certain kind with a certain quality of love—and his poem has really nothing to do with the Bill of Rights. Freedom, some would say, is more important than poetry—hence the comparative shortage of freedom poems, because the lovers of freedom would rather work for it than play with the idea (freedom *songs*, of course, are in a different category, for they are themselves weapons in the struggle for the real thing). In any case, the point, says the immanentist, is that poetry and bills of rights are different things, with different uses. And to enjoy poetry *as poetry* you have to abstract from practical affairs and be prepared to contemplate patterns of concepts and of emotions, of images and of experiences, for their own sake, as patterns. For that is what a poem is—and that is all it is.

The immanentist, then, sees works of art as variegated wholes, as more or less coherent and complete complexes of elements and qualities, which present themselves to us for absorbed contemplation. Their apparent references are pseudo-references; they are, so to speak, transformed into qualities. Just as the statue uses only the shapes of people, not people themselves, so the literary work uses only the possibilities of human action and experience, the surface and contour and texture and emotional impact of ideas, but not their living substance—that is, their capacity to compel belief, to work practical results. How else could we enjoy the horrors of tragedy? How else could we even laugh at comedy, which is composed, in the last analysis, of the same unhappy elements—deceit, misunderstanding, failure of purpose, helplessness under chance and fate, the painfulness of guilt and shame?

IV

What is the fundamental character of the dispute between the significance theory and the immanence theory? That is one of my main questions, but it will be approached by stages.

First, it is to be noted that the significance theory accepts all the examples in Group II above as making good sense. Either the painting—probably titled "O Pioneers!" or "The Last Stand on the Prairie"—does represent (in this case, I use the term "depict"[5] a Conestoga wagon, or it does not. And, at the other end of the list, either the music refers to the fear of death or it does not. Of course, it may be hard to tell, and there may be borderline cases, where the graphic depiction or the musical reference is so gentle or subtle as to escape the detection of all but the most sensitive and sharp-eyed critical interpreter. But there is at least one kind of meaning in every work of art, and it can in principle always be disclosed.

The immanence theory, on the other hand, must make some distinctions. Statements such as II.1 have a clear status. It is either true or false to say that a painting with a general term as cap-

---

5. See *Aesthetics*, pp. 269–78, where "depiction" and "portrayal" are distinguished.

tion (the newspaper ad that says "Turkeys 69¢ a pound") depicts a turkey; it is either true or false to say that a painting with a singular term as caption (the newspaper photograph with "Krushchev") portrays Krushchev. But it is always false to say that a painting without a caption depicts or portrays anything. The immanence theory must undoubtedly accept such statements as II.2—that is, explications of metaphors—as true or false; however, it treats them not as interpretations but as descriptions. And I think that examples II.3 to II.6 would be regarded as neither true nor false by the immanence theory. Though the key terms, "symbolize," "denote," and "refer," have legitimate uses in other contexts, they would be said not to make sense as applied here.

In short, the significance theory declares all works of art to be interpretable (in principle), and the immanence theory considers no work of art, taken by itself, as being interpretable (unless the explication of metaphor—and, it might be added, the elucidation or analysis of implied character and motive in novels—be considered interpretation). Evidently, to adjudicate this dispute we must take a closer look at interpretation.

As I have defined it for present purposes, interpretation is essentially connected with meaning, in a broad sense. One who advances an interpretation tacitly claims correctness for it, and thus allows the logical possibility that it may be incorrect. He purports to be giving information about the work he is interpreting, and one who accepts a new interpretation typically feels that he thereby learns something (perhaps even something valuable and interesting) about the work that he did not know before. When an interpretation is challenged, the interpreter has the responsibility of backing it up by appeal to the work in question; it is understood to be checkable in some way. There must be, in other words, criteria of interpretation.

All this follows from the connection of interpretation with meaning. As far as linguistic meaning is concerned, its dependence on linguistic rules is now widely agreed upon. I don't say the thesis goes unchallenged, but it seems clear that, in the customary phrase, the use of language is a rule-governed or rule-guided activity, and linguistic meaning is best understood in terms not merely of regular but of regularized use. Much thought, of course, has been given to the indicia of regularized behavior—though more is needed. How do we know when someone recognizes a rule, acknowledges an obligation to obey it, takes responsibility for certain conditions that are required in order for his linguistic performance to be correct?[6] We inquire whether he can state the rule as a rule. And, if not, we see whether he follows a fairly constant procedure, admits the possibility that he might be going wrong, gives evidence of a sense of requiredness, feels regret and tends to correct himself when he deviates, is able to settle disputes in an orderly fashion, and so on. In the light of such an inquiry, we may be able to say that infant speakers of a language are following syntactical rules even when they cannot formulate them, just as in playing a simple game they may follow rules that remain largely unspoken—except when violent disagreements occur.

If the concept of meaning is generalized by the art critic from certain linguistic contexts to more specialized linguistic contexts (poems and novels) and to the nonlinguistic contexts (paintings and music), the regularization of use must accompany it. Otherwise, the corresponding activity of interpretation will lack criteria of correctness. Now, it is well known that activities may vary considerably in the degree to which they are regularized. There are at least two dimensions of this variation—degrees, let us say, of rule government and of rule guidance. A person's actions are rule governed to the extent to which his acceptance of certain rules leads him to follow them. His actions are rule guided to the extent to which he subscribes to rules. It is this second feature that concerns us most here. Between a neighborhood game of hide-and-seek, whose participants often think of things to do that nobody has prohibited but some object to, and, say, baseball, where practically anything that could conceivably happen is provided for in the rulebook or in the ground rules, there are many possibilities. One of the points I want to argue is that this range of variation is also to be found in interpretation of the arts. As we go down the list of examples in Group II, from 1 to 6, the rules of use (so to speak), and consequently the criteria of interpretation, become less and less stringent. Therefore what the critic is doing deserves less to be called interpretation at all, since the act of interpreting becomes itself less rule guided. I believe that a recognition of this point will clarify some puzzling features of art criticism, and will dispose of some unnecessary conflicts. To make

---

6. See William Alston, *Philosophy of Language* (Englewood Cliffs, N.J., 1964), pp. 41–44.

it stick would require a much fuller argument than I shall give, but perhaps brief remarks about a few of the examples in Group II will show the plausibility of the general line of argument.

Starting at the top, it seems to me that statements about what paintings represent (in the sense of depicting) are probably the most thoroughly regularized of all interpretations. Not that there are no paradoxes and difficulties about depiction.[7] But both in the practice of fine arts critics and in analytical studies by aestheticians, it is very clear for the most part when a painting depicts a Conestoga wagon and when it doesn't. And (usually) if a dispute occurs, it can be settled by methods agreeable to all. The main problem about depiction arises in the following way. Let us say that objects of a certain kind, whether existing ones or imaginary ones possessing a defined general name, have visual aspects (the term comes from Paul Ziff)—that is, all the different ways they might appear at various angles, in various directions, under various atmospheric and lighting conditions. When a painting presents one of the visual aspects belonging to the set of visual aspects associated with a Conestoga wagon, then the painting may be taken to depict a Conestoga wagon. But it may happen that there is some other kind of object, X, the set of whose visual aspects overlaps with that of Conestoga wagons, and that the visual aspect presented in the painting belongs both to those associated with Conestoga wagons and those associated with X's. In that case (and it is the usual case) there is apparent ambiguity of depiction; and if that is all that can be said, the ambiguity is real and no decision is possible. However, as Ziff has cogently argued, a decision can be made if, on a frequency basis, the probability that the particular visual aspect is associated with a Conestoga wagon is greater than that it is associated with an X. In that case, we will say that the painting depicts a Conestoga wagon, rather than an X.

This analysis of depiction could be refined further, but surely it is a very good description of the grounds on which we actually decide what pictures are pictures of. Consequently, it makes explicit the operative criteria for interpretation statements of this sort; it shows that within fairly narrow limits there are generally accepted rules for determining what is depicted. Moreover, these

---

7. See, for example, Paul Ziff, "On What a Painting Represents," *Journal of Philosophy* 57 (1960): 647–54.

rules refer to quite objective features of the world. They do not depend on verbal captions (except in the case where the painting portrays a nonexistent individual person). Nor do they depend on intention. Concerning one of his most famous cartoons, James Thurber explained to Harold Ross "that I had tried to draw a wife at the head of the stairs—at the head of a flight of stairs waiting for her husband. Having no skill in draftsmanship, I lost perspective and the stairs turned instantly into a bookcase or what looked like a bookcase, if you made transverse lines—so I made it into a bookcase—and there was this naked lady on top of a bookcase."[8] It is an important rule about the general use of the term "represent," in the sense of "depict," that a drawing can represent something accidentally. The sole test is a relationship between the visual design and its object. There are other tricky points that a full analysis would have to clear up—for example, when a visual design depicts another depicting object:[9] say a photograph of a waxwork effigy of Mahatma Ghandi. But perhaps they can be taken care of by the principle of frequency—the only way one could unambiguously depict a waxwork effigy would be by giving it a stiff and glassy quality that would not be as likely to appear in a visual aspect of human beings.

The problems about representation in the visual arts may serve to point up one way in which some of the conflicts between the significance theory and the immanence theory might be resolved. We can say a painting depicts a house, or that it portrays the White House; it can't do the latter without doing the former, but it can depict *a* house without portraying any particular house. These two notions can be compared to familiar ones: the depiction is the *sense* of the picture (Mill's connotation), whereas portrayal is *reference* (denotation). Or it might be more correct to say something different: A picture depicts in virtue of its characteristics and those of the world (including worlds already imagined or described previously). So depiction *is* like a sense. But portrayal is a *use* of the picture. If it *has* a sense, then it can be used to portray. And a good support for this view can be found in the woodcuts in *The Nuremberg Chronicle*, where the same cut (that is, many tokens of the same type woodcut) is used over and over to

---

8. Interview with Henry Brandon, *New Republic*, May 26, 1958, p. 12.
9. It was David Lewis who, as a student at Swarthmore College, showed me this difficulty.

portray (inaccurately) a number of different cities, by being given a different label, though it always depicts (by definition) the same kind of city. So perhaps the significationist is right when he says that paintings can depict, and perhaps the immanentist is right when he says that they do not in themselves portray anything.

I believe that explications of metaphors in poetry (such as the example in II.2) are only slightly less well provided with criteria than statements about depiction. A study of the actual practice of literary explicators—their manner of explicating, and of defending and attacking proposed explications—reveals a fairly definite commitment to some general rules. The essential point is that the emergent meanings of the metaphorical construction are treated as functions of the standard meanings of the constituent words. The nature of this function is still subject to dispute among those philosophers who have tried to formulate it. And it is not conceived so exactly that no metaphors defy explication, and no unresolvable disagreements arise, and there are no residual ambiguities. Nevertheless, I believe this activity is largely rule guided, and since it has been discussed in some detail elsewhere, I set it aside here.[10]

My example II.4 should really be a series of examples, for when we get this far down on the list the regularization of interpretation begins to relax considerably. In this category, we are dealing with representational paintings (and sculptures), and with critical statements to the effect that some depicted object symbolizes some abstract quality or condition. (There are other complications about symbolism, of course, but we will have to ignore them here.) At the upper end of II.4, we would still have fairly circumscribed interpretations—examples of traditional iconography. The symbolic reference of the emblems of the saints is thoroughly regulated—there are official rulebooks. Toward the lower end of the series we come to what might be called *free symbolism*—for example, the interpretive writing currently pouring forth about Pop art. The hundredfold repeated tomato soup can, the blown-up comic strip frame, the life-size wooden caricatures of people, with real dirty sneakers on—these things are said to have enormous symbolic weight, carrying the burden of such abstractions as the conformism of modern life, the loss of individuality, the growth

---

10. See *Aesthetics*, Chap. 3; "The Metaphorical Twist," pp. 263–80, this volume; Alston, *Philosophy of Language*, p. 96.

The Limits of Critical Interpretation 181

of *Angst*. "The ten photographed images of forgotten men (pasted in a row on the ten white spools, one photo to a spool, arranged in two rows, on two platforms, of five each) express the Existential situation with poignant, noble, bittersweet clarity" (*Art News*, April 1962, p. 23).

We need not deny that in such art, and in such criticism, there is a species of exhaustible fun. But the nature of that fun becomes understandable, I think, when we take such statements at their face value and look for criteria of interpretation, or rules of symbolic reference. For, in the first place, there is one sort of rule that continues to operate—as it has for a long time in pictorial art. Roughly, it is that any object prominently displayed in depiction, given special emphasis, is worthy of particular attention and has symbolic significance. To multiply the tomato soup cans, or to magnify the comic strip, is to claim and insist that there is meaning here, beyond what would ordinarily be noticed by the grocer or weary businessman. It is only the general acceptance of this rule, as part of the game of fine arts viewing, that gives momentary interest or excitement to the work. But, in the second place, there are no distinct rules to guide us in deciding *what* the symbol means. We know the soup is symbolic, but we can't know what it symbolizes—that is the irony, the mystery, and the amusement. Of course, we can think of what it *might* or *could* symbolize: anything we can associate with tomato cans, if we have the strength and patience, may be brought in. But there is hardly any restraint on the harassed reviewer for *Art News* when the time comes for him to retire to his desk and compose his lyric little paragraph. I do not say that there is no restraint at all, for the interpreter takes off from an intelligible and often familiar object, and there hovers about his symbol reading the shadow of a methodology that suggests some sort of line. Tomato soup cans cannot possibly symbolize, I suppose, the pioneer spirit, any more than Conestoga wagons can symbolize the affluent society.

Yet the rules are so lax and the license has such latitude that this sort of symbol reading cannot be said to be very regularized. It reminds me of the struggles of poor Ishmael in *Moby Dick* (Chap. 3) to make out the subject, and then the significance, of that grimy painting in the Spouter-Inn.

> But what most puzzled and confounded you was a long, limber, portentous, black mass of something hovering in the center of the picture over three blue, dim, perpendicular lines floating in a name-

less yeast. A boggy, soggy, squitchy picture truly, enough to drive a nervous man distracted. Yet was there a sort of indefinite, half-attained, unimaginable sublimity about it that fairly froze you to it, till you involuntarily took an oath with yourself to find out what that marvellous painting meant.

For the most part, there is no way of disqualifying anyone's guess, and therefore there can be little achievement in maintaining one. The participants—neither the painters, the critics, nor the dealers—have hardly any rules, so what they are doing hardly deserves to be called the interpretation of meaning. The talk goes on, but it is a mug's game.

Somewhat more respectable than this free symbol reading in painting, because more ancient and generally more self-restrained, is the interpretation of "meaning" in music. It is my view about music—and here I am speaking of music without words—that we have not even the first sort of rule that exists for allegedly symbolic depictions: we have no warrant for taking a musical composition to refer to anything at all outside itself. If we did, we would perhaps not be much worse off than with Pop art. That is, if music has to refer to something, we could certainly find *less* appropriate things to say, for example, than that "the agony with which Mahler viewed the subject of death is undoubtedly expressed in" the Andante of his last symphony (this from Winthrop Sargeant), or that grief for their daughters "colors," or is "reflected" in, certain works of Smetana (Op. 15) and Dvořák (String Quartet in E Major), as we are told in the Penguin volume *Chamber Music* (1957).[11]

Here, it seems to me, if not in the case of symbolic meanings ascribed to Pop art (and to nonrepresentational designs; see II.5), we must call a halt. Certainly anyone who wishes can ask himself whether the music reminds him of something, and can put down what comes to mind as his "interpretation." But the term is badly misused, for it involves a claim to criteria distinguishing correct from incorrect ones. Since there are no rules for musical significance, there is no such thing as interpreting music.

11. Remarks like these do not have the complete freedom from rule guidance that we find, for example, in Titchener's image of "but" as the back of a speaker's head or Kandinsky's association of green with bourgeois smugness, because in it the "concentricity" of blue is locked in a static and nullifying mixture with the "eccentricity" of yellow.

V

It has long been realized that there is a curious division in discourse about music. The majority of competent critics and musicologists write as though it would hardly occur to them to take music as referring to something external to it—though some of them, like Sir Donald Tovey, may use rather elaborate, or even whimsical, metaphorical phrases to describe what they hear the music doing. But those who do find musical references write as though there were a fairly clear-cut rule, as though they knew what they are up to and are only doing their duty. True, they may contradict each other, but this does not seem to discourage them. Should we say that *they*, at least, do have rules, and do engage in interpretation, even if the others don't?

Let us see where this thought might lead. What if there were a rule for meaning in music? What would it have to be like to justify the sort of interpretation we find some critics giving? Since in discussing music we are at the bottom of my list of examples in Group II, this question can be broadened by a kind of a fortiori reasoning. If music has interpretable meaning, there shouldn't be any difficulty about those examples higher on the list. What we are asking for, then, is a defense of the entire significance theory. On what general principle could it be argued that there is in fact a rule for interpreting all art?

The relevant point of view might be summarized this way: Works of art are made by human beings; they are characteristically fashioned with care. To make any object deliberately is implicitly to claim that it *has* a purpose and a value. But, generally speaking, works of art are, by intention, incapable of fulfilling any practical need, or at least designedly poor at it. They seem bent to the will of the maker rather than to the demands of the environment. The maker has put something of his own, indeed of himself, into the object. Thus for him to publish or exhibit or perform it can only be to call attention to his own experience, his thoughts or feelings, and indirectly to the world around him (and us), for this is the world his thoughts and feelings are *about*. In short, a manmade object must be a sign if it is nothing else. Now every work of art resembles something in the world to some extent, and what it resembles it can be taken to refer to. Therefore every work of art is an intentional object—it makes a reference to the world and to the human condition. It cannot help being so, for it has to be something (it claims to be something) and it is prevented from being anything but a seeming, a show, a likeness. To draw a picture of a house under conditions when we can neither live in the picture nor use it for finding our way, for building or buying—this can only be to suggest something about houses, or some houses, and the way one can feel about them. And to compose a passage of sorrowful music can only be to allude to grief.

The significationist will need two general rules. The first might be called the rule of indication (for music and visual designs): Whenever an object satisfies the following conditions: (1) it has been made deliberately by a human being, (2) it serves no practical end, and (3) it resembles, in form or regional quality, something already found in the world or in human experience, then we may take it that the object indicates what it resembles. By this rule, paintings can be said to depict, and abstract designs and musical compositions to have not only a quality but a meaning. The second rule might be called the rule of (free) symbolism: Whenever an object that plays a role in human life is depicted in a painting or introduced into the world of a literary work, then we may take that the object symbolizes any general qualities that can be connected with it via the activities in which it usually plays a part.

But the permissive phrase "we *may* take it that" makes these rules too weak. Consider the second one. We may, if we wish, take absolutely anything as in some way symbolic. The cheerful suburbanite can cook on his barbecue pit and toss his salads without a qualm after a hard day's work. But his college-age son who comes home fresh from a course in sociology sees the barbecue pit as the symbol of an other-directed culture, the hearth of the home moved outdoors in full view of everyone. He notes the conspicuous waste of steaks that fall into the fire, sending up their aromatic smoke as a visual and olfactory signal to the neighbors. And to him the tossed salad marks the family's status in the higher echelons of middlebrow culture. Many of the 1,200 car salesmen who were lured into becoming agents for the ill-fated Edsel some years ago thought that they were selling a car—but to its more dedicated promoters it was mainly a symbol of the younger executive's "upward mobility."

In such cases as these it is evident that making a symbol consists in getting people to take something as a symbol—that is, to approach it with that peculiarly detached, searching, and diffuse attention that enables us, with a little imagination, to transform any object into a symbol by dwelling on its relation to forms of human life. And so the phrase required for these rules is not permissive but injunctive: "we are to take it," or "it is to be taken." Thus Rule 1: Works of art, as nonutilitarian human artifacts, are to be taken as indicating what they most resemble in form or regional quality. Rule 2: Utilitarian objects prominently depicted or described in works of art are to be taken as symbolizing the dominant qualities of the activities in which they usually function.

The basic character of the significance theory and the immanence theory can now be made plain. For these two rules, which in effect define the significance theory, have a peculiar status. There is no doubt that some critics (allowing this term to encompass all who talk much about works of art) more or less tacitly subscribe to these rules, and follow them as best they can much of the time. And there is no doubt that other critics do not follow them at all, and would repudiate them if explicitly invited to adopt them. We cannot say that critical activity in general is guided by these rules. And we therefore cannot escape the question whether or not it ought to be. In short, if taken as general theories about art, the significance theory and the immanence theory are, at bottom, not descriptions of what in fact prevails, but recommendations about how works of art are best approached. And more fundamentally still, they are pedagogical proposals about how people should be induced to approach works of art. Should we teach children to look for meaning in music or not? Some of the older psychological research on responses to music led the investigators to the conclusion that there are different types of listeners, but the evidence never (as far as I can see) showed any more than that people can be taught to expect different things from music and to make something different of it.

The significationist, then, is recommending that we follow his rules; and the immanentist is advising us not to follow those rules. A modified immanentist, of course, might accept Rule 1 as far as representation in painting is concerned (II.1) and Rule 2 as far as symbolism in literature is concerned (II.3), but reject them for free symbolism in painting and for music and nonrepresentational painting. The crux of the issue is really whether the rules are to be extended to II.4, II.5, and II.6. How, then, is a dispute over art education to be resolved? Evidently by going back to the question of aesthetic value. If both parties can agree on what aesthetic value consists in, and on the elements of art and of aesthetic experience that contribute to it, then it will become a factual question whether or not, in the long run, aesthetic value is maximized by following the two meaning rules. If it turns out that besides the aesthetic value of art there are other extremely important values, the question might be whether these other values can be realized best with or without the rules.

The kind of thing I have in mind here can be illustrated by an example from Bernard Bosanquet, expounding his "festal or social view of art": "Suppose a tribe or a nation has won a great victory; 'they are feeling big, and they want to make something big,' as I have heard an expert say. That, I take it, is the rough account of the beginning of the aesthetic attitude. And according to their capacity and their stage of culture they may make a pile of their enemies' skulls, or they may build the Parthenon."[12] Whether or not this is the beginning of the aesthetic attitude, it is certainly an instance of what might be called the *commemorative impulse*, of which Dewey has so much to say in his *Art as Experience*. Satisfying our need for a symbolic intensification and a lasting reminder of social achievement is one of the values that art can provide, even when it is not great art (the campus statue of a departed university worthy may be no great shakes as sculpture, after all). In order to recognize the commemorative character and appreciate the commemorative value of that pile of skulls, we would have to approach it under the guidance of the rule of symbolism.

If there are both aesthetic and nonaesthetic values in art, then there is the possibility of a conflict of interest—and this conflict may be reflected in some areas of disagreement between the significance theory and the immanence theory of art. In that case, the issues between these two theories will require even more delicate adjudication. Should we, for example, approach music in churches under the rule of indication, but lay that rule aside when we enter the concert hall?

These normative problems underlie the problem I have been discussing—though not quite in the way argued by Charles Stevenson, who was the first to explore carefully the interrelations of interpretive and normative issues (in "Interpretation and Evaluation"). My conclusion differs from his in that I do not regard each interpretation statement as normative (it does not have to be for-

---

12. *Three Lectures on Aesthetics* (London, 1915), p. 75.

mulated with an "is to be" or "is properly interpreted as"), but only the underlying theories of interpretation. But one of the main implications of Stevenson's work still holds good, I believe—that until we are reasonably confident that we know what aesthetic value is, the nature of interpretation will continue to puzzle us.

11: *Intentions and Interpretations: A Fallacy Revived*

I

ONE of the greatest satisfactions of the philosopher is to expose the fallacy in what has hitherto been accepted as a conclusive argument; and I suppose this can be as selfless as any satisfaction in making a contribution to the general welfare. Equally satisfying, and equally altruistic, is to expose the fallacy in the fallacy—to demonstrate that it is not a fallacy after all, or not the sort of fallacy it was claimed to be. By this turn of the wheel, what was worth saving in the original argument gets rehabilitated, though it will never look quite the same.

An instance of this dialectical, or zigzag, pattern of philosophical progress—suitable for the climbing of steep slopes to truth—is the "intentional fallacy," articulated and named over thirty years ago as a kind of banner, or rallying cry, for those literary theorists who could no longer put up with the mishmash of philology, biography, moral admonition, textual exegesis, social history, and sheer burbling that largely made up what was thought of as literary criticism in academic circles, as well as in the wider world of letters. The rather youthful authors of this designedly subversive and unpleasantly provoking essay were out to insist on some distinctions and were convinced that various intellectual confusions and invalid reasonings sprang from a failure to mark those distinctions. They were concerned with the logical relevance of information about the intentions of an author to the interpretation and the evaluation of his work. And they took the position that there is no such logical relevance.

Over the years, as these problems have been discussed by numerous other writers, it has turned out that the issues are a good deal more complicated and subtle than had been acknowledged. It has been argued that the anti-intentionalist position is unquestionably sound; it has been argued that the position is probably false or incoherent; and practically every plausible compromise has also been espoused. I have followed these developments with much interest, mainly from the sidelines. However, the recent publication of a lively collection of essays on the subject[1] has roused me to take another look at the issues, or some of them anyway. I shall not deal with the question of evaluation here, but stick to interpretation—which offers difficulties enough. I am still attacking intentionalism (by which I mean the view that interpretations of literature can be supported by appeal to knowledge of authors' intentions), but with concessions and qualifications that I owe to my critics (and thank them for) and, I hope, with help from some more recent work on language that I believe places the anti-intentionalist position in a clearer and more favorable light.

II

There have been complaints—some of them surely justifiable—about the slackness of the word "intention" in the phrase "the author's intention." And even without complaints, the need for tightening the original use has been revealed by various objections that rest on taking the author's intention in a wrong way. Thus a certain amount of confusion has been caused by recurrent use of such expressions as "what the author meant" and "what the author intended." In the last analysis (on my view), it is only doings that can be intended; strictly speaking, one does not even intend states of affairs, rather one intends to bring about states of affairs.[2] What, then, does an author, in meaning something, actually intend to do?

I shall use the term "author" for anyone who intentionally produces a text: that is, a syntactically ordered sequence of words, spoken or written, in a natural language. To produce a text intentionally, on my view, is just to produce the text while wanting to

---

1. David Newton-De Molina, ed., *On Literary Intention* (Edinburgh, 1976). Wimsatt has also taken another, careful look at the problems in "Genesis: An Argument Resumed," in *Day of the Leopards: Essays in Defense of Poems* (New Haven, 1976).
2. See "Intending," in *Values and Morals*, ed. Alvin I. Goldman and Jaegwon Kim (Dordrecht, 1978).

do so and knowing that one is doing so. (This formula requires a little refinement, but is nearly correct, I believe.) A somnambulist, for example, may produce a text while unconscious; but he does not do so intentionally. When wide awake, however, one may produce a text and intend to *say* something in producing that text; and this is the way I shall understand "meaning something." More generally, the case in which I can truly be said to mean something is the case in which I intentionally perform an action of some kind and also intend to *say* something in performing that action. For example, I wave my hand to say good-bye. But I am concerned here only with the narrower case in which the action performed is that of producing a text—more precisely, a token (that is, an inscription or an utterance) of a text type. The author's intention in producing a text is his intention to say certain things in producing that text.

I use the word "say" in a convenient, though perhaps uncommonly broad, way, to include two very different kinds of speech act.

First, the word is to cover illocutionary actions in general. What the author intends to say may consist in giving unsolicited advice, protesting a rise in taxes, recommending for a job, authorizing the disbursement of company funds, or some such thing. Using another term, we might say he is voicing advice, or a report, or a request, or a threat. On my view of illocutionary actions, they are generated (in Alvin Goldman's sense of "act-generation") by text production under certain conditions, according to certain language conventions.

Thus, *if* Jones speaks in a serious tone to Smith, and Smith hears and understands Jones's words, and Jones owns a watch, and Jones believes that his watch has been stolen, *then* in saying the words "You stole my watch!" Jones is accusing Smith of theft. His act of producing the text, under those conditions, generates an act of accusing. These are the same action, on my view, but the action that is of the one kind becomes an action of the other kind when performed under the requisite conditions. I may not have stated here all of the requisite illocutionary-act-generating conditions, but I think I have. Perhaps some of those I have stated are not absolutely necessary. You may question whether Jones must believe his watch to have been stolen in order to accuse Smith of stealing it. But suppose this episode occurs onstage, in a play: then Jones is not really accusing Smith, even though Jones has a watch, uses the right tone of voice, and secures what J. L. Austin called "uptake" (his text is heard and understood). The difference seems to be that in this case Jones does not really believe his watch is missing. On the other hand, of course, for the act of accusing to occur it is not necessary that Smith actually stole the watch; a false accusation is still an accusation.

Second, the word "say" is to cover the special case of refraining from illocutionary commitment in order to produce a fiction: this is the representation, rather than the performance, of an illocutionary action. Thus in Margaret Drabble's most recent novel, there is this passage: "'Never recommend your secretary to anyone,' said Len, still giving Maureen the eye, 'or they get stolen, didn't you know? We'll have her off you, if you don't keep an eye on her.'"[3] In writing the words between quotation marks, the author is not herself advising anyone, but she is representing an advising.

Verbal representation, or the representation of an illocutionary action, comes under the same general concept as pictorial representation (in the sense of depicting an acrobat or an anatomy lesson) and dramatic representation (playing a role on stage). In all these forms, the representer produces something that falls short of being the real thing, but provides certain features distinctive or characteristic of its kind, which thus refer (indefinitely) to something of that kind. Following in the wake of *Languages of Art*, there has been a great deal of dispute about pictorial representation, and I can't do justice at the moment to the many arguments that flourish. My own view, despite the powerful attacks of Nelson Goodman and his followers, is still that representation (in this sense of depiction, as I call it) involves *selective similarity*: the mime can represent himself as, say, climbing a ladder—without climbing and without actually having a ladder—but only by selecting certain movements that are characteristic of ladder climbing, rather than, say, riding a bicycle or milking a cow. So the draftsman can sketch a horse race, with perhaps an incredibly few lines, by selecting shapes and shape combinations that can be perceived as *telling* elements that would be present in an actual horse race.[4] And so a poet may write

---

3. *The Ice Age* (New York, 1977), p. 54.
4. See "*Languages of Art* and Art Criticism," *Erkenntnis* 12 (1978): 95–118.

> Milton! thou shouldst be living at this hour:
> England hath need of thee—

and by selecting words that could be used, under appropriate imaginable conditions, to perform an illocutionary action, he can represent an action of that sort—namely that of expressing a wish that the addressee were on hand to remedy the deplorable state of the nation. But of course the mime who mimes ladder climbing does not actually climb; the picture of a horse race is not a horse race; and Wordsworth, for all his passionate intensity, is not performing an illocutionary action in writing these words, since they are ostensibly addressed to a long-dead poet and could not be expected to secure uptake.

We must allow, of course, for a distinction between a *failure* to perform an illocutionary action and a *refraining* from one. One who fires a gun at another and misses is failing if he intended to hit, I suppose; but one who fires a gun knowing that it is loaded with blanks, while on location making a Western movie, is only representing a shooting. On the other hand, one who fires a gun in anger without knowing it is loaded with blanks might, under certain circumstances, try and fail to shoot someone, but *also* unintentionally represent a shooting. I claim that the term "represent" in pictorial contexts is not essentially tied to intention: a person might make marks on paper intending in doing so to depict a horse, but in fact depict a mule. So one might write certain words intending in doing so to make them a passage of praise, but for one reason or another they may turn out to represent a subtle insult.

In order to accommodate these and other distinctions, we must, I think, consider representation in any of its forms a kind of reference—but, as I suggested above, an indefinite reference, where what is represented is not this or that X, but *an* X. I don't have a full account of this form of reference, but I think it must involve at least two elements, a form of synecdoche, or letting part stand for whole, and a transformation that might be called the "detachment of reference." The basic notion of reference is no doubt reference by persons: in using such-and-such symbols (words, pictures, gestures) someone refers to something. Much representational reference must be intentional in order to get a *practice* of representing going. One lets it be understood that the lines of a sketch are to be taken as a picture of a whole face, from which these few curves and angles have been culled; and the convention becomes accepted that an actor on the stage is not pouring poison in the porches of his brother's ear, but intends us to take his movements as a representation of an action of that kind. But once these representing practices are established, reference is detached from the referrer to the symbol; in a new sense the marks or gestures themselves are said to refer, and quite apart from any intentions. The part (if *indicative*, if selective enough) can be taken for the whole, as in synecdoche: so the firing of a blank cartridge onstage represents a shooting, and the writing of Wordsworth's apostrophe to Milton represents a wish expressing.

III

Sketchy as it is, this account of "saying," and the distinction between two sorts of saying, may serve to pin down adequately the issues over the intentionalist thesis about literary interpretation—that is, the thesis that facts about the author's intention, or facts tending to show that the author probably had such-and-such intentions, can give evidential support to the claim that a particular interpretation of a literary work is true or correct. To interpret a work is to declare what it says, in my broad sense. Of course it will make a great difference to the way we conceive of the interpreter's task whether the text to be interpreted is one whose production was the performance, or the representation, of an illocutionary action. On my view, lyric poems (for example) are representations, not performances—though this view is certainly debatable, and calls for a great deal more argument than I shall provide here.[5] When Wordsworth, in the sonnet I quoted earlier, goes on to say of England that

> she is a fen
> Of stagnant waters: altar, sword, and pen,
> Fireside, the heroic wealth of hall and bower,
> Have forfeited their ancient English dower
> Of inward happiness,

it is tempting to say that in writing *these* words, Wordsworth was castigating England, or something of the sort. But my view is that in writing these words, Wordsworth was representing an illocutionary action of castigating England.

Of course to say that castigation is represented is not much of

---

5. See "Fiction as Representation," *Synthese* 46 (1981): 291–314.

an interpretation, and would not be very helpful to a reader. It is the precise nuances of the illocutionary actions in the poem, the delicate shadings and subtle distinctions, that may call for comment. Why is England a "fen," not a "swamp"? What exactly is covered by "altar, sword, and pen," for example? What is the "heroic wealth of hall and bower"? What sort of happiness is "inward happiness," how is this a birthright of the English—and how could it have been forfeited? To answer such questions is to make plain what is being said, but not what is obviously or bluntly said.

Most intentionalists have not made, or at least featured, the distinction between performing and representing. And indeed I think that this omission has contributed to the plausibility of their view. For if we learned from letters, diaries, or the recollections of Wordsworth's friends that in 1802 he was distinctly alienated from the England of his day and believed, as he adds in the poem, that "we are selfish men," then it may seem that this information is evidence about the sorts of illocutionary actions he might *intend* to perform if he got to discussing the sorry state of things. Even here we should avoid the leap from what Wordsworth intended to what he actually did. The precise illocutionary contribution made by the metaphorical word "fen" is not affected by Wordsworth's intention, but is a function of its literal sense, its verbal context, and the conventions for grasping metaphorical senses. But if I am right in regarding this poem as a *representation* of an illocutionary action, the relevance of biographical information becomes even more remote. Even if Wordsworth in fact took a dim view of England in 1802, does that make it more likely that he would intend to *represent* a castigation? And, of course, even if we knew what Wordsworth *intended* to represent, we would still have to study the poem to see what he *did* represent.

The connections between saying and intending are, I think, often misunderstood; they are more complex than is generally realized. I disagree with those who have argued, along with Quentin Skinner, that "to know a writer's motives and intentions is to know the relationship in which he stands to what he has written. To know about intentions is to know such facts as whether the writer was joking or serious or ironic or in general what speech-act he was performing."[6] I agree that knowing whether a writer is

---

6. "Motives, Intentions and the Interpretation of Texts," in *On Literary Intention*, ed. Newton-De Molina, p. 215.

serious is knowing something about his intention. The question of irony I shall come to shortly. As regards speech acts, if this means illocutionary actions, I differ. To know what illocutionary action was performed is to know what action the production of such a text generated by the appropriate conventions. I believe it is a misunderstanding of J. L. Austin's position to read him as holding "that an understanding of the illocutionary act being performed by an agent in issuing a given utterance will be equivalent to an understanding of that agent's primary *intentions* in issuing that particular utterance."[7]

Three comments seem to be called for.

First, we should note one necessary role that intention plays in illocutionary performance: to perform an illocutionary action in producing a certain text one must intend to produce that text: only intentional text production can generate illocutionary actions.

Unless George Washington intentionally produced the words of his Second Inaugural, his utterance of those words was not (among other things) a warning against foreign entanglements. But I don't think this principle applies to the *representation* of illocutionary actions, if we allow for the detachment of reference. Consider that once we establish the practice of depicting objects by line drawings and shading (that is, set up a system of representation), we can find pictures in clouds and window frost. Of course we cannot speak of an *act* of representing here, but we can say that in virtue of the existence of a system of representation, and in terms of that system, the marks made by nature depict a weasel or a mountain range.

So if, as I have suggested, a poem is (typically) a representation of an illocutionary action, it is not surprising that computer-generated poems, in which the selection of syntax and of lexis is random (within a range of choice), can also be said to represent illocutionary actions. Of course we might treat the programmer as a poet, despite his diminished role in the determination of the final product; but if we do not, we are left with a printout that has some analogy with clouds and window frost. And I see no objection to regarding even the verbal output of a myna bird as crude verbal depiction of illocutionary actions: the bird does not actually greet you or curse you but gives a pretty good imitation of it.

Second, the existence of a certain intention may be one of the requisite conditions for the performance of some illocutionary

7. Ibid., p. 216.

actions. It could be argued that an intention to assign moral or legal responsibility is a condition of performing an accusation; but I am inclined to say that this is really the same thing in different words, another way of (partially) describing what it is to accuse, not a *condition* of accusing. Perhaps one has to intend to deceive in order to lie, in the same way one has to intend to kill in order to commit murder—except, of course, in those jurisdictions where the legal definition of murder makes it include various kinds of homicide committed, even unintentionally or even by someone else, in the course of a felony.

Even if one must have a particular intention to *perform* a certain illocutionary action, it does not follow that one must have that intention to *represent* that action. This error in inference might seem too elementary to make, but even literary critics who hold, in general, that poems are fictions (and hence, I would say, representations) sometimes treat biographical facts about the author as relevant to the interpretation of his poem in a way that would make sense only if the poem were a performance rather than a representation.

Third, although most illocutionary actions can be performed intentionally—that is, with the intention of performing that action—that cannot be one of the *conditions* for performing the action. I will explain why.

There are illocutionary actions of a sort that are usually, but not always, performed intentionally. For example, suppose Jones believes that Smith has already laid a bet on Black Beauty in the third race at Liberty Bell, but conversationally passes on inside information that another horse in the same race, Bucephalus, is certain to lose. As a matter of fact, Smith has not yet laid his bet, and was inclined to back Bucephalus. Under the circumstances, we might say that Jones has unintentionally warned Smith against betting on Bucephalus. (If there had been no chance of Smith's betting on Bucephalus, Jones's remark would not have been a warning.) If you object to this analysis, I suppose you could argue that what happened here is that Jones unintentionally *alerted* Smith to his danger (a perlocutionary action) without warning him, though not without performing the illocutionary action of *reporting* Bucephalus' chances.

We cannot say that an illocutionary action is necessarily intentional (and hence that it is the intention that conclusively decides what sort of illocutionary action is being performed), because that would make intending to perform an action of a certain kind a requisite condition of performing it, and this would be circular and lead to conceptual confusion. You cannot intend to ride a horse, say, unless you understand what riding a horse consists in; so to ride a horse intentionally is not the same thing as to ride a horse. Even if in practice it turns out to be difficult, or empirically impossible, to ride a horse unintentionally, the distinction between riding a horse and riding it intentionally remains. I want to argue the same distinction for illocutionary actions: between performing the action and performing it intentionally—that is, with the intention to perform an act of that kind. (I do not mean to ride roughshod here over the distinctions among the three locutions I have used—say, accusing intentionally, accusing while intending to accuse, accusing with the intention to accuse—but I hold that each of these illocutionary actions connects with the others. And I distinguish them all from accusing.)

In any case, it is of course plain that *representing* an accusation cannot have as its condition an intention to accuse, and indeed these are somewhat at odds, for to take the representational stance is to renounce or withhold or suspend the illocutionary action. Yet strangely enough, this suspension is an extremely important and central feature of the process of poetic creation, which very often is a process in which real moral indignation, real grief, real affection, real religious devotion, real horror even, is made use of, is transformed into material for aesthetic representation and thus given a form that can long outlast the transient occasion of its birth.

IV

I turn now to consider some other pro-intention arguments that have been pressed in recent years, and see how they look in the light of my general principles.

One way of blowing up the importance of intention is to crowd under that label various considerations that really don't belong there. I give an example from an essay by Graham Hough:

> The intentionalists are right to maintain that the basic intentional act performed by the author in writing must be correctly identified. They are right too in maintaining that this frequently requires a search for evidence outside the text. . . . Literary conventions, prevailing cultural assumptions, are not contained within the poem,

but are necessary to its proper understanding. What could *Lycidas* mean to a reader who knew nothing of the long tradition of pastoral elegy? A good deal, no doubt, but half its significance would escape him, and some of its most prominent features would remain impenetrably obscure. . . . We need prior and external evidence about the poet's intentions.[8]

Let us agree at once that important parts of what *Lycidas* says depend on certain conditions external to it—literary traditions and conventions. To write the words of the poem was to say those things, among others, but only because the writing occurred against the background of those traditions and conventions. No doubt Milton was aware of them and knew what he was doing, but this knowledge on his part has no bearing on what he said in writing the words. Even if he had been ignorant of those traditions and conventions, he would still have been saying the same things—the "prominent features" Hough alludes to would still have been there. In just the same way, someone who enters a room and says, "The Phillies are leading," may be contradicting a previous speaker, though he is not aware of this, since he did not hear what the previous speaker said.

Another kind of example of how considerations get illegitimately listed under intention is provided by A. J. Close. He lists a number of statements about *Don Quixote*, of which he says:

> While I believe that all the above statements are at least arguably true, I maintain that (a), (b), (c), and (d) are either truisms or demonstrable truths. The fact is significant because it presupposes that one may state truths about the artist's intentions in doing what he does. Before this assertion the extreme forms of anti-intentionalism collapse.[9]

I don't know that anyone has ever been so "extreme" as to deny that "one may state truths about the artist's intention in doing what he does"—even those who doubted that we can *know* the artist's intentions very specifically when they fail to be realized in

---

8. "An Eighth Type of Ambiguity," in *On Literary Intention*, ed. Newton-De Molina, p. 233. Hough holds that illocutionary actions are "intentional by definition" (p. 235). John Reichert argues in a similar way in *Making Sense of Literature* (Chicago, 1977), chap. 3, esp. pp. 62–63. Like Reichert (p. 63), Mary Sirridge holds that "recourse to the author's motivations" (in her broad sense) "is *the right standard* for determining whether we are faced with irony, sympathy or simple illustration" (*British Journal of Aesthetics* 18 (1978): 150).

9. "Don Quixote and the 'Intentionalist Fallacy,'" in *On Literary Intention*, ed. Newton-De Molina, p. 185.

the work. But consider the four examples he refers to as "truths about the artist's intentions":

> (a) *Don Quixote* is a work of comedy (genre-identification). (b) Cervantes often adapts rhetorical techniques of amplification and reduplication for ends of burlesque bathos (analysis of style). (c) Sancho Panza is an illiterate rustic simpleton (character-evaluation). (d) Sancho Panza's comic attributes are essentially those of the foolish funny servants—the *bobos* or *simples*—of sixteenth-century Spanish Drama (source-identification).[10]

Only one of these statements even mentions Cervantes, and that is not about his intentions but about his works. Granted that Cervantes intentionally made Sancho Panza an illiterate rustic simpleton; we do not need to know whether this making was intentional in order to know that Sancho Panza is an illiterate rustic simpleton.

Much more challenging—because more penetrating and more rigorously argued—is a recent essay by William E. Tolhurst, which defends a very persuasive theory of what the meaning of a literary text (its "utterance meaning") consists in. The essay has too much substance to be adequately considered in this context, and in part what it shows is that certain information about the circumstances or occasion of producing the text may be required to interpret it correctly (a thesis I do not contest). But its bearing on the problems of intention deserves to be acknowledged, as well as its force, even though with brief and inadequate comments.

> What we now argue is that utterance meaning [i.e., the meaning of a literary text] is best understood as the intention which a member of the intended audience would be most justified in attributing to the author based on the knowledge and attitudes which he possesses in virtue of being a member of the intended audience.[11]

This thesis is clearly and carefully guarded from potential confusions; it does not, for example, identify utterance meaning with "utterer's meaning" (i.e., what the author meant). Taken as a material equivalence, it is nearly acceptable, for in fact the meaning of a literary text will almost always be just the meaning that the intended audience would in fact be most justified by their characteristic qualities in attributing to the author. But as an *analysis* or *definition* of textual meaning I think it does not quite hold

10. Ibid.
11. "On What a Text Is and How It Means," *British Journal of Aesthetics* 19 (1979): 11.

up. Imagine a would-be writer of children's stories who intends his book *Pinny the Who?* for an audience of eight-year-olds, but who woefully overestimates the range of their vocabulary. The actual meaning of this work may not correspond to the meaning that the intended audience would be most justified, in virtue of their skills and experience as eight-year-olds, in attributing to the author. Of course another audience could read the book aright; but the argument suggests to me that the reference to the "intended audience" does not belong here, and without it utterance (textual) meaning does not seem definable as most plausibly attributed utterer's meaning.

There has been much discussion of *allusiveness* in poetry, and a frequent intentionalist challenge: to recognize that, say, the words "Sweet Thames, run softly till I end my song" in *The Waste Land* as an allusion to Spenser's "Prothalamion" is to recognize Eliot's intention to allude to Spenser. Now there is no doubt that allusion in poetry is a form of reference; and I believe it is a form of the same synecdochic reference, from part to whole, that we have been talking about: the line occurs in Spenser's poem and is a distinctive, discriminative part of it, so it picks it out. Of course the possibility of allusion depends on the prior establishment of poetic quotation as a mode of reference, but given the general convention, there is again detachment of reference from the person to the vehicle or symbol itself. In his judicious discussion of these matters, Michael D. Wheeler quotes R. W. Stallman as proposing a distinction between "literary parallelisms" and "literary sources," including allusion; the distinction is that the latter are "conscious."[12] I don't deny the difference, but we need—and I think we have—a concept of allusion that does not require it. If we should, surprisingly, discover that Eliot never read or heard a line of Spenser, we would have to say that *Eliot* did not allude to "Prothalamion," but we could still *also* say that *The Waste Land* alludes to it.

Another recurrent argument for intentionalism is based on the so-called indeterminacy of poetry, and the supposed need to reduce it by appeal to the "will" of the author. This is a favorite theme of E. D. Hirsch, and I have discussed it elsewhere.[13] Here I

---

12. See "Biography, Literary Influence and Allusion as Aspects of Source Studies," *British Journal of Aesthetics* 17 (Spring 1977): 152.
13. See *The Possibility of Criticism* (Detroit, 1970), chap. 1.

only want to note its connection with what I have been proposing, and consider its relationship to illocutionary action theory. When the poet writes, "Gather ye Rose-buds while ye may," and we try to interpret this imperative, we can easily see in a general way what kind of illocutionary action is being represented. But can we be more specific? Is the speaker (the fictional utterer of the words) advising, or urging, or pleading, or commanding, or suggesting, or what? The very success of the poem may depend on getting the tone just right—and that means deciding precisely what sort of illocutionary action (or perhaps group of illocutionary actions) is represented. Especially if we wish to give an oral performance of the poem must we make up our minds about such matters.

Now if we are anti-intentionalists, all we can do is study the whole poem to find clues in the context of the first line; and I should think in this case that will tell us a great deal. According to E. D. Hirsch, it will never tell us enough—that is, there will always remain possible doubts as to whether the poem's opening action is, say, sage counsel or lighthearted teasing. At this point the two schools of interpreting part company. According to Hirsch, we must pursue the question beyond the reaches of the poem into the author's private life, so far as we can; when we find out what sort of person Robert Herrick was, we infer what sort of illocutionary action he would intend to perform, and conclude that this is what he did perform. (Hirsch treats poems as performances and performances as intended performances.) To my mind, it is more reasonable to conclude that our question is left undecided by the text, hence undecidable. The "indeterminacy" in the work cannot be replaced by the author's mental states. But of course oral performers are left free to present the poem in any way they wish, within the bounds set by the poem itself. That is why different oral performers can give quite different but equally satisfactory performances of the same work.

Some significant differences between the intentionalist and the anti-intentionalist perspectives are rather sharply brought out by a question about the explication of Yeats's "Leda and the Swan" (1924).

> A shudder in the loins engenders there
> The broken Wall, the burning roof and tower
> And Agamemnon dead.

Suzanne S. Dean, in a term paper for a graduate seminar at Temple University, has argued that the word "tower" could be read as referring, *inter alia*, to the Tower, a card in the Tarot deck with readily connectable meanings. The argument for such a reading is that in earlier drafts of the poem Yeats capitalized "Tower." How should we reason in such a case—what is the proper interpretive inference from this evidence, if any? The intentionalist will say that the capital *T* makes the word refer to the Tarot card, shows that Yeats had such a reference in mind, and so permits us to conclude that "tower" in the final version carries this reference and the associated or consequent meanings. The anti-intentionalist will say that if the capital *T* was significant in the early draft, then the lowercase *t* is, by the same token, equally significant in the final draft. So whether Yeats intentionally changed the text from *T* to *t* or this happened by some accident, the change deleted the reference to the Tarot deck; and since there is no other warrant in the poem for such a reference, there is no justification for the intentionalist's reading.[14]

Another recurrent argument for intentionalism is based on the apparent possibility of private or idiosyncratic meanings: the poet who uses a word to which he is said to give a sense quite different from any of its standard senses, and whose contextual sense cannot be derived from any of its standard senses. Clear-cut cases are hard to find, even in Yeats. But suppose Yeats attached a wholly special meaning (as people are wont to say, though oddly) to one of his pet words, such as "gyre," and we know of this only because he wrote it in a letter or told it to a friend. Then it would seem that to interpret correctly a poem in which this word appears we must have recourse to Yeats's intention, and that appeal will be decisive.

Outside of poetry, the classic case, of course, is that of Humpty-Dumpty, and some years ago Keith Donnellan gave the right solution to that problem, in an exchange concerning reference.[15] I recast his proposal in terms of my own account of intention, but the substance is nearly the same. Humpty-Dumpty's own position is really inconsistent. His first claim is that when he said,

---

14. For some discussion of Yeats's use of the Tower card in general, Suzanne Dean has referred me to Thomas R. Henn, *The Lonely Tower* (London, 1950), pp. 124ff.

15. "Putting Humpty-Dumpty Together Again," *Philosophical Review* 77 (1968): 211–15.

"There's glory for you," he meant "There's a nice knock-down argument for you." This is the claim to be questioned in a moment. But, second, he admits that Alice could not know what he meant by "glory," as she complains, until he has provided a stipulative definition—which he proceeds to do. The illocutionary action in question is that of boasting that his argument for the superiority of unbirthdays to birthdays is a conclusive one. The question is whether he can really intend to perform this action *in* producing the words "There's glory for you!" *before* giving a stipulative definition. Intending involves both wanting and believing: if you intend to go to a movie tonight, you desire to go and you believe you will go.[16] Now it may be possible for Humpty-Dumpty to *want* to boast in uttering those words, but it is not possible for him to *believe* that he *will* boast in uttering those words, because he knows that Alice has no way of assigning the novel sense to "glory," and therefore that he cannot secure the requisite uptake. And if he cannot intend to boast in uttering those words, he cannot boast intentionally in uttering them. So if to mean is to say intentionally, then Humpty-Dumpty cannot mean a nice knock-down argument by the word "glory," under the conditions given. As Donnellan says, if he had *begun* by offering the stipulation that in the ensuing conversation "glory" would be synonymous with "a nice knock-down argument," he would have made it mean what he wanted it to mean, because he would have provided conditions for securing uptake. But absent that stipulation, as lawyers say, he could not intend to do what he could not believe he would do.

V

This principle has a wider and more significant application to another recurrent thorn in the side of anti-intentionalism, namely the problem of irony. I should like to say something about this topic, which has been most interestingly discussed by three recent writers.

Although careless definers of literary theoretical terms still are wont to say that we have irony when we have a text of which the intended meaning is opposed to that expressed by words, in practice this crude description yields to a more defensible account. We

---

16. See "Intending."

look for tensions within the text—including those internal tensions that come about because of external conditions, for example, the political environment in which the text is produced. It is only because there exist texts designed to attract followers of various religious and quasi-religious sects, and these texts have the features they have, that it becomes possible to write an ironic invitation to join a sect. But then to say, with irony, that one should join a sect is (1) to perform the locutionary action of uttering such a sentence as "Drop what you're doing and give your all to the Reverend Moon," and (2) *in* performing this action, to perform the illocutionary action of urging people *not* to join the sect. The locutionary action (1) is performed *with* irony; the illocutionary action (2) is performed *through* irony.

The problem for the anti-intentionalist is said to be posed by the existence of texts that are ironic but are free of such inner tension, and hence can be recognized as ironic only by appeal to the author's intended meaning: how he intended the text to be read. Swift's *Modest Proposal* is the most familiar example, though there is growing and already wide agreement, I think, that it does not fully qualify—that it, so to speak, signals its ironic character. Another is the nineteenth-century Samuel Butler's book *The Fair Haven* (1873), an ostensible defense of Christianity designed to destroy its miraculous foundations. This book was first published anonymously and widely taken at face value.[17] E. D. Hirsch has discussed Defoe's tract *The Shortest Way with the Dissenters*, in which Defoe argued that dissenters deserved the worst that could be done to them; but Defoe was presumably trying to gain sympathy for them. Many took him seriously, and when he was discovered to be the dissenting author, he was jailed for the offense. This text, according to Hirsch, "clearly did *not* contain stylistic give-aways. . . . I cannot find a single stylistic barrier to a perfectly straightforward interpretation, and the historical evi-

---

17. See the judicious discussion of this work by Ina Rae Hark, "Samuel Butler and the Gospel of No Gospel," in *Interspace and the Inward Sphere*, ed. Norman Anderson and Margene Weiss (Macomb, Ill., 1978). She brings out Butler's conflicting purposes that make the book work against itself. One conclusion: "Butler exercises much skillful irony outside the 'memoir' [which prefaces the main text], but he never gives it free enough rein to assure detection by those not in on the joke from the start" (p. 128). "Irony" here, I take it, refers to features of the work which would subtly but distinctly signal the reversal of assertion if they were not countered by opposing signals.

dence constitutes a prima facie case against any stylistician who claims to find such a linguistic barrier."[18]

Let us assume that Hirsch is right when he says there is nothing in the work to mark it as ironic. The question is, then, whether the tract *is* ironic. He concedes that the *only* ground for saying that it *is* ironic is that it was intended by Defoe to be ironic. I think this is no good ground, but I agree there is no other ground. Then was it intended to be ironic? According to my view, this would entail that Defoe intended to say that dissenters deserved better treatment and he intended to say this in writing a text containing sentences that would normally be used in saying that dissenters did *not* deserve better treatment. Now perhaps he *wanted* to do this; one can want the impossible. But he could not *believe* he was doing this; for if he took pains to exclude from the text (and title page) every hint of reservations about, or detachment of belief from, the ostensible attack on dissenters, he must know that he would not secure uptake from the reader. And thus he could not expect the illocutionary action of pleading for dissenters to be completed. Therefore the work was not intended to be ironic, and since there is, by hypothesis, no evidence in the work that it is ironic, there is no reason to believe that it is ironic. Consequently, it will not serve as an example of an ironic text whose irony requires to be discovered by appeal to evidence of what was intended.

Once we see that we must renounce the Hirschian path, we see that the definition of literary irony need make no reference to intention. Our task as interpreter is not to find out what was going on privately in the author's mind that he did not choose to reveal in his text, but to find out what is going on in the text to make it turn itself upside down or inside out and say the opposite of what it seems, on the surface, to say. Here I disagree with Göran Hermerén, who quotes a remark about Beckett's poem "Ooftisch": "We recognize the bitter irony that mimics cruelty partly in rage, partly in the certainty of understanding the case, partly to jolt the reader into awareness; and we can guess the mixture of personal pain and pugnacious courage in a pun like 'cough up your T. B.'"[19] Unlike Hermerén, I don't see that this

18. *The Aims of Interpretation* (Chicago, 1976), pp. 24–25.
19. "Intention and Interpretation in Literary Criticism," *New Literary History* 7 (1975–76): 74.

depends on a distinction between what is said and what was intended, but only between levels or layers of what is said.

Jonathan Culler's comments are sound, I think, but need to be supplemented by the other side of the coin.

> Kierkegaard maintains that the true ironist does not wish to be understood, and though true ironists may be rare we can at least say that irony always offers the possibility of misunderstanding. No sentence is ironic *per se*. Sarcasm may contain internal inconsistencies which make its purport quite obvious and prevent it from being read except in one way, but for a sentence to be properly ironic it must be possible to imagine some group of readers taking it quite literally. Otherwise there is no contrast between apparent and assumed meaning and no space of ironic play.[20]

Kierkegaard's remark is characteristically paradoxical and self-defeating. Swift, Defoe, and Butler were "true ironists," if anyone ever was—and if they did not wish anyone to understand their real feelings, they were playing a most peculiar and incomprehensible game. Irony must offer the possibility of misunderstanding (yes, if all that means is that we can *imagine* someone missing the irony); it also must offer the possibility of *understanding*, it seems to me, for if we and the author cannot imagine anyone taking it ironically, it can hardly have been intended as ironic, and there would be no reason at all to believe that it is.

In considering these fascinating examples, we must bear in mind that they are not works of fiction. They serve here as data for an a fortiori argument. The question about them is whether the author is actually performing the illocutionary actions of condemning, ridiculing, pleading, or whatever, and doing so through irony. And if *this* question is not to be settled by appeal to the author's intentions, how much less will that appeal decide what is being *represented* in works of fiction—as, for example, in the celebrated and not-to-be-forgotten case of A. E. Housman's poem on Queen Victoria's Golden Jubilee.[21] The irony representer certainly cannot

---

20. *Structuralist Poetics: Structuralism, Linguistics, and the Study of Literature* (Ithaca, 1975), p. 154.

21. My treatment of this example (in *Aesthetics: Problems in the Philosophy of Criticism* [New York, 1958], pp. 25–26) has been critically discussed by A. J. Ellis in "Intention and Interpretation in Literature," *British Journal of Aesthetics* 14 (1974): 322–23. Despite his confident statement that "there is no such thing" as the (ironic) meaning of this poem—"One might ask: Did Housman intend the lines to be ironical? . . . Or one might ask: How should we read them, how do they sound best? . . . But there is not some third question: Are the lines ironical?"—I still think there is a good question: Was Housman, in composing this poem, saying—or

rely on the existence of his masked attitudes (however displayed to actual friends and foes) to give his work the second layer of verbal action. His reliance must be on verbal signals that delineate someone mimicking a performance but refraining from it—and make it possible (even if difficult) for the reader to determine just what is done and what is withheld and what is said thereby.

Well, then—to turn back to the beginning briefly by way of conclusion—is there an intentional fallacy after all? (Is there really, we might ask, a naturalistic fallacy, a genetic fallacy, a fallacy of misplaced concreteness, a fallacy of the suppressed correlative, a logocentric fallacy . . . ?) Perhaps the returns are not all in. I think we know enough to concede that the intentional fallacy is not as distinctly marked and bounded as, say, the post hoc, ergo propter hoc fallacy, or the fallacy of composition. But the term still points, sternly and unwaveringly, at a small cluster of errors in inference that center around the concept of the author's intention. The errors can be formulated as confusions: of illocutionary-act performance with illocutionary-act representation, of authorial meaning (what was intended to be said) with textual meaning (what was actually said), of the ostensible speaker of a poem with the biological author, of the subject of the poem with the occasion of its composition. One or more of these confusions seem to be implicated in the characteristic and central form of inference that the anti-intentionalist calls fallacious: from premises about the intentions of the author to conclusions about the meaning (that is, the saying content) of the work. Generally the argument has three stages, or two steps: from biographical data of various kinds to the probable intention, and from the probable intention to the proposed interpretation of the work. With the first step per se I have no quarrel, though its results are often rather unreliable and speculative; it is the second step whose logical legitimacy I still find very doubtful.

---

representing someone as saying—that Queen Victoria did not deserve all that adulation for building the Empire (this being said through irony, i.e., as opposed to the plain sense of the words)?

12: *The Generality of Critical Reasons*

IF giving reasons for an assertion consists in making other assertions and also asserting that they support it, then critics evidently give reasons for their judgments of art. To doubt this is to urge a stricter concept of reason giving, according to which not every proposition that is alleged to be a reason actually is one. But then, using the narrower definition, we can still say that critics wish to give reasons, and think they are doing so, whether or not they succeed. Whichever way we put it, the critic implicitly makes the same essential claim: namely, that his judgments can be supported in some way by other propositions.

This claim is challenged by the critical skeptic. The form of his challenge depends on the latitude given to the term 'reason,' but its substance is the same. A few years ago, a colleague of mine and I engaged in correspondence with an English gentleman, author of a monograph titled *Shakespeare's Hyphens*,[1] who pointed out to us that Shakespeare used a great many hyphenated words and that this practice was also followed by Walt Whitman and Dylan Thomas. Our correspondent argued at one point: the more hyphens, the greater the poet. Now, suppose a critic were to propose the following: This poem is poor because it is deficient in hyphens. We may choose to say that this is not a reason at all, because it is so wildly irrelevant; in this sense of "reason," the skeptic's position is that no reasons can be given for critical judgments. On the other hand, we may take a more charitable view, and call this a reason simply because it is offered as one; in this broad sense, the skeptic's position is that no good, or cogent, reasons can be given for critical judgments.

The critical skeptic may remind us of Wordsworth's assurance,

---

1. L. C. Thompson, *Shakespeare's Hyphens* (London, n.d.).

in his 1800 Preface, that he was not "principally influenced by the selfish and foolish hope of *reasoning* him [i.e., the reader] into an approbation of these particular Poems."[2] Now this was a somewhat peculiar remark in the first place. The hope of reasoning someone into an approbation might conceivably be "selfish" (if Wordsworth were merely aiming to increase his royalties), but it is "foolish" only if we take 'approbation' in the sheer sense of *liking*. "How can anyone be *argued* into liking Wordsworth's 'We are Seven'?" the skeptic asks. But I should think that the aim of the reasoner—that is, the critic armed with reasons—is not to get people to *like* the poem, but to get them to acknowledge that it is good. And the question is whether his reasons—or alleged reasons—are of service to him in this enterprise.

I don't think that the skeptic's position, Cartesian though it may in some respects appear, can be disposed of by a simple appeal to paradigm cases. We might try this argument against him: Granted that the number of hyphens does not make a poem poor (or good), still that's not the sort of thing critics usually say. Consider a principle enunciated by Cleanth Brooks: "A poem, then, to sum up, is to be judged, not by the truth or falsity as such, of the idea which it incorporates, but rather by its character as drama—by its coherence, sensitivity, depth, richness, and toughmindedness."[3] Now, suppose the critic says, "This poem is poor because it is incoherent." If that is not a good reason for condemning a poem, what *could* be a good reason? Doesn't critical skepticism imply that the expression 'good reason' has no application at all in critical discourse? But surely this term must have some application, or we would never have learned how to use it.

If this sort of argument is ever persuasive, I'm afraid that aesthetics is the last place in which to employ it. Probably a fair number of philosophers would be quite ready to label the whole body of critical reasoning a misuse of language. Let us assume that there must be *some* examples of good reasons, if we can speak intelligibly of good reasons; but it might well be that all of the examples are to be found in fields other than criticism, and that none of the arguments in, say, *The Well Wrought Urn* come near to meeting the high standards that are exemplified in legal reasoning, or ethics, or the game theory of nuclear deterrence.

2. Preface to *Lyrical Ballads* (1800), in *Complete Poetical Works* (Boston, 1911), vol. 10, p. 5.
3. *The Well Wrought Urn* (New York, 1947), p. 229.

No—if we are going to be able to make sense of what the critic does when he gives reasons, and back him up with a philosophical account of how those reasons work, we must grapple more closely with the skeptic's arguments.

II

The general problem of justifying the critic's appeal to reasons is, of course, large and complex. I propose to deal with only one of its parts, but one that has received some attention in the past few years.

To pass over a number of preliminary matters, let me first say that I hold that the critic does make value judgments and does sometimes adequately support them by good reasons. A reason is some descriptive or interpretive proposition about the work under consideration—"The poem is incoherent," for example. Thus a reason always cites some property of the work, and we may say that this property is then employed as a *criterion of value* by the critic who presents that reason. Criteria cited in reasons supporting favorable judgments are merits; criteria cited on behalf of unfavorable judgments are defects. If the critic says, "This poem is poor because (among other things) it is incoherent," then he is treating incoherence as a poetic defect. A critical criterion is thus a feature that helps to make the work good or bad, better or worse; it adds to or detracts from its aesthetic goodness.

This is the position that the skeptic rejects. He holds that, in the sense proposed, there are no criteria of aesthetic value, that is, of goodness or badness in poems, paintings, plays, music, and so on. Some skeptics like to invoke John Wisdom's distinction, in another context, between what he called "dull" and "interesting" ways of talking about art. A book about art, says Wisdom, "is dull when it tries to set out in general terms what makes a good picture good" by giving "rules" or "canons."[4] This, by itself, is something of an obiter dictum, but it can be given plausible and perhaps rather convincing support.

If one proposition is a reason for another, in the sense of actually supporting it, then there must be a logical connection of some sort between them. And, being a logical connection, it must relate

---

4. See his paper in the symposium "Things and Persons," *Proceedings of the Aristotelian Society*, suppl., 22 (1948): 207.

general concepts in an abstract way. Thus, for example, if a certain degree of sharpness is a merit in knives (we can think of a particular sort of knife, such as the butcher's), then to say that a knife has that degree of sharpness must *always* be a reason to support the conclusion that it is good, and it must apply to *all* knives of the relevant sort. This reason may not be enough to *prove* that the knife is good, since the merit may be outweighed by serious defects, but sharpness to that degree will always make its contribution to the goodness of the knife. It will, at least, never be a fault in a knife: that is, we cannot say, "That knife is poor just because it is exactly that sharp." And of two knives similar in all other respects, if one is sharp and the other is not, the former will be a better knife than the other. Thus sharpness is a *general* merit in knives.

Generality of this sort appears to be essential to reasons in the logical sense, and if critical criteria are defined as features citable in reasons, then there must be an important sense in which such criteria are general, too. Thus the view that there *are* reasons that support the critic's judgment entails the view that there are general criteria of evaluation. Let us call this view the general criterion theory. It is a main target of the critical skeptic's attack.

As my main text for examination, I shall select the very forthright statement by Mr. William E. Kennick in his article "Does Traditional Aesthetics Rest on a Mistake?"[5] In this article, Mr. Kennick holds that there are no "general rules, standards, criteria, canons, or laws applicable to all works of art by which alone such critical appraisals can be supported." And he goes on to say this:

> Ordinarily we feel no constraint in praising one novel for its verisimilitude, another for its humour, and still another for its plot or characterization. . . . Botticelli's lyric grace is his glory, but Giotto and Chardin are not to be condemned because their poetry is of a different order. . . . Different works of art are, or may be, praiseworthy or blameworthy for different reasons, and not always for the same reasons. A quality that is praiseworthy in one painting may be blameworthy in another; realism is not always a virtue, but this does not mean that it is not sometimes a virtue.[6]

---

5. *Mind* 67 (1958): 317–34.
6. Ibid., pp. 329, 331. See also Mary Mothersill, "Critical Reasons," *Philosophical Quarterly* 11 (1961): 74–79; this is a reply to Dorothy Walsh, "Critical Reasons," *Philosophical Review* 69 (1960): 386–93: "There is *no* characteristic which is amenable to independent explanation and which by its presence enhances the aesthetic value of paintings or of any subclass of paintings" (77).

The problem, then, is this: Do critical reasons have a kind of generality of application, so that it makes sense to try to formulate principles of criticism? I believe they do. Mr. Kennick, like a number of other recent writers, believes they do not. Now, if they do not, there are two possibilities. Some philosophers, including Mr. Kennick, hold that we can still talk of giving reasons in particular cases (that is, supporting the judgment that this or that poem is good or poor) without committing ourselves to any general principles at all. Others, however, hold (and I think with more reason) that some form of generality is essential to reason giving, and therefore that if there are no general criteria, there can be no critical criteria at all. My aim is to examine the arguments against the general criterion theory.

Before coming to them, however, it may be helpful to remind ourselves that the issue has two close analogues in other fields of philosophy, no less troublesome elsewhere than this is here. First, there is the problem of the universalizability of ethical judgments. Some writers have contended that it is precisely the difference between ethical judgment and critical judgment that one is general and the other is not,[7] but there does seem to be a similar problem in ethics. When we blame someone for not keeping an appointment, are we committed to the universalization of an implicit principle? Most moral philosophers would say we are; and the principle is something like: Anyone else in circumstances that do not differ in relevant ways from this one would be equally to blame. The problem is to provide an adequate criterion of relevance, without circularity. We want to say, for example, that having a different color skin is not relevant, while having been knocked down by a truck *is* relevant. Is there an analogous kind of implicit commitment involved in criticism? (And I don't mean when we blame the painter, but when we set a low estimate on his work.)

Second, there is the problem of the relation between singular causal statements and general laws. According to the traditional view, singular causal statements (such as "Dropping caused that pitcher to break") are, and must be, applications of universal law-like statements, even if we cannot formulate the latter completely ("Whenever a pitcher of this sort is dropped in this way, it will

---

7. The writer most often quoted is Stuart Hampshire, "Logic and Appreciation," in *Aesthetics and Language*, ed. William Elton (Oxford, 1954).

break"). But in recent years some philosophers have suggested that we may be able to know singular causal statements without relying on *any* general laws. Historical explanations are sometimes alleged to be of this sort. I would be happy to avoid this broad and complicated issue, but there is more than an analogy between my aesthetic problem and the causal problem: the former is in fact a special case of the latter. For, speaking very sketchily, I conceive the peculiar aesthetic goodness of a work of art to consist of its capacity to provide experiences with certain desirable qualities; and the criteria of critical evaluation are simply features that tend to contribute to or detract from this capacity. Hence, according to my theory, there is a causal relationship involved in the notion of critical criteria. And since I side with those who think that some generalized lawful relationships are essential to individual causal actions, by the same token I must suppose that a criterion can be relevant to the value of a particular work of art only if some generality of bearing lurks (so to speak) in the background.

III

A fundamental point alleged against the general criterion theory is that works of art are unique. Frequent repetition has not worn off the oddness of this statement. It can be construed in several ways, of which the most sensible are the most pointless. Mary Mothersill and Ruby Meager have analyzed and criticized it very effectively, and I need not review what they have said.[8] No doubt works of art—if we confine our attention to the good ones—tend to have a comparatively high degree of individuality, at least as compared with knives and typewriters. Because there are many human acts that may be called acts of promise keeping, we can speak of general moral rules. But perhaps there are no genuine classes of aesthetic objects, such as poems and paintings (this seems to be the extreme neo-Crocean view)—or perhaps the members of each class differ so much from one another that no features can be found that are desirable in all or most of them.

But there *are* genuine classes of aesthetic objects, and their

8. See Ruby Meager, "The Uniqueness of a Work of Art," *Proceedings of the Aristotelian Society* 59 (1959): 49–70, and Mary Mothersill, "'Unique' as an Aesthetic Predicate," *Journal of Philosophy* 58 (1961): 421–37. See also Albert Tsugawa, "The Objectivity of Aesthetic Judgments," *Philosophical Review* 70 (1961): 3–22, esp. 11–12.

members share important properties. I don't see why we cannot admit that visual designs vary enormously in many ways, without denying that certain fundamental laws of perception may be at work in all of them. I should think that people and their moral predicaments are at least as different as poems, yet we can say that courage is a virtue in anyone in whom it may be found.

There is an interesting phrase that turns up here and there. For example: "A good critic is one who can discern the *peculiar* excellence of a particular work."[9] Now what is meant by "the peculiar excellence" of a work? If it means (as I should think it must) an excellence that no other existing work happens to have, then of course many works do have peculiar excellences. (Many also have excellences that are not peculiar to them.) But the existence of such excellences does not in any way contradict the general criterion theory. On the other hand, if it means instead a quality that is an excellence in this work, but that, if it appeared in any other work, could *not* be an excellence, then I have seen no convincing proof that there are "peculiar excellences" in this sense.

Let us now turn back to Mr. Kennick's propositions and examples. I think his paper contains at least four distinguishable arguments against the general criterion theory, each going a little beyond the previous one.

The first argument is this: The general criterion theory can't be true because there are no single features of poetry, for example, that are either necessary or sufficient conditions of goodness.[10] That no single feature is sufficient I am prepared to grant at once. That there is no necessary feature I am not prepared to grant without qualification: for example, I have argued that some degree of coherence is a necessary condition of being a poem at all, and a fortiori of being a good poem.[11] I suppose, however, that it could be replied, by way of putting this qualification in its place, that no *special* degree of coherence is necessary to make a poem a good poem. In any case, I shall waive my objection and concede for the sake of argument that there are no necessary or sufficient single

---

9. See Mothersill, "'Unique' as an Aesthetic Predicate," p. 428; this sentence appears in her formulation of the argument for the less radical form of the autonomy theory.

10. This seems to be the main point of A. G. Pleydell-Pearce, "On the Limits and Use of 'Aesthetic Criteria,'" *Philosophical Quarterly* 9 (1959): 29–45.

11. See "The Definitions of the Arts," *Journal of Aesthetics and Art Criticism* 20 (Winter 1961): 175–87.

conditions of poetic goodness. Does it follow that the general criterion theory is wrong?

The answer seems sufficiently obvious. Though a given feature may be present in some poor poems and absent from some good ones, so that it neither guarantees poetic goodness nor is indispensable to it, nevertheless it may contribute to the goodness of any poem that contains it and thus may be citable as a merit wherever it can be found. A person may be good without being magnanimous, and he or she may be magnanimous without being good; but that doesn't show that magnanimity is not a virtue in anyone who has it, and to the degree in which it is had. So, too, not every good poem has "depth," to recall one of the terms quoted from Cleanth Brooks above, and not every deep poem is good—yet depth may always be a good thing, as far as it goes.

The second argument given by Mr. Kennick involves a shift of ground: What if different features are merits in different contexts?—humor in one case, he suggests, tragic intensity in another. Or lyric grace in one painting, heroic strength in another. Does this refute the possibility of general criteria? I think not. Lyric grace may nevertheless always be a good thing when it can be had, and heroic strength likewise—only it may turn out that they cannot both be had in the same painting, or not without being watered down or confused. The general criterion theory certainly need not deny that there are qualitatively different merits that cannot always be combined. We admire one person's physical courage and another person's sensitivity to others, but we find few, if any, who combine both of these virtues to a high degree. So with two of Brooks's criteria, "sensitivity" and "toughmindedness": poems that excel in one of these qualities are perhaps not likely to excel in the other.

The third argument is also Mr. Kennick's, and this time he belongs to a larger company.[12] What if there are features that are merits in some works, but not merits at all in other works? Take realism, Mr. Kennick suggests: sometimes it is a merit, sometimes not. But this argument does not tell against the general criterion theory if we complicate the theory in an easy and convenient way. There are features of poems, and there are pairs and clusters

---

12. For example, Helen Knight, "The Use of 'Good' in Aesthetic Judgments," in *Aesthetics and Language*, ed. Elton, pp. 155–56; J. A. Passmore, "The Dreariness of Aesthetics," in ibid., pp. 49, 51–52; J. Kemp, "Generalization in the Philosophy of Art," *Philosophy* 33 (1958): 152.

of features. And some contribute value, so to speak, on their own, while others do so only in combination. This principle has an application in many walks of life, as G. E. Moore pointed out some time ago. It's like saying that you don't want butter without bread or bread without butter, but only the two together. We can say that bread is not desirable and butter is not desirable, but bread-and-butter is desirable; or we can say that butter is sometimes desirable (namely, when there's bread) and sometimes not (namely, when there isn't).

Thus we should not be surprised to find specific features that may be good in one poem but neutral in another: their goodness depends on association with other cooperative features. Mr. Kennick's example, realism, is a broad notion, so it's not clear exactly what sort of judgment he has in mind when he says that "realism is not always a virtue." In some of its senses, I'm not sure that realism is *ever* a strictly literary virtue (or, as I would prefer to say, merit—Mr. Kennick's moralistic terms 'virtue' and 'blameworthy' do not seem to me appropriate to the critical context). But a critic might justifiably cite an author's discriminating ear for four-letter words as a merit in, say, *Tropic of Cancer*, where certain types of situation and character are present, without, of course, wishing to say that their introduction would improve *The Wings of the Dove* or *The Mill on the Floss*.

IV

The fourth argument against the general criterion theory takes us a little beyond the third—though, in fact, the examples I have just given would serve for it as well. Suppose there are features that are merits in one work and actually *defects* in another. The touch of humor that is just right in one play is just exactly wrong in another—and so with the four-letter words. How, then, can there be any general criteria, or true propositions of the form: 'Humor is always a good-enhancing feature'? The general criterion theory can meet this objection by one more complication that is natural and sensible. Some criteria are subordinate to others, as constituting their perceptual conditions. For example, suppose the touch of humor (the gravedigger's gags, the drunken porter at the gate) is a merit in one context because it heightens the dramatic tension, but a defect in another context, where it lets the tension down. Then we may admit that the touch of humor is not a general merit, but only because we also admit that something else *is* a general merit (in a play, that is)—namely, high dramatic tension. Remember that this does not mean that dramatic tension is either a necessary or sufficient condition of being a good play, nor does it mean that this desirable feature can be combined with all other desirable features, nor does it mean that all plays that lack a high degree of it would necessarily become better if it were increased, for some plays might thereby lose some other quality that especially adorns them. The point is that the general criterion theory can easily take account of such variations as the skeptic points out—providing it is allowed to fall back on more general and, so to speak, more fundamental criteria.

We may distinguish two ranks of critical criteria, then, in the following way: Let us say that the properties A, B, C are the *primary (positive) criteria* of aesthetic value if the addition of any one of them or an increase in it, without a decrease in any of the others, will always make the work a better one. And let us say that a given property X is a *secondary (positive) criterion* of aesthetic value if there is a certain set of other properties such that, whenever they are present, the addition of X or an increase in it will always produce an increase in one or more of the primary criteria.

Notice that each of these definitions is formulated in such a way that it contains the word 'always' in an important position, and therefore that they both define *general* criteria in an important sense. But the secondary criteria are subordinate and conditional: it is only in certain contexts that, for example, elegant variation is a fault of style. (However, some of these secondary criteria, on the other hand, always contribute positively to the value of a work, insofar as they are present. And their absence is always a deficiency, however it may be made up in other ways. Thus I think that Paul Ziff is precisely correct when he says: "Some good paintings are somewhat disorganized; they are good in spite of the fact that they are somewhat disorganized. But no painting is good because it is disorganized, and many are bad primarily because they are disorganized."[13] Disorganization, by this exact description, is a primary (negative) critical criterion.

There is a danger that such a discussion as this may unintentionally confirm John Wisdom's remark that talk about "canons"

---

13. "Reasons in Criticism," in *Philosophy and Education*, ed. Israel Scheffler (Boston, 1958), p. 220.

and "rules" is "dull." I don't insist that it is interesting, only that it is possible and reasonable. The act of judging—in the sense of appraising—works of art is certainly not a purely intellectual act, and many elements of talent and training are required to perform it well. But it is, in part, a rational act, for it involves reasoning.

13: *The Relevance of History to Art Criticism*

I

QUESTIONS of relevance, though among the most important we ask, must be handled with care if they are not to occasion pointless and fruitless disputes. When clearly articulated, they are seen to be either causal or logical—that is, they concern the influence one event or state of affairs exerts on another or they concern the logical support one proposition gives to another. Being a philosopher, I am naturally more interested in connections of the latter sort than in those of the former. This bent, with its consequent narrowing of focus, will be evident in the course of my essay. I discuss the bearing of history on art criticism (whatever art may be in question) by asking: What sorts of historical information, if any, are required to justify our acceptance of particular sorts of statement made by critics?

I trust it will not be taken amiss if I forestall what may seem a very remotely possible misunderstanding by remarking that I am not concerned here with the relevance of historical information to art history. It is a truism—though not, I think, a trivial one—that if you ask a historical question you will need historical evidence to answer it. Take, for example, a question of influence. According to Erwin Panofsky, Dürer's drawing *The Death of Orpheus* "derives from a Mantegnesque prototype transmitted through a North Italian engraving and probably inspired by a poetic source such as Politian's *Orfeo*."[1] This conclusion must have been established (if it

---

1. "Albrecht Dürer and Classical Antiquity," in *Meaning in the Visual Arts* (Garden City, N.Y., 1955), p. 239. For many other examples, see Göran Hermerén, *Influence in Art and Literature* (Princeton, 1975).

really *was* established) by a study of other objects besides the drawing itself and by inferences about presumable causal connections. Perhaps it is not necessary to defend here my terminological decision to separate art history from art criticism; the usage is convenient and does not commit anyone to substantive implications. My concern at the moment is to make an initial concession that if we want to know whether a North Italian engraving was in some way *causally* relevant to the existence and character of Dürer's drawing, then certain facts of history will be logically relevant, as supporting reasons, to a hypothesis we propose to prove.

There is another important kind of historical question that obviously calls for a historical—in this case, also, a specifically art-historical—inquiry. Part of our understanding, in a broad sense, of the artwork is seeing it in its significance for an artistic development: what it tells us about a particular stage in the painter's career (it may mark the emergence of a new style or subject matter), in the fulfillment or decline of an artistic period, in the history of the art of painting itself. It is light on such relationships that we perhaps principally hope for from art historians.

Setting explicitly and plainly historical questions aside, then, we turn to criticism proper. More interesting, and more debatable, is the claim that certain ahistorical questions can be answered only by appeal to historical evidence—or, more radically, that questions we have taken to be ahistorical are really historical questions in disguise. But at this point we need further distinctions. For there are several kinds of statement that occur characteristically in the discourse of critics, and what is relevant to one kind may not be relevant to another. The only safe course here, pedestrian as it may be, is to take these kinds one by one, or in closely related groups. My examples will be chosen from pictorial art, but I am assuming that many of the problems they raise have analogues in other arts.

II

First, there are questions of meaning—semantic questions, in a broad sense. These may appear to be quite distinct from historical questions, since they are not questions about influence or significance, yet when we analyze them we may discover that they call for information about semantic conventions or rules of interpretation that were in force during some past period—conventions whose authority and jurisdiction can be established only by historical inquiry. For example, if we look into the meaning of the ostrich egg that hangs from the ceiling in a famous altarpiece by Piero della Francesca, we will find (according to the late art historian Millard Meiss) that ostriches were believed to be forgetful of their eggs, though later minded of them, and that consequently in the Middle Ages ostrich eggs were hung in churches to show how man, forgetful of his God, may, when illuminated by the Divine Light, return to God and be cherished.[2] (This is a good deal to make an egg mean, but after all, ostrich eggs are large.) To interpret the egg in the painting is to say what such eggs meant in a particular religious community at the time the work was painted. It is historical scholarship that provides us with the rule of interpretation.

The symbolic ostrich egg exemplifies one familiar and important kind of artistic meaning. But we must not rush to generalize the conclusion to other kinds of meaning or reference. For example, before we can interpret the ostrich egg we must recognize that it *is* an ostrich egg; to establish this fact, however ("The painting represents an ostrich egg"), we appeal to knowledge, not of history, but of oölogy. To be sure, we must know something of ostrich eggs, but only in a timeless way: that there are such things and that they have a certain size and shape.

Do we not have to know at least this much of history: that a fifteenth-century Italian painter could have had access to ostrich eggs, or could have at least read about them, even if he never saw one? Here we encounter one of those unresolved issues that aesthetic questions are bound to lead to if they are faithfully pursued. One way to put the problem is to ask whether something can be represented unintentionally. Suppose it could be proved, by historical inquiry, that Piero never saw and never heard about ostrich eggs: would we then have to conclude that the figure in his painting cannot represent an ostrich egg? I don't think we would. No doubt it is a little odd to think of someone's representing an object inadvertently, and this is perhaps very unlikely to happen; but I see no contradiction in the supposition. Dr. Seuss

---

2. See "*Ovum Struthionis*: Symbol and Allusion in Piero della Francesca's Montefeltro Altarpiece," in *The Painter's Choice: Problems in Interpretation of Renaissance Art* (New York, 1976), p. 107.

could conceivably invent an animal that later turns out to exist after all, though it is highly improbable that any of his creatures are really, as they say, viable. And Piero della Francesca could paint a shape that is a picture of an ostrich egg, though neither he nor his contemporaries could have recognized it as one—in which case, of course, it would not have the symbolic significance that Millard Meiss found, or at least suggested.

I want to defend a general claim here, in terms of a distinction that I have urged between portraying and depicting.[3] Briefly, what a painting portrays is this or that individual object or event: the Virgin Mary, the Annunciation. What it depicts is *an* object or event of a certain kind: a woman, an announcement by an angel. In general, to know what a painting portrays we must connect the painting with its object—we must know that the painter intended his work to refer to Mary and to a momentous event in her life, in which he believed and in which he expected his audience (vidience?) to believe. So—in general—our understanding of what is portrayed rests essentially on historical knowledge of what once happened at some time prior to the painting of the work or of what was believed at the time of painting. But—again in general—our understanding of what is depicted is independent of historical knowledge. History is irrelevant to the question whether a painting depicts a woman or an ostrich egg.

But, you may say, what about angels? To recognize a depiction of an angel, we must know that angels have wings; and this knowledge does not come from personal observation. It is only by placing the artwork in a particular religious iconographic tradition that we can see it as depicting an angel rather than just as some strangely winged man. Now, insofar as we appeal to existing texts about angels, we are not consulting history, but angelology, a branch of theology. But it seems that we require more than this: we need to know what rules or conventions for depicting angels were accepted and employed in the time of the painting in question. And so it appears that angels, at least, may be an exception to my general claim about the ahistorical character of depiction.

Even if you are inclined to grant my general claim about the depiction of natural (or supernatural) things, you may argue that it breaks down when we turn to human artifacts. Imagine, for

---

3. Monroe C. Beardsley, *Aesthetics: Problems in the Philosophy of Criticism* (New York, 1958), chap. 6.

example, a painting that represents a trolley car (it might be a mural painting in the transportation building of some world's fair). Now, if you live in a city in which this mode of transit is not yet extinct, you clearly need no historical information to understand what the painting depicts. There are, of course, deep current issues about the precise nature of pictorial representation and whether or not it essentially involves a selective similarity between the picture and its object.[4] But in any case, your familiarity with the way trolley cars look enables you to read the picture. Even if the ruthless hand of progress has cleared the streets of trolley cars, one of them may be preserved as a curiosity in a municipal museum. And though you may learn some history by going to the museum, you don't require that history to see that the object in the museum is of the sort depicted in the painting.

But suppose the trolleys are all gone, and all you know of them comes from a history of your city, with descriptions, perhaps illustrated by photographs, of what they once were like. Then, in a sense, you are using historical knowledge to determine what the painting depicts. But only, I think, in too weak and insubstantial a sense to count against my claim that in general understanding of depiction does not depend on historical knowledge. For the only information that is relevant here is that such things as trolley cars have existed and have had certain characteristic features (wheels, windows, trolleys, front–rear symmetry, etc.). Knowledge of this sort is not strictly historical knowledge, since it is essentially dateless: you don't need to find out *when* the trolley cars came and went, or how or why, any more than you need to find out when ostriches first appeared to recognize an ostrich-egg depiction.

All this fussiness about exactly which statements about paintings are, and which are not, supported by historical information may seem unnecessary. But once we raise the question of the relevance of history to criticism, we have, I believe, no alternative to patiently considering what critics would want to say and how they know these things to be true. We have not made any discoveries of great significance or novelty. Yet I think our distinctions can contribute toward fostering a greater judiciousness than

---

4. See Nelson Goodman, *Languages of Art* (Indianapolis, 1968), chap. 1. See also Monroe C. Beardsley, "*Languages of Art* and Art Criticism," *Erkenntnis* 12 (1978):95–118.

sometimes characterizes discussions of our central question. It is easy to point out examples of historical relevance and then to wave the hand and conclude that practically every question for the critic is historical, or in the end reduces to history. My aim is to counteract this tendency, to try to carve out limited domains of independence for the critic—to see what is, in this respect, autonomous in art.

III

To point out what a painting depicts or portrays, and interpret its symbolic significance, is surely (when such remarks are called for) within the province of the critic. Beyond that, we expect (both in the sense of predicting and in the sense of desiring) judgments of artistic goodness or aesthetic value. For example, in his book *On Quality in Art*, Jakob Rosenberg tells us that a drawing of an oriental head by Martin Schongauer is a better drawing than another on a similar subject by one of his pupils. And he tells us why. Among other things,

> there is no doubt that the Schongauer head has more plastic life, more surface animation and organic coherence than the other drawing. The whole and the parts are better related. . . . Altogether [in the pupil's work] we miss the graphic charm, the decorative coherence of the design, and the human animation that Schongauer achieves.[5]

There might be some question about the correctness of Rosenberg's descriptions of the two drawings, and it must be conceded that the descriptions are quite general and somewhat vague. Nevertheless, Rosenberg is giving reasons for his conclusion, and relevant ones—and the conclusion of his argument appears to be independent of any historical evidence.

But perhaps this appearance is misleading. On one view of critical value judgments—a view that is, I believe, more common among historians of visual art than among historians of music or literature—a work of art is (or is to be regarded as) the solution of a "problem." Such problems are conceived in different ways, but the following may serve as examples: to create a satisfactory composition of two adults and a child, to capture the impression of

---

5. *On Quality in Art: Criteria of Excellence, Past and Present* (Princeton, 1967), p. 133.

bright sunlight on calm water, to break up a human body into an assemblage of cubist forms that shall suggest fundamental relationships of mass and at the same time make a coherent pattern. James Ackerman cites the illusionistic imitation of nature as a recurring artistic problem, and even proposes in such terms his account of style: "A style, then, may be thought of as a class of related solutions to a problem—or responses to a challenge—that may be said to begin whenever artists begin to pursue a problem or react to a challenge which differs significantly from those posed by the prevailing style or styles."[6] If the problem is one posed by the art-historical situation at the time the work was created, then the artistic goodness or badness of that work is (or depends on) its success in solving that problem. It follows that one cannot judge an artwork until one has established, by historical inquiry, the nature of the problem it was designed to solve. We would have to know that the two drawings discussed by Rosenberg were both attempts to solve the same problem before we could determine which was the more successful, and why.

For various reasons, I do not accept this view of critical judgments, nor do I believe that even art historians could consistently adhere to it. In the first place, we often know nothing definite about the problems that may have existed and, existing, presented themselves to the artist and were acknowledged and addressed by him or her. Yet in such cases we often believe ourselves able to make judgments. Of course, given any painting, we may conceive and formulate some problem to which it can be regarded as a solution, just as, given any proposition, we may conceive of a question to which it could be an answer. But then we are really trying to decide what the work does that is worth doing, and the reference to a "problem" is otiose.

In the second place, we would often be able to think of various problems to which the painting could be a proposed solution; so we would get a multiplicity of perhaps conflicting judgments, among which we could not choose. Which suggests—to me, at least—that this is not the way to go about setting up the evaluative task.

In the third place, even when we *can* fix the historical context and the painter's intentions so that we can say quite exactly and

---

6. James S. Ackerman, "A Theory of Style," in *Aesthetic Inquiry*, ed. Monroe C. Beardsley and Herbert M. Schueller (Belmont, Calif., 1967), p. 64.

confidently what problem he was trying to solve, success or failure in this enterprise cannot determine artistic goodness. Depending on the fruitfulness and depth of the problem, a successful solution may be a magnificent or a trivial work of art.

Hence talk about historically set "artistic problems" readily passes out of the historical plane. Panofsky, for example, who speaks of such "problems," proceeds along these lines:

> When we call a figure in an Italian Renaissance picture "plastic," while describing a figure in a Chinese painting as "having a volume but no mass" (owing to the absence of "modeling"), we interpret these figures as two different solutions of a problem which might be formulated as "volumetric units (bodies) *vs.* illimited expanse (space)." . . . Upon reflection it will turn out that there is a limited number of such primary problems, interrelated with each other, which on the one hand beget an infinity of secondary and tertiary ones, and on the other hand can be ultimately derived from one basic antithesis: differentiation *vs.* continuity.[7]

But it is clear that now we are no longer appealing to external historical information: the "problem" is derived from the painting itself, by applying a theoretical system articulating all possible "artistic problems." Of course it is true that we must have knowledge of many artworks to judge a particular artwork—we need a repertoire as background. But if the artworks in the repertoire (those from which Panofsky's system is derived) need not be of any particular time and place, we are not making use of them in their *historical* aspect. We have removed the concept of an "artistic problem" from something in the actual life world of the painter, open to historical inquiry, to an ahistorical dimension or parameter of the art of painting.

I do not deny that we can frame various restricted or guarded sorts of value judgment that essentially involve historical comparisons; I hold out only for the existence of other value judgments ("This drawing is better than that") that are, so to speak, history-free, yet intelligible and arguable.

IV

There is another way in which judgments of artistic value may be thought to rest on historical facts. Among the reasons that can be

---

7. "The History of Art as a Humanistic Discipline," in *Meaning in the Visual Arts*, p. 21.

given in support of critical praise or denigration, as we see in the passage from Rosenberg, are descriptions of the artwork in terms of its expressiveness, or what are now widely called "aesthetic qualities." "Plastic life," "organic coherence," "graphic charm" are noted by Rosenberg as desirable qualities, found to a higher degree, or more intensely, in one drawing than in the other. But suppose it could be shown that we must undertake historical inquiry to discover whether in fact an artwork has such qualities, or whether it has them to a marked degree; then, indirectly, our evaluations would rest on historical evidence after all, for we could not know that Schongauer was a better draftsman than his pupil unless we could be confident that our perception of these qualities is not an illusion but historically correct.

It is E. H. Gombrich who has opened up this extremely important and challenging line of argument. Though my formulation may reach a little beyond what he has explicitly stated, I hope it is free from distortion; in any case, it is well worth careful consideration on its merits. The conclusion is validly derived from three premises that are to be found in the final searching chapter of *Art and Illusion*.[8]

1. Expressiveness involves matching; more explicitly, to say what a painting expresses we must select a description (or, more generally, a label) for its aesthetic quality. Thus, in Gombrich's celebrated example, a well-known painting by Mondrian is titled *Broadway Boogie-Woogie*, which assimilates it to Fats Waller playing "Doin' the Uptown Lowdown," rather than, say, to Pablo Casals conducting Bach's First Brandenburg Concerto. We match the description with the painting.

2. Matching involves a selection among alternatives within sets of comparanda, that is, potential matchees and potential matchers. Thus, Gombrich says, we will accept the label "Boogie-Woogie" for this painting if we have to choose between this painting and a characteristic example of Mondrian's extremely still and rigid style; but we will accept the label "First Brandenburg Concerto" for this painting if we have to choose between this painting and an example of the futurist Severini's feverish dynamism; and then we will willingly move the old label "Boogie-Woogie" over to the

---

8. "From Representation to Expression," in *Art and Illusion*, 2d ed. (Princeton, 1961); see also several of the essays in *Meditations on a Hobby Horse*, 2d ed. (London, 1971).

Severini. It is in contrast to other Mondrians that this painting is boogie-woogie-like and in contrast to Severinis that this painting is First-Brandenburg-Concerto-like.

From the first two premises Gombrich concludes that "we cannot judge expression without an awareness of the choice situation, without a knowledge of the organon."[9] Mondrian could make his multiplicity of red and yellow squares boogie-woogie-ish only because he was confining himself to a rectangular style in which most of the paintings consisted of fewer and larger elements.

3. To know the comparanda that the painter actually had at hand—his range of objects to be matched and his repertoire of items to match with them—is to possess historical knowledge. Therefore, without appropriate historical knowledge we cannot determine what is expressed. Gombrich does not deny that we can often perceive aesthetic qualities in works of whose historical and cultural position we know nothing—say, Central African masks. But this is a mere impression, requiring to be confirmed, sometimes corrected, by historical inquiry, which sets bounds to what *could* be expressed at that time and place.[10] So a future visitor to the Museum of Modern Art might well notice a certain liveliness in the Mondrian painting, but he could not confidently call it "jazzy" unless he knew not only how this painting compared with other Mondrians but also how jazz (at the time it was painted) compared with other music.

This is a powerful and illuminating argument. Its only vulnerable, or at least questionable, point is the first premise. If that holds up, the conclusion seems secure.

Does expressiveness involve matching? If expressiveness consists in the exemplification of metaphorical labels, as in the theory of Nelson Goodman,[11] the answer is clearly yes. But if we distinguish between properties and the predicates that are used to describe them, we must say that the *properties* need not involve matching merely because the application of *predicates* involves a matching of words to things. This issue need not detain us, however, for the distinction, even if sound, will not help much. We got into the problem of expressiveness, you will recall, by considering the reasons that Rosenberg gave for his comparative value judgment: the thesis we started out to investigate is that artis-

9. *Art and Illusion*, p. 376.
10. Ibid., p. 388. See also *Meditations*, pp. 96–97.
11. *Languages of Art*, chap. 2.

tic value judgments indirectly rest on historical evidence because some of their reasons (that is, those ascribing aesthetic qualities) do. When we give a reason—when we say that the Schongauer drawing has "surface animation" (like *Broadway Boogie-Woogie*)— we are clearly matching a description with an object, and if this matching requires historical knowledge, Gombrich's conclusion must be accepted.

The equation has two ends; let us begin by looking at the predicates that are to be selected from. No doubt our descriptions of aesthetic qualities are implicitly comparative; Rosenberg's decision to build his book on pairs of readily comparable artworks takes advantage of this fact. We speak of paintings as more or less animated, as hardly at all animated, or as highly animated; and no doubt in such judgments we have in the back of our minds a rough norm or standard, either medium or extreme cases. Moreover, "animated" belongs to a family of predicates, the rest of which we more or less consciously rejected: "static," "sluggish," "turbulent," and so on. Now it might be argued that our choice from among those predicates must be at least partly governed by historical considerations, since we must limit ourselves to predicates (or to synonyms of predicates) that were available at the time the painting was painted; or that we have no right (it would be anachronistic) to call the painting "animated" unless we know that the painter could have intended his audience to describe it by this or some equivalent term.

The rationale for such a view would presumably be based on some notion of "communication"—a slippery term in contexts such as this. One would say that the painter intended to convey the concept of animation, and had to know that those who would see his painting could read this concept off it: so if asked what the painting expressed, they could say it was "decidedly animated," or something of the sort. But I think this model of painting and of painting appreciation has serious difficulties and unduly limits the art itself. A painting may have subtle and valuable aesthetic qualities that we have no very apt labels for; the purpose of painting cannot be to get people to utter descriptions. And it may have qualities that viewers many years later can describe more fully and more precisely than could the painter or his contemporaries (for example, because jazz and the word "jazzy" have come into existence). So I see no solid justification for imposing on our descriptions of paintings such historical limits.

I turn now to the works themselves: what must we know about their historical context in order to choose correctly from among the descriptive predicates now available? One line of argument on this point is that we must know what alternative ways of painting were open to the painter, considering the art-historical situation, the style in which he chose to work, the range of qualities possible to his medium, and so on. Thus if we learned that the Schongauer drawing was the *most* animated one that could be made by him, we should apply our most extreme predicate and describe it, say, as "turbulent." This argument cannot be right, for its conclusion is absurd. Anyone who holds that to describe an artwork correctly we must contrast it with others painted at its time or just before—call this a "contrastive class"—must tell us how to form the proper class. Shall we select only works of the same artist? But then we shall not be in a position to describe his style generally, in contrast to other styles—to speak, for example, of a painting as one of Perugino's "utterly serene compositions."[12] If we admit to the contrastive class all contemporaneous paintings, we shall not then be able to say that in general the period featured certain aesthetic qualities to a high degree. The only unquestionable contrastive class is the class of all other paintings; but in this class no painting has a privileged place on account of its historical position.

The problem of specifying the contrastive class[13] is brought out by one of Gombrich's very interesting examples, which we should perhaps not take too seriously. He discusses a painting by Kandinsky, called *At Rest* (1928, Guggenheim Museum), in which, according to one authority, Kandinsky "wanted the shapes themselves to suggest and convey the feeling of calm or repose." These are Gombrich's words,[14] and I regard them as a little misleading: it is not that Kandinksy wanted his painting to make the viewer *feel* calm, but that he wanted his painting to *look* calm, to have the quality of repose. This is no verbal quibble, for Gombrich claims that Kandinsky did not succeed: "I certainly doubt that even the most sensitive beholder would feel 'at rest' in front of this picture." I doubt that, too, but it doesn't mark the painting as a failure, for it is equally true of any painting you can name. I am

12. *Meditations*, p. 91.
13. This problem is also discussed in Richard Wollheim, *Art and Its Objects* (New York, 1968), pp. 48–57.
14. *Meditations*, p. 67.

sure Gombrich would agree that paintings are not sedatives or tranquillizers. The real question, then, is whether, by arranging the rectangles and triangles that make up his vaguely suggested harbor scene, Kandinsky succeeded in giving his picture the emergent aesthetic quality of calm or repose.

Though Gombrich apparently does not think we can see restfulness in this painting when we consider it by itself, he does think we can come to see it if we approach the painting with the relevant historical (here, biographical) knowledge.

> It so happens, however, that we can restore a clear expressive meaning to Kandinsky's composition by placing it in its historical context. During the 'twenties, the artist worked side by side with Paul Klee at the *Bauhaus,* and the two were friends. . . . Now, in 1927, Klee . . . had experimented with the suggestion of movement in ships, first in a drawing of slightly swaying sailing boats and then in a larger harbour scene which he called "Activity of the Port" . . . (1927, Berne, Klee Foundation). It is a witty experiment in conveying the bustle and restlessness of the harbour by novel graphic means. What is relevant to our context is only how much Kandinsky's work, painted a year later, gains in intelligibility when placed side by side with Klee's. Suddenly the massive rectangular forms acquire indeed the dimensions of heaviness and calm. . . .[15]

This is an interesting experiment, but what does it prove? It proves that if you approach Kandinsky's painting after just having looked at one with a great deal of busy movement in it, it will look very calm—more than if you had just been looking at a gallery full of Ruisdael landscapes. But, first, I doubt that this would happen if the Kandinsky did not already have a good deal of stability and fixedness in its forms and composition. And second, I don't see that the historical context is at all essential; the same effect can be achieved by first looking at any painting that is full of activity; the historical facts that Klee was a friend and that his painting was done in 1927 don't seem to matter. And third, I note that Klee's painting is described as restless and bustling (or at least these are qualities conveyed); but apparently the perception of *these* aesthetic qualities does not depend on a historical contrast with any earlier picture.

My treatment of Gombrich's account of expression must leave out of account many of the provocative and penetrating points he has made in various essays, and it must also resist the temptation

15. Ibid., p. 68.

to open up further discussion on other points that I would like to see more fully explained. I have been convinced by Gombrich that artistic expressiveness is sometimes closely related to—and even bound up with—communication, in what is now its technical Colin Cherry sense. One of Gombrich's best examples of contrast in communication is from Ali Baba: when the thief marked one door with chalk, the sign value of that mark, since it depended entirely on contrast with the unmarked doors, was easily destroyed by marking all the other doors in the same way.[16] The signification of the X depended on contrast; but signification is not, of course, the same thing as expressiveness. The Ali Baba example does not involve expressiveness at all. A Quaker meetinghouse signifies its builders' commitment to a way of life just by virtue of its contrast with the more elaborate churches and chapels of other sects;[17] but the expressiveness of any particular Quaker meetinghouse is not canceled by the building of others no less plain, sturdy, simple, and spare. Thus I can't help thinking that Gombrich goes too far in his understandable effort to counteract art historians who have not understood the essential role of choice in artistic signification. Discussing a book by Charles Stirling, he quotes some of the author's descriptions of seventeenth-century Dutch paintings, and comments:

> All these descriptions depend on the author's knowledge of alternatives. What was "bourgeois opulence" in seventeenth-century Holland would have been beyond the dreams of a twelfth-century nobleman. But the "intimacy" of these motifs still stands out when compared to the typical repertoire of contemporary Flemish artists, the peacocks, game and silver dishes of Snijders. Naturally these in their turn would not be particularly "heroic" (no courage was needed to paint them) if they were not so much larger and louder than the average Dutch counterpart, in other words if their deviation from some expected median were not felt to be equivalent to the similar deviations of other "heroic" genres in literature or music. Likewise, if there is indeed "serenity" in Caravaggio and humility in Spanish still lifes this character must also spring from their place within the field of possibilities. For neither the words nor the labels used by the critics have any of these meanings inherently and by themselves. They only communicate meaning within an articulated tradition.[18]

16. Ibid., p. 111.
17. Compare ibid., p. 17.
18. Ibid., p. 100.

The problem of the contrastive class is that of specifying the relevant "field of possibilities," short of considering the entire range of existing paintings as constituting that field. I do not see what the criterion could be. Meanwhile, it is certainly true that an animal that is large compared to mice may be small compared to elephants, but we can still convey the size of an animal roughly by saying that it is about as large as a breadbox. And the statement that one painting is more serene than another may hold up whatever other paintings may come into our ken.

I do not, of course, consider myself to have disproved Gombrich's account of expression. My concern has been to articulate some of the difficulties I find in it, in the hope of contributing to their resolution, by that account or another.

V

Though it will add nothing substantive to my argument, I hope I may be indulged in one more example, which I offer as a final warning against overemphasis on the relevance of historical knowledge to art criticism. As a foil to my little sermon, I begin with a quotation from that admirable critic, Frank Getlein, writing in *The New Republic* about the Archives of American Art, which the Detroit Institute of Arts set up as a repository of historical facts about the works of American painters, including tape recordings of interviews with painters and their companions. Getlein remarked that some might regard all this as beside the point, but "everything we know about an artist or his times contributes something to our understanding of his work."[19] It is always easy, and therefore unrewarding, to overturn such sweeping universal generalizations, but in this case I want not only to state explicitly that Getlein's statement is false but also to add that it would be more nearly true if he had added "or *mis*understanding" to "understanding."

Some years ago there was an interesting symposium, later published, at a meeting of the American Society for Aesthetics, in which Picasso's painting *Night Fishing at Antibes* (Museum of Modern Art) was discussed by a psychologist, a philosopher, and

19. June 27, 1960.

an art historian.[20] What the art historian, George Levitine, said is, to my mind, a direct counterexample to Getlein's generalization, though I don't think it did any real harm, except insofar as it distracted attention from the work at hand. In search of understanding, he cast about for a "filiation," or possible source, to compare with the Picasso. He was reminded of paintings by Raphael and Copley, but without enthusiasm; finally he came up with a seventeenth-century Dutch painting in the Louvre, *The Bathers*, somewhat hesitantly attributed to Nicolas Maes. It shows a bunch of country boys swimming off an old boat. Unfortunately, there is no fishing in it, but there are features that are vaguely similar to those in *Night Fishing*. Levitine concluded that Picasso had been influenced by this painting, and suggested that the recognition of this influence "can perhaps cast a light upon the mechanics of some of Picasso's distortions."[21]

There is no doubt that there are distortions—the flounder that is being speared is no Mediterranean species, but only a Picasso species, and the girls watching from the jetty are most unusual, despite the normality of the double ice cream cone: one has seven fingers on one hand, the other has an eye that seems to have dropped to her chin. But what are these distortions distortions *from*? In paintings that are explicitly allusive—as in Picasso's series of variations on *Las Meninas* or on *The Woman of Algiers*—an acquaintance with the original painting is called for, so we may see what changes Picasso made for his own purposes. But the expressiveness of the distortions in *Night Fishing*, as far as I can see, does not depend on its deviation from earlier pictures or styles of depiction, but from flounders and females as we are acquainted with them in the real world. Levitine said many interesting and helpful things about *Night Fishing*, but I believe none of them owes anything to the art history he invokes.

Rudolph Arnheim, in his discussion, made many perceptive comments on the shapes and figures in the painting, but when he came to the "paradoxical contradiction between the nature of the action represented and the dynamics of the shapes representing,"[22] he was suddenly moved to reflection of a very different sort.

20. Rudolf Arnheim, Douglas N. Morgan, and George Levitine, "Picasso's *Night Fishing at Antibes*," *Journal of Aesthetics and Art Criticism* 22 (Winter, 1963):165–75.
21. Ibid., p. 174.
22. Ibid., p. 166.

> It seems legitimate to remember here that the painting was done in August, 1939, when the imminence of World War II darkened the horizon. In this ominous light, the murder of the fishes, portrayed in our painting, acquires a particular meaning. Watched with noncommital curiosity by the girls, whom we described as creatures of pleasure and luxury, the prospect of slaughter appears unreal, paralyzed in its impact by its remoteness, by the incompatibility of violence with the gay setting of the Mediterranean harbor. . . . The foreboding of violent, but unknown, things to come emerges as the dominant theme of the painting.[23]

Here are two historical facts: (1) that the painting was painted in August 1939, and (2) that the Germans invaded Poland on September 1. This is the knowledge, I would say, that serves only to darken our understanding of this painting.

If we were not told beforehand that we must look at this painting in an "ominous light" and find it full of "foreboding" and "violence," I think we would find it most delightfully cheerful. True, the man on the right (unlike his apparently seasick and retching companion) is certainly concentrating with fierce—even with absurd—intensity on spearing the flounder. But can we describe this imminent capture as "murder" and "slaughter"? This flatfish is the most unlikely symbol of suffering humanity that one could conjure up. It reminds me of what Harold Ross once said about the classic *New Yorker* cartoon in which one enthusiastic duelist severs his opponent's head and cries, "Touché." The cartoon was originally drawn by Carl Rose, but Ross thought it was too gruesome. Let Thurber draw it, he said; "Thurber's people don't bleed." We may be sure that Picasso's fish doesn't bleed, either. As for the girls—one of whom does indeed give ambiguous promise of pneumatic bliss, like T. S. Eliot's Grushenka—they are hardly to be cast in the role of those who dance into the dawn of disaster, like Byron's midnight revelers before Waterloo, or Shaw's doomed denizens of *Heartbreak House,* or the traveling players in *Idiot's Delight.*

Of course knowledge is, from the most fundamental perspective, always better than ignorance. We cannot have too much. But knowledge misdirected can lead to its polar opposite, which is not ignorance but false belief. And misdirection is always a matter of taking as logically relevant what is in fact not so.

23. Ibid., p. 167.

PART III

Creativity and Metaphor

14: *The Creation of Art*

I

FROM the times of Homer and Hesiod, creative artists have wondered about the source of their power to summon into existence things hitherto unseen and even unthought. In our day, it has begun to seem feasible to solve this problem with something like conclusiveness. Yet much of its mystery remains.

A number of distinct questions are involved here, only one of which I shall take up. For example, I shall not inquire why the artist creates in the first place—what obscure impulses compel him to make shapes or melodies, to dance or tell stories. This question has been given two sorts of answer. The first is in terms of conscious motives (the artist wants fame, money, love, power, etc.), and here it seems pretty evident that there must be a vast variety of true answers, depending on the artist, the work at hand, and even the time of day or night. The second is in terms of unconscious needs and drives, and this I am not competent to pursue. Again, I shall not inquire how the creative process begins—what evokes the first stroke of the brush, the first words of the poem. In the creation of every work, no doubt something does come first, perhaps a single little fragment, perhaps a rush of ideas. This initial element of what later becomes the work has been referred to by various metaphors, some of them misleading, as we shall see—*germ, cell, seed, nucleus*; I will call it the *inceptive element*, or, for short, *incept*. The incept of the work may simply pop into the artist's mind—like Mozart's melodies or Housman's verses—or it may come from external sources, accidentally, like the notes struck by a cat on the keyboard or the pattern made by mud in the gutter. When it does come from within, it no doubt has preconscious causal conditions, though to trace them would surely be a difficult undertaking.

What I mean by the creative process is that stretch of mental and physical activity between the incept and the final touch—between the thought "I may be on to something here" and the thought "It is finished." My problem is about what goes on in this interval—how the work of art itself comes into existence and takes on its character through the stages or phases of this process.

II

Many students of art have assumed, or expected to find, that there is such a thing as *the* process of art creation—that is, a pattern universally or characteristically discoverable whenever substantial works of art are produced. They would allow, of course, for many differences between one creative process and another, depending on the artist's habits and temperament, the medium in which he moves, and the demands of the particular work in progress. But they argue that beneath these differences there is what we might call the *normal creative pattern,* and that to understand this pattern would contribute much to our understanding of the finished product.

Nor is it unreasonable to suppose that there is such a creative pattern to be isolated and described. First, it might be said, the common character of works of art in all media—whatever it is that enables us to class them together—presents a prima facie case for a creative pattern. For things that are alike may well have been produced in a similar way. Second, there is the analogy with aesthetic experience. For if there is a pattern of appreciation common to the arts, then why should there not be a pattern of creation, which would, in a sense, be its inverse? Third, there is the analogy with other kinds of creative activity. Dewey's classic description of the process of inquiry, or problem solving, remains the standard one, though it has been refined and extended since its first appearance in *How We Think.* Practical and scientific problems differ considerably among themselves, just as works of art do, and if there is a common pattern of thought provoked by the former, there may be a common pattern of activity required for the latter.

It is true that the theory of a common character of the arts and the theory of a special aesthetic experience have been questioned in recent years.¹ I appreciate the force of the objections, which I won't go into here, but, like many others, I am not ready to abandon either of the theories. In any case, of course, the three arguments I have mentioned above are not conclusive; they are but suggestive analogies. If there is a common creative pattern, then it can be discovered only by direct study of creative processes. And we might expect to find three main sources of evidence: the artist, the psychologist, and the philosopher.

Our first inclination, of course, is to turn to the creative artist himself, for he ought to know, if anyone does, what is going on in his mind during that mysterious interval between the first pinfall or brickfall of an idea and the final laying down of pen or brush. And it is true that much of our best and most useful information about creative processes does come from artists. The trouble is that, for reasons of their own, they are often inclined to the most whimsical and bizarre statements, and seem to enjoy being deliberately misleading. For example, Christian Zervos tells us that Picasso once said to him: "I take a walk in the forest of Fontainbleau. There I get an indigestion of greenness. I must empty this sensation into a picture. Green dominates it. The painter paints as if in urgent need to discharge himself of his sensations and his visions."² But this is a most curious description of the creative process. If the painter suffers from a surfeit of green, does he avoid looking at green any more for a while? No, he goes to his studio, squeezes out the green pigment, and proceeds to cover a canvas with it. This is like drinking grapefruit juice to cure an acid stomach. To make the indigestion theory of artistic creation plausible, the green-surfeited painter would surely go off to paint a *red* painting—red being the chromatic analogue of sodium bicarbonate.

We have had, by the way, many other metaphorical models of the creative process or the mind during creation, though perhaps none more colorful than Picasso's heartburn. The famous treatise

---

1. The former by Paul Ziff and Morris Weitz, whose views I have discussed in "Art and the Definitions of the Arts," *Journal of Aesthetics and Art Criticism* 20 (1961):175–87; the latter by George Dickie, in "Is Psychology Relevant to Aesthetics?" *Philosophical Review* 71 (1962):285–302, "The Myth of the Aesthetic Attitude," *American Philosophical Quarterly* 1 (January 1964):56–65, and "Beardsley's Phantom Aesthetic Experience," *Journal of Philosophy* 62 (1965):129–36.

2. Brewster Ghiselin, ed., *The Creative Process: A Symposium* (Berkeley, 1952), p. 51.

of John Livingston Lowes, *The Road to Xanadu*, is full of them—the "hooked atoms" jumbled about, the "deep well" of the unconscious into which the poet dips, the imagination as "loom." Once we read of Shelley's "fading coal." Now it is the digital computer that furnishes the most tempting figure.

Or consider a famous statement by Henry James, in his preface to *The Spoils of Poynton*.³ He begins by saying that the "germ" of his novel, as he called it, lay in a story told at a dinner party in London. James dilates upon "the sublime economy of art," which starts with such a "prick of inoculation," when the virus is communicated, and then goes on to build a work out of itself. The lady who told the story began by mentioning a woman at odds with her son over the furniture in an old house bequeathed to the son by his father. James remarked, "There had been but ten words, yet I had recognized in them, as in a flash, all the possibilities of the little drama of my *Spoils*, which glimmered then and there into life." James says he didn't want to hear any more of the story, because the germ was complete in itself; the seed had been "transplanted to richer soil." This claim has often been repeated and taken as a text. But, as S. P. Rosenbaum has shown, if we look in James's *Notebooks*, where he tells a good deal about the process of writing *The Spoils of Poynton*, we find that in fact, on the day after the party (December 24, 1893), James wrote down not only the germ but the whole story, as it was told him, and that in fact many other germs came into the picture before very long, as well.⁴

Probably the greatest contributions made by creative artists to the solution of our problem are not their own theories about what they do, but the records they leave us in the form of sketches and early drafts. We cherish, for example, the notebooks of Beethoven, the sketches and studies in which Picasso worked out his ideas for *Guernica*, and the rich materials contributed to the special collection at the University of Buffalo by living poets who are willing to allow scholars to study their methods of work, their ventures,

---

3. Henry James, *The Art of the Novel*, ed. R. P. Blackmur (New York, 1934), pp. 119–24.

4. *Notebooks*, ed. F. O. Matthiessen and Kenneth Murdock (New York, 1947), pp. 136–37. For further stages in the development of this novel (tentatively titled *The House Beautiful*), see the references on p 138. See also S. P. Rosenbaum, "Henry James and Creativity: 'The Logic of the Particular Case,'" *Criticism* 8 (Winter 1966):44–52.

erasures, substitutions, corrections, and revisions. I shall have occasion to make use of these materials later.

As for the psychologists, despite the considerable effort (or at least speculation) that has gone into the study of the artist's unconscious, not much is available by way of well-established conclusions about the way the poet's or painter's mind is actually working when he is on the job.[5] Some of the most interesting contributions have been made by gestalt psychologists—for example, Rudolf Arnheim, in his psychological study of some materials in the Buffalo collection, and in his study of *Guernica*.[6]

Among the most valuable of the psychological investigations are those undertaken nearly thirty years ago by Catharine Patrick.[7] She first secured a group of 55 poets (with 58 "non-poets" as a suitable control group), and, after putting them at ease, confronted them with a certain picture and made them write a poem about it. She asked them to talk aloud as they thought, and took down their words in shorthand. Then she went to the painters, and, tit for tat, presented them with a part of a poem by Milton, which they were to illustrate in some way, while again she took down their vocal musings, and also kept note of what they were drawing, as time passed. Every encounter was carefully timed. And the results were supplemented by questionnaires.

These interviews resulted in a good deal of very interesting material. Professor Patrick set out to determine whether the typical process of artistic creation passes through the four stages classically distinguished by Graham Wallas in his book *The Art of Thought*—the stages of preparation, incubation, inspiration, and elaboration. And she concluded that these stages can indeed be distinguished. But the most remarkable feature of her material, it seems to me, is precisely the opposite. All four of these activities are mixed together; they are constantly (or alternately) going on throughout the whole process.

When we turn to the philosophers, we find a few who have tried to bring together into something of a general theory the

---

5. Douglas Morgan, "Creativity Today," *Journal of Aesthetics and Art Criticism* 12 (1953):1–24; and Stuart E. Golann, "Psychological Study of Creativity," *Psychological Bulletin* 60 (1963):548–65.
6. *Poets at Work* (New York, 1948), by various authors, and *Picasso's "Guernica": The Genesis of a Painting* (Berkeley, 1962).
7. *Creative Thought in Poets*, Archives of Psychology, no. 178 (1935); "Creative Thought in Artists," *Journal of Psychology* 4 (1937):35–73.

insights of artists and psychologists. They, too, of course, have their own occupational hazards, or professional vices, and are too readily drawn away from contact with actual works of art into theorizing about what might ideally be true. For one who has a metaphysical ax to grind, it is easy enough to find a congenial formula to describe the creative process. Depending on the angle of approach, the artist will be said to be converting sensations into intuitions, receiving divine inspiration, reshuffling the atoms of immediate experience, embodying the ideal in sensuous form, working out the consequences of an initial postulate, or affirming the authenticity of existence. But I am looking for less ambitious theories than these.

III

Philosophic reflection on the available empirical data has given us two widely held accounts of the creative process. When we consider any artistic work of major proportions, whose creation we know something about, we are often struck by the gap between the final achievement and its humble incept. Clearly, the process between can be said to have moved in a desirable direction. Now in the usual case, although lucky accidents may make an important contribution, this process appears to be at least partly controlled. The problem for the aesthetician is, then: What is the nature of this control?

The earliest people who raised this question—Homer, Hesiod, and Pindar—were inclined to give it a supernatural answer, attributing their own feats to the intervention of the Muses. And the theory of divine inspiration, often in a pantheistic version, remains with us. But if we insist on a naturalistic theory of artistic creation, we find two main ones. And these are distinguished in a way familiar to other branches of philosophy.

According to what I shall call the propulsive theory, the controlling agent is something that exists prior to the creative process, and presides over it throughout. According to the finalistic theory, the controlling agent is the final goal toward which the process aims. No doubt the two theories run into each other in the minds of some philosophers, and perhaps we need not strain to keep them wholly distinct. But even if there are not two theories, there are at least two errors, and this is what I am most concerned to note.

The theory of art as expression is probably the most popular form of the propulsive theory of the creative process. And I shall take R. G. Collingwood as representative of expressionism at its best. "When a man is said to express emotion, what is being said about him comes to this. At first, he is conscious of having an emotion, but not conscious of what this emotion is. All he is conscious of is a perturbation or excitement, which he feels going on within him, but of whose nature he is ignorant."[8] Before the emotion is expressed, the artist is oppressed by it; he works so his mind will become "lightened and eased" (p. 110). His aim is to make his emotion clear to himself (pp. 111, 114)—indeed, to discover what the emotion is (p. 111). Thus Collingwood postulates a single emotion that preserves its identity throughout the process of creation—if the work is to be genuine—and determines the main course of that process.

The first difficulty with this theory is that no principle of identity can be provided for this emotion. "If artists only find out what their emotions are in the course of finding out how to express them, they cannot begin the work of expression by deciding what emotion to express" (p. 117). Well said. But, on the other hand, after the artist has expressed his emotion, and come to experience it clearly, how does he know it is the same emotion he started with? He cannot compare them, since the other was unknown to him. How does he know that the emotion he feels now is not a new and different emotion—an emotion that is perhaps felt as the *effect* of the finished work, rather than its cause? As far as I can see, Collingwood has no answer to this. And, moreover, in order to preserve his theory he has to say some rather surprising things. For example, "No artist, therefore, so far as he is an artist proper, can set out to write a comedy, a tragedy, an elegy, or the like. So far as he is an artist proper, he is just as likely to write any one of these as any other" (p. 116). I am sure that statement would have startled Sophocles or Shakespeare, not to mention Racine and Molière. According to Collingwood, the genuine artist says, "I feel an emotion coming on; no telling what it is until I write something (or paint it, or compose it); how will I know what I've felt until I see what I've done?" If he insists from the start on writing a tragedy, he will be forcing his emotion into some channel, and the result cannot be art.

8. R. G. Collingwood, *The Principles of Art* (Oxford, 1938), p. 109. See also Alan Donagan, *The Later Philosophy of R. G. Collingwood* (Oxford, 1962), chap. 5, §3.

The whole concept of *clarifying* an emotion is itself very obscure. I have a suspicion that when Bruckner finished one of his enormous symphonies, his emotions were no more clear to him than they were at the start. At least, they are no more clear to me. They are big emotions; anyone can see that. But clarity is hardly the word for them. On the other hand, nothing could be more clear than the special quality of the opening of Mozart's G-Minor Symphony; but what reason do we have for thinking that Mozart's composition of this symphony began with some obscure or indescribable emotion, rather than with the subject of the first four bars? And what about artists who have spent years on a single work—are we to say that the very same emotion was there throughout, striving to clarify itself?

An interesting and well-worked-out version of the finalistic or goal-directed theory of art creation has been presented by David Ecker.[9] He describes the creative process as "qualitative problem solving," borrowing the concept from John Dewey. The stages of the process, he says, consist of a series of problems and solutions: if I use this cool green here I can get this plane to recede; "this jagged shape contrasts sharply with those open volumes" (p. 235), and so on. Now he makes it clear that the problems posed are within the work itself: "Artistic problem solving takes place in the artist's medium" (p. 285). The problem need not be verbally formulated (p. 286), and various logical terms that might be applied to the process (such as "verification" and "hypothesis") are "grossly misleading" (p. 288). But the process is to be analyzed in terms of the categories of means and end; the choices involved, and the general direction, are controlled by the previsioned goal. (It is plain that Ecker's account would be strongly repudiated by Collingwood; according to Ecker, the poet *must* begin by intending to write a tragedy, or comedy, or something, for otherwise he has no problem to solve.) Ecker quotes a very illuminating passage from the sculptor Henry Moore:

> ... I sometimes begin a drawing with no preconceived problem to solve, with only the desire to use pencil on paper, and make lines, tones and shapes with no conscious aim; but as my mind takes in what is so produced a point arrives where some idea becomes conscious and crystallizes, and then a control and ordering begins to take place.

9. "The Artistic Process as Qualitative Problem Solving," *Journal of Aesthetics and Art Criticism* 21 (1963):283–90.

Or sometimes I start with a set subject; or to solve, in a block of stone of known dimensions, a sculptural problem I've given myself, and then consciously attempt to build an ordered relationship of forms. . . .[10]

The first part of this statement is very clear, and restricts one side of Ecker's theory. There may be, says Moore, no "preconceived problem to solve"; the only problem, if there is any, arises after the occurrence of the incept, the first lines of the drawing. The "control and ordering" begins with the elements of the work itself. The second part of the statement can be understood, it seems to me, in a similar way. Sometimes, says Moore, he starts with a subject—say, he is to make a reclining figure. Or a set of outside dimensions within which to work. But basically this is the same sort of thing; the incept can be some lines randomly drawn on paper, or the subject, or the block of untouched marble, with its own particular size and shape.

The trouble appears when this is called a *problem*. What is the problem? It might be: "How can I make a good drawing using these lines I've already drawn?" Or "How can I make a good sculpture of a reclining figure?" Or "How can I make a good sculpture out of this block of marble?" But these are queer things to call *problems*: they are really *tasks*, the terms of which are voluntarily accepted by the artist. The main question involved in each of them is simply: "What do I do next?" A problem arises out of a conflict of some kind—a goad that the sculptor does not require. And it calls for a specific and determinate solution or set of solutions—which is not what the sculptor achieves.

Elsewhere I have stated my objections to the end–means terminology in art.[11] Actually, when Ecker gives his examples of ends and means, it is clear that he is not really talking about these at all, but about the relation between what I call regional qualities and their perceptual conditions. The cool green is not a means to the receding plane; it is one of the localized features of the visual design that help to make the plane recede. The recession of the plane, to put it another way, is a comparatively large-scale property of the work, which depends (in part) on a comparatively small-scale property, the cool green. Now, if we ask which the artist first intended and has as an "end-in-view," it is tempting to say, with Ecker, that the artist "arranges qualitative *means* such as

10. Ghiselin, ed., *The Creative Process*, p. 77.
11. *Aesthetics: Problems in the Philosophy of Criticism* (New York, 1958), pp. 78–80.

lines, colors, planes, and textures, to achieve his qualitative *end*, which we might name 'cubist,' 'impressionist,' or 'expressionist'" (p. 287). But Ecker has already conceded that the end-in-view may be "some intended order" as well as a "pervasive quality" (p. 286). It may often be the case that what the artist is consciously after is a certain arrangement of lines, colors, planes, and textures, and the resulting regional quality is unexpected. It is odd to speak of the color as a "means" when it is chosen for no ulterior motive.

The error here is a subtle one, but a very crucial one in talking about art. It consists in jumping from the fact that regional qualities depend on their perceptual conditions to the conclusion that the former are therefore always ends-in-view and the latter means in the process of creation. Perhaps no great harm would usually be done, but this way of speaking leads to an impasse, which is fully exhibited in a sentence quoted from John Dewey by Ecker: "The doing or making is artistic when the perceived result is of such a nature that *its* qualities *as perceived* have controlled the question of production.'"[12] Take the finished painting; note its quality. Now suppose we have photographs of various stages of the work, taken at daily or hourly intervals, let us say, while the painter was working. None of these, of course, has the *specific* quality of the finished painting. But Dewey says this quality was all along controlling the artist's work. Since the quality did not exist until the painting was finished, it could only have been in the artist's mind. Does that mean that from the earliest stages of a painting, from the incept onward, the painter has definitely in mind some regional quality that he is trying to bring into existence on the canvas? It is conceivable that this is sometimes the case, but most of the experience of artists goes against it: it would be remarkable if the exact regional quality of the final painting were that plain to the painter from the start.

Now, Dewey's statement can be interpreted in a somewhat more plausible way if we introduce the notion of degrees of intensity for these regional qualities. The final painting, let us say, is characterized by a firm semigeometrical solidity and rigidity, with decisive lines and interlocking forms. We look at the first tentative strokes put down by the painter, in the earliest photograph, and we see that somehow, dimly but unmistakably, this

---

12. *Art as Experience* (New York, 1934), p. 48.

final quality is foreshadowed in the early draft—a touch of it is already there, though nothing like the way it is there at the end. So the process of creation lying between these stages could be described, at least in part, as one in which a regional quality hit upon early in the game is gradually intensified with the complication of new lines and colors. So in this sense, it could be that the final quality has been at work throughout—not as a foreseen goal to which the process is heading teleologically, but as a present quality whose immediately perceivable value suggests to the painter that it would be even more valuable if there were, so to speak, more of it.

There is no doubt that something like this does often happen. Sometimes we can see in the earliest stages of a great work that the quality we value so highly in the finished product has begun to emerge. But this is not always the case, by any means. Sometimes the quality that appears most definitely at the start turns out not to be fruitful; the artist's attempt to intensify it leads to radical formal rearrangements that end by destroying the original quality and substituting a very different one. The melody that was first tried out as a quick rondo theme becomes the subject of a slow movement, almost unrecognizably altered. The poem that started out as a few ironic lines about a current political issue transforms itself, almost against the poet's will, into a moving meditation on the human condition. Nor is such a process—contrary to what Dewey implies—any the less artistic because not the same, but different, qualities have been active in generating the process at different stages.

Vincent Tomas has effectively criticized the finalistic view that artistic creation is "a paradigm of purposive activity."[13] There is a sense of "heading somewhere," though without a given goal in terms of which success or failure can be defined as it can when a torpedo is launched toward a target. Yet, paradoxically, "the artist *can* say that certain directions are not right." And Thomas' solution, sound so far as it goes, is to emphasize the critical ingredient in creation. His theory is that creation is a self-correcting process, in which the artist constantly redirects its aims. Tomas does not show in detail how the artist does this. But I believe that he is right, and I will try to develop and defend this theory.

13. "Creativity in Art," *Philosophical Review* 67 (1958):1–15; "A Note on Creation in Art," *Journal of Philosophy* 59 (1962):464–69. The former is reprinted in *Creativity in the Arts*, ed. Tomas (Englewood Cliffs, N.J., 1964).

IV

The real nature of the artist's control over the creative process will elude anyone who looks for a single guiding factor, whether a need or an end. It is internal to the process itself. I do not plan to argue for a single creative pattern, but to show how, in the absence of any such general pattern, each individual process that eventuates in a work of art *generates* its own direction and momentum. For the crucial controlling power at every point is the particular stage or condition of the unfinished work itself, the possibilities it presents, and the developments it permits. There are three things to discuss here, and I will say something about each—the incept, the development, and the completion of the work.

The first control over the artistic process is set up by the incept itself. And I want to emphasize, as I have said before, that the incept may be any sort of thing: the first sentence of a story or the last, a simple plot situation, a character, theme, scene, figure of speech, or tone or style. Paul Valéry has told us, instructively:

> My poem *Le Cimetière marin* began in me by a rhythm, that of a French line . . . of ten syllables, divided into four and six. I had as yet no idea with which to fill out this form. Gradually a few hovering words settled in it, little by little determining the subject, and my labor (a very long labor) was before me.[14]

Elsewhere, Valéry adds that his playing around with possibilities of this rhythm led to a certain kind of stanza; then

> between the stanzas, contrasts or correspondences would be set up. This last condition soon required the potential poem to be a monologue of "self," in which the simplest and most enduring themes of my affective and intellectual life, as they had imposed themselves upon my adolescence, associated with the sea and the light of a particular spot on the Mediterranean coast, were called up, woven together, opposed. . . . All this led to the theme of death and suggested the theme of pure thought.[15]

This is exactly opposite to the usual idea that the poet must begin with his theme, or thesis, and that he characteristically then devises a suitable subject or set of images, and finally settles on the appropriate stanzaic form and meter. Now, I'll have to con-

---

14. "Poetry and Abstract Thought," in *The Art of Poetry*, trans. Denise Folliot (New York, 1961), p. 80.
15. "Concerning 'Le Cimetière marin,'" in *Art of Poetry*, p. 148.

fess at this point that I am wide open to one kind of skeptical criticism. Considering that this particular poem is one of the most obscure poems in the French language, it might be said that we can draw no general conclusions from Valéry's method of composing it—what can you expect from a poet who begins with rhythms and ends with themes? Still, Valéry's account shows there is no one, privileged order in which a poem has to get written. And even in the composition of more conventional poems, many different items (including metrical patterns) actually come first. Stephen Spender, for example, tells us in an essay that one of his poems began with a vision of the sea, and that another time, the words "a language of flesh and roses" came into his head as the incept of a possible poem while he was standing in the corridor of a train looking at a landscape of pits and pitheads—though at the time he was writing his essay, the words had not yet grown into an actual poem.[16] From a famous essay by Allen Tate, we gather that two elements of his "Ode to the Confederate Dead" were present from the start, the idea he calls "solipsism" and the idea of the dead, though it took ten years to fuse them together.[17] And according to Muriel Rukeyser, her poem "Orpheus" began with a sudden terrifying image of disintegration that came to her as she walked along a crowded street in New York.[18]

One of the most important questions about the role of the incept in the creative process is this: Does it exercise a pervasive influence throughout? If the propulsive theory is correct, one would expect to find the incept dominating the whole process, for whatever appears first would presumably be closely related to the original emotion. On second thought, I am not sure this really follows; it is hard to say what can be predicted from Collingwood's unknown and unknowable emotion. Again, if the finalist theory is correct, one would also expect the incept to dominate, for it would presumably embody the original problem or goal that directs the process to the end.

Now, one thing is evident: once an element is chosen, it sets up

---

16. "The Making of a Poem," *Partisan Review* 13 (1946):294–308 (also in Tomas, ed., *Creativity in the Arts*).
17. "Narcissus as Narcissus," in *On the Limits of Poetry* (New York, 1948).
18. Frank Barron, *Creativity and Psychological Health* (Princeton, 1963), p. 229n. For examples of fiction incepts see Malcolm Cowley, ed., *Writers at Work* (New York, 1959), esp. pp. 7–8.

demands and suggestions as to what may come next, and also places limits on it. Draw a single line on a piece of paper. If you do not think what you have there is worth much attention, the question is what you can do next to improve upon it. You can balance it, cross or oppose it by other lines, thicken and emphasize it, transform it into a more complex line or shape, and so on. Or, of course, you can erase it—but then you are rejecting it as an incept, and putting an end to that particular creative process. That every stage of the process powerfully affects the succeeding stage is plain; but our present question is whether the first stage is somehow dominant over all. Artists have spoken rather differently about this. For instance, Picasso once said that "basically a picture doesn't change, that the first 'vision' remains almost intact, in spite of appearances."[19] But he also said that a picture cannot be thought out ahead of time, and "changes as one's thoughts change." The sketches for *Guernica* do have a notable continuity despite all the changes. The bull and the horse were there in the first sketch, and a woman appeared in one of the later sketches done the same day.

Another example is provided by Beethoven's long series of sketches for the spacious melody that he used for the variations in the slow movement of his string quartet in E-flat, Opus 127. These sketches have been studied by Victor Zuckerkandl.[20] When they are placed side by side, they illustrate the force of the incept very clearly. The first full bar of the final melody, with its stepwise motion upward from A-flat to F, is there almost complete from the very first sketch, though with a slightly different rhythm; and the rest of the story is a struggle, resumed from time to time over a long period, to find an adequate continuation and completion of that incept. Beethoven tries various ways of carrying on the melody, and abandons them; he tries the initial bar in the key of C, in duple tempo, with turns and rhythmic alterations, to see if it can be made to move into the long flowing line that the incept seems to call for. The whole keeps changing its regional character as it grows, yet some of its outstanding final qualities can be described as intensifications of qualities that were there in the first sketch. But this is by no means true of all of Beethoven's work; Allen Forte, a careful student of the piano sonata opus 109, has re-

---

19. Arnheim, *Picasso's "Guernica,"* p. 30.
20. I am referring to a lecture given in the spring of 1963 at Swarthmore College.

marked that "in many instances one can hardly recognize the final version from the initial sketches."[21]

Indeed, an incept that initiates a successful creative process may become almost lost in it. Of course there must be some continuity from incept to final work, otherwise we could not say that the incept was the start of that particular work. But there is a wide range of deviation from the straight line of development. An ingredient that has one quality as it first appears to the artist may later find a context that alters its quality completely. Dostoyevsky's novel *The Idiot* is an interesting case in point. We have a large collection of manuscript notes and drafts to tell us the agonizing story of Dostoyevsky's working out of that novel. In the very early stages, the Idiot (as he is called from the beginning) is "described as a powerful, proud, and passionate individual. There is something Byronic about him, and he resembles those criminal, self-willed creations Valkovski and Svidrigailov. He is sensual, performs extravagant actions, and perhaps his most marked trait is egoism."[22] Could anything be farther from the Idiot of the final novel? For two months, through eight detailed plans for the novel, Dostoyevsky worked toward the deadline for the first installment (published January 1868). As the plans succeed each other, we see certain characters take on the Christlike characteristics of Prince Myshkin as we now have him, and we see the Idiot developing a double nature that prepares the way, in the eighth plan, for his reversal of personality. Even so, the novel was still significantly changing between the first installment and the later ones.

Once the work is under way, with a tentative commitment to some incept, the creative process is kept going by tensions between what has been done and what might have been done. At each stage there must be a perception of deficiencies in what now exists, plus the sense of unrealized possibilities of improvement. The motivating force, as Tomas says, is a negative critical judgment. And this same point has been made by Valéry. To understand poetry, he remarks, we must study "word combinations, not so much through the conformity of the meanings of these

---

21. *The Compositional Matrix* (Baldwin, N.Y., 1961), p. 4. See also Ernst Krenek's analysis of the sketches for the false entry of the subject in the Eroica: "The Problem of Creative Thinking in Music," in *The Nature of Creative Thinking*, a symposium published for the Industrial Research Institute, Inc. (New York, 1952), pp. 54–57.

22. Ernest J. Simmons, *Dostoyevsky* (Oxford, 1950), p. 202. See his whole book for very illuminating accounts of Dostoyevsky's creative processes.

groups to an idea or thought that one thinks should be *expressed*, as, on the contrary through their effects once they are formed, from which one chooses."[23] In other words, as the poet moves from stage to stage, it is not that he is looking to see whether he is saying what he already meant, but that he is looking to see whether he wants to mean what he is saying. Thus, according to Valéry, "every true poet is necessarily a first rate critic"—not necessarily of others' work, but of his own.[24]

Each time the artist—whether poet or painter or composer—takes a step, he adds something to what is already there (A), and makes another and different object (B). If he judges B worse than A, he must go back. If B is better than A, the question is whether it is good enough to stand alone as a work of art. If not, the question is whether B can be transformed into still another and better object C. If this is impossible, if every attempt to improve it only makes it worse, then the whole project is left unfinished, for it is unfinishable.

One of the most puzzling questions about the creative process is how the artist knows when to stop. If the propulsion theory is correct, the answer is that he stops when his original impulse has exhausted itself. If the finalistic theory is correct, then the artist compares his work at every stage with the intact memory of his original vision of his goal, and when they match, the work is done. But without these theories, it becomes more difficult to explain what it means to come to an end of a creative process.[25]

There are really two questions here: how the artist knows when *he* is finished, and how he knows when the *work* is finished. The first question is no doubt the easier. The artist comes to a point when he can no longer think of any way to improve his work.

---

23. "A Poet's Notebook," p. 178. Compare John Dryden's dedication of *The Rival Ladies* (in Ghiselin, *The Creative Process*, p. 77): "When the fancy was yet in its first work, moving the sleeping images of things toward the light, there to be distinguished, and then either chosen or rejected by the judgment." The drafts of Yeats's "Sailing to Byzantium," written on loose-leaf pages over several years, show how fertile he was in alternative possibilities for lines we now know so well, and that his problem was to select and combine; see Curtis Bradford, "Yeats's Byzantium Poems: A Study of Their Development," *PMLA* 75 (1960):110–25. (I am indebted to Robert Daniel, of Kenyon College, for this example.) See also Martin K. Nurmi, "Blake's Revisions of *The Tyger*," *PMLA* 71 (1956):669–85.

24. "Poetry and Abstract Thought," p. 76. This is echoed by Richard Wilbur in *The Nature of Creative Thinking*, p. 59, and by Ben Shahn in *The Shape of Content* (see selection in Tomas, ed., *Creativity in the Arts*, p. 20).

25. I. A. Richards, "How Does a Poem Know When It Is Finished?" in *Parts and Wholes*, ed. Daniel Lerner (New York, 1963).

This becomes more and more difficult as the work progresses. In the early stages, lines and colors, stanzas and melodic fragments, can be added quite freely to see whether they can be assimilated. But in the later stages, as the work becomes more complex, the effect of every addition or alteration is more serious; a wrong line or color, a wrong word or melodic figure, can throw the whole thing badly off. Of course, the artist can never be certain he has done all he can. Happy is the painter who can say, with Matisse, "Then a moment comes when every part has found its definite relationship and from then on it would be impossible for me to add a stroke to my picture without having to paint it all over again."[26] Many a painter has been notorious for a never-say-die determination to hang on to his paintings in the hope that he will think of a way of bettering them—unless extreme poverty or a wily dealer induces him to part with them. (Valéry, by the way, says he wouldn't have published "Le Cimetière marin" when he did had it not been snatched from him. "Nothing is more decisive than the mind of an editor of a review," he remarks—though perhaps he could have put up more of a fight.)[27]

The artist generally knows, then, pretty well whether *he* is finished, but that is not the same as saying that the *work* is finished. For when the artist has done all he can, the question remains whether the work has enough to it, whether it is worthy of standing by itself, as an object of aesthetic enjoyment. If he judges so, the artist says it is done. If he judges not, the artist says it is unfinished. And of course the threshold of contentment varies enormously from artist to artist.

These points are illustrated by the famous puzzle of Schubert's Unfinished Symphony. Unlike most great unfinished works, it was not cut short by death (Schubert had six more years to live), but simply abandoned by the composer after he had completed two magnificent movements. Hans Gál has proposed an interesting solution.[28] Schubert began a scherzo in B-minor, which would have been the third movement. In the manuscript, the parts are at first quite fully indicated, then they drop out, as the composer loses interest, and the movement trails off in the trio. The trouble

---

26. "Notes of a Painter," in *The Problems of Aesthetics*, ed. Eliseo Vivas and Murray Krieger (New York, 1953), p. 259.
27. "A Poet's Notebook," p. 144.
28. "The Riddle of Schubert's Unfinished Symphony," *Music Review* 2 (1941): 63–67.

is that the opening subject is one of startling emptiness and dullness—and yet it is a compulsive theme, hard to get away from once it is started, especially if the scherzo must be in the conventional key. "Those obtrusive four bars," as Gál calls them, get a grip on the composer; he cannot shake them off, or, apparently, find a way of starting anew so long as every time he picks up the manuscript they stare him in the face. If we agree with Gál's hypothesis, the scherzo is a formidable example of a composition that cannot be well finished, even by a master. It must have required a powerful force indeed to make a composer leave off a symphony so excellently begun.[29]

In one respect, the foregoing account diverges from a remark by Rudolf Arnheim in his study of Picasso's *Guernica*. Arnheim speaks of the creative process as being "goal-directed throughout"[30]—a view I challenged earlier. And summing up the whole process, he says, "A germinal idea, precise in its general tenor but unsettled in its aspects, acquired its final character by being tested against a variety of possible visual realizations. When at the end, the artist was willing to rest his case on what his eyes and hands had arrived at, he had become able to see what he meant."[31] I would not put such stress on the words if these two sentences had not been so exact and eloquent up to the final clause. But the words "become able to see what he meant" seem to imply that what Picasso ended with was an expression, an explication, an embodiment, a realization, or whatever of what was already in his mind at the start. Better, I think, to say that he had become able to mean something much better than he was able to mean a few months before, and that what he now was able to mean—that is, to make—was enough.

To draw together these remarks and examples, perhaps we can decide how far to generalize. Though there are no universal *stages* of the creative process, there are two clearly marked *phases*, which constantly alternate throughout. They involve an interplay between conscious and preconscious activities. There is the *inventive* phase, traditionally called *inspiration*, in which new ideas are form-

---

29. It is harder to understand what distractions led Mozart to abandon the more than 100 unfinished compositions (not counting the *Requiem*) that his widow preserved for us. Perhaps they simply looked less promising financially than other projects, and he never found the time to turn back to them. See Erich Hertzmann, "Mozart's Creative Process," *Musical Quarterly* 43 (1957):187–200.

30. Arnheim, Picasso's "Guernica," p. 134.

31. Ibid., p. 135.

ed in the preconscious and appear in consciousness. And there is the *selective* phase, which is nothing more than criticism, in which the conscious chooses or rejects the new idea after perceiving its relationships to what has already tentatively been adopted.

The problem of what goes on in the preconscious is apparently still unsolved. We would like to know how it is that a composer, having sung two bars to himself, suddenly thinks of a way to continue it; or that a painter, having outlined a figure, thinks of certain colors that might be added; or that a poet may look at a line he has just written and think of possible substitute words. To take a few examples from R. P. Blackmur,[32] suppose the poet has written "breathless tiptoeing," and it occurs to him that "flowering tiptoeing" might be better; or suppose he has written "chance deepening to choice" and substitutes "chance flowering to choice." Whether the new words are better than the old is the question to be decided by his conscious mind, but why one set of words rather than another comes to consciousness is the more mysterious question.

The psychological dispute seems to be formulable this way: to what extent are the preconscious processes associative; to what extent do they involve closure or strengthening of gestalts?[33] As far as I can make out, both of these processes seem necessary to account for what the preconscious presents to the conscious. If, for example, "flowering" replaces "deepening" because of some meaningful connection of this figure with other images earlier in the poem, then we can say that the unconscious has found some degree of closure. On the other hand, the substitution may have only a very remote relationship to other words already set down, but it may serve to break down an existing gestalt, to introduce a more unstable cluster of meanings, which may lead to a more inclusive synthesis later. In this case, the word "flowering" would be described as due to free—or at least freer—association. It seems evident, in any case, that unless the preconscious can produce both kinds of ideas—those that close a gestalt and those that break one—poems could not get composed, nor could paintings or musical works.

32. *Poets at Work*, p. 48.
33. This is the point at issue, for example, between Lawrence S. Kubie, *Neurotic Distortion of the Creative Process* (Lawrence, Kans., 1948), esp. pp. 53–61, and Arnheim, *Picasso's "Guernica,"* p. 70.

V

It is no doubt high time to face up to the question that is bound to arise after all these reflections and speculations about the creative process: what is the point of them? Or, in other words: what difference does it make to our relationship with the arts that we understand the creative process in one way or another? And here my answer is brief and unequivocal. It makes no difference at all. I think it is interesting in itself to know, if we can, how the artist's mind works, but I do not see that this has any bearing on the value of what he produces. For that value is independent of the manner of production, even of whether the work was produced by an animal or by a computer or by a volcano or by a falling slop bucket.[34]

This statement would be vigorously repudiated by some who have studied the creative process: they claim that their studies throw light on the "meaning" and "beauty" of poems, to use the words of Donal Stauffer in "Genesis, or the Poet as Maker."[35] If we knew, says Stauffer, the genesis of a poem by Housman, it would "enable us to interpret this particular work with more precision." But his method puts the enterprise in none too favorable a light, it seems to me. Digging through the early stages of the composition of Marianne Moore's poem "The Four Songs," he finds a typescript in which the poem is titled "Poet to Lover (Admitting Limitations)." Moreover, he turns up other titles that the poet considered and rejected: "Poet to Plain-Reader," "Poet to Ordinary Man," and, oddly, "Asphodel." (This poem has as many titles as the White Knight's song "A-sitting on a Gate.") All these titles, says Mr. Stauffer, "should prove of value in interpreting the complete poem,"[36] and he proceeds to put them to use. But think of the implications. The poet discards the titles, and the genetic interpreter plucks them out of the wastebasket and uses them as though they had not been discarded. This is a pretty high-handed way to treat Marianne Moore. The logic of the situation is clear. Either the title of a poem makes a difference to the way it is read or it does not. If not, then knowing the discarded titles has no effect on our interpretation. If so, then each title makes a slightly different poem, and Mr. Stauffer is simply re-

---

34. For a decisive argument along this line, see John Hospers, "The Concept of Artistic Expression," *Proceedings of the Aristotelian Society* 55 (1955):313–44.
35. In *Poets at Work*, p. 43.
36. Ibid., p. 63.

fusing to read the poem that Miss Moore wanted us to read. Granted that her choice does not have to be final; some of the titles she threw away could conceivably be better than the one she kept. (After all, remember the time she was commissioned to suggest names for a brand-new car that the Ford Motor Company was planning to bring out. She came up with some lovely ones, but in the end they called it the Edsel.) But if you do not accept her title, then at least do not pretend that you are interpreting her final poem.

The informed observer will, of course, detect in these genetic maneuvers a particularly persuasive form of that vulgar error which William Wimsatt, Jr., and I stigmatized some years ago as the intentional fallacy. I do not know whether it is in good taste for me to rake over these old coals, but whenever a fallacy gets to be so old-fashioned and so familiar as this one, it is always heartening to find new instances of it, so that you know you are not beating a dead horse—even if he is not exactly the picture of health. What we attacked under a single name (intentionalism) was in fact two closely related forms of unsound argument: that which attributes a certain meaning to a work on the ground that the artist intended the work to have that meaning, and that which appraises the work at a certain value on the ground that it does or does not fulfill the artist's intention. If we took to interpreting poems in terms of what they were like before they were finished, we would be turning the whole creative process upside down, by refusing to consider the final product on its own terms. Let this method become popular, and you can expect poets, painters, and musicians to keep their wastebaskets emptied by burning their early sketches just as soon as possible.

Is this our final conclusion, then—that questions about creativity are irrelevant to questions about actual works of art? Somehow it does not seem enough. From the beginning of thought about art, though in many different forms, the creativity of art has been noted and pondered. Associationists, intuitionists, romantics, and idealists have offered explanations. In the making of such works, something very special seems to be happening; something fresh is added to the world; something like a miracle occurs. All this is true. There is such a thing as creativity in art, and it is a very important thing. What I want to say is that the true locus of creativity is not the genetic process prior to the work but the work itself as it lives in the experience of the beholder. Let me explain—all too briefly and puzzlingly, no doubt—what I mean.

To begin with, what is a melody? It is, as we all know, a gestalt, something distinct from the notes that make it up, yet dependent on them for its existence. And it has its own quality, which cannot be a quality of any particular note or little set of notes. Recall that melody from Beethoven's E-flat quartet—grave, serene, soaring, affirmative, yet in a way resigned. Now when we hear a melody, however simple, we hear two levels of things at once: the individual notes and the regionally qualified melody that emerges from them. We hear the melody being born out of the elements that sustain it; or we hear the elements, the tones and intervals, coming together in an order that calls into existence an entity distinct from them, and superior to them. In the experience of a melody, creation occurs before our very ears. And the more intense the created qualities, the more complex the sets of cooperating elements, the tighter their mutual relations, the more fully we can participate in that basic aesthetic experience.

I need not argue in detail that the same holds for works of fine art. The essential feature of such a work—I am tempted to say, but recognizing that I am likely to sound dogmatic—the essential feature is not merely that certain visual elements (lines, shapes, colors) are assembled together, but that as we concentrate on their natures and relations, we become aware, suddenly or gradually, of what they add up to as a whole. For what they add up to is not an addition at all, but the projection of a new pattern, a new quality of grace or power.

When we consider a poem in this perspective, we see again that the important creativity is in the operation of the work itself. The sound qualities, such as meter and rhyme patterns, are one sort of emergent quality; more important, the interactions and interinanimations of words, in figurative or unusual language, create hitherto unmeant meanings; and more important, the objects and events of the poem mysteriously are made to accumulate symbolic reverberations, by which they seem to have a significance far beyond themselves. And this takes place in the act of reading; the excitement of seeing it happen is precisely the peculiar excitement of reading poetry.

The British literary critic L. C. Knights has made some comments that seem to me very similar to what I want to say, in a special issue of *The Times Literary Supplement*, on "The Critical Moment."[37] His example is from Wordsworth's famous sonnet

---

37. July 26, 1963, p. 569.

> Dull would he be of soul, who could pass by
> A sight so touching in its majesty.

That is a strange combination of ideas—"touching" and "majesty." Knights says this:

> The peculiar pleasure of that last line—though the pleasure is independent of conscious recognition of the source—comes from the movement of mind by which we bring together in one apprehension 'touching' and 'majesty': feelings and attitudes springing from our experience of what is young and vulnerable, that we should like to protect, fuse with our sense of things towards which we feel awe, in respect of which it is we who are young, inexperienced or powerless.

The "movement of mind" of which he speaks, in bringing these two opposed feelings into a fusion, through the words of the poem, is an act of creation, for out of that fusion comes a new, complex, vital feeling that has elements of both and yet is reducible to neither. So, says Knights, the creative use of words "energizes" the mind—"new powers of vision and apprehension come into being."

It may seem that this way of looking at artistic creativity demeans the artist by making not him, but the work itself, the creative thing. But I do not think so. I do not forget that man is the maker—of nearly all the great works we have, or are likely to have. but the finest qualities of a work of art cannot be imposed on it directly and by fiat; the artist can, after all, only manipulate the elements of the medium so that *they* will make the quality emerge. He can create a solemn melody only by finding a sequence of notes that will have that quality. The powers he works with are, in the end, not his own but those of nature.[38] And the miracle he makes is a miracle that celebrates the creative potentialities inherent in nature itself. But when in this way the artist makes

---

38. This is a good place to recall those marvelous words I have quoted elsewhere: the reply of Polixenes, in *The Winter's Tale*, when Perdita says she cares not for the "streak'd gillyvors / which some call nature's bastards":

> *Perdita.* For I have heard it said
> There is an art which in their piedness shares
> With great creating nature.
> *Polixenes.* Say there be;
> Yet nature is made better by no mean
> But nature makes that mean—so, over that art,
> Which you say adds to nature, is an art
> That nature makes. . . .
> The Art itself is nature.

plain to use over and over the marvelous richness of nature's potentialities, he also presents us with a model of man's hope for control over nature, and over himself. Artistic creation is nothing more than the production of a self-creative object. It is in our intelligent use of what we are given to work with, both in the laws of the universe and in the psychological propensities of human beings, that we show our mastery, and our worthiness to inhabit the earth. In this broad sense, we are all elected, or perhaps condemned, to be artists. And what keeps us going in the roughest times is the reminder that not all the forms and qualities and meanings that are to emerge in the fullness of time have already appeared under the sun—that we do not know the limits of what the universe can provide or of what can be accomplished with its materials.

15: *The Metaphorical Twist*

I

OF all the questions about metaphor that interest the literary theorist or philosophic aesthetician, the foremost—that is, first and fundamental—one is, of course: what is it? To give an adequate account of metaphor as linguistic phenomenon, on which to base our account of it as poetic phenomenon, is to say what is peculiar to metaphorical expressions, how they differ from literal ones, how we recognize them and know what they mean.

It is not easy to say exactly what are the issues over this problem. There are several ways of describing metaphor, some of them going back to ancient times, that are so familiar and so confidently echoed from one writer to another that they all have the air of being roughly equivalent. But there is, I believe, an important distinction among them, and part of my purpose here is to drive a wedge—to separate things out more sharply than has been done. I want to distinguish what might be called a thing approach and a word approach to the problem of analyzing metaphor.

According to one of these views, taken broadly, the modifier (as I call it) in the metaphor—for example, the word "spiteful" in "the spiteful sun"—retains its standard designative role when it enters into the metaphor and therefore continues in that context to denote the same objects it denotes in literal contexts. Thus the metaphor is an implicit comparison, an elliptical simile, and says in effect that the sun is like a spiteful person. The spiteful person is referred to, in this context, just as is the sun—there are two objects. The metaphor, as Johnson said, "gives you two ideas instead of one." John Crowe Ransom has classified metaphors as

"Importers" that introduce "foreign objects" into the "situation"[1]— I guess he was thinking of those fancy importers of exotic foodstuffs, like truffles and candied bees. The metaphor, in his view, drags an alien and uncalled-for object into the context (delighting us, the eighteenth-century theorist might say, by its charm and novelty), and thereby adds to that "local texture of irrelevance" that Ransom considers so essential to poetry.

Let us call this the object-comparison theory of metaphor. According to its rival, the verbal-opposition theory, no such importation or comparison occurs at all, but instead a special feat of language, or verbal play, involving two levels of meaning in the modifier itself. When a predicate is metaphorically adjoined to a subject, the predicate loses its ordinary extension because it acquires a new intension—perhaps ones that it has in no other context. And this twist of meaning is forced by inherent tensions, or oppositions, within the metaphor itself.

I propose to give reasons for rejecting the object-comparison theory, both in its general form and in a special form that has recently been offered. Then I shall explain more fully the verbal-opposition theory, and defend it against some possible objections.

II

Now up to a point, I admit, it does not matter whether you talk of metaphors in the object fashion or in the semantical fashion. But only up to a point. Thus suppose the word "briar" is introduced metaphorically into a certain context, as, say, in "East Coker"— the reference to

>   frigid purgatorial fires
> Of which the flame is roses, and the smoke is briars.[2]

You can start your explication either in object language (talking about the characteristics of briars) or in metalanguage (talking about the connotations of the *word* "briars"). You can say, "Briars have the capacity to scratch people, to retard their progress, to be made into pipes," and so on. Or you can say, "The word 'briars' connotes such properties as being scratchy, retarding progress, being made into pipes," and so on. But though these two ways of

---

1. "William Wordsworth: Notes Toward an Understanding of Poetry," *Kenyon Review* 12 (Summer 1950):498–519.
2. T. S. Eliot, *Four Quartets* (New York, 1953), p. 16.

speaking overlap, since in part the connotations of the *word* derive from what is generally true of the *objects*, they do not coincide completely.

For the connotations are controlled not only by the properties the object actually has but by those it is widely *believed* to have—even if the belief is false. This is my first argument against the object-comparison theory, then—that a consistent adherence to that theory would produce incorrect or incomplete explications of metaphors in cases where the modifier has connotations, applicable in that context, that are not common accidental features of the objects denoted. For example, some of the important marginal meaning of "briars" in the Eliot poem comes, of course, from the way the crown of thorns figures in the Christian story. And quite apart from its historical truth, the existence of that religion is sufficient to give the word that meaning. If in explicating this line we limit ourselves to what we know about briars, we will not fully understand it.

My second argument against the object-comparison theory is that once we commit ourselves to finding, or supplying, an object to be compared with the subject of the metaphor (that is, in I. A. Richards' terms, a "vehicle" to make it go), we open the way for that flow of idiosyncratic imagery that is one of the serious barriers between a reader and a poem. Consider an example also discussed by Ransom, the lines about Brutus' sword in Anthony's speech:

> Mark how the blood of Caesar follow'd it,
> As rushing out of doors, to be resolv'd
> If Brutus so unkindly knock'd or no.   [III, ii, 178]

Ransom speaks of the "shift" from the tenor (the blood) to a "page" opening the door, the page being the vehicle.[3] Now there is obviously no page in these lines, any more than there is a rudely awakened householder or soon-to-be-embattled farmer alarmed by Paul Revere. Where does the page come from? The tenor–vehicle terminology, with its underlying assumption that the metaphor must be a comparison, tempts the explicator to invent, where he cannot discover, a vehicle; and so we get the page. But "rushing out of doors" is not exactly synonymous with "page rushing out of doors," as applied to Caesar's blood. And it is the first

---

3. "Poetry: I. The Formal Analysis; II. The Final Cause," *Kenyon Review* 9 (Summer 1947):436–56; (Autumn 1947):640–58.

meaning that the explicator is to keep his eye on, not the further meaning imported—a good description—by his own fancy. Quoting a characteristic metaphor of Samuel Johnson's, "Time is, of all modes of existence, most obsequious to the imagination," William K. Wimsatt, Jr., remarks, "We need not imagine Time as a butler bowing to his master the Imagination."[4]

My third argument against the object-comparison theory is that it tends to lead to the unfortunate doctrine of "appropriateness." If a metaphor is a comparison, it is possible to ask whether the comparison is apt or farfetched. We see this in Aristotle's fourth type of bad taste, his objection to the phrase of Gorgias "events that are fresh and full of blood."[5] If we take Macbeth's words (II, iii)

> their daggers
> Unmannerly breech'd with gore

to be comparing bloody daggers and breeched legs, and if we inquire into its appropriateness, we are likely to say, like the nineteenth-century critic quoted by Cleanth Brooks,[6] that Shakespeare "disgusts us with the attempted comparison." But the correct question is what is *meant* by the words—what properties are attributed to the daggers via the marginal meanings of the metaphorical attribute. It is of no moment whether bloody daggers in general are best so described; the question is what we learn from this description about *these* daggers, and their role in the whole story—or about the speaker who describes them this way.

To put the point more generally: suppose the poet remarks, "My sweetheart is my Schopenhauer." According to the comparison theory we are to ask what his sweetheart and Schopenhauer have in common. But we don't *know* his sweetheart, so how can we answer this question until he tells us, by the metaphor itself, what she is like? The correct question is what possible meanings of "Schopenhauer" can apply to the sweetheart, and are not ruled out by the context.

4. *The Prose Style of Samuel Johnson*, Yale Studies in English, vol. 94 (New Haven, 1941), p. 66.
5. Lane Cooper, trans., *The Rhetoric of Aristotle* (New York, 1932), p. 192.
6. *The Well Wrought Urn* (New York, 1947), p. 29. The New Variorum Edition, ed. H. H. Furness, 5th ed., (Philadelphia, 1915), pp. 160–61, shows amusingly what a nagging puzzle this metaphor has been to Shakespearean explicators.

III

My general objections to the object-comparison theory apply, I believe, with like force to the very interesting form of this theory that has been advanced by Paul Henle: the iconic signification theory.[7] Henle actually seems to hold both of the theories that I have named. His version of the verbal-opposition theory, however, is described in terms of the reader's response—his "shock" at the "clash of meanings."[8] I prefer to state the theory as a theory not about the effect of metaphor, but about the linguistic structure that causes the effect—about the "clash of meanings" itself. Henle says little about this, and he does not say why there should be any shock, or any clash, if the other is correct.

Henle holds that "there is an iconic element in metaphor," and he proposes to analyze metaphorical attributions in terms of the concept of iconic signs. In this example from Keats, "hateful thoughts enwrap my soul in gloom," he says there are two relationships: first, the word "enwrap" designates a certain action—"envelopment in a cloak." Second, this action is made an iconic sign of gloom.[9] "In a metaphor, some terms symbolize the icon and others symbolize what is iconized."[10]

We might begin by asking how the cloak gets into this explication. The iconic theory seems to import an alien object of some sort—like Ransom's page—and it is subject to the difficulties in the theory of importation. Henle has even yielded to the "appropriateness" doctrine, which, as I suggested, the comparison theory at least makes tempting. Thus he says that "it would not have done to speak of hateful thoughts *entrapping* the soul in gloom," because traps "are all sharp, with definite edges, and this spoils the correspondence with gloom."[11] Perhaps I should not put so much stress on this remark, but I must say that it would generalize into a most astonishing critical principle. For my part, I think the question whether wraps or traps are better iconic signs

---

7. In his chapter on metaphor in *Language, Thought, and Culture*, ed. Paul Henle (Ann Arbor, 1958), chap. 7, a development, and also a modification, of the view earlier set forth briefly in his presidential address to the Western Division of the American Philosophical Association, "The Problem of Meaning," in *Proceedings and Addresses of the American Philosophical Association* 28 (Yellow Springs, O., 1954).
8. *Language, Thought, and Culture*, pp. 182–83.
9. Ibid., pp. 177–79.
10. Ibid., p. 181.
11. Ibid., p. 180.

of gloom is a wholly unanswerable question, and fortunately it does not need to be asked. If the speaker in the poem had been trapped in gloom, rather than wrapped in it, that would simply have said something different about him, and about how he felt and came to feel that way—which might have made a worse poem or a better one, depending on several other things.

Henle cites one of Aristotle's examples of the way in which "proportional analogies" can be inverted: another is that we can say either that the shield is the bowl of Ares or the bowl is the shield of Dionysus.[12] "That such inversion is possible is of course a consequence of the iconic character of metaphor," says Henle.[13] And maybe it does follow from any object-comparison theory, for if A can be compared to B, why not B to A? And a statement of likeness is equivalent to its own converse. But if it follows, that is a fatal objection to the theory. Now Henle realizes that there is a difficulty, and so he says that though metaphors are always reversible, sometimes the "feeling tone is different." I don't believe this will do: the difference between "this man is a lion" and "that lion is a man"[14] is in what the different metaphorical modifiers attribute to the two subjects. In the verbal-opposition theory, it does not follow that because A's are metaphorically B's, therefore B's are metaphorically A's. That is just the difference between a metaphor and Aristotle's proportional analogy, or relational simile—even if Aristotle himself thought the difference was not great. And surely the verbal-opposition theory is correct in this consequence, while the iconic theory, if it entails that in calling men lions and lions men we are in both cases attributing the same properties, is clearly false.

One other objection can, I think, be fairly made against the iconic signification theory. It should be counted as a merit in a theory of metaphor that it can analyze metaphor in the same terms that will do for oxymoron. This makes for economy of theory, and it fits in with the evidently deep affinities between these two types of expression. Now the iconic theory is somewhat handicapped here, for it does not seem to work well for

---

12. Lane Cooper, trans., in ibid., p. 193.
13. *Language, Thought, and Culture*, p. 190.
14. I take this example, but not his explanation, from R. P. Blackmur, "Notes on Four Categories in Criticism," *Sewanee Review* 54 (October 1946):576–89. It would be, by the way, interesting to hear a defense of the reversibility of Ezra Pound's "Your mind and you are our Sargasso sea."

oxymoron. In "mute cry" (if that may be taken as an example), we should have to say that a mute person was being made an iconic sign of something that is not mute: soundlessness becomes a sign of sound. This is not very convincing. The truth seems rather to be that in oxymoron we have the archetype, the most apparent and intense form, of verbal opposition.

IV

If we turn from the objects referred to in the metaphor and consider the significations of the words themselves, we must look for the metaphoricalness of the metaphor, so to speak, in some sort of conflict that is absent from literal expressions. One direction in which this conflict has been searched for may, I think, be quickly marked off as a dead end. This approach contrasts the meaning of the expression itself and the idea in the speaker's (or writer's) mind. To call *A* a *B* metaphorically, on this view, is to say that *A* is a *B* without meaning it—metaphor is a form of irony.[15] The implicit appeal here is to intention, and the theory suffers from all the ills associated with that notion in the context of literary interpretation. We do not decide that a word in a poem is used metaphorically because we know what the poet was thinking; rather we know what he was thinking because we see that the word is used metaphorically. The clues to this fact must somehow be in the poem itself, or we should seldom be able to read poetry.

There is a hint of a similar view in the excellent account of metaphor in Isabel Hungerland's book.[16] In the metaphor, she says, "there must be some ascertainable point in the deviation from or violation of ordinary usage—another way of putting it is that the violation must be deliberate." Hungerland has since said that the second clause here was inadvertent; I mention it only to empha-

---

15. Anthony Nemetz, in "Metaphor: The Daedalus of Discourse," *Thought* 33 (Autumn 1958):417–42, bases his argument on the formula that "a metaphor consists of two parts: 1. What is said; 2. What is meant" (p. 419); the question is, then, what is the relation between them? But this formulation gets the inquiry off on the wrong track. A metaphor is a "saying," just as a literal expression is: we can say things either literally or metaphorically, and in either case we can be understood to mean only what we can say. In a sarcastic remark, what is suggested is opposed to what is stated, but if we do not let the word "say" cover both, we are sure to think that interpreting the remark is a process of getting *around* it to a hidden intention behind.

16. *Poetic Discourse* (Berkeley, 1958), pp. 108–10.

size that the two clauses are surely far from equivalent, because accidental or unintended metaphors are perfectly possible.[17]

The opposition that renders an expression metaphorical is, then, within the meaning structure itself. The central features of such a verbal-opposition theory I have already expounded elsewhere,[18] but I should like to recapitulate them briefly here. In that version, I said that the possibility of the metaphorical performance—the opportunities that a living language presents for fooling around with meanings in this particular way—depend on a felt difference between two sets of properties that (at least in a given sort of context) are taken to be necessary conditions for applying the term correctly in a particular sense (these are the defining, or designated, properties, or the central meaning of the term in that sort of context); second, those properties that belong to the marginal meaning of the term, or (in the literary critic's sense of the word) its connotation—properties that a speaker can, in appropriate contexts, show that he attributes to an object by using that term without claiming to follow a rule that he would not apply the term to that kind of object if it did not have that property. I said that when a term is combined with others in such a way that there would be a logical opposition between its central meaning and that of the other terms, there occurs that shift from central to marginal meaning which shows us the word is to be taken in a metaphorical way. It is the only way it can be taken without absurdity. The term "logical opposition" here includes both direct incompatibility of designated properties and a more indirect incompatibility between the presuppositions of the terms—as when our concept of the sun rules out the possibility of voluntary behavior that is presupposed by the term "spiteful." The logical opposition is what gives the modifier its metaphorical twist.

A metaphorical attribution, then, involves two ingredients: a semantical distinction between two levels of meaning, and a logical opposition at one level. Thus there is no question of "spiteful," in a metaphorical context, denoting spiteful people and in-

---

17. See Walker Percy, "Metaphor as Mistake," *Sewanee Review* 66 (Winter 1958): 79–99. Percy shows interestingly how there can be "mistakes which . . . have resulted in an authentic poetic experience" (p. 80). Yet he too seems to weaken at the end, when he speaks of "that essential element of the meaning situation, the authority and intention of the Namer" (p. 93).
18. See *Aesthetics: Problems in the Philosophy of Criticism*, (New York, 1958), chap. 3.

jecting them for the purpose of comparison; the price it pays for admission to this context is that it function there to signify only its connoted characteristics.

Such is the simple verbal-opposition theory as I have defended it, and it seems to me to be right up to a point. That is, I believe that the phenomenon it describes, the shift from designation to connotation, actually occurs. But I am afraid it is not enough. Something else that is very important also happens in at least some metaphors, I now think.[19] And to explain it, we must make (or make more explicit than was done in the earlier version) two distinctions.

The connotations of a word standing for objects of a certain kind, it will be agreed, are drawn from the total set of accidental properties either found in or attributed to such objects. Let us call this set of accidental properties the *potential range of connotation* of that word. At a given time in the history of the word, however, not all of these properties will perhaps have been made use of. Thus, think of a number of properties characteristic of trees, though not necessarily present in all: leafiness, shadiness, branchiness, tallness, slimness, having bark, suppleness in the wind, strength, and so on. Some of these properties, such as leafiness, shadiness, tallness, clearly belong among the recognized connotations of "tree," readily called into play in familiar metaphors. They may be called *staple connotations*. Other properties, such as perhaps slimness and having bark, do not seem to be staple connotations, though they may be sufficiently characteristic of trees to be available in the potential range of connotation. They may wait, so to speak, lurking in the nature of things, for actualization—wait to be captured by the word "tree" as part of its meaning in some future context.

My first distinction, then, is between two sets of accidental properties—not a sharp distinction, not one that can always be cut with confidence, but still objectively determinable. My second distinction is between two kinds of metaphor, and it is subject to similar qualifications.

---

19. The part that is new (to me) in my present account of metaphor did not occur to me until after, and in the light of, the papers by Henle and Hungerland, who were my fellow symposiasts when the present paper, in a different form, was read before the 17th annual meeting of the American Society for Aesthetics, Cincinnati, October 29–31, 1959. Henle's crticisim of the verbal-opposition theory as incapable of explaining the element of novelty in metaphorical meaning, and the discussion that followed the papers led me to the present line of thought.

Suppose we begin by trying to divide metaphors into two classes. Let us try putting into Class I such metaphors as "smiling sun" and "the moon peeping from behind a cloud." Note that these are not dead metaphors—that is not the problem involved here. They are live, but somehow they are different from those we might put into Class II: "the spiteful sun," "unruly sun," "faithful sun," "inconstant moon." We recognize, it seems safe to say, that those in Class II are more interesting than those in Class I—which is not, of course, to say that they are better in every poetic context. But what is the difference?

Now, in terms of the simple verbal-opposition theory, something can be said by way of explanation. The Class II metaphors are more complex than the Class I metaphors. They seem to say more about the object. They are thus more precise, more discriminating, as descriptions. To speak of the sun as "smiling" is to imply a broad contrast with a sun that does not succeed in smiling, perhaps, or that is angry and beats down on the desert. but to speak of the sun as "unruly" is to imply a sharper distinction between this quality and other qualities conceived with comparable specificity: obedience, punctuality, deference to one's wishes. Now the verbal-opposition theory, even in its simple form, allows degrees of complexity, and so perhaps it can at least partly explain the difference between the two classes. Yet there seems to be more to the matter even than this.

It is at this point that we encounter a very tricky question indeed. For one suggestion that seems obvious enough is this: the Class I metaphors are trite and banal; the Class II metaphors are fresh and novel. If there is truth in this description, it can be won and kept only by skillful maneuvering around some deceptive shoals. In the first place, we must not, I think, suppose that it is a matter of mere repetition. Perhaps "smiling sun" has been said more often than "inconstant moon," but even if we were to repeat the phrase from *Romeo and Juliet* over and over until we were tired of it, and therefore were in no position to attend to its meaning, that would not alone make it trite. In any case, if triteness is a frequency notion, then it is not what makes the difference here. Yet in the second place, the nature of a particular metaphor cannot be entirely independent of its date in the history of English literature. For what it does mean, or can mean, at a given time must depend to some extent on what other contexts the words have appeared in, and what analogous or parallel expressions exist in the language.

V

Let us suppose that when the metaphor "th' inconstant moon" is first constructed in English, it is the first time that "inconstant" has been used metaphorically—or at least the first time it has been applied to an inanimate object. (This, of course, does not preclude the possibility that it may originally have applied *only* to inanimate objects, say, to their rotational motion; if at some time it came to have the psychological or behavioral meaning as its primary one, then we can speak of the first metaphorical use after this time.) At this moment the word "inconstant" *has* no connotations. When, therefore, we find "inconstant moon," we seize upon the verbal opposition, all right, but when we look for relevant connotations we are balked. How, then, can we explicate it? Given the surrounding syntax and the prevailing tone, it claims to make sense; therefore we must try to make it make sense. And so we look about among the accidental or contingent properties of inconstant people in general, and attribute these properties, or as many of them as we can, to the moon. And these properties would, for the moment at least, become part of the meaning of "inconstant," though previously they were only properties of those people. Then we might say that the metaphor transforms a *property* (actual or attributed) into a *sense*. And if, taking their lead from this license, other poets were to find other metaphorical applications for "inconstant," which employed the same properties and created similar, or overlapping, senses, then those senses might become closely enough connected with the word so that they would be relatively fixed as connotations of that word. In this way the metaphors would not only actualize a potential connotation, but establish it as a staple one.

Here is where the object-comparison theory makes its contribution after all. For it is correct in saying that sometimes in explicating metaphors we must consider the properties of the objects denoted by the modifier. But those objects are not referred to for comparison: they are referred to so that some of their relevant properties can be given a new status as elements of verbal meaning.

Let us suppose that at a given time in the history of the English language we have already in existence such metaphors as "smiling sky," "smiling sea," and "smiling garden." The modifier cannot, of course, mean exactly the same thing in all these contexts, but there will be some meaning in common. And let us suppose this common meaning is already established as the connotation of "smiling." When a poet for the first time speaks of a "smiling sun," what will happen? The logical opposition is plain, so we turn first to the staple connotations of "smiling" and apply them to the sun (as the simple verbal-opposition theory says). But we go no further. Perhaps we cannot go further; perhaps we are just not forced to. In any case, we see that it is a metaphor, and we can read it correctly, but we do not take it as *creating* meaning in the same way as Class II metaphors. It is merely borrowing its sense, relying on what is already established and available.

The revised theory can be well illustrated by a very interesting metaphor that I have borrowed from Paul Henle. In one of his devotional works, Jeremy Taylor says that "chaste marriages are honourable and pleasing to God," that widowhood can be "amiable and comely when it is adorned with gravity and purity," but that "virginity is a life of angels, the enamel of the soul."[20] This was not the earliest metaphorical use of "enamel"; we learn from the NED that Donne, in 1631, had already used the phrase "enameled with that beautiful Doctrine of good Workes," and that Evelyn, in 1670, had used the phrase "enamel their characters." Moreover, Taylor himself, in the dedication to his *Sermons*, spoke of "those truths which are the enamel and beauty of our churches." Perhaps such usages had already established some of the properties of enamel as staple connotations of the word; perhaps not. We would have to know this in order to know exactly how definitely in Class II was the metaphor "the enamel of the soul" in the context of Taylor's *Of Holy Living*. But of our own time we can make a surer judgment. Enamel is hard, resistant to shock and scrape, applied with labor and skill, and decorative. I should think some of these are not fully established as recognized connotations of the word. Yet to speak of virginity as the enamel of the soul is surely to say (as Henle points out) that it is a protection for the soul, and that it is the final touch of adornment on what is already well made. Thus this metaphor does not merely thrust latent connotations into the foreground of meaning, but brings into play some properties that were not previously meant by it.

It seems to me that we probably have to distinguish at least three stages in this metamorphosis of verbal meaning, even though

---

20. *Of Holy Living*, chap. 2, sec. 3, in *Works*, ed. C. P. Eden, vol. 3 (London, 1847), p. 56. Henle used this example in his symposium paper.

the points of transition are not clearly marked. In the first stage we have a word and properties that are definitely not part of the intension of that word. Some of those properties are eligible to become part of the intension, to join the range of connotation. In order to be eligible, they have to be fairly common (actual or imputed) properties, typical properties—not just in the statistical sense, but normally or characteristically present in the objects denoted by the word. Thus, for example, suppose someone said that whiteness could become a connotation of "enamel." This could happen, I should think, if most or all enamel were white, or if enamel were usually white except when affected by external conditions, or if the best enamel were white, or if the whitest white things were enameled things.

When the word comes to be used metaphorically in a certain sort of context, then what was previously only a property is made, at least temporarily, into a meaning. And widespread familiarity with that metaphor, or similar ones, can fix the property as an established part of the meaning. It is still, in this second stage, not a necessary condition for applying the word. Even if "tree" connotes tallness, there is no contradiction in speaking of a short or stunted tree. Still, if someone said that his tree was a tree "in the fullest sense" (compare "He is in every sense a man"), we should, I think, be justified in taking him to be saying, among other things, that it had reached a good height, at least for its species.

When a connotation becomes so standardized for certain types of context, it may be shifted to a new status, where it becomes a necessary condition for applying the word in that context. It then constitutes a new standard sense. This third stage is illustrated by the dead metaphor: "tail," used in connection with automobile lights, now owes nothing to animal tails, and its meaning can be learned by someone who never heard that animals had tails. Not all connotations, of course, pass into this third stage, but some are always doing so.

Perhaps some portion of this history can be traced in words, such as "warm" and "hard," that are taken over from the sensory realm and applied to human personality—as apparently happens in many languages.[21] I should think that the first application of

---

21. These personality metaphors have been interestingly investigated by Solomon E. Asch in "On the Use of Metaphor in the Description of Persons," in *On*

"warm" to a person had to change some accidental properties of warm things into part of a new meaning of the word, though now we easily think of these properties as connotations of "warm"—for example, approachable, pleasurable in acquaintance, inviting. These qualities were part of the potential range of connotation of "warm" even before they were noted in warm things, which may not have been until they were noted in people and until someone, casting about for a word that would metaphorically describe those people, hit upon the word "warm." But before those qualities could come to belong to the staple connotation of "warm," it had to be discovered that they could be *meant* by the word when used in an appropriate metaphor. Finally, although it has not happened yet, "warm person" may come to lose its metaphorical character, with the present connotations of "warm" changing into a new designation. It would then be a dead metaphor.

If the revised verbal-opposition theory is correct, it would account for a good deal. It does better than the simple theory at explaining the remarkable extent to which metaphor can expand our verbal repertoire beyond the resources of literal language.[22] It allows for novelty, for change of meaning, even for radical change. It admits the unpredictability of metaphor, the surprising ideas that may emerge even from chance juxtapositions of words. It shows that a metaphor can be objectively explicated, for the properties of things and the connotations of words are publicly discoverable, and disputes about them are in principle resolvable.

Expressive Language, ed. H. Werner (Worcester, Mass., 1955), and "The Metaphor: A Psychological Inquiry," in *Person Perception and Interpersonal Behavior*, ed. R. Tagiuri and L. Petrullo (Stanford, 1958). See also Roger Brown, *Words and Things* (Glencoe, Ill., 1958), pp. 145–54.

22. This is the way I interpret Wallace Stevens' poem "The Motive for Metaphor" (in *The Collected Poems of Wallace Stevens* [New York: Alfred A. Knopf, 1955; copyright 1923, 1931, 1935, 1936, 1937, 1942, 1943, 1944, 1945, 1946, 1947, 1948, 1949, 1950, 1951, 1952, 1954 by Wallace Stevens], p. 286): metaphor enables us to describe, to fix and preserve, the subtleties of experience and change ("the half colors of quarter-things" in springtime), while words in their standard dictionary designations can only cope with

> The weight of primary noon,
> The A B C of being,
> The ruddy temper, the hammer
> Of red and blue. . . .

It seems to me quite correct to say that new metaphors enlarge our linguistic resources, even if they do not "expand meaning" in the narrow sense objected to by J. Szrednicki in "On Metaphor," *Philosophical Quarterly* 10 (July 1960):228–37.

And it explains the comparative obscurity, or momentary puzzlingness, of the Class II metaphor, which may take time to understand completely.

VI

It seems that, in its revised form, the verbal-opposition theory may go a long way toward providing a satisfactory account of metaphor—if it can be defended against two possible lines of objection that are suggested by recent developments.

The first objection might be raised by those who are committed to an extensionalist philosophy of language. The verbal-opposition theory cannot be formulated without speaking of properties. Could we not, one might ask, get along without the concept of incompatibility, and treat metaphors as simply a special case of materially *false* statements? Of course there is a difference between saying that someone is bald when he isn't and saying that he is a lion when he isn't. But perhaps the difference is merely that the latter is more surprising, more obviously and certainly known to be untrue. We see how the speaker might make a mistake about baldness, but we don't see how he could confuse a man with a lion, and so it is the sheer improbability of the latter remark (in the light of common knowledge) that makes us reject it literally and take it metaphorically, rather than any internal opposition of meaning.

We could make out a case for this improbability theory of metaphor, and we can even support it by examples of certain degenerate cases of metaphor that may be analyzable in this way. For example, the joker says, "I was in Philadelphia once, but it was closed."[23] Is this really self-contradictory? True, the word "closed" is ordinarily, and most appropriately, applied to individual enterprises, such as stores and museums, which have doors that can be locked and bolted. But perhaps without stretching the term very much, a whole city could be literally closed, too. Let us suppose so. In that case, the peculiar metaphorical effect—the denigration of the vitality of Philadelphia night life—must depend on our rejecting the statement as false out of hand, because it is

---

23. Another example has been given by Kenneth Burke in "Semantic and Poetic Meaning," in *The Philosophy of Literary Form* (Baton Rouge, 1941), p. 144: "New York City is in Iowa" can mean that the influence of New York stretches out, like its railway tracks, into the West.

so absurdly unlikely. Yet granting that this verbal maneuver occurs, it does not cover all the cases. At the opposite extreme is oxymoron. A reviewer in the *Reporter* a while back described the literary figures of the Beat Movement as "writers who don't write who write." That is not merely improbable. And it seems to me that metaphors, for the most part, have something of this built-in self-controversion, quite distinguishable from the Philadelphia crack. Borderline cases there of course must be, where there is a not-too-remote possibility of taking the modifier in a way that will literally apply to the subject: for example, the phrase "bak'd with frost," in Shakespeare's *Tempest* (I, ii, 256), where "bak'd" could mean "thickened," and so the whole expression could have been literal in Shakespeare's time.[24]

The second objection to the verbal-opposition theory might be put this way: even if there are properties to be opposed, they are not, in ordinary language, so fixed in the designation of general terms that sharp and clear contradiction can occur. It is conceded that "brother" and "male sibling" may be practically perfect synonyms, as far as their central meanings are concerned (ignoring their connotations), and so "female brother" is internally contradictory—though not much of a metaphor, of course. But the thesis is that for most of the interesting words, the rules are not so definite, and so when these words are used metaphorically it cannot be because we detect an incompatibility of meaning on the level of designation.

Michael Scriven[25] has argued that the word "lemon" has, in fact, no defining properties in the traditional sense—that is, properties that *must* be present if the word is to be correctly applied to an object. He quotes Webster's definition, "the acid fruit of a tree (*citrus limonia*), related to the orange," and this does not seem to give necessary conditions of lemonness, since it would not be a contradicton to say that a lemon grew on a banana tree, or no tree at all. Scriven, however, goes further, and claims that there is no single property of lemons that is individually necessary, if many others are present. And he holds that the same is true of most

---

24. See the interesting papers by Allan Gilbert, "Shakespeare's Amazing Words," *Kenyon Review* 11 (Summer 1949):484–88, and Andrew Schiller, "Shakespeare's Amazing Words," *Kenyon Review* 11 (Winter 1949):43–49.
25. "Definitions, Explanations, and Theories," in *Concepts, Theories, and the Mind-Body Problem*, ed. Herbert Feigl, Michael Scriven, and Grover Maxwell, Minnesota Studies in the Philosophy of Science, vol. 2 (Minneapolis, 1958), pp. 105–7.

general terms in common use. They designate what he calls "cluster concepts," and have "criteria" of application, but not necessary conditions.

This important idea, if it can be sustained, would require some reformulation of the verbal-opposition theory as I have stated it above. It would not destroy the theory by implying that if the theory is true then the word "lemon" cannot be used metaphorically—as it evidently can. Scriven himself speaks of literal meaning as having "a shifting boundary beyond which only misuse and metaphor lie."[26] If "lemon" has no necessary conditions, then it cannot be placed in a verbal context where some necessary condition is logically excluded, but it may be placed in a context where so many of its criteria are excluded that it cannot be literally applied—as when a secondhand car turns out to be a lemon.

I am not convinced that "lemon" and other ordinary words have *no* necessary conditions, and Scriven now holds his former view only in a modified form. I should think, for example, that having a certain organic texture—instead of being made of wood or wax—would be a necessary condition of lemonness. Surely being a material object is a necessary condition—a "spiritual lemon" would either be not literally a lemon or not literally spiritual. The questions involved here are subtle, too subtle for this occasion. For example, if I were suddenly to come upon an object otherwise exactly like a lemon, but six feet in diameter, I suppose I could be persuaded to call it a giant "lemon"—I really haven't made up my mind. Does this show that I now use the property of being small-sized only as a "criterion," but not as a defining property, of lemons? Perhaps so—yet if someone says an object is a lemon *without* adding any remarks about its unusual size, I am justified, I think, in deducing that it is small. Perhaps we could follow a suggestion of Arthur Pap[27] and others who have discussed the "open texture"[28] of empirical terms, and weight the criteria as more or less required: distinguishing "degrees of meaning." Then we might identify a metaphorical modifier as one placed in a context where one of its more stringently required conditions is

26. Ibid., p. 119.
27. *Semantics and Necessary Truth* (New Haven, 1958), p. 327.
28. Friedrich Waismann, "Verifiability," in *Proceedings of the Aristotelian Society*, suppl. vol. 19 (London, 1945), pp. 119–50. See also Georg Henrik von Wright, *A Treatise on Induction and Probability* (London, 1951), chap. 6, sec. 2; and Pap, *Semantics and Necessary Truth*, chaps. 5, 11.

excluded. Even if small size is not an indispensable property of lemons, it might be a fairly central one, in which case a context that opposed this property would be enough to throw the word into a metaphorical posture.

This question I leave open here, satisfied for the present if I have shown that the verbal-opposition theory not only explains quite well a number of acknowledged features of metaphor, but makes no assumptions that a sound philosophy of language would be unwilling to grant.

PART IV

Some Persistent Issues in Aesthetics: Further Reflections

Introduction

PHILOSOPHERS who cling to their doctrines, resisting change through all vicissitudes, even in the face of cogent criticism, are charged with excessive stubbornness and a taint of dogmatism, while those who wear their doctrines lightly, eagerly rejecting or recasting them with every adverse breeze, are castigated for their fickleness and superficiality. Perhaps there is no perfect path between these philosophical vices, but one ideal acknowledges the claims of both correlative virtues: a willingness to enter into genuine discussion and to learn from others in a way that makes philosophy a social enterprise, and a sustained effort to see how far a particular position or line of argument can be maintained, can meet objections, can be patched and mended without becoming unwieldly and ramshackle—giving it (to the benefit of us all) the best possible run for its money, such as only a proud partisan can do.

The earliest essays reprinted in this volume were written nearly twenty years ago, and I am glad to say that I have succeeded, with notable help from students and colleagues on many campuses, in changing my mind (I believe for the better) on a number of the issues that I—along with many others—have been thinking about over these two decades. Many of my basic views, though by no means all, were formed before the impact of several developments in aesthetic theory that have rightly become the center of much discussion: Sibley's work on "aesthetic concepts," Arthur Danto's and George Dickie's work on art as an institution, E. H. Gombrich's work on the role of schemata in visual perception and representation, Nelson Goodman's revolutionary proposals for a new semiotic aesthetics, the emergence of structuralism and the philosophy of action as significant methods and conceptual schemes, especially in literary theory, the development of new and interesting forms of Marxism, extensions of Wittgenstein's notion of "seeing as," from *Philosophical Investigations*. Those views of mine were also formed before the most far-out sorts of contemporary experimentation in all the arts became familiar and were taken seriously by philosophers. All of these developments, as well as the essays and books of many other philosophers and art theorists, have modified my understanding of various matters and changed my mind on various points.

Yet there seems to have been a strong central thread of concern and inquiry running through my work in aesthetics since I first began teaching this subject regularly in 1947; and, looking back, I can see now that it was the articulation of the distinctively aesthetic point of view, together with systematic solutions to the various problems attendant upon this enterprise. Several fundamental views that I came to hold during the 1950s have been occasionally placed in jeopardy, yet I have not found it reasonable—yet—to abandon them, and some have even (in my judgment) been corroborated by later developments, or at least have proved readily adjustable, with minor necessary improvements, to those parts of the newer work that, in their turn, seem to hold up under critical scrutiny. Even if these fundamental views are mistaken, and will at some later time have to be scrapped, I believe it is worthwhile to see how far they can be carried, without being overcomplicated or trivialized into tautology. They still commend themselves strongly to me as taking up into themselves ideas of many other aestheticians, past and present, and giving reasonably clear and defensible answers to the most serious questions in aesthetics or the philosophy of art.

In the following essays I do not of course propose to review all the issues on which there have been interesting developments in the past twenty years and on which my views have been affected. Rather, I select a few connected issues that are still plainly basic, that are the focus of much discussion, and that I dealt with in one or more of the earlier essays in this volume. I welcome the opportunity to try to articulate my more recent thoughts on these issues, responding from time to time to criticisms or to alternative proposals (but in a rather selective manner that I hope will not be taken as a disparagement of the very many other writings I could well have commented on).

16: *Aesthetic Experience*

THOUGH some members of each opposing party would impugn so balanced a judgment, it is in my opinion still an open question whether it is possible—or, if possible, worthwhile—to distinguish a peculiarly aesthetic sort of experience. The question of possibility involves the debatability of the claim that there is a common character that is (1) discernible in a wide range of our encounters with the world and (2) justifiably called "aesthetic." The question of worthwhileness involves the debatability of the further claim that, once distinguished, this character is sufficiently substantial and noteworthy to serve as the ground for important theoretical constructions such as we shall come to in subsequent essays.

Before we begin our own search for this character, or inquire whether it has already been found, we ought to consider carefully what it is we are searching for, and how we shall know that we have found it. Our hope is to end up justified in saying that some experiences are marked by aesthetic character and some are not; and of those that have it, that some have it more markedly than others. Experiences with such character need not be universally associated with objects that belong to familiar artistic categories. (It is convenient to have the term "artkind instance" to cover poems, paintings, sculptures, musical compositions, dances, and so on, without—at this stage—raising or begging questions about the definition of art in general.) But to deserve the epithet "aesthetic," such experiences ought (1) to be obtainable commonly through, or in, the cognition of artkind instances, (2) to be obtainable in their most pronounced character from artkind instances that have been judged to be outstanding examples of their kind, and (3) to be obtainable in some degree from other objects or situations (especially natural objects) that are often grouped with artkind instances in respect to an interest we take in them.

It is not surprising that it has proved very difficult to distinguish and articulate an aesthetic character of experience. Accurate phenomenological description, especially of common strains in so richly varied a class of phenomena, requires more care and effort than (I am afraid) many of us have been willing to make, and perhaps were too easily discouraged because we often had unreasonable expectations of exactness in our results. It is also, and consequently, not surprising that there has been a good deal of honest difference of opinion about what the aesthetic character is, even among those who agree that there is such a thing. But here we must not follow those who have magnified and emphasized these differences in order to cast doubt on the whole inquiry. Some features very widely and frequently found in experiences of artkind instances have been noted by perceptive aestheticians, and very often their divergent descriptions, when carefully analyzed in relation to the examples offered, turn out to be quite close in meaning. Moreover, if we do not insist a priori that the aesthetic character must be a single and simple one, but look instead for a set of central criteria, we may find that we can accommodate and reconcile insights and discoveries from several quarters.

This last conclusion, I must confess, is one that I have come to only over a long period of intermittent reflection on the problem and after a gradual recognition that my earlier attempts to capture the aesthetic character were defective and incomplete in ways that either became apparent to me as I tried to apply them and work out their consequences or were thoughtfully called to my attention. My struggles with the problem have taken two forms, which are not utterly hopeless, but which have not managed to satisfy me fully.

For some time I tried working with the concept of *aesthetic experience*, trying to make the most of Dewey's inspiring ideas (as they have always struck me) by sharpening them and seeing how they can actually be applied to concrete artkind instances. In my *Aesthetics*,[1] I made a somewhat sketchy attempt to fix this concept usably, and ten years later, in Essay 5, I tried to revive and renew it, after it had wilted somewhat in the intervening climate of opinion. I must say that I am still a partisan of aesthetic experi-

---

1. *Aesthetics: Problems in the Philosophy of Criticism*, 2d ed. (Indianapolis, 1981). See "Postscript 1980."

ence; I don't fully understand how anyone could deny that there are clear and exemplary cases of such experience, described in Dewey's words (at least as supplemented and qualified by mine!). And if there are such experiences, I do not understand how anyone could reasonably refuse to call them "aesthetic." But I have come to see that, even so, only a very limited account of our aesthetic life can be given in such terms. Aesthetic experiences—one of Dewey's most insistent and most eloquently made points—have an unusually high degree of unity in the dimension of completeness, and when you listen, for example, to an entire string quartet, the experience has this character to a very marked degree. But even if you tune in the quartet in the middle, and listen for a minute or two before you are torn away, there is no doubt that something aesthetic has happened to you—without completeness or consummation. During that stretch of time, your experience has taken on a character (and not just the property of being a music-hearing experience) that is strongly different from what was present before you tuned in or after you tune out—though some of it, of course, may linger even as you turn to the jangling telephone or the inopportune (even if welcome) television repairman at the door. So it seems important, indeed essential, to introduce a broader concept of the aesthetic in experience, while reserving the term "aesthetic experience," as a count noun, for rather special occasions.

It was such considerations as these that led me, as in Essays 1 and 2, to explore the possibility of treating the aesthetic character as a species of hedonic quality, working with the terms "enjoyment," "satisfaction," and "pleasure." Here I believed myself to have a good deal of support from a number of eighteenth-century thinkers, especially in Great Britain. And again, I am still persuaded that there is important truth in this doctrine: I haven't found any serious and cogent refutation, at least, of the proposition that experiences with aesthetic character *are* intrinsically enjoyable (which is not to say they are intrinsically valuable, of course; see Essay 3). Examples of unpleasant objects that have been placed in galleries (for example, the famous figures of decaying corpses by Gaetano Zumbo—but choose your own examples; they are not hard to find these days) only go to show that unpleasant objects have been placed in galleries, unless we go on to argue (1) that our experience of them has aesthetic character and (2) that, taken all in all, our experience of them does not involve an enjoyment that encompasses or assimilates the disgust (the small size of Zumbo's figures creates a certain detachment). Still, enjoying is taking pleasure in, and a particular kind of enjoyment must in the end be a function of the kind of thing in which pleasure is taken. There is something threateningly reductionistic about taking the defining feature of aesthetically characterized experiences to be a particular kind of pleasure; and there are theoretical problems that arise in relating such a view to the justification of reasons in art criticism (see Essay 2). So I have thought it worthwhile to cast about for a promising alternative.

My present disposition[2] is to work with a set of five *criteria of the aesthetic character of experience*. I suggest that we apply these criteria as a family, with one exception of a necessary condition: an experience has aesthetic character if and only if it has the first of the following features and at least three of the others. (But I am not wedded to a particular formula, rather trying to open up a line of further inquiry; it may be that the list of criteria should be expanded or that the number of features specified for the application of the term "aesthetic character" should be decreased.)

1. *Object directedness.* A willingly accepted guidance over the succession of one's mental states by phenomenally objective properties (qualities and relations) of a perceptual or intentional field on which attention is fixed with a feeling that things are working or have worked themselves out fittingly.
2. *Felt freedom.* A sense of release from the dominance of some antecedent concerns about past and future, a relaxation and sense of harmony with what is presented or semantically invoked by it or implicitly promised by it, so that what comes has the air of having been freely chosen.
3. *Detached affect.* A sense that the objects on which interest is concentrated are set a little at a distance emotionally—a certain detachment of affect, so that even when we are confronted with dark and terrible things, and feel them sharply, they do not oppress but make us aware of our power to rise above them.
4. *Active discovery.* A sense of actively exercising constructive powers of the mind, of being challenged by a variety of potentially conflicting stimuli to try to make them cohere; a keyed-up state

---

2. First presented in a presidential address to the Eastern Division of the American Philosophical Association, December 1978 ("In Defense of Aesthetic Value"); see *Proceedings and Addresses of The American Philosophical Association* 52 (1979):723–49. See also Essay 6, sec. 2.

amounting to exhilaration in seeing connections between percepts and between meanings, a sense (which may be illusory) of intelligibility.
5. *Wholeness.* A sense of integration as a person, of being restored to wholeness from distracting and disruptive influences (but by inclusive synthesis as well as by exclusion), and a corresponding contentment, even through disturbing feelings, that involves self-acceptance and self-expansion.

Each of these features calls for a little commentary; and the last one takes us back to a continuing controversy that I should like to resume briefly.

The first feature, object directedness, is one on which I believe general agreement can be had. It is, of course, framed to apply quite broadly. I have in mind not only the plain and obvious cases where we are intensely absorbed in the contemplation of a painting or paying close and undivided attention to the course of a musical composition, but also other cases where the object or situation in question is merely intentional: we are concerned with what is happening in the world of a novel, we are thinking intensely and seriously of the symbolic significance of a figure in a painting, or, confronted with an instance of conceptual or "idea" art, we consider a proposition or a theme or a possible state of affairs the artist brings to our attention. When the work embodies instructions for apprehending it in a determinate serial order, we follow the way it works itself out, and this is a process of discovery; but even in the case of a painting or a sculpture there is of course the same process of discovery, of gradual revelation of its nature as we explore it probingly; and thus there can be the same controlling or emerging sense that something is worked out and is accepted for what it is. This willing surrender, limited and actively engaged as it is, has often been noted as characteristic of our experience of artkind instances. And, as I suggested above, it seems to me plainly present even when what we are dealing with is a tragedy of horrors or a poignant and (by itself) painful reminder of real evils about us. If we are repelled and turn away, of course there can be no claim that the experience, even while it lasted, had aesthetic character (we looked because we were forced to, or ordered to, or in some other way involuntarily, not because we willingly accepted the object's control over our mental states). If we choose to continue the experience because we must actually see and feel the working out of what is there, and the rightness of that working out, then our experience satisfies at least the first—and necessary—criterion of aesthetic character.

Felt freedom is perhaps the hardest feature to talk about very definitely. I point to it as a notable ingredient in that experience I alluded to earlier, of turning on the radio and suddenly hearing, say, the first-movement second subject of Mozart's String Quartet in A: that lift of the spirit, sudden dropping away of thoughts and feelings that were problematic, that were obstacles to be overcome or hindrances of some kind—a sense of being on top of things, of having one's real way, even though not having actually chosen it or won it. Much deeper senses of "freedom"—metaphysically and epistemologically speaking—have been invoked in talking about the arts, by Kant and Schiller and others; I am staying with what I take to be phenomenology here, however, without moving to transcendental psychology (of course there is a good deal of valid phenomenology in Kant and Schiller, too). It is, I take it, this felt freedom that has been so feared and condemned by the Puritan—religious or political—as a temptation to dangerous escapism and failure of nerve amid the actual trials of the religious or the revolutionary life. And he is right to be concerned. For it is in respect to this second feature that art has affinities with certain drugs, which can also generate (though of course not through their mere cognition) intense forms of felt freedom. It is in this respect that art can be enervating and antisocial, and many other unfortunate things it has often been accused of. I am convinced that this second feature is real and significant. Nevertheless, I do not want to make it a necessary condition of the aesthetic; in our encounter with artkind instances that are intricate and puzzling and hard to make out, that offer resistances and obstacles to understanding or perception, this felt freedom may be absent or at a low pitch. Yet even such experiences may have the aesthetic character if they meet the other criteria.

The element of detachment in aesthetic experience, under various terms, such as "disinterestedness," "psychical distance," and "will-less contemplation," has very often been remarked, and (at least before the post–World War II avant-garde) has very often been considered central to its nature. I do not wish to formulate this feature so that it becomes enmeshed in the controversies surrounding the terms in which it has been described, or in such a way that it is tied to any particular metaphysical or epistemological or ethical theory. The heart of the matter is that when we view, say, the Gaetano Zumbo sculptures, however strongly or even violently we may respond, it is still true and highly important to add that we do not confuse them with genuine corpses, that we can avoid feeling full emotions as we naturally would do with corpses, that our feelings are therefore somewhat muted, gently screened from direct contact with reality outside the sculptures themselves. In many different typical ways, instances of artkinds are designed to lend some degree of detachment to the affects they produce: giving an air of artifice, of fictionality, of autonomy and reflexiveness, of separation from other things, and so on. But of course this is not always true, and as has also often been pointed out, there is often the attempt at a kind of brinkmanship, coming close to the borders of the seeming-real and risking the disappearance of detachment. Even so, artists generally try not to come as catastrophically close as, say, when the high-wire artist falls to his death, or the realistic life-size imitation of a museum guard is asked for directions to the men's room. Sergei Eisenstein remarks that when he staged Tretiakov's play *Gas Masks* (1923–24), about a gas factory, in an actual gas factory, it was a failure—I take it, from the aesthetic point of view. Now, it might not have been a failure even if the setting proved too realistic to preserve detachment of affect, provided it had something else to offer in the way of aestheticity; so I do not propose to make even this important and extremely common feature of art experience a necessary condition.

It is extraordinarily difficult to capture in words the exact ways in which the practical or technological aspect of an object can and cannot enter into the experience of it if that experience is to have this third feature of detached affect. Even so excellent a phenomenology of aesthetic experience as that presented by M. J. Zenzen—drawing upon Heidegger and Merleau-Ponty—exhibits these difficulties. For example, he remarks that "unlike the case of normal perception where objects are always experienced as systems of instrumentality, in an aesthetic experience the object is stripped of its instrumental 'values.'"[3] It is true that in detached affect there is a lack of concern about the instrumental values, but

---

3. M. J. Zenzen, "A Ground for Aesthetic Experience," *Journal of Aesthetics and Art Criticism* 34 (1976):471.

there need not be a lack of awareness of such values—and in the aesthetic experience of architectural works, for example, such awareness ought to be present. Zenzen also holds that in aesthetic experience of a painting the knowledge "that the work at which I am looking can be taken as canvas and paint . . . must be forgotten and transcended to the painting as art-work. . . . [It] must hide itself in order for the art-work to show itself; but in hiding itself the knowledge must not be lost."[4] Here the paradoxical language, I think, helps to bring us close to a grasp of the subtle difference between the way in which the knowledge is present and the way in which it is absent.

It seems to me that I have always thought of the act of apprehending an artkind instance as basically a cognitive act, though I may have insufficiently stressed this point or failed to grasp its consequences. Certainly I did not adequately understand the importance of this fact until such thinkers as Gombrich, Goodman, and Arnheim taught it to me in recent years. At any rate, I see now more clearly than I ever did before that one of the central components in art experience must be the experience of discovery, of insight into connections and organizations—the elation that comes from the apparent opening up of intelligibility. I call this "active discovery" to draw attention to the excitement of meeting a cognitive challenge, of flexing one's powers to make *intelligible*—where this combines *making sense of something* with *making something make sense*. In this aspect, experiences with aesthetic character overlap with experiences of empirical scientists and mathematicians; here is the link between them. There is a common thrill—speaking as always phenomenologically, and reminding ourselves that the enjoyment of emerging intelligibility or order or system may be exactly the same, even for the scholar or scientist, whether the order turns out to be empirically real (such as the table of the elements, the taxonomy of animals and plants, and the progression of artistic styles from 1350 to 1650) or an illusion (such as the classification of people according to the signs they were born under, the distinction of autonomous Spenglerian cultures, and the Baconian cypher). In some artkind instances on the minimalist side, the experience is mainly, or at least primarily, one of coming to see how some few things are related, and this by itself doth not an aesthetically characterized experience make.

4. Ibid., p. 477.

In other artkind instances, the intellectual element is too small to attribute this feature of active discovery, though of course there must always be *something* there to be apprehended, and there is always something going on that can be called, in a broad sense, understanding.[5]

The fifth feature, wholeness, is surely very central to any acceptable account of the aesthetic character—so much so that it may well deserve to be ranked with the first as essential. In trying to clarify this concept for myself as well as others, I have (gratefully) bowed to well-formed criticisms, especially those of George Dickie, and steered away from unity in the dimension of completeness in order to concentrate on unity in the dimension of coherence. And I want to keep in view two levels of this wholeness: the coherence of the elements of the experience itself, of the diverse mental acts and events going on in one mind over a stretch of time; and the coherence of the self, the mind's healing sense (which, again, may be illusory) of being all together and able to encompass its perceptions, feelings, emotions, ideas, in a single integrated personhood. To a large degree this feature of the usual art experience may be a consequence of other features; but it is, I think, distinct. It is found, of course, in many other regions—in commerce with nature, in certain kinds of religious experience, in the exciting climaxes of games, and even in concentrated intellectual activity, though in these latter cases there is a tendency to achieve unification of experience and of self through narrowness of focus and the pushing away of intrusive elements, rather than through the widening and deepening of a pattern or network of relations to take in contrasting elements.

The legitimacy of this concept of the unity of experience (in a phenomenological rather than a Kantian sense) has been a point of contention between George Dickie and myself through a debate that has continued intermittently and happily for many years—part of a genuine dialogue between us that has been one of my most cherished memories. Since Dickie, at the time of this writing, has had the latest word,[6] I think it's my turn to carry the debate into another round, by responding briefly to a few of the interesting new criticisms he has offered.

5. See "Understanding Music," in *On Criticizing Music: Five Philosophical Perspectives*, ed. Kingsley Price (Baltimore, 1981).
6. In the 1st chapter of *Art and the Aesthetic: An Institutional Analysis* (Ithaca, 1974).

My concept of experiential coherence is that of the elements of experience having the appearance of belonging together: some parts of the phenomenally objective (perceptual or intentional) field with other parts, some feelings with other feelings, some thoughts with other thoughts—and each of these sorts of mental element with the others (see Essay 5).

> The first difficulty with Beardsley's view is that there are many cases regarded by everyone as aesthetic experiences but having no affective content caused by a work of art. . . . I have in mind, for example, the experience of a certain kind of abstract painting which has a good but simple design and which can be taken in, as it were, at a glance.[7]

This comment is to the point, and helps me to clarify my view, as well as to defend it. First, I should like to formulate my fifth criterion of the aesthetic in experience so as to render it immune to this criticism: *if* there are experiences with aesthetic character that are affect-free—that include no feelings at all—then whatever elements they *do* include may still more or less cohere. The criterion can still be applied, only there will be less to apply it to, fewer sorts of element to take into account. But second, and more important, I cannot bring myself to accept the antecedent of the above conditional. If the design of a painting is in fact "taken in at a glance," I agree that there may be no affect, but I don't think there is an aesthetically characterized experience, either—one could do no more than scan and mentally classify, and that doesn't give room for a buildup of the features I have described. If, on the other hand, we stay with the picture—"such paintings frequently repay continued attention," Dickie says[8]—something more could happen, an intensification of interest, an increasingly keen appreciation of the color relationships, a feeling of uneasiness about the violent hard-edge contrasts, a touch of vertigo, or an unanticipated calmness. If Dickie is "inclined to think that many of our aesthetic experiences are without affective content, not just a few ones of abstract paintings,"[9] it may be, as his examples (from Goya and Arthur Miller) of affective works suggest, that he thinks of feelings as like full-fledged emotions, whereas I do not.

Finally, Dickie is still doubtful about the concept of a coherence of emotions, when they vary and succeed each other. Of *Hamlet*

7. Ibid., p. 189.
8. Ibid., p. 190.
9. Ibid., p. 191.

he says: "During the course of the play I might have felt fear, anger, distrust, irritation, pity, indignation, excitement, pity, and sadness, not to mention the many other feelings the play might produce in a spectator. How does this sequence of affects constitute a unity?"[10] This is a difficulty, but I think not a fatal one—even if we do not invoke the nonnecessity of my fifth criterion. These emotions directed to the events of the play are indeed, I would say, brought into coherence in the playgoing situation far more than they would be in ordinary life. First, they are all muted by a degree of detachment through the fictionality of their objects, and this helps to keep them from flying off in different directions like "real" emotions. Second, to the extent to which the events of the play are tied together by psychological inevitability (and *Hamlet* is no doubt not the best example of this!), the emotions themselves can be felt to follow naturally upon one another. Third, the emotions, when considered in their specific quality as well as in their intensity (as responses to the developments in the plot), form certain patterns, rhythms of contrast and curves of strength. Fourth, involved in all the different emotions, continuing from one emotional phase to the next, and underlying their differences, there are other important feelings—a gradually growing concern that Hamlet will not extricate himself from his situation without bringing tragedy to himself and others, along with a gradually growing feeling of acceptance of this tragic denouement as a release from torment, and as an inevitable expression both of Hamlet's brilliance and sensitivity and of his fatal limitations. These pervasive feelings give the experience of the play much of the unity that it has.

When we look again at the five criteria, we see, I think—for all their intended tentativeness—that they may well prove to be not unuseful. They are vague, of course; but that is to be expected at this stage, and perhaps to a considerable extent at any stage. They cannot be used in certain convenient ways that would be open if we had a set of necessary and sufficient conditions; but it seems that we must be content with what we can find. They show how, and in what ways, aesthetically characterized experience overlaps with experiences obtained in areas of life quite remote from art; they allow for the evident fact that we even find the aesthetic character in unexpected places. In a recent essay,

10. Ibid., p. 192.

Joel J. Kupperman has commented on my earlier remarks about aesthetic experience, especially in Essay 5; quoting my characterization of aesthetic experience,[11] he writes: "This definition on one hand appears too broad, since it could apply to a sexual experience as well as an aesthetic experience. On the other hand the requirement of unity appears unwarrantedly to legislate *a priori* that aesthetic experiences have firm boundaries."[12] I am not fully convinced of either of these charges. But if my earlier wording does admit sexual experience, I hope that the new criteria reveal both the ways in which aesthetic experience differs from, and some features it may share with, sexual experience. Moreover, if the earlier formula did insist too much on completeness, that insistence has been properly withdrawn.

In any case, the proposed account of aesthetic character does enable us to admit numerous clear-cut cases of artkind instances to the class of things capable of providing experience with this character (it would be absurd if it turned out that a competent hearing of Mozart's A-major string quartet had no aesthetic character after all). And it shows us how to rule out other phenomena that either have some pretensions to provide aesthetic character or may be expected or mistakenly believed to do so. I cite two examples.

Commenting on an exhibition of "color-field optical paintings" by Wojciech Fangor, David L. Shirley writes:

> If Mr. Nangor has masterfully used space and color to create a very special experience, albeit at times unpleasant, the experience is no more than just that. Attempts to dazzle, blind, overwhelm, even in such a spectacular way, are still attempts to dazzle, blind, and overwhelm. Even when the canvasses are generating their own particular environments, they are much closer to artifice than to art.[13]

I make no assumptions, of course, either about the paintings, which I have not seen, or the critic, whom I know little about. But if he is right in his account, the experience of viewing these paintings does seem not to be an aesthetic one, by my criteria. (Whether the paintings are art is another question, to be taken up in the following essay.)

---

11. See p. 81 above.
12. "Art and Aesthetic Experience," *British Journal of Aesthetics* 15 (1975):34.
13. *New York Times*, December 19, 1970.

Somewhat later, commenting on a show by G. E. Moore, the same critic says it contains

> a sustained, sinister threat of imminent destruction. . . . The works that pose a threat to the viewer are a pile of rough-hewn bricks stacked up on a glass plate that leans out toward the viewer, a low glass bench that, if sat upon, could splinter into painful pieces, a doorway stretched tight with rubber strips that pinch and press when you try to go through them and two sets of blinding hot lights set up on door jambs so as to cause great discomfort when you pass them. . . . There is nothing visually exciting but the conveyor belt that sweeps through the air with the élan of a trapezist and the bricks that have a kind of power in their potential movement. If the other works happen to threaten us on a physical level, they never challenge us on an esthetic level.[14]

This is the sort of discrimination that critics are called upon to make—distinguishing as clearly as possible between those works that push aesthetic experience into new directions, expanding the range of qualities it can encompass, and those works that renounce their interest in aesthetic experience and abandon it in favor of something else, something quite different. Such an alternative, for example, is also described by Shirley, recalling, in the same review, a "Destruction in Art Symposium" in 1969 at Finch College, in which a live chicken was beheaded with a pair of scissors and "several artists scratched, beat, and punched one another until their clothes were in shreds and their flesh running with blood"—these "realizations" accompanying an exhibition of "dismembered mannequins, slit and gouged canvases, gutted furniture, defaced books, plastic dresses burnt full of holes, and new violins that had been shattered into splinters."

14. *New York Times,* January 23, 1971.

17: *Redefining Art*

THE prize (if there were one) for the most vexing, the most widely and constantly worried question in aesthetics over the past three decades—at least in English-speaking countries—would surely go to the question "What is art?" That is, how should we define that term seemingly most central and indispensable to this branch of philosophy? Having followed the course of this incessant controversy as a rapt spectator—for I made no direct positive contribution to it—I am uneasily aware that concise proposals and restricted arguments may prove utterly inadequate to the accumulated complexities of this issue. Nevertheless, I shall try on my own proposal for defining "artwork" (now a common abbreviation), and defend my definition. My argument will rest heavily on meta-aesthetic considerations about the appropriate—or at least some defensible—grounds on which such a definition is to be accepted within an aesthetic theory.

There is no need to remind ourselves of the enormous and even ridiculous variety of objects, events, situations, texts, thoughts, performances, refrainings from any performance, and so on that have, in recent times, drawn the label "artwork" from their authors, admirers, or patient endurers. I yield but once to the temptation to cite a colorful example: an artist of SoHo, John Halpern, who not long ago was detained by the police (and naturally sent to Bellevue for psychiatric study) because he arranged an explosive device consisting of rockets, cherry bombs, batteries, radio receiver, and two pounds of gunpowder atop one tower of the Brooklyn Bridge, and who told a press conference that the contraption was a "relatively harmless work of art."[1] *Was* it a work of art? If so, why? If not, why not? The question may be academic

---

1. *New York Times*, August 5, 1979.

(but in the best sense of the word), since it is not clear how establishing the bomb's artistic status would affect his attorney's conduct of the defense, but it seems an askable question, and of all people, aestheticians, you might think, should be ready with a reasonable answer.

Though the procedure involves some risk of alienating the reader's attention and forfeiting credibility before getting into the substantive discussions, I think it best to be forthright and lay out succinctly my proposed definition of "artwork" before undertaking to explain the meta-aesthetic considerations that have guided me in formulating it. I say that an artwork is *either* an arrangement of conditions intended to be capable of affording an experience with marked aesthetic character *or* (incidentally) an arrangement belonging to a class or type of arrangements that is typically intended to have this capacity. There are a lot of things I would hasten to add if they could all be said at once, but the commentary must be orderly and somewhat drawn out; so all I can hasten to add at the moment is that it is to be understood from the start that the arrangements I speak of often are created with more than one intention, but what makes them art, on this definition, is that the aesthetic intention described above is present and operative.

The first meta-aesthetic consideration is that the definition chosen for a role in an aesthetic theory should mark a distinction that is theoretically significant (i.e., significant for aesthetic theory). Here I am very much in accord with some remarks by Kendall Walton. Noting that artists themselves may have many acceptable reasons for calling *outré* objects "artworks," he adds: "But their objectives are not those of philosophers. They do not have our interest in an elegant, comprehensive theory. So it would be naive and foolish of philosophers to accept uncritically their way of classifying things."[2]

Perhaps I do differ with Walton on the desirability of having *some* definition of "artwork." "What about defining 'art?' My own view is that the search for a definition is a philosophical dead end. We do not need one—not, at least, a definition of 'art' in the contemporary sense that Dickie is trying to capture."[3] There is some indecisiveness in this passage, so I take the liberty of read-

---

2. Review of George Dickie's *Art and the Aesthetic*, in *Philosophical Review* 86 (1977):100. (A similar view is defended by Milton H. Snoeyenbos in "On the Possibility of Theoretical Aesthetics," *Metaphilosophy* 9 (1978):108–21.)
3. Ibid., p. 99.

ing it my way. I agree that we can get along without a definition that is designed to encompass all the kinds of things that somebody at one time or another has called an "artwork." The class is just too heterogeneous to have any theoretical value and there are too many vested interests in appropriating the label, which is so easily switched from a descriptive to a commendatory or even commercial use. I do not question the value of studying and analyzing ordinary uses of the term, or deny that this sort of lexicographical inquiry can pay off in important insights. But it is a quite different inquiry from that of constructing aesthetic theory. Given more stable linguistic conditions, I would invoke a second meta-aesthetic consideration: that in selecting key terms for aesthetic theory we ought to stay as close as convenient to ordinary use. But the most I can claim—and I think I can claim it—is that my proposed definition captures reasonably well a use that has been prominent for some centuries and still persists quite widely today, outside the speech and writing of or about the avant-garde.

Among the well-considered views about the definition of art that I find myself departing from here is that set forth in a thoughtful essay by Haig Khatchadourian. He recommends that we (i.e., philosophers of art) follow a "principle of extension by resemblance or analogy" which he finds in general use through much of the history of art, and by which the extension of the term "artwork" is constantly and conveniently widened, but in a controlled and reasonable way. The principle requires that we ascertain whether a new object or whatever (X) proposed for admission into the class of artworks "shares any qulaities with or has any qualities appreciably similar to the A- and N- features [i.e., aesthetic and nonaesthetic qualities] of what the judge regards as paradigms of art_1, $music_1$, etc.; and balancing these features against X's dissimilarities to the latter's A- and N- features." He finds the unity of the class of artworks, even when indefinitely extended by this principle, in "a certain *general kind* of complex impact which art aims at *qua* art. . . . For I believe that, as traditionally conceived in the West, art has probably always aimed at the stimulation of the audience's intellect, the broadening of its imaginative horizons, and the broadening and deepening of its emotional experience."[4] And he finds these aims still widely present in avant-garde artistic activity.

4. "Art: New Methods, New Criteria," *Journal of Aesthetic Education* 8 (1974):71, 75.

Khatchadourian's proposal is attractive, and I wish I could find it satisfactory. But, first, I cannot see that the principle of extension gives us useful guidance or exercises any real control over the way in which the concept of art may be expanded: anything new will surely have *some* qualities similar to, and some qualities different from, those of objects already classified as artworks, and since both aesthetic and nonaesthetic qualities are to count, it is hard to see how the "balancing" is to be carried out. One of his more far-out examples is that of the person who periodically changes his name and regards the legal procedures involved in doing so, as well as the name change itself, as part of his artistic activity and output.[5] This performance is rather different from Shakespeare or Shaw, you might say—but on the other hand, he is enacting, and presumably in a sort of public or publicized way, a certain (somewhat repetitive) plot, so his activity is *something* like drama (and if drama keeps developing in certain directions, it will become more like drama). Are the similarities more decisive than the differences? How can we tell?

But, second, I wonder whether the general "aims" of "art" really help to provide a usefully unified set. Presumably Khatchadourian does not claim that *every* individual artwork must have all three aims (perhaps this is the point of talking about the aims of "art" rather than of artists). So we seem to have a disjunction, rather than the conjunction expressed. Then anything that affects *either* the intellect, the imagination, or the emotions in the stipulated way is an artwork? That is surely too much art.

Another definitional proposal that is in some ways like Khatchadourian's, but in others more in harmony with mine, is that of Jerrold Levinson. His argument is admirably conducted, and in the course of it he defends a number of important points that I thoroughly agree with and that fit in with my definition of art. The important point on which we differ arises because he has concluded that the intention whose presence in the arranging of something makes it the arranging of an artwork cannot be the intention to afford a particular kind of "pleasure/experience."[6] He seems skeptical of the existence of such a special experience; to this doubt I would only address the considerations in Essay 16. He also points out that a "stone which, when rubbed, would provide a pleasure/experience akin to what one can have by listening intently to Beethoven's Quartet in C# minor, Op. 131" would

5. Ibid., p. 76.
6. "Defining Art Historically," *British Journal of Aesthetics* 19 (1979):235.

not be an artwork; the artist is "concerned intentionally with what is to be *done* with the object, as opposed to what might be *got* out of it," so that it is the way something is intended to be treated that is art indicating. I'm not sure I picture this stone properly; if it actually made us *hear* the quartet it would be a new kind of long-playing record, and if it didn't make us hear it, what *other* experience would be "akin"? But the point about the aesthetic experience being one in which participation is active and searching is one I agree with.

Levinson develops his definition carefully, point by point. X is an artwork at *t* if and only if "X is an object of which it is true at *t* that some person or persons, having the appropriate proprietary right over X, non-passingly intends (or intended) X for regard-as-a-work-of-art, *i.e.* regard in any way (or ways) in which objects in the extension of 'art work' prior to *t* are or were correctly (or standardly) regarded."[7] "The notion of correct regard for an art work is a difficult one to make out," Levinson concedes in a footnote.[8] But it is one of the crucial elements of the definiens. Since he makes it clear that "commonly" or "rewardingly" cannot be substituted for "correctly," I am inclined to fear a dilemma here. Either we give a general account of "correctly" in terms of some version of taking an aesthetic interest in X or else we make an open-ended list of specific "ways of regarding" that have been permitted in the past and that will among them probably permit just about anything in the future. In the end, this definition may be no more usable than Khatchadourian's.

If, as I have argued, there is such a thing as aesthetic experience, then we can identify an aesthetic interest as one among the manifold interests of human beings. If, as I have not yet argued here, this interest is an important part of human life and culture, then the endeavor to satisfy it is a fundamental one for aesthetic theory to recognize and to study. Therefore if we use the term "artwork" to label those objects, in any society or at any epoch, which are designed for this purpose, it will mark a distinction of considerable theoretical significance. Such objects may be expected to have a distinctive function in the culture of the society, to be closely connected with certain institutions and roles, to deserve particular attention from sociological and anthropological

7. Ibid., p. 240.
8. Ibid., p. 248n.

students of the society, and so on. It will be useful to have a term for talking about them.

It makes no difference (this seems a good point at which to warn against a recurring historicist fallacy) whether the society or epoch we are studying has its own term that corresponds to our term "artwork." If it does have a term that comes quite close in its intension, that will be of great interest and will simplify our task of understanding. But there may be reasons why the society has not evolved such a close synonym, even if the distinction we want to mark is significant for that society. A historicist, for example, may protest if in studying eighteenth-century literature we employ a concept of literature, hence a definition of "literary work," that eighteenth-century poets and critics would not have employed. But evolving a better literary theory (with the aid of better concepts) than they had will not prevent us from grasping their beliefs. After all, they thought that whales are fish, but that does not oblige us to adopt their definition of "whale" in studying the early stages of the whaling industry. What we want to understand in such cases, as historians or anthropologists, is what is going on—in the texture of social relations, in the minds of individuals. For this difficult inquiry we need the best conceptual tools and most reasonable theory we can lay our hands on.

It is also to be borne in mind that alleged conceptual gaps between ourselves and other societies are sometimes overstressed in order to support philosophical commitments: to a "mythical" way of treating cultures or to a radical relativism. There is a wise passage in E. H. Gombrich's review of André Malraux, replying to his claim that we wrongly impose our own concepts of art on medieval artifacts.

> "A Romanesque crucifix," Malraux opens his book, "was not regarded by its contemporaries as a work of sculpture; nor Cimabue's *Madonna* as a picture."
>
> As a protest against the neglect in expressionist literature of the social setting and function of images, that sentence must surely stand. But if Malraux wishes to imply, as he appears to, that the whole notion of art is the creation of the last, godless centuries, he is mistaken. Did not Oderisi da Gubbio tell Dante in the *Purgatorio* that Cimabue thought that he held the field *in painting*? And when the same Oderisi humbly admits that the pages illuminated by Franco Bolognese "smile more" than his own, he compares them as *art* and not as sacred images. Clearly neither Pliny nor Vasari could have written their accounts of the rise of the arts without the no-

tion of contributions to "art" made by individual masters—a notion that is not incompatible with a religious setting.⁹

Which leads me to my third meta-aesthetic consideration: that the definition of "artwork" should be of the greatest possible utility to inquirers in other fields besides aesthetics—fields to which aesthetics itself should (sometimes) be thought of as a support and underpinning. Two are particularly relevant here: art history and anthropology.

It stands to reason that someone starting out to write a history of (visual) art would want to have a reasonably definite idea of what it is that he is writing a history of. Yet art historians are wont to spurn the friendly offers of aestheticians to help them out.¹⁰ What often happens, of course, is that the art historian either tacitly accepts the conventional categories of his profession or, if he ventures into less trodden ways, does so with little or no rational justification. Enormous numbers of visually interesting, even striking, objects produced in the past never get into histories of visual art. I suggest that one justification of this exclusion might reasonably appeal to the absence (or near absence) of any detectable aesthetic interest from the processes of their creation and social use.

My proposal seems to be in close accord with the views of Erwin Panofsky.

> An art historian, then, is a humanist whose "primary material" consists of those records which have come down to us in the form of works of art. But what is a work of art?
> A work of art is not always created exclusively for the purpose of being enjoyed, or, to use a more scholarly expression, of being experienced aesthetically. . . . But a work of art always *has* aesthetic significance (not to be confused with aesthetic value): whether or not it serves some practical purpose, and whether it is good or bad, it demands to be experienced aesthetically.¹¹

Panofsky explicates his concept of demand in terms of the scholastic notion of intention, but what it comes down to is the modern notion of intention. He points out, very appositely, that evi-

---

9. *Meditations on a Hobby Horse* (London and New York, 1963), pp. 81–82.
10. See, for example, H. W. Janson's comments on my essay "The Aesthetic Point of View," in *Perspectives in Education, Religion, and the Arts*, ed. Howard E. Kiefer and Milton K. Munitz (Albany, 1970), pp. 295–311; reprinted in *Metaphilosophy* 1 (1970), with my reply, pp. 63–65.
11. *Meaning in the Visual Arts* (Garden City, N.Y., 1955), pp. 10–11.

dences in an object of careful attention to and concern for form are signs of the maker's purpose:

> If I write to a friend to ask him to dinner, my letter is primarily a communication. But the more I shift the emphasis to the form of my script, the more nearly does it become a work of calligraphy; and the more I emphasize the form of my language (I could even go so far as to invite him by a sonnet), the more nearly does it become a work of literature or poetry.
>
> Where the sphere of practical objects ends, and that of "art" begins, depends, then, on the "intentions" of the creators.[12]

The relevant intention, in my opinion, is the intention to provide a possible source of aesthetically qualified experience, and this intention can comfortably coexist with the intention to get someone to come to dinner. So I would want to adjust Panofsky's last sentence: the letter does not become less of a communication when written in verse, though I think that a letter written in verse, taken out of the context of dinner invitations, and so on, is not a communication, but a fictional text.[13] That, however, is another story.

It may be thought that the art historian is in trouble if he takes on the task of determining the intentions that went into the creation of the artworks he discusses. Determinations of intentions are, of course, often difficult. But intentions (especially in the form of motives) are the very stuff of history in general, since they explain why people did the things they did. And the art historian is deeply implicated with them anyway, insofar as he traces influences and stylistic developments and rebellious innovations. One thing, as noted by Panofsky, that makes his task easier (and here he is simply making use of ordinary psychological knowledge, like any other historian) is that there are reasonably plain signs of intention. We can discern in the subject of a painting by Rubens that it was intended to depict vividly a particular martyrdom, and we can discern in its composition and color harmonies that someone must have been interested in giving it exciting and moving aesthetic qualities. (We are here considering only proximate or first-order intentions, which affect the actual character of the painting directly—not longer-range intentions, such as to fulfill a contract with a Jesuit chapter or to maximize profits for the atelier.)

12. Ibid., p. 12.
13. See my "Fiction as Representation," *Synthese* 46 (1981):291–314.

A second way of easing the historian's task is provided by the second half of my proposed definition of "artwork"—the half that may well have seemed somewhat odd without explanation. Many artworks fall into classes or genres that get labeled as such and are recognized as such—sculptures, rope designs, etchings, manuscript illuminations, hard-edge abstractions, and so on. We may call these "artkinds." What establishes an artkind, on my view, is that a good many of its individual instances are created with the intention (perhaps among others) of making aesthetic experience obtainable. The intention must be present. But once an artkind gets socially established, its label is readily and conveniently extended to new instances of it, as they turn up, whether or not they are individually intended to be aesthetic sources. The same thing happens in general with manmade objects. After the kind is established, it becomes possible for new instances to be produced inadvertently or accidentally. So the art historian or archeologist, unearthing a new Minoan sculpture, or some fragment of it, can treat it as an artwork without knowing anything of its maker's actual intentions—and even without being able (since it is so fragmentary) to observe strong indications of an aesthetic intention.

So much talk of intention in this context may trouble readers who have learned to be wary of committing the so-called intentional fallacy. I think I should insert a reminder here that the intentional fallacy applies to the interpretation and the evaluation of artworks, not to their identification. There is no logical disharmony in maintaining that intentions are crucial in making something an artwork but irrelevant to determining what the artwork means and how good it is. This point was most helpfully clarified by Maurice Mandelbaum in a well-known essay,[14] and what he says about it correctly represents my view.

The anthropologist, it seems to me, is no less in need than the art historian of a good definition of "artwork," and his need provides an even better test for any proposal. Plainly unsatisfactory ones are not hard to expose. If we were told of objects made in a certain society, collected and occasionally attended to, in whose formal organization and regional qualities no one takes the slightest interest, we would, I think, be rightly hesitant to translate the society's name for such objects by our term "artwork." If the

---

14. "Family Resemblances and Generalization Concerning the Arts," *American Philosophical Quarterly* 2 (1965):5n.

members of that society never spend any time in contemplation of these objects, and never praise any of them as more deserving of such contemplation than others of the same general type, and show no enthusiasm about their being fashioned, preserved, and made available, we *might* have to conclude that the members of that society simply do not have aesthetic experience. On the other hand, of course, we would not want to impose narrow restrictions on the range of experiences we are prepared to recognize as aesthetic; if they are indifferent to Schubert or Mendelssohn but seem to get a great deal of enjoyment out of their wailing and drumming, I hope we might recognize a kindred spirit across the cultural barrier.

The problem comes in with the enormously varied ways in which aesthetic interests are mingled, sometimes indissolubly combined, with other interests, so that it may take a deep understanding of the society and its culture in order to discriminate the different strands. Here it is tempting to make hasty judgments. For example, that most sensitive anthropologist, Dorothy Lee, remarks that Navajo sand paintings are so permeated with religious (and also medical) purpose and function that "what we classify as art is actually religion"; and the same is true, she suggests, of Hopi drama and clowning to make the corn grow or participate in its growing.[15] As she develops her account, however, it is clear that she is not speaking exclusively. "The sand-paintings are *no more art* than they are ritual, myth, medical, practice or religious belief"; the clowning "is not *mere* art" (my italics). To say significantly that "art and agriculture and religion are part of the same totality for the Hopi" presupposes that we can distinguish these enterprises even though they are bound together, so the question "What is art?" is still admissible, and even pressing.

One writer who has come to grips with the problem is George Mills. "Such a definition should enable us to distinguish artistic activity from other activities, but it should also help with the specifically anthropological problems mentioned at the start of the paper: relating art to the rest of culture, and making available the methods and conclusions of art historians, aestheticians, and psychologists of art." Mills frames a concept of "controlled qualitative experience," borrowing from Dewey, and offers a definition that is of the same general character as mine: "Art then is the creation,

---

15. *Freedom and Culture* (Englewood Cliffs, N.J., 1959), pp. 166–67.

by manipulating a medium, of public objects or events which serve as deliberately organized sets of conditions for experience in the qualitative mode." He concludes that "though many cultures do not have a concept of art, all cultures produce art objects" (which may have other functions as well).[16]

If Mills is right in saying that there are many examples of artworks whose production and enjoyment are unaccompanied by any concept of art (and thus a fortiori of any theory of art), then Arthur Danto must be mistaken in his well-known view that it is theories that make art "possible." Danto says, "It would, I should think, never have occurred to the painters of Lascaux that they were producing *art* on those walls. Not unless there were neolithic aestheticians."[17] Perhaps so; but it does not follow that they were not producing art. An art theory may make the *concept* of art possible, but that's not the same as making *art* possible. Unless there were neolithic microbiologists, it would not have occurred to the cave dwellers that their illnesses were caused by microorganisms; nevertheless they died from them.

Mill's definition of "artwork" in terms of "affective response" is criticized by Richard L. Anderson in his very interesting book; but I think the criticisms can be met or set aside. First, since continuing investigation reveals variations in response to art from culture to culture, "it seems imprudent to assert that we currently know just what the essence of art is." Well, when anthropologists discover the essence of art, as Anderson apparently anticipates, we can move to a better definition; meanwhile, it matters much that our definition lay hold of a fundamental, practically universal, and highly important cultural phenomenon. Second, "individuals' subjective states are notoriously difficult to ascertain, especially if the states tend to be fleeting and personal in nature, as is the case with the affective response to art."[18] If the anthropologist gives up on discovering the "subjective states" of members of a society, including shares and repeated states connected with observable objects and events, there doesn't seem to be much else of interest he can tell us. And as a matter of fact there is indeed much about such states in Anderson's book.

Anderson's own proposal is to define "art" in terms of "skill":

16. "Art: An Introduction to Qualitative Anthropology," *Journal of Aesthetics and Art Criticism* 16 (1957):7, 15, 17. See also Warren L. d'Azevedo, "A Structural Approach to Esthetics: Toward a Definition of Art in Anthropology," *American Anthropologist* 60 (1958):702–14.
17. See "The Artworld," *Journal of Philosophy* 61 (1964):572, 581.
18. *Art in Primitive Societies* (Englewood Cliffs, N.J., 1979), pp. 16, 17.

those things are considered to be art which are made by humans in any visual medium and whose production requires a relatively high degree of skill on the part of their maker, skill being measured, when possible, according to the standards traditionally used in the maker's society.[19] But this definition seems to give up on the very distinctions we seemed to need, say, for such activities as the Navajo sandpainting: the skill is used to produce an object that satisfies both a religious and an aesthetic interest. Anderson makes no distinction among crafts in general, whatever their social purposes. Of course there is a live sense of the term "art" that makes it practically synonymous with "skill," but it would be most confusing in our culture to call everything fashioned with skill an artwork, and I should think it would be no less confusing to rely on this notion in discussing Navajo practices.[20]

Another extremely thoughtful and interesting proposal has been made by Ellen Dissanayake: "artistic behavior" consists in conferring "specialness" on an object or activity, or in recognizing its "specialness"; it "shapes and/or embellishes everyday reality with the intention of constructing or manifesting (or recognizing) what is considered to be another 'level' from quotidian practical life."[21] Dissanayake shows how her definition fits well the ethological contexts in which art is intimately combined with ritual or other cultural actions. But her definition seems to entail the idea that we have art *only* when there is something else (something significant religiously, agriculturally, militarily, or whatever) whose importance is acknowledged and is to be pointed up by the behavior of "making special." In her commendable desire to escape "the culture-bound preconceptions of modern Western aesthetics," which reflect "art produced and appreciated by an infinitesimal number in both time and space,"[22] she seems unfortunately to de-

19. Ibid., p. 11.
20. I think I can claim *some* support for my argument in the interesting though not very coherent discussion of cave drawings by Herbert Read in *Art and Society* (New York, 1966; first published 1936), Introduction and chap. 1. Read discerns a plain aesthetic intention in these works, distinct from magical purpose; and though he begins by identifying the essence of art in terms of the cognitive function of revealing a higher than scientific universal truth (pp. 2, 7), he seems to consider the drawings artworks on account of their "vitality, vividness and emotive power, which are precisely aesthetic qualities" (p. 11).
21. "Art as a Human Behavior: Toward an Ethological View of Art," *Journal of Aesthetics and Art Criticism* 38 (1980):401.
22. Ibid., p. 404. I want also to call attention to an essay by Denis Dutton, "Art, Behavior, and the Anthropologists," *Current Anthropology* 18 (1977):387–407 (with his reply to a number of comments). It sharply exposes fallacies in some anthropological approaches to the arts of primitive societies and defends the artistic

fine culturally independent artworks out of existence. By this, of course, I do not mean to suggest that there can be artworks that have no internal relations with the rest of culture (see Essay 20), but only that our appropriate experience of a contemporary work such as Jackson Pollock's "Lavender Mist," in the National Gallery, is not intimately connected with religious ritual, political ideology, warfare, and so forth. Certainly we require a definition of art—such as the one I have offered—that allows us to discover and discuss cultural situations in which artworks are never just artworks, but I think we should not adopt a definition that rules out artworks that have a fairly specialized and independent function.

This anthropological context seems appropriate for a discussion of George Dickie's "institutional" definition of art, which has played such a prominent role in recent discussion. Perhaps the context is unduly narrow for a proposal that has been discussed in a few hundred thousand words, but I think it is a sort of test case, and it will provide an opportunity for three critical comments (not new, but not yet exhausted either).

Dickie's definition, it will be recalled, stipulates that something is an artwork only if "some person or persons acting on behalf of a certain institution (the artworld)" have conferred upon some of its aspects the status of "candidate for appreciation."[23] That's not the whole story, but it is the part I begin with—especially the central concept of the "artworld." The artworld is a "social institution," a "bundle of systems" (such as theater and painting). It clearly encompasses some distinctive practices, or at least activities, of members of a social group or groups. I have been troubled by the apparent circularity introduced by this segment of the definiens, and Dickie has acknowledged its presence while playing down its harmfulness.[24] But from the point of view of the anthropologist trying to understand the major segments of culture in a strange society, Dickie's definition may prove less helpful than one could wish. How is he to determine which are the artworks in that society? By discovering which "artifacts" have had a certain status conferred on some of their aspects in the name of the

---

status of such artworks in an argument that is, to my mind, eloquently humane and philosophically wise.
23. *Art and the Aesthetic* (Ithaca, 1974), p. 34.
24. See ibid., pp. 43–44.

artworld of that society. How, then, does he determine which persons, in which roles, engaged in which activities, belong to the artworld? The activities themselves are extremely varied, and may, as we have seen, be closely intertwined with nonartistic activities, so the best way to discriminate them is to see which artifacts they deal with, and which aspects of those artifacts primarily concern them. Here the circle closes. If there is a way of opening it up, I have not found it in Dickie's system.

Dickie's concept of something's being a "candidate for appreciation" has been subjected to much critical discussion.[25] By defining "appreciation" in terms of value ("in experiencing the qualities of a thing one finds them worthy or valuable"),[26] he aims to bypass the line of thought reflected in my proposal, which leads to a distinction between *aesthetic* appreciation and other forms or types— or at least to an attempt at such a distinction. But despite all the difficulties, some of them well urged by Dickie over the years, some distinction of this sort still seems to me indispensable. For one thing, Dickie's definition of "appreciation" makes no adequate provision for a distinction between intrinsic and extrinsic interest, and I don't see how it rules out the idea that, say, in seeing and responding to ("experiencing") the changing colors of a traffic light I find them valuable as signs for regulating traffic. The anthropologist's informants in a preliterate society may assure him that the carvings on a totem pole or the colors on a tribal mask are regarded as extremely important, are respected and cherished by members of his community, but such an account of their "appreciation" will still not tell us whether their interest is aesthetic or religious or medical or political.

Dickie's stipulation that artworks must be "artifacts," the product of intentional human activity, is to my mind sound. If I have

---

25. See, for example, Ted Cohen, "The Possibility of Art: Remarks on a Proposal by Dickie," *Philosophical Review* 82 (1973):69–82; Dickie, "A Response to Cohen: The Actuality of Art," in *Aesthetics: A Critical Anthology*, ed. George Dickie and Richard J. Sclafani (New York, 1977), pp. 196–200; Richard J. Sclafani, "Art as a Social Institution: Dickie's New Definitions," *The Journal of Aesthetics and Art Criticism* 32 (1973):111–14; Sclafani, "Art Works, Art Theory, and the Artworld," *Theoria* 39 (1973):18–34; Timothy W. Bartel, "Appreciation and Dickie's Definition of Art," *British Journal of Aesthetics* 19 (1979):44–52; Gary Iseminger, "Appreciation, the Artworld, and the Aesthetic," in *Culture and Art*, ed. Lars Aagaard-Mogensen (Atlantic Highlands, N.J., 1976), pp. 118–30; Anita Silvers, "The Artworld Discarded," *Journal of Aesthetics and Art Criticism* 34 (1976):441–54; Jay Bachrach, "Dickie's Institutional Theory of Art," *Journal of Aesthetic Education* 11 (1977):25–36.

26. *Art and the Aesthetic*, pp. 40–41.

suggested the broader term "arrangement," it is to include activities, earthworks, smoke rings, ideas not carried out but recorded on paper, and other items that may be artworks but don't fit very easily under the rubric of "artifact." Of course when we decide to limit artworks to products of human effort we stir up another set of problems about how much effort, deliberation, skill, intelligence, passion, knowledge, and so on we wish to insist upon before we admit these products to the category of artworks. Or, coming from the other direction, we may want to rule out wholly accidental objects (the patterned shards of an unintentionally dropped ceramic pot), yet admit even a considerable amount of accident of which the artist makes use. I don't know that we have to try to draw sharp lines here, and I am personally inclined to be quite generous. But I think it is a mistake to confer artistic status on found objects untouched by human hands, or arrangements, however aesthetically interesting, in the genesis of which no intentions at all played a part. Perhaps there is place here for the moral concept of responsibility; not that we need to find someone to blame if things go wrong, but that to be a genuine work of art, an object or arrangement must be something for which some person or group of persons takes responsibility, stands behind. Without that, we are back to nature.

My fourth meta-aesthetic consideration in framing a definition of "artwork" is that I think art and the aesthetic should be conceptually linked. Not that all art is aesthetically successful, or that everything of aesthetic interest is art; but our concept of the aesthetic basically derives from and gets its primary use from our experience of artworks, and the main and central (though of course by no means the only notable) function of artworks has *always* been, and remains, the aesthetic function. So, at least, I maintain. And I regard it as a merit of my proposed definition that it provides a linkage of the right degrees of intimacy and of looseness.

But here I come up against a very strong and, some think, permanently significant trend in current artistic practice and theory—a trend that has perhaps reached its philosophical high watermark in the eloquently and cogently argued thesis of Timothy Binkley that art in our time has succeeded in severing its connection with the aesthetic, so that the two concepts are completely independent.[27] It is easy to exaggerate the amount of contemporary

---

27. Others who have interestingly disputed about this connection are Robert MacGregor, "Art and the Aesthetic," *Journal of Aesthetic and Art Criticism* 32 (1974):

art (so-called) that is excluded by a proposal such as mine. Many conceptual "pieces" are quite amusing, and the comic is a form of aesthetic experience. Many of the ideas they evoke have a striking character, of irony or impressive grotesqueness or teasing complexity, that caters to aesthetic interest; and many of the projected ideas have "intentional objects" (in the phenomenological sense) that, as miniature fictional worlds, can be regarded with profit from the aesthetic point of view. But it is true that my proposal rules out pieces that are *solely* designed to protest social injustice, to make a philosophical point, to thumb a nose at conventional art, to induce extreme boredom or depression, to arouse a morbid curiosity. I don't say that such things are not worth doing—not at all. Nor do I deny that objects, including written texts and wall scrawls and piles of trash, can usefully be classed together, say as "exhibition pieces," in that they are made or arranged to be shown to a putative public in a gallery or suitable public outdoor space. But the difference between the artworks (in my sense) and the rest, even conceding the inevitable borderline cases, seems to me too important, too vital, to lose its most convenient and natural marking label.

The disconnection of art from the aesthetic has been hailed as the most significant development in contemporary visual art, as a final freeing of the artist from all obligation. It is expressed in the celebrated dictum of the painter Donald Judd: "If someone calls it art, it's art." This statement has a nice ring to it, but there is less in it than meets the eye, for it makes the speech act of "calling" a pseudo-performative. It sounds as though the act of calling something art *makes* it art, but since there are, on this view, no enabling or requisite illocutionary conditions for performng the act of calling something a work of art, it turns out that calling something a work of art only makes it something that has been called a work of art. Which no doubt can happen to all sorts of things these days, but which still doesn't settle the question whether it *is* art.[28]

It is Binkley's important contribution to this issue that he has provided the most sophisticated and carefully reasoned philosophical defense of the idea that artworks are "created" by fiat.

549–59; "Dickie's Institutionalized Aesthetics," *British Journal of Aesthetics* 17 (1977): 3–13; Robert A. Schultz, "Does Aesthetics have Anything to Do with Art?," *Journal of Aesthetics and Art Criticism* 36 (1978):429–40.

28. See Richard J. Sclafani's vigorous argument in "What Kind of Nonsense Is This?," *Journal of Aesthetics and Art Criticism* 33 (1975):455–58.

He provides a method for demonstrating that "art cannot be defined" by showing how any possible definition can be upset by a counterexample.[29] Whatever is ruled out from the class of artworks by a particular proposal (say, as in one of his examples, your grandmother's arthritis) can be made an artwork by recourse to an act of artwork specification. "Anything can be art if it is indexed or catalogued as art. All one needs to do is make clear what he intends the piece to be. Artists since Duchamp have revelled in this realization." To use a current "piece-specifying convention," or establish a new one, is to say something like "I hereby specify the piece (I am now creating) to be my grandmother's arthritis."[30] Such a declaration creates the new artwork (it does not affect the arthritis one way or the other). But though this procedure is said to follow a "convention," apart from the wording of the formula there doesn't seem to be anything in the way of a rule to be followed. The formula can be applied to anything you can think of or refer to or describe; there are no conditions, and so there is no possibility of misfiring. It is hard for me to understand how such an empty verbal gesture can accomplish anything substantive, such as increasing by one the number of artworks in the world. It's a bit like calling spirits from the vasty deep.

But Binkley argues that this is now the operative rule governing the word "art" among those who have the authority to make the rules. Such conceptual art pieces as grandmother's arthritis are created every day, and philosophers are in no position to question them. "And I don't know what to say except that they are made (created, realized, or whatever) by people considered artists, they are treated by critics as art, they are talked about in books and journals having to do with art, they are exhibited in or otherwise connected with art galleries, and so on."[31] Of course these considerations must carry some weight in making philosophical decisions about definition, even if we are not simply surveying actual usage. I would be more inclined to pay attention to them if I were convinced that this avant-garde actually *has* a usage.[32] But if all that is meant by art-gallery proprietors, writers for certain pe-

---

29. See "Deciding About Art," in *Culture and Art*, pp. 92ff.
30. Ibid., p. 102.
31. Ibid., p. 95.
32. According to Richard Hertz, "Philosophical Foundations of Modern Art," *British Journal of Aesthetics* 18 (1978):237–48, the thrust of recent movements is to erase any distinction between art and nonart.

riodicals, specifiers of conceptual pieces, and so on when they use the word "art" is that something has been specified as a piece, and especially if Binkley is right in saying that they accept *no* definition of "art," then I don't feel dogmatic in deciding to employ a definition useful for purposes of aesthetic theory—or the philosophy of art.

Developing his theory in a later essay, Binkley introduces the term "indexing" for this verbal mode of art creating. Art is a cultural activity, a set of practices. "An artwork is a piece. The concept 'work of art' does not isolate a class of peculiar aesthetic personages. The concept marks an indexical function in the artworld. To be a piece of art, an item need only be indexed as an artwork by an artist"—but the last requirement is empty, for anyone who indexes anything (even if he or she is only "recategorizing an unsuspecting entity," as Duchamp did with the *Mona Lisa* and many other things) is thereby an artist. "The fact that someone could be an artist by just christening his or her radio or anxiety may seem preposterous. However, the case of the Sunday Painter who rarely shows his or her paintings to anyone is not substantially different."[33] But this is just what I think we have to resist. The difference is that the Sunday painter, however modest, at least typically is trying to create something with the *capacity* to provide aesthetic experience. And this, to my mind, is a *substantial* difference. Actions generally have a point, and that's what makes them differ importantly, I suppose. I don't know what the point of indexing one's anxiety would be; Binkley says that the point of the real examples he gives is to convey information.[34] As, for example, when On Kawara creates his works by sending postcards each day noting the time he gets up. I suppose this is information in some sense, even if it's not exactly the answer to anyone's burning question. (What information is conveyed by indexing a case of arthritis?) But the point is *not* "to proffer aesthetic delights." The difference is one that Binkley marks by calling it "nonaesthetic art"; and I might be persuaded to adopt this terminology if I were convinced that there is any real genus left for the term "art" once it has been severed from all connection with aesthetic interests and turned over to the indexers.

33. "Piece: Contra Aesthetics," *Journal of Aesthetics and Art Criticism* 35 (1977):273, 274.
34. Ibid., p. 272.

18: *Critical Evaluation*

IT has seemed clear to me for a long time that philosophical aesthetics must be conceived as having a very intimate connection with art criticism. Dedication to this principle may have been carried to excess twenty years ago when I suggested that we might reasonably identify aesthetics with metacriticism, and wrote: "As a field of study, aesthetics consists of a rather heterogeneous collection of problems: those that arise when we make a serious effort to say something true and warranted about a work of art."[1] Not that I am leading up to an act of contrition; I still think this is a good focus, although I am not so wedded to the formula that I cannot accept qualifications. It may be true, for example (and I never wished to deny this), that even if we had no artworks at all, we might take the sort of interest in selected aspects of nature that could arouse philosophizing about art. There is controversy over the extent to which the aesthetic appreciation of nature is parasitic upon or an extension of the experience of artworks—controversy that I shall (somewhat regretfully) stay out of in these pages. It is also true that philosophers who have declined to adopt the philosophical analyst's "semantic ascent"—recasting object-language questions as metalanguage questions, in the hope of rendering them more manageable—have been able to get a fair amount of mileage, and also to discover some things worth knowing, by asking such questions as "What is beauty?" and "Is art a form of knowledge?" without translating them into such contemporary idioms as "What is meant by saying 'X is beautiful,' and are such sentences verifiable?" and "What are the truth conditions of such critical remarks as 'This music shows (or affirms, or proclaims, or hints . . .) that God is merciful?'" Still, genuine prob-

---

1. *Aesthetics: Problems in the Philosophy of Criticism* (New York, 1958), p. 3.

lems stated in the ordinary form can always be preserved in the metalinguistic form; and I retain enough confidence in the virtues of philosophical analysis to think that its method has often led to better understanding of the questions we are trying to answer and to better answers to those questions. So it could still be true that the range of problems properly gathered under the rubric of "aesthetics" can be picked out as those discoverable in art criticism—even if not *only* in art criticism.

I don't have any great ego involvement in my earlier definition of aesthetics, and I certainly do not insist that all aesthetic problems be formulated metalinguistically. But I do think it important to emphasize the relationships between aesthetics and criticism and to do aesthetics with one eye, quite frequently, on critical practice. For, first, what critics say about artworks is at least a major source of fruitful philosophical puzzlement; and some aesthetic problems can be reached *only* by this path, I think—as, for example, when Aristotle, in his *Poetics* (Chapter 25), classifies unfavorable criticisms of tragedies under five headings. (He adds that there are twelve ways of replying to such criticisms—some of which he had previously cited—but unfortunately the text breaks off at this point.)

Second, besides being an important *source* of aesthetic problems, the general practices of art critics provide important *evidence* for testing the truth of proposed aesthetic theories. The relationship here is somewhat delicate: it is surely not up to the aesthetician to provide a justification of every sort of thing we find critics saying—the topics they select for discussion, the value judgments they make, the reasons they give, and so on. On the other hand, if an aesthetic theory were to entail, say, that the degree of unity of an artwork has nothing whatever to do with its artistic goodness, so that it is always logically irrelevant for a critic to praise a poem or a sonata on the ground that it is highly organized and coherent, then that theory would run counter to widely established critical practice, and would, I think, thereby come to grief.[2] Given the divergences in critical practice, and the influence of nonlogical factors such as the power of art dealers, advertisers, corporate taste molders, and fashion promoters, this sort of evidence must of course be used with care. But it cannot be ignored.

---

2. For further consideration of this point, see "*Languages of Art* and Art Criticism," *Erkenntnis* 12 (1978):95–118.

Third, a major—perhaps the chief—benefit to be hoped for from aesthetic inquiry is improvement in the way we think and talk and write about artworks—that is, in criticism. Taking a longer-range and wider-scoped view, we might well want to make out a case for other valuable contributions that may be demanded from aesthetics. Using the term "criticism" in a narrower way, such as I have occasionally pleaded for, and distinguishing it from *aesthetic education*, we might decide that in the longest run and widest view, the greatest thing that aesthetics can do for us is help us devise the very best possible aesthetic education.[3] But for the moment, in this paragraph anyway, I am taking "criticism" to cover a lot of talk about artworks, and that includes the important talk of aesthetic educators as well as teachers of the arts. And even if we want to add that in the end we hope aesthetics can contribute to the flourishing of the performing arts, the spread of creativity, the improvement of the environment, and the growth of a spirit of community in the world, I suppose these contributions would come about through its influence on criticism, broadly speaking. For criticism just reflects our understanding of what the arts are, what their point is, why they are worth having; and to improve criticism is to improve this understanding.

Turning from these general, perhaps overambitious reflections, we may next consider more closely what art criticism is in the narrower, stricter, more useful sense I have alluded to. For this is a sense we should not lose track of. There are many ways of talking about artworks, some more worthy of encouragement than others, but one of these ways in particular seems to me to deserve—or to deserve best—the name of "criticism," and unless talk of this kind is included in it, talk about artworks fails to do this central, quintessential job.

To get the right perspective on art criticism, I think, we should see it as one species of a generic and fundamental activity of evaluating selected portions of our surroundings in order to make reasonable choices among the things they have to offer. (This perspective is also a prophylactic against the incursion of the wilder current forms of verbal activity that are palmed off as criticism.) Wherever we can articulate and anchor a definite point of view—moral, legal, medical, pedagogical, financial, or whatever—

---

3. A proposition to which I am confident Ralph Smith would agree; see his editorials in *The Journal of Aesthetic Education* since 1966.

we can make value judgments from that point of view, in the expectation that such judgments, if sound, will help us to make reasonable decisions about what it is best to do.[4] In this perspective, artworks constitute one of the noteworthy classes of things we encounter and must make choices about—between one artwork and another, sometimes; between an artwork and something of another kind, quite often. It is the direct central function of criticism, I would say, to provide guidance for such choices. So we can speak of moral criticism, legal criticism, technological criticism, environmental criticism, and the rest, because (a) different classes of things (objects, actions, events, situations, proposals, motives, states of affairs, or whatever) or (b) different features of these things (parts, aspects, inner relations, references, qualities) are being singled out for attention in the criticism. But we must not forget that there can be overlapping in both respects: (a) many, perhaps most, things can be criticized from more than one point of view and (b) some features of things may be relevant to more than one species of criticism.

What is distinctive of criticism, on my view, is that it aims to discover those features of a thing that call for admiration or condemnation—if these terms, so well suited to strong moral contexts, may here be allowed to embrace also much weaker and more casual attitudes, as when we think some feature is a good thing, a plus, an asset, a decided advantage, meritorious, worth having; or a fault, a flaw, a defect, a deficiency, a disadvantage, undesirable, regrettable. Thus there are two levels to the critic's task, each involving the other. We ask the critic to give us, as definitely as possible (though we must be willing to accept quite indefinite ones in many cases), *critical judgments,* or evaluations of artworks as wholes. And we ask for what might be called *normative explanations*: calling attention to features whose presence accounts for the thing's being better or less good than it might be or than something else is—from a certain point of view. "Legally, Snodgrass was within his rights in bringing suit, *because* the statutes allow for recovery in such cases, though morally his suit was objectionable, *because* he was motivated solely by spite in this attempt to bankrupt his former wife."

If this is what criticism in general is (though rather tersely described), it plainly involves two basic elements: a kind of value on

4. See Essay 9 above and "The Name and Nature of Criticism," in *What is Criticism?*, ed. Paul Hernadi (Bloomington, Ind., forthcoming).

which attention is focused and a set of features that are believed to affect the degree to which this value is found in the thing criticized. The term "value" is not, I hope, unduly strained to cover the entire range of criticizable things: there is the political value and there is the moral value of a rule for a national political convention; there is the financial value and there is the medical value of a pound of aspirin. The *grounds* of value (or the antigrounds: the features that inhibit or diminish it) are those appealed to in the explanation, those that are alleged to *make a difference* value-wise (say, the properties of being permitted by statute and of being motivated solely by spite to injure someone financially).

It is in this context of a concept of criticism in general that I present the species *aesthetic criticism*, or criticism from the aesthetic point of view, and that I propose to define *art criticism* as the aesthetic criticism of artworks. The purpose of my detour was not to obscure the distinctive nature of aesthetic criticism, but to display this nature in its true colors by providing the proper background of contrast, and thereby establish its respectability. For the reader who has been persuaded that there *must* be such a species as aesthetic criticism has reached the proper frame of mind for being favorably disposed toward accepting my theory of what that species involves. Aesthetic criticism, too, must assume a kind of value: aesthetic value. And at this point something should be said about that.

I have tried working with a few slightly different versions of aesthetic value, as some essays in this volume attest; I have even tried getting along without any version, though these failures are not recorded herein. At the present time, I regard aesthetic value as that value which something possesses in virtue of its capacity to impart, through cognition of it, a marked aesthetic character to experience.[5] Or we might say that aesthetic vaue is value conferred by the capacity of the object to provide aesthetic experience when accurately and adequately apprehended—where to apprehend accurately is to perceive or understand what is actually there in the object, and to apprehend adequately is to apprehend so much of what is there that further discoveries would not noticeably affect the degree to which the experience is aesthetic.

5. See "In Defense of Aesthetic Value," *Proceedings and Addresses of the American Philosophical Association* 52 (1979):723–48; Noël Carroll's comments on this essay have been very helpful to me in reflecting further on its argument.

This capacity to afford aesthetic experience (I use this term for brevity) is, when considered by itself, an empirical property, not a value. But it is a value on the assumption, which I make, that aesthetic experience is worth having; for on this assumption the capacity to provide such experience is a way of being worthwhile. Since one experience may be more aesthetic than another—more intensely or extensively or pervasively imbued with aesthetic character—aesthetic value has degrees. Thus the aesthetic critic's double task is (a) to estimate (even if only roughly) the aesthetic value of the object and (b) to explain why the object has so much (or so little) aesthetic value by pointing out those features that contribute to or interfere with the thing's possession of aesthetic value. These normative explanations have been called "functional explanations" by Leonard Meyer,[6] in the development of his theory of music criticism: they show the specific musical (or literary, or other) role that a given feature plays in bettering or worsening the work. On my view they have two sides, which appear in different critical contexts: (a) If we accept the critic's general judgment of the work, then we are ready for his or her normative explanations; and these serve both to help us understand why the work is as good (or poor) as it is and to justify (or condemn) the presence of the features that help to make it that good (or poor). (b) If we doubt, or are in doubt about, the critic's judgment of the work, then the normative explanations serve as reasons to support that judgment, and may help to convince us that it is right.

It is time to quicken these abstractions by examples, and I choose them from what lies conveniently at hand: an issue of *Artforum*, containing typical avant-garde talk about avant-garde artworks. Concerning a movement of a musicwork for solo organ, Philip Glass's *Dance No. 4*:

> Among the new and rather striking techniques introduced here is the extensive use of more or less traditional harmonic progressions borrowed from tonal music. The sonic plateaus created through these tonal shifts help define and support multiple levels of activity which often shift back and forth quite rapidly, acting in various ways as foils to one another. Furthermore, certain changes are given added emphasis through the use of strong harmonic rela-

---

6. See *Explaining Music: Essays and Explorations* (Berkeley, 1973). Meyer's views are critically discussed in my essay "The Role of Psychological Explanation in Aesthetics," in *Art and Perception*, ed. John Fisher (Philadelphia, 1980); but I did not there fully appreciate the significance of Meyer's concept of "functional explanation" in criticism.

tionships. . . . One finds that certain harmonic relationships employed are much stronger than others. This, coupled with the varying quality and intensity of the rhythmic activity involved, helps to define the hierarchical relationships heard among the different plateaus. . . . As is often the case [with rapid cross-cutting] in film, the high contrast felt between certain changes adds to the dramatic importance of the scenes involved.[7]

According to the critic, certain features of the work (rhythmic and harmonic) explain how it also possesses another feature, articulated "hierarchical relationships . . . among the different plateaus." There is a tacit but clear assumption that these relationships are, in turn, worth having, that is, worth hearing—that they constitute a musical structure of some kind, and that they are highly dramatic, and in virtue of these properties the work has (aesthetic) value.

Concerning paintings by Stewart Hitch:

> The more obvious dynamism of the "flying" shape that characterized some of his earlier starburst paintings here informs instead the motion and direction of strokes within the shape, and with a greater ambiguity in the reading. The central shape can now be interpreted as a figure on a ground and as a hole in a plane, as both expanding and contracting, as a living organism and as something crushed or sheared off (Still's shapes). In terms of value, the figures in these paintings should be holes in the canvas, but the issue is confused by their density and animation, and by the layered edges that place them in front of warmer, lighter, normally more positive, ground colors. In certain paintings the sense of tension and movement may even suggest animate life, as if the figure were an individual going two separate ways.[8]

Here, it seems, a comparatively high level of "ambiguity" (which here I take to mean multiple suggestiveness) is explained by the brush strokes, and the assumption seems to be that what makes the painting (aesthetically) good, or gives it such goodness as it has, is that multiple suggestiveness, animation, tension, movement, dynamism.

It may be suspected that I am reading unwarranted meanings into these passages in respect to two points. First, it may be said that the passages can be read as sheer description of what is going on in the work, or at most an explanation of the way re-

---

7. Thomas DeLio, "Avant-Garde Issues in Seventies Music," *Artforum* 18 (September 1979):64.

8. Anita Feldman, "Space and Subjectivity: Four Painters," *Artforum* 18 (September 1979):52.

gional qualities are produced by local features: why do we have to take these remarks as implicit evaluations? For two reasons. One: when a critic singles out certain features of an artwork for careful and explicit discussion, there is always, surely, the presumption that he regards these features as worth noting and discussing; and what would make them worth noting and discussing is their having some bearing on the value of the artworks discussed. Two: even if this were not true in general, it would be true in the present cases; for these essays are developed as demonstrations of the importance of the creative artists discussed; their demeanor is favorable, and such evaluative terms as appear ("interesting" is one of them) are positive. But second, it may be said that even if these critics do impute value to the artworks they describe, it may not (for all they say) be *aesthetic* value they have in mind. I suppose this doubt is legitimate, and I do not claim to read their minds. Still, since they do not warn us against drawing this conclusion, and the primary grounds they cite are quite in line with features of musicworks and paintings that have long and commonly been cited in support of explicit judgments of aesthetic value, we seem to be justified in finding an implicit appeal to aesthetic value.

I do not want to distort the problem here. There are complications typical of present-day critical discourse. We find, for example, the first critic saying the following about a performance at the Kitchen by Robert Ashley of his work *The Wolfman*:

> The excruciating noise from the tape and organ, of course, made the audience terribly uncomfortable. Many, in fact, either left or covered their ears. Meanwhile, Ashley rather deliberately and self-consciously acted out their projected responses.
>
> . . . In *The Wolfman* the composer plays with that very special relationship that exists between an audience and a performer. As the audience became self-conscious it became very aware of those restrictions under which it functions in any concert situation where it typically finds itself in the role of the silent observer of actions in which it may never participate.[9]

There is still, I think, the implication that something worthwhile was to be gained by staying through this performance, despite the decibels, so this is criticism in that it points out those features that are the grounds of value—the "excruciating noise" and the composer's acting out of the audience's responses. But is this

9. DeLio, "Avant-Garde Issues," p. 66.

aesthetic criticism? Hearing excruciating noises and watching someone on the stage mimic the defensive gestures of a much put-upon audience apparently is to pay off in becoming "very aware" of the restrictions of normal concert situations (which, I guess, means that people at concerts are so polite you have to work hard to drive them out). If such awareness is valuable, its value seems to be psychological or sociological, rather than aesthetic. I can't help suspecting that if it were plainly stated that the value of this artwork lies in its informativeness, it would become all too evident that the value is slight—though I may be unfair here. (Michael Wreen has shown me how a plausible case can be made for claiming that this performance calls attention to a number of tacitly accepted conventions of concertgoing and might indirectly contribute to the aesthetic education of the audience.) In any event, I believe that critics would do us a service to distinguish the kinds of value they are remarking and the kinds of criticism they are engaged in, especially when several kinds are combined in the same critique.

Avant-garde critics often seem to be satisfied with so little—it is odd to read that "among the new and rather striking techniques introduced" in the musicwork called *Dance No. 4* are "traditional harmonic progressions"! Perhaps we ought to envy this ability to be pleased and impressed so easily, but the consequence is that the pages of avant-garde periodicals do not provide the most clear-cut examples of criticism. Explicit evaluations are somewhat rare, though not absent; there is some shyness about speaking directly of aesthetic considerations; and much of the usually limited space has to be taken up with conveying to those who were not present at the performance or the exhibition a sense of what was coming down. In any case, clear-cut examples are plentiful elsewhere—as, to cite one source, in Charles Rosen's chapter on Mozart's piano concertos, in which numerous features of "the six great concertos of 1784" are cited to explain their greatness.[10]

My examples were chosen to show that my conception of criticism is not historically limited: it applies to contemporary artworks of every kind. It is *always* in order to consider what's aesthetically good in an artwork and what features of it account for its being that good, in that way, and for its not being better. No matter that the artist may beg to be excused from such judgments:

10. *The Classical Style* (New York, 1972), p. 227.

if he issues forth his work, publishing, exhibiting, showing, performing, or whatever, then he invites us to attend to it, places it within our living space in relation to (in competition with) other things, and exposes it to our need to make discriminations of value and choices based on them. No matter if the work is highly aleatoric: although it may seem strange to inquire what aesthetic value is achieved by having just these events or features, when the artist did not consciously choose them, nevertheless we can ask, we must ask, whether the work is worth it—whether its features play a part in making enough aesthetic value accrue to it to warrant our effort to experience and understand it.[11] When you are invited to sit through "excruciating noise," it is idiotic not to ask what you can expect to receive in return. The answer, if one is forthcoming, need not be in terms of aesthetic value; if it is not, we have passed from the realm of aesthetic criticism, though not of criticism.

Perhaps I should add that even if I do not see a good reason why any artworks should be exempt from aesthetic criticism, I am prepared to admit other limitations of the critical enterprise. I do not claim that judgments of aesthetic value can always be made precise, or that they can always be made with confidence, much less that critics are infallible. Further experience, better analysis, a broader background of relevant knowledge can correct our judgments or at least improve them. I am in fact rather uneasy about using the term "evaluation" in this connection, since it has been so widely appropriated by the applied social scientists—for example, those who practice "policy evaluation." The aim there, and not improperly, is to find ways of measuring the desirable features of what is done in putting policy into practice; and of course many such features can be quantified (we can count the number of children who went through the Head Start Program, the improvements in grades, the tons of spaghetti served in school lunches, etc.). But such quantification is always an act of abstraction, which loses while it gains, and even the policy evaluators are frequently deluded in thinking that what they ignore is less important than what they have figured out how to count and measure. So I do not wish to suggest that art criticism could be, or should be, quantifiable, and would willingly speak instead of "ap-

11. A point very nicely made by Edward T. Cone in his essay "One Hundred Metronomes," *American Scholar* 46 (1977):443–57; *Journal of Aesthetic Education* 13 (1979):53–68.

praisal" or "assessment," except that these words, too, have a tinge of quantity. (My phrase "estimating aesthetic value" still strikes me as the safest I have seen.)[12] Yet I cannot bring myself to doubt that some artworks are aesthetically better than others; some are much better than others, and quite obviously so; many are better at later stages than at earlier stages of their creation, or have been improved by revisions; and many have serious flaws that bar them from being among the very best or even among the decidedly good.

It should be plain—at least after a few supplementary comments—why I can't accept any of the alternative accounts of critical judgments that have been championed in recent years. Important cues to the right view are obtained by a careful examination of the actual practice of critics. For, as I said earlier, although we need not suppose that everything critics say is true or reasonable, we can and must appeal to procedures widely followed, to forms of argument that hold up under philosophical analysis, to typical features of the critic's illocutionary situation with respect to his or her readers, to those sharp edges of intercritical conflict where one critic's modus operandi is seriously questioned by another. I do not promise to list all of the rejected alternatives, but I hope I shall have included at least the favorites.

1. Critical judgments are not predictions, as suggested, for example, by Hans Eichner and Jerome Stolnitz.[13] An estimate of the value (or *a* value) of something carries no implications about the number and type of persons who will be in a position to take advantage of that value—to cook according to the recipe, to wield the pitchfork skillfully, to appreciate the dancework. A critic can hardly be in a position to make predictions about what his or her readers will appreciate when they are totally unknown to him; and even to make statistical predictions he would have to be in possession of a wide range of empirical knowledge, sociological and psychological, that surely is no part of the critic's requisite equipment. Eichner succeeds in giving some slight plausibility to his view only by framing the alleged prediction—that the reader will like the work "if your experience of art is wide enough"—in a

---

12. It is analyzed further in *The Possibility of Criticism* (Detroit, 1970), pp. 68–72.
13. See Eichner, "The Meaning of 'Good' in Aesthetic Judgments," *British Journal of Aesthetics* 3 (1963); Stolnitz, *Aesthetics and Philosophy of Art Criticism* (Boston, 1960), chap. 15 (the latter incidentally in the course of defending an "objective relativist" account of aesthetic value that is fundamentally in accord with mine).

way that seems to reduce it to a tautology. If prediction were the name of the critic's game, we would expect critical discourse to be far different from what it is: that is, heavily laced with statements about the probable likes and dislikes of various types of people—statements such as only occasionally, casually, and incidentally occur.

2. Aesthetic value is not a tendency, as suggested, for example, by Michael Slote.[14] Dispositional properties are either tendencies or capacities, and many with a single name (such as poisonousness) can be analyzed in either way. Critics may sometimes speculate about how long a novel is likely to stay on the best-seller list or a Broadway play on the stage; but this speculation may have little to do with the work's aesthetic value, and is more the exercise of a reportorial than a critical function. What we want to know from the critic, and what he or she should be in a position to tell us, is what the artwork in question *can* do, when approached in whatever way it takes to get the most out of it. A critic who fails to apprehend the work accurately and adequately may easily underestimate or overestimate its value—this is his occupational hazard. But the kind of knowledge and training that he brings with him to the work, and the methods he uses to make his apprehension of it as accurate and as adequate as he can, relate to gaining knowledge of its capacity to provide aesthetic experience, not its tendency.

3. Critical judgments should not be confused with verdicts. Granted that the word "verdict" has a loose general use that tempts some philosophers to extend it to estimates of aesthetic value; but the air of judicial inquiry and of handing down a decision in response to a preexistent social need is highly misleading here. Judges of artistic competitions render verdicts, may even award Grammies or blue ribbons, and may (as we hope) base their verdicts on sound critical judgments. But the judgments are not verdicts, and can be made in situations where nothing like a verdict is called for, but only (if I may use the term) information: this is, about the value of the artwork at hand, about how good (or poor) it is, and why. The critic is asked for knowledge, I would say, not to make a choice or a decision tied to social consequences. His answer to our question informs our choice, makes us abler to choose wisely, but leaves us wholly free.

14. "The Rationality of Aesthetic Value Judgments," *Journal of Philosophy* 68 (1971):821–39.

4. Critical judgments are not the same as aids to apprehension. The idea that the essential point of criticizing an artwork is to call our attention to what we had missed, to open our eyes or ears, to tell us how to look or listen or read in some preferred way—this idea keeps cropping up. And understandably so, since there is no doubt that one of the valuable side effects of good critical discourse can be precisely this; and criticism that does not satisfy this need is much impoverished. Still, criticism is only one of the ways to do this: pointing, muttering, shouting with enthusiasm, playing the piece over and over, demonstrating the important movements of the dance also open our eyes and ears. What makes criticism criticism is that it does this in the course of providing estimates of aesthetic value along with normative explanations that both support these estimates and help to make them clear and definite.

5. Critical judgments are not necessarily personal endorsements. One provocative line of thought that has been developed in recent years takes off from a somewhat restricted view of the critic's illocutionary situation with respect to the artwork he or she is about to appraise. Presumably a person who is knowledgeable about cars may be able to evaluate a new model, even though he has never driven it, if he observes its performance when driven by expert drivers and solicits their explicit and reliable testimony. Of course when he drives it himself he can do something more, namely give it a personal endorsement: he now knows some of its virtues from experience. Now suppose I am thinking of a certain painting that I have never seen and I want to know whether it is a good one (so I can decide whether to go see it). If I can obtain a reproduction, I will have pretty good evidence, though in some respects distorted. Suppose I talk with people who have seen it and whose artistic judgment I respect, and they tell me their appraisals and supply normative explanations that function for me as reasons for belief. Will I not then be in a position to make a judgment of the painting, however cautious and tentative? It seems to me I will. I grant that being in a position to speak from direct experience is especially crucial in matters of art, and unless my judgment is connected somehow with *someone's* experience of the painting, it is not worth much, and perhaps does not even deserve to be called a judgment. But it *is* an estimate of aesthetic value, based on evidence, and capable of being tested, in its way.

This essentially impersonal view of critical judgments—that their essential character is independent of the status or situation of the judger, and that they can constitute a kind of knowledge capable of being shared with others—has been challenged, first by Guy Sircello and more recently by Alan Tormey.[15] There is a line of thought here that is tempting and deserving of consideration. It starts with the distinction between judging as an illocutionary act and merely reporting someone else's act of judging: my judgment has to be *my* judgment, not someone else's. Hence, it is thought, my judgment cannot be merely a repeating or copying or echoing of another's judging, but must be based on my own experience. So Sircello says "we would be surprised" if someone who had never seen a painting asserted that it is good, and it would be "hardly less strange" if someone who had never read a certain Kafka story said that it is an excellent work.[16] But what *kind* of oddities are these? The claim seems to be (to put it in more current language) that these speakers have somehow failed to fulfill the illocutionary-act conditions of judging, if they are merely going by the testimony of others, so that when they perform the locutionary action of uttering the words "The painting [or story] is good" they simply do not succeed in judging.

But why should we accept this conclusion? Agreed: a report of a judging is not a judging; but if I repeat someone else's judgment in agreement with it, am I not judging likewise? My commendation of a painting or story may not be worth a great deal if I have no experience of what I am judging, but can it fail to be a judgment? Both Sircello and Tormey admit (parenthetically) that I can judge a painting—however incompetently—from a reproduction, and this seems to me to give their case away. A reproduction gives me some information about the original, but so does a description by an art historian who has studied the painting—especially if he supports his judgment of it by normative explanations. Relying on reproductions and relying on expert testimony differ only in degree of directness; how can the former, but not the latter, convert a locutionary action into an illocutionary action of judging?

Tormey's argument is more complex: it aims to undermine the view (which I have been maintaining) that we have knowledge of

---

15. See Sircello, "Subjectivity and Justification in Aesthetic Judgments," *Journal of Aesthetics and Art Criticism* 27 (1968):3–12; Tormey, "Critical Judgments," *Theoria* 39 (1973):35–49.
16. Sircello, "Subjectivity and Justification," pp. 6, 7.

artworks' aesthetic value by arguing that the judgments in which such knowledge would be expressed lack the transmissibility that knowledge requires. The critic can know that the painting is a masterpiece, after experiencing it, but he cannot pass that knowledge along to me, because for me to know this, I would have to experience the painting and make my own judgment of it. "Acquaintance with the object"—that is, "direct perceptual access to the object"—is a "condition that is presupposed whenever we offer or accept an utterance as a genuine critical judgment, whatever the actual merits of that judgment may be."[17] Now it may be that only one who has confronted the painting is in a position to contribute his or her own facts about it, or normative explanations, to a group discussion; but that does not entail that confrontation is an illocutionary-act condition of judging. And indeed if I, who have not seen the painting, reflect on what I know about it and come to believe, for these good reasons, that the painting is a fine one, how can I *not* be judging (and perhaps even expressing my knowledge) when I say the painting is good?

As Tormey has pointed out in a letter to me replying to some earlier comments on his most interesting essay, he holds that our perplexities over these problems derive from admitting the terms "true" and "false" (as implicit in "knowledge") into our picture of critical judgment, and this skeptical doubt, of course, raises some very fundamental questions. I do not share his doubt—partly because I do not see how, on his own view, critical judgments could even function as personal endorsements unless they had truth value. But since he has this doubt, and it is shared by Joseph Margolis in an essay that has provoked some discussion,[18] I may as well place on the record one more mistaken view that I reject.

6. Critical judgments are not truth valueless. Margolis' brief discussion of his view does not clarify or support it much, but in gist, it apparently assimilates critical evaluations to what he calls "appreciative judgments," which (a) are neither true nor false but (b) take other "values." Margolis gives samples but no definition or characterization of the class of predicates that are "values" in this special sense. "With respect to such judgments, I claim, we may say only that it is reasonable, extreme, eccentric, etc. to *say*

---

17. Tormey, "Critical Judgments," p. 38.
18. "Robust Relativism," The *Journal of Aesthetics and Art Criticism* 35 (1976):37–46; reprinted in *Philosophy Looks at the Arts,* Joseph Margolis, 2d ed. (Philadelphia, 1978).

that a work has this or that degree of merit rather *than* that it demonstrably *has* it."¹⁹ The word "demonstrably" is diversionary here; the question at issue in his discussion is not whether we can *demonstrate* that *Paradise Lost* is a great poem but whether we "may say" this, in that we would be saying something true or false. I must confess that I do not understand why (a) "we may say . . . that it is reasonable . . . to say" that *Paradise Lost* is great, but (b) we may *not* say that *Paradise Lost* is great. And if it is "eccentric" to say that *Paradise Lost* is literary trash, this is surely not because there is anything wrong with the grammar (category mistakes, Austinian illocutionary misfirings, etc.) but because it is so plainly false.

If I have overlooked other accounts of critical judgment that conflict with the one I have expounded and defended, but that deserve at least the attention of rebuttal, I ask to be excused for my negligence. Perhaps I have said enough, both on behalf of my own view and in reply to others, so that it can be inferred how I would deal—or ought to deal—with the missing accounts.

19. Margolis, ed., *Philosophy Looks at the Arts*, p. 42.

19: *The Relevance of Reasons in Art Criticism*

THE character of serious and informative critical discourse shows even in such capsule examples as these: The popular paintings of children by Walter Keane are aesthetically execrable *because* of their "appalling sentimentality" (John Canaday). Vladimir Nabokov's *Pale Fire* is "one of the very great works of art of this century" *because* it is "a creation of perfect beauty, symmetry, strangeness, originality, and moral truth" (Mary McCarthy). Elgar's Cello Concerto "impresses not only as Elgar's finest work, but also as one of the most perfect and intense pieces of its kind ever written" (at least partly) *because* "it has unity from beginning to end, and poignant melody and personality and depth" (Harold C. Shoenberg). We don't have to endorse either the critical judgments or the subordinate clauses to use these examples, which are surely representative. As we saw in Essay 18, what follows the connective "because" is, from one perspective, a normative *explanation* (or partial explanation): the fact that the painting is appallingly sentimental explains (or largely explains) the fact—assuming it *is* a fact—that the painting is aesthetically execrable. So, at least, the critic affirms. From another perspective, however, what follows "because" is a *justification* (or partial justification) of the judgment: the fact—assuming it *is* a fact—that the painting is sentimental supports the judgment. It is a reason for believing that the painting is bad, and if it is a very good reason, it can convert the belief into *knowledge*.

The logical principle involves a close relationship between explanation and justification. There is no circularity, but there is mutual reinforcement. If we think the painting is bad, if it strikes us as horrible at first sight, we may wonder what makes it so. If we then discover that it is extremely sentimental, and if the extreme sentimentality would largely explain its badness (if it is bad), then the fact that it is sentimental lends support to the conclusion that it is bad. The critic who goes through such a process of reacting and analyzing and explaining is now in a position to cite the sentimentality as a justification for his judgment—and to offer it to others, even to someone who has not yet seen the painting but may be grateful to be warned away, as a reason for believing that it is bad.

I am sorry to complicate this account, but I think no simpler one will suffice. And if it is acceptable, it suggests that we may have one valuable criterion for deciding what can count as a reason to support critical judgments. But we must not be in a hurry to leap to conclusions here; we may require more distinctions. So for the moment let us tentatively adopt just these cautious principles:

> *Any* fact about an artwork that would help to explain its goodness (or poorness) can be used as a reason to help justify the judgment that it is good (or poor).
>
> *Some* facts that may be used as reasons for judging an artwork to be good (or poor) are facts that would help to explain its goodness (or poorness); let us call such reasons "explanatory reasons."

Explanatory reasons are justifications (at least partial) that also explain; we may take explanation here as a relation between facts and as transitive. Thus suppose the fact (F_1) that the children in Walter Keane's paintings are very sentimental, and the fact that the paintings are very sentimental (F_2) helps to explain the fact (F_3) that they are aesthetically bad; then indirectly F_1 helps to explain F_3. So the range of justificatory reasons that are explanatory—and are justificatory *because* they are explanatory—is considerable, and may include information about the smallest details of an artwork.

Nonexplanatory reasons—justifications that do not explain why the work is good (or poor)—can, I think, be divided into two groups. Some are *authoritative* and some are *circumstantial*. An authoritative reason is a fact about someone's beliefs that counts as a reason because that person is a reliable authority. Consider the fact that Mary McCarthy has praised *Pale Fire* highly. I suppose this fact does not help to explain why *Pale Fire* is very good, but it could still be a (partial) justification for the reader of her review in *The New Republic* to judge that the work is very good. And it could be a quite *good* reason, that is, one that counts strongly or weightily. But what gives it this strength or weight is that Mary McCarthy's authority in the particular matter of *Pale Fire* derives from her ability to provide *explanatory* justifications of *her* judgment: she offers normative explanations of the work's aesthetic value in terms of its "perfect beauty" and so on. So the reasons in this subclass of nonexplanatory reasons depend on *someone's* having explanatory reasons.

Circumstantial reasons, on the other hand, are neither explanatory nor authoritative. Someone might infer that a piece by Elgar must be good because it was written during a period when he was generally doing fine work, or because it was publicly performed a hundred times over a few decades, or because it was commissioned by and dedicated to a celebrated cellist. No doubt such facts are evidence of a sort, and could be reasons for the conclusion. But a good deal of what we know about the individuality of musicworks, the creative process, the economic and personal factors that affect performances and commissions goes to show that circumstantial reasons can seldom, if ever, be very *good* reasons (that is, strong or weighty ones). So let us set this subclass aside, as of little interest or moment to a study of critical reasons. It would be difficult to lay your hands on a piece of criticism that takes such facts very seriously, at least by themselves. One might write: "As we would expect, considering that this is one of the last complete works of Mozart, it is splendid"—but the real justification for this judgment would have to be supplied by explanatory reasons or authoritative reasons, which are just borrowed explanatory reasons.

Donald Callen has called my attention to the difficulty of finding a place in this classificatory scheme for the familiar kind of reason that consists in appealing to the "verdict of history," that is, enduring interest taken in an artwork. The fact that the work has continued to be enjoyed and praised over a long period of time does seem to constitute a legitimate ground for praise. Such reasons are plainly not directly explanatory, but their force (when they have force) depends, I think, on their combining some assumed authority with their circumstantiality. Thus if the fact is simply that the work has remained in print or on the stage or on the walls of an art museum, it can only be a purely circumstantial reason; but if we know enough to infer that its longevity has depended to some extent on the positive judgments of those in a position to judge soundly, the verdict of history reflects the existence of good reasons on its behalf. Though the persistent approval does not help to explain the excellence of the work, the excellence of the work can be taken to explain its persistent approval.

Here we must note another ambiguity in "reasons": there are facts that are *offered* as reasons, and there are facts that *count* as reasons, because they are logically relevant to the judgments they are alleged to support.

In the *Lesser Hippias* Socrates says to Eudicus: "I have heard your father, Apemantus, declare the the *Iliad* of Homer is a finer poem than the *Odyssey* in the same degree that Achilles was a better man than Odysseus; Odysseus, he would say, is the central figure of the one poem and Achilles of the other."[1] Here is a critical judgment accompanied by a forthright reason that most contemporary critics would consider wildly irrelevant to it. And on the face of it, Achilles' moral superiority does not seem to have any bearing on the aesthetic superiority of the Iliad; it seems as irrelevant as the fact that the Iliad is longer (by some 3,000 lines, I believe). It is tempting to dismiss this passage (especially since the Platonic dialogue is of doubtful authenticity) as an abandonment of the aesthetic point of view for the moral point of view.

For comparison, consider a judicious passage in which Samuel Johnson answered critics who objected to Edmund's role in *King Lear*:

> The injury done by Edmund to the simplicity of the action is abundantly recompensed by the addition of variety, by the art with which he is made to co-operate with the chief design, and the opportunity which he gives the poet of combining perfidy with perfidy and connecting the wicked son with the wicked daughters, to impress this important moral, that villainy is never at a stop, that crimes lead to crimes and at last terminate in ruin.[2]

Here the point of view seems to shift from a consideration of formal properties of the play to its use in promulgating the moral that crime does not pay. We might wonder whether the fact that the play has an acceptable moral is a relevant reason for praising it, or judging it better than other critics have realized—especially since the play seems also to suggest that virtue (such as Cordelia's) cannot be depended on to pay either.

How shall we decide such questions? By discovering whether

---

1. *The Dialogues of Plato*, trans. Benjamin Jowett (New York, 1937), bk. 2, p. 715.
2. W. K. Wimsatt, ed., *Samuel Johnson on Shakespeare* (New York, 1960), p. 97.

the fact whose relevance is in dispute can help explain the play's capacity (or the limits of its capacity) to provide experience with aesthetic character. It is not hard to show that the first part of Johnson's sentence is relevant in just this way. The fact that Edmund's actions are present in the play does not detract significantly from unity, since his actions are thematically related to the main plot, while they increase variety, extending the range of human experience presented for our contemplation. Thus Edmund's presence helps to explain the complexity of the work, which in turn helps explain why the work is capable of moving and absorbing us and calling on some of our deepest emotions and thoughts. But the fact (if it *is* a fact) that the play is a warning against perfidy and crime does not seem to connect in this explanatory way with those features of aesthetic experience that we considered above, in Essay 16.

It may be that, on further reflection, our dismissal of Apemantus' idea will seem too hasty. Perhaps I am not enough of an admirer of Achilles or enough of a student of Homer to make as much of a case as could be made. It would be the critic's task to discover exactly how the characters of the epic heroes are connected with other features of the work and give it its aesthetic capacity. Suppose we could agree on what virtues make Achilles the better man than Odysseus; we then could ask what precise roles these traits play in the plot. One thing we are sure to find is that neither plot could be possible unless Achilles and Odysseus had some moral virtues and some moral defects. Odysseus is required to be the more interesting, the more complex character, and perhaps he even has to have more faults, some of them consequent upon his central drive to get home, some of them needed in the plot to get him into and out of situations that delay his return. If he were less tricky or less courageous, the poem would be less great. His good and bad points are both needed. On the other hand, the conflicts in the *Iliad*, between persons and between peoples, rise to a level of grandeur that helps to give this work a sublimity unmatched by the *Odyssey*, and for this purpose it is necessary to have heroes who are larger than life, whose deeds are the stuff of song and legend. Perhaps Apemantus (unless Socrates is indulging in irony) was thinking along lines that could be recast in our terms: the fact that Achilles, central to the *Iliad*, has heroic virtues to a high degree helps to explain the fact that the *Iliad* has sublimity to a high degree. To which we might then add: the fact that the *Iliad* is sublime helps to explain the fact that it has the capacity to provide experience with extremely marked aesthetic character.

Since the marks, or criteria, of the aesthetic character of experience are varied and vague, we cannot, of course, expect to draw a sharp line between relevant and irrelevant reasons. But if, as I suppose, the burden of proof (in case of a dispute) rests on the claim to relevance, we have a procedure we can recommend in order to show that a particular kind of reason is indeed relevant. Somewhere along the line the property (of an artwork) that the reason cites should be connectable with some element of the aesthetic character. The route may be long, involving several stages; even the fact that the *Iliad* is 3,000 lines longer than the *Odyssey* might be shown, by some perceptive critic, to help to give it the room required for the development of its epic power and hence for acquiring the capacity to concentrate and intensify the elements of our experience of the poem—in which case the length would become a partial explanation of the work's aesthetic value. Any fact about the *Iliad* could conceivably be relevant, but not all really are—including some that are of a sort on which certain critics are wont to dwell.[3] The procedure I propose is generous and flexible, allowing a very wide range of reasons; it leaves criticism open to future artworks with properties not yet imagined. But it does make a distinction and draw a line, so that it is not unuseful.

But is there a way of sharpening this distinction a little—of providing the critic with more directly applicable criteria for determining the relevance of reasons? I think there is, though I am aware that some joints in the argument are not yet perfectly fitted. To make the case as clear and convincing as possible, let us begin by going back for a moment to fundamentals.

An artwork is an arrangement made in order to provide occasions of aesthetic experience, but its special nature makes an encounter with it an occasion in a peculiarly intimate sense. The work must be actively and generously present in the experience; that is, many of its properties must be open to cognition and must be the direct objects of attention and of enjoyment. These properties always include at least some perceptual properties—those that

---

3. For many interesting examples see Renata Adler's dissection of a volume of film reviews *When the Lights Go Down*, by Pauline Kael: "The Perils of Pauline," *New York Review*, August 14, 1980, pp. 26–35.

can be grasped in perception—and very often, too, of course, various kinds of semantic properties: something is referred to (denoted, represented, symbolized, suggested, etc.). What is given is a manifold, the proper cognition of which can become the core element of an aesthetic experience. However much may be referred to, and thus be brought into the compass of the experience, something must be *presented* in perception, and what is referred to depends on and builds on this perceptual base. Thus those properties of the artwork that either are perceptual or are connected with its perceptual properties through reference are the properties that can actually do the work required—can induce, by entering into, an aesthetic experience.

When we consider the manifold of properties in an artwork, both perceptual and semantic, we may inquire into its basic dimensions: the most general and important ways in which one such manifold can be compared with another. I find three such basic dimensions. Although from time to time I have been (like others) afflicted with doubts about this suspiciously tidy scheme, I keep returning to it; there is something *almost* a priori about it. Given perceptual-semantic manifolds that are designed for aesthetic experience, and setting aside particular differences in content, in order to focus on features common to all, though varying in degree from one manifold to another, we come up with three dimensions: they vary (1) with respect to their degree of unification or integration (as opposed to disunity or disorganization), (2) with respect to their degree of complexity or multiplicity of varied parts and internal relations (as opposed to simplicity), and (3) with respect to the intensity (as opposed to the weakness or insipidity) of their affirmative regional qualities—that is, those qualities that spread out through the artwork or some major portion of it and that have a positive character.

When we consider these three dimensions with respect to the requirements for providing aesthetic experience, we can take guidance from the prevailing (though not universal) practice of art critics, noting what sorts of thing they tend to single out for attention in their criticism. We can also consider the nature of aesthetic experience and what properties of artworks can be expected to enhance and encourage it. So it is the unity, rather than the disunity, of an artwork that can make it capable of a strong and concentrated impact and hold our attention within the limits of its manifold, while it works upon us. It is the complexity, rather than the simplicity, of an artwork that can give enrichment, excitement, challenge, and adventure to the experience of it. It is the intensity rather than the vapidity of regional qualities that can be interesting, can claim and reward lingering attention, arouse our affection, and dominate our response.

All this is sketchy, to be sure, but what it sketches is the outline of a defensible line of thought. The conclusion to which that thought leads is that we can explain *how* an artwork becomes capable of affording aesthetic experience, or more capable than another, when we see how unified and complex it is, how intense its affirmative regional qualities are. Thus the critic's explanations have to *go through* these three basic properties. The critic explains how good, or how poor, the work is by showing how certain noteworthy features of the work contribute to making the work more or less unified, complex, and qualitatively intense. All critical explanations that bear on these three dimensions are logically relevant to the critic's overall evaluation. And I think—though this is more debatable—that *only* explanations that bear on these dimensions are logically relevant.

Such, at least, is the principle that I proposed some time ago, and have been defending against the natural, and proper, suspicions it occasionally arouses. To put this triadic principle directly, I say that a feature of an artwork is a normatively explanatory feature with respect to its degree of aesthetic value (so that a reason citing it is judgmentally relevant) if and only if it is

1. *unifying* or *disunifying*: that is, its presence causally contributes toward increasing or detracting from the work's coherence or completeness; or
2. *complexifying* or *decomplicating*: that is, its presence contributes toward giving the work range, scope, variety, subtlety, contrast, or depth, or restricting it in one of these respects; or
3. *intensifying* or *enfeebling* of the work's affirmative regional qualities.

When a critic offers the fact that an artwork has a certain feature as a reason for a judgment, hence as an explanation (generally partial) of the work's degree of aesthetic value (it is excellent, very poor, magnificent, aesthetically negligible, fair, etc.), that feature can *be* explanatory only if it is capable of influencing the work's degree of unity, complexity, or intensity of affirmative regional quality.[4]

Undoubtedly some of the key terms in the triadic principle are philosophically puzzling and give rise to difficult questions, which I have been trying for many years to resolve, though as yet not to my complete satisfaction. The word "affirmative," for example, is needed to hold a place open for a distinction in segment 3 that is still puzzling. It is evident that some regional qualities are directly citable in this explanatory role: that the work is highly elegant, for example, must go some way toward accounting for its being good, if it is good—and this is true whether or not you happen to be in favor of producing elegant works or of having them around. But that the work is awkward (not a character in it, but the work itself) can never help to explain its goodness, only its poorness. This distinction is one I have labored over on earlier occasions,[5] and I hold out for an important difference between, say, elegance and awkwardness—the former being full of positive phenomenal content, thus in my metaphorical sense "affirmative," or life-enhancing; the latter being a sort of deficiency or deprivation.

Again, with respect to segment 2, it might be remarked that complexity is all very well in some very loose sense, but when it comes down to all the many ways in which an artwork can be complexified, there is some question about how far we can go to establish objectively that one artwork is more complex than another. Of course this doubt is valid, so such comparisons wane in objectivity and usefulness as the differences between the comparanda increase. Still, similar works can quite easily be compared with respect to complexity, and every form of complexity in a work is, taken by itself, something that counts in its favor.

Perhaps the concept of unity has been the target of the greatest skepticism, though the skeptics have not been as forthcoming with arguments as they might be. Very often, I am afraid, their objections amount to hand wringing and sounds of distress, which are rather difficult to answer logically. I offer a recent example,

---

4. I hope I am allowed—if I can obtain brevity without risking unintelligibility—to speak occasionally of "features" and of "states of affairs" (the presence of a feature) and of "facts" as explanatory. Strictly speaking, it is states of affairs and events that affect or influence other states of affairs and events, and it is facts that explain facts—at least I am using this defensible conceptual scheme here.

5. See Lecture 4 of *The Possibility of Criticism* (Detroit, 1970).

just come to hand, from a review of Joseph Margolis' collection of readings in aesthetics, *Philosophy Looks at the Arts* (revised edition), which begins with the essay that opens the present volume.

> For instance, M. Beardsley's 'The Aesthetic Point of View' is, in itself and unintentionally, a refutation of the professionalism of aesthetics. Without proper reference to the traditions of its problem, the article undertakes a regressive, definitional exercise culminating in the unexplained ideas of 'formal unity' and 'regional intensity.' These ideas, though unclear, are hardly new. If there is professionalism it is unnecessary, because the content is not being invented but regurgitated (untransformed), and the methodology is a naive definitionalism which advances argumentatively by means of a simplistic confrontation with counterexamples.[6]

True, not much had been said in the essay to clarify the concepts of unity and of intensity of regional quality, though something had been done elsewhere; but apart from not being new, I wish the reviewer had told me what's wrong with these ideas. (I would also like to know what definitionalism is, so that I can henceforth shun it, at least in its naive form.)

Besides the internal troubles with my attempt to set the bounds of relevance for critical reasons, there are external ones that may be even more serious, and something needs to be said here about them. If, as some have protested, I have set the bounds too narrowly, then there will be kinds of reason that are inadmissible by my principle though essential to the critical enterprise. In that case, the principle must be rejected or revised. There are widely used critical concepts that I have rejected as irrelevant to critical judgment,[7] but that deserve another careful look to round out the present argument. The pressure to widen, almost indefinitely, the bounds of relevance has been intensified in recent years by two developments: a growing sense that avant-garde artistic movements call for many more critical grounds than my principle provides, and a resurgence of philosophical interest in the problems presented by forgeries, reproductions, copies, and restorations of artworks.[8]

6. Roger L. Taylor, in *British Journal of Aesthetics* 19 (1979):381.
7. See, for example, *Aesthetics: Problems in the Philosophy of Criticism* (New York, 1958), pp. 457–61.
8. See, for example, the collection edited by Denis Dutton, *The Forger's Art: Forgery and the Philosophy of Art* (Berkeley, 1982).

The concept of originality has come into frequent use as a ground for praise among avant-garde art critics: sometimes about the only nice thing you can say about a new offering is that no one ever did *that* before. But my main interest here is in the continuity, rather than the breaks, in art criticism. One of the things I had in mind in giving examples of current criticism in Essay 18 was to show that even in a representative sample of avant-garde criticism we find appeals to the three fundamental pairs of properties built into the triadic principle. First, our critics are evidently much concerned with intensity of affirmative regional qualities—with the "dramatic" character of the musicwork and the "dynamism," "tension," and suggestion of "animate life" in the painting. Second, they are concerned with complexity—with the contrasts provided by "tonal shifts" between "plateaus," and with the multiplicity of suggestion ("ambiguity") in the painted shapes. Third, I think I even descry here some concern with unity. It is of course true that present-day critics are not much on unity; they are often content with a comparatively low degree of unity if it seems to them that unity has been sacrificed for intensity of regional qualities or for great complexity—or for some nonaesthetic achievement, such as making the audience aware that the normal concert situation is constraining. But our music critic does find a structure of "hierarchical relationships," which might introduce a sense of order; and the changes and contrasts are all of a piece, so to speak, as shifts from plateau to plateau, so that what is happening could have coherence. And our painting critic apparently sees a clear relationship between figure and ground persisting throughout the various "readings" of their suggestiveness. If avant-garde art tends to be little unified, it does not follow that it is necessarily bad, or that its disunity is what makes it good, or that such unity as it has is not an important element in contributing to its capacity to move us aesthetically by means of its fascinating complexities or vital regional qualities.

On a philosophical plane, the concept of originality has been given thoughtful consideration in recent years, and has been endorsed as a critical criterion by able aestheticians. Thus Haig Khatchadourian has argued that to be an artwork at all, an object must exhibit some "minimal achievement in originality and freshness"; but to be a *good* work of art, it must go further and be capable of "enlarging our aesthetic experience, of widening and deepening our perceptions."

A work of art may also be judged to be good art if it is regarded as productive of new and fresh kinds of effects, if it employs new materials or media, new techniques of organization, or new subject-matter. . . . But again, originality in technique and in the use of materials is generally regarded as aesthetically valuable, as meriting the application of the epithets "good," "very good," only when it is believed to be aesthetically effective. Originality for originality's sake, novelty for novelty's sake, is ordinarily disparaged rather than praised.[9]

I have some difficulty with this passage, as with many other discussions of the relevance of originality to aesthetic value. The first sentence seems clearly to say that the fact that an artwork is original ("new" in one or more of the specified ways) may be offered as a reason—a good, even conclusive, reason—why it is a good one. But what if the "effects" are deplorable, the "materials or media" unpromising for the achievement of aesthetic value, the "techniques" fumblingly used, and the "subject-matter" totally confused and disorganized? Will the originality save the work? I doubt it. And indeed, Khatchadourian himself seems to doubt it, too, when later he endorses the disparagement of "originality for originality's sake"—which I take to be originality separated from other features that would admittedly count as helping to give the work aesthetic value.

Here it will be useful to remind ourselves of the distinction between two kinds of facts about an artwork (including its relationships to other artworks and to actual or potential receivers). There are facts about features that increase or diminish (so that their presence helps to explain) the aesthetic capacity of the work. And there are facts about features that increase or diminish (so that their presence helps to explain) the ability of a *receiver* to appreciate the work. It may sometimes be difficult in practice to decide, when the interaction is defective, whether it is the work's aesthetic capacity or the receiver's aesthetic ability that is at fault; but the distinction is crucial to an adequate theory of criticism. For example, obscurity, or difficulty of apprehension, makes the work harder, or even for some impossible, to derive aesthetic satisfaction from, but it does not detract from its capacity to provide aesthetic experience so long as some people are able to overcome the barriers. Now one thing we can say about originality (freshness, novelty, pleasant surprisingness) is that it can affect the

9. "Art-Names and Aesthetic Judgments," *Philosophy* 36 (1961):38.

receiver's ability to appreciate an artwork, just as the overfamiliarity of works of a certain kind can jade the appetite, dull perception, produce stock responses triggered by a casual, hasty, inadequate apprehension of the work. Two paintings of (roughly) equal aesthetic value might fare differently with a particular viewer if only one is strikingly and interestingly different, in form or quality, from what he has heretofore known.

I believe my distinction has an important bearing on a point that has been well made, by Nelson Goodman and others: that perceptions of an artwork are sometimes strongly affected by shifts of belief about its genuineness (that is, its having, in Goodman's term, the "history of production" it purports to have): they cite the critics who, after the exposure of Van Meegeren's forgeries, came to see aesthetic faults and un-Vermeerlike features that they could not see before the exposure. What is the import of this psychological fact? One reasonable response to it is to deny that Van Meegeren's forgeries either objectively have or objectively lack these fickle features, and to insist on relativizing them to the states of belief: the paintings look stylistically coherent to one who believes that they were painted by Vermeer, but stylistically incoherent to one who believes that they were painted by Van Meegeren. But these two relativized statements, if taken generally, are not true; and in any case there is no need for them if we are willing to allow the possibility of perceptual error in such cases. So my alternative response is to say that someone was deceived—although, of course, it may be very difficult to decide whether these critics were overinfluenced by their awe of Vermeer in the earlier time or by their disgust with Van Meegeren in the later time (or by both). Perception of such qualities as stylistic coherence is delicate, and sensitive to cognitive background, but I assume here that it is itself a cognitive act capable of informing us about the painting. So we might say that the fact that the work was painted by So-and-so, when believed by a viewer, may affect that viewer's ability to apprehend the work accurately and adequately. But it does not strictly affect, and therefore does not help explain, the artwork's capacity to provide aesthetic experience; so it is not a relevant reason for a value judgment.

But perhaps I am reaching this conclusion too hastily. How might the case for originality as a critical criterion be advanced? Suppose we try the following thesis, in defense of the relevance of originality:

The fact that X is more original than Y (or is original though Y is not) helps to explain why X is aesthetically better than Y.

As I remarked earlier, I think it is up to the defender of the originality criterion—whom I should like to call an originalitarian—to show how this explanation works. One way I can try to make things hard for him is to bring in my triadic principle and insist that the originality of an artwork can affect (and therefore can explain) the artwork's aesthetic value only via one or more of the three pairs of features embedded in the triadic principle. If the originality helps to make it more (or less) unified or complex, or helps to strengthen or enfeeble one or more of its affirmative regional qualities, then it *is* relevant to the judgment. If not, not. One thing the avant-garde visual and aural artists (and of course playwrights and choreographers too) have shown us is that you can make a novelty of simplicity and poverty that cannot help but be unified, of chaos, of negative regional qualities that inhibit affirmative ones, of utter blandness and vapidity. So this doesn't look like a very promising line of argument for the originalitarian.

Suppose, however, that he evades our trap by rejecting the triadic principle and claiming that originality is one of those features of an artwork that contributes to its aesthetic value *without* affecting unity, complexity, or regional-quality intensity. He might insist:

> Even if X is no more unified, complex, or intense in affirmative regional qualities than Y, if X is more original than Y, then X is aesthetically better than Y.

To such a thesis we might pose counterexamples. The first and second editions of Kant's *Critique of Pure Reason* are fairly equal in unity, complexity, and intensity of affirmative regional quality—never mind that in the third respect both may be somewhat deprived. The first edition is far more original than the second; but is it aesthetically better? It won't do, I think, for the originalitarian to reply that the question is inappropriate, for anything can be regarded from the aesthetic point of view, and when so regarded the *Critique of Pure Reason* is seen to be not lacking in aesthetic value, which comes, among other things, from the dramatic development of its argument and the intricate architecture of its system of thought. But if it seems fairer to stay within the realm of art, we may admit that the *Odyssey* is a good deal more original than the *Aenead*. Must we then concede that if it turned out that the latter had been written first, we would have to revise our comparative judgment of these poems? I don't see why.

We may now take a look at some recent discussions of the problem and consider how well they fare if the problem is posed the way I suggest. One remark may be made by way of introduction: at the risk of brief monotony, since I have been insisting on this point for some time, I say once more that we must keep a distinction here between judging the artwork and judging the artist, and this has not proved easy to do because the word "original" slides so readily back and forth. Consider this example:

> Sirs: I do not question Frank B. Warnke's comments on Gilbert Highet (July 18); but I do dissent from his statement that Richard Rodgers is inferior to Samuel Barber as a composer because he is trivial and shallow—and presumably because Barber is serious and deep. I contend that there is value in Rodgers' light songs for *Pal Joey* and *The Boys from Syracuse,* but none in Barber's unoriginal and eclectically imitative serious music.[10]

Coming from a conscientious and perceptive music critic, whom I respect, this note should carry some weight, but it unfortunately illustrates exactly the slide I am concerned to warn against. The thrust of the passage is clearly a comparison of two *composers,* and here the comparative originality (or alleged originality) of their work is certainly relevant to a judgment. It is a quite different matter to say that Barber's music lacks (aesthetic?) value, and to try to explain this lack of value by asserting that his music is unoriginal. That only makes it less interesting to a music critic—which is not the same as being no good.

In a brief discussion of originality as a critical ground, H W. Janson concedes that it is often difficult to apply, "but it does seem a bit more manageable than perfection, coherence, unity of form and content, balance, and similar criteria."[11] I hold no brief for "unity of form and content," which I think is a snare and a delusion, and I am puzzled about perfection, but the main point is that manageability is hardly the central issue here. Logical relevance is. Janson seems to endorse the art historian's concern with originality, at least in the sense of getting at the original work: for this expert, "as long as we see it 'merely' as a forgery, it is assumed to have no aesthetic value at all. . . . Next in rank are

10. B. H. Haggin, in *New Republic,* August 15, 1960.
11. "Originality as a Ground for Judgment of Excellence," in *Art and Philosophy: A Symposium,* ed. Sidney Hook (New York, 1966), p. 28.

copies: here the assumption is that no copy can capture the essence of the original, hence the more faithful the copy, the lower its aesthetic value."[12] No support is given for these assumptions, and the second one is certainly paradoxical: it's like saying that since ersatz coffee can never "capture the essence" of real coffee, the more successfully it imitates the latter's flavor, the worse it is. Surely there is some value that an excellent reproduction shares with its original, and what more appropriate name for that value than "aesthetic"?

In response to a critical discussion by James Walsh of his book *Thought and Action*, Stuart Hampshire remarks that "any critic of the art of the past, or of his own time, looks for originality as one of the values of art. Originality is the opening of new possibilities in the use of the medium and, therefore, of new uses of the imagination, both for artists and for their public."[13] The point is well taken and the formulation judicious. It is to be noted, however, that originality is given rather more content here than in ordinary language: it's not just being different from what has gone before, but being different in a *desirable* way—the artist who opens "new possibilities" (Cézanne is his example) does not accomplish this feat merely by novelty, but by producing some first-rate work in the new manner, thereby demonstrating that it actually *has* possibilities. In this sense, originality is itself a value, as Hampshire says, because value is built into its definition. And certainly a critic or an art historian must be concerned with originality in this sense. But note that nothing Hampshire says implies that the aesthetic value of an artwork can be explained (even in part) by the fact that it is original, in the sense of being of a hitherto uninstanced kind.

In a discussion of Nelson Goodman's views on authenticity, Richard Rudner distinguishes between judgments of aesthetic value and judgments of artistic value, and assigns considerations of originality and authenticity to the latter type of judgment. Artistic judgments belong rather to ethics than to aesthetics, he holds, because they apply to situations in which we need to do something with or about or to artworks.[14]

There is another group of interrelated concepts, of which *skill*

---

12. Ibid., pp.-26, 27.
13. "Reply to Walsh on *Thought and Action*," *Journal of Philosophy* 60 (1963):422.
14. "On Seeing What We Shall See," in *Logic and Art: Essays in Honor of Nelson Goodman*, ed. Richard Rudner and Israel Scheffler (Indianapolis, 1972), pp. 169–72.

is best taken as representative, that deserve discussion here, especially in view of Jerome Stolnitz's valuable treatment of the issues.[15] Following Ingarden, he uses the term "artistic values" for such properties of an artwork as skill, virtuosity, deftness, adroitness, economy.[16] As he says, it may be a fact about a musicwork that "the transition . . . is skillfully managed," a statement that seems to me to be a combination of two distinguishable facts: one about the audible character of the transition (that it is smooth, neat, carried through without wasted or dull passages, or whatever), and one about the genesis of the transition (that its character is due to the exercise of skill on the part of the composer). As he notes—but I am recasting in my own language of action theory—an action is an event in which something changes state (say, the staffs on the music paper fill up with notes as the composer writes the score), and the final state, the *terminus ad quem*, of the action, what the action issues in, may be called the "result" of the action. This final state is not the *effect* of the action, but its deposit in the world: the act of shutting a door results in a door's being shut. So we can think of the act of composition as resulting in a musicwork.

Now Stolnitz is chiefly concerned, first, to correct some current misunderstandings—including real deficiencies in my own earlier discussion of the topic—and, second, to show that "the appreciation of skill or virtuosity is a well-defined sector of aesthetic experience generally. . . . Judgments of artistic value are therefore a subclass of aesthetic judgments."[17] What concerns me is a question that may not be exactly Stolnitz', but is certainly closely related: whether the fact that something in an artwork is done skillfully can be a reason in support of the judgment that the work is good. And it seems quite clear—contrary to my earlier view—that it can. The objective part of the fact—for example, that the transition has a certain character—can certainly be a (partial) explanation of the music's goodness. And the genetic part—for example, that the composer possessed skill in designing transitions—also helps to explain, though more indirectly, how it comes about that the music is good. But of course the second part, by itself, is not a very informative explanation; it doesn't tell us what the composer

---

15. "The Artistic Values in Aesthetic Experience," *Journal of Aesthetics and Art Criticism* 32 (1973):5–15.
16. Ibid., p. 7.
17. Ibid., p. 15.

actually *did* (the result of his act of composing) that helped make the work good. It is the first part of the fact, concerning the character of the transition as we hear it, that carries the main explanatory weight, in informing us, say, why *this* transition is so superior to those in some of the composer's other works. And the objective result stands on its own feet: if the same transition had been hit upon by luck or chance or pedestrian trial-and-error rather than skill, it would have been no less a merit and a ground of praise *of the work*.

If we single out just the fact that the artist exercises skill in creating a work, that is perhaps more like a variable than a constant, a schematic way of pointing out that there is some character of the work that is worth noting as a ground of its aesthetic value. In experiencing the work, we may make the inference that some admirable feature was due to the artist's skill, and this may make us extend our admiration to the artist. Stolnitz may be quite right that such admiration is neither necessary to aesthetic experience nor excluded from it; I am not convinced, however, that the work's capacity to make us admire the artist contributes to the work's capacity to afford aesthetic experience. One way in which it might do so is by transforming the opportunity for causal inference into a semantic relation of reference: if we could say that one of the things the artwork refers to is the artist's skill, so that grasping this reference is part of apprehending the work. Stolnitz does not take this road, but it has recently been taken in an original and carefully argued essay by Thomas Carson Mark.[18]

"Works of virtuosity," on Mark's proposal, are those of which a central feature is "displayed skill," that is, skill exhibited as an end in itself.[19] The thrust of his argument is that in the case of some artworks "technical skill . . . penetrates and partly determines the nature of the artwork itself," and hence its artistic goodness.[20] The argument begins with the claim that an essential feature of artworks is that "they admit of having a subject, of being about something"—that is, "it is never out of place" to ask what an artwork is about, even though it may in fact be about nothing.[21] A work of virtuosity, then, is distinguished by its possession of three properties: (1) it is a work "for which skill is a necessary

18. "On Works of Virtuosity," *Journal of Philosophy* 77 (1980):28–45.
19. Ibid., p. 29.
20. Ibid., pp. 28, 33.
21. Ibid., p. 33.

condition" (some artworks require skill and some don't); (2) it "must take the skills that are its own necessary conditions as its subject," or one of its subjects; and (3) "it must display the skills it is about."[22] The third condition is fulfilled when an artwork is an instance of what it is about, as (Mark claims) an impressionist picture can instantiate what it is about: namely, the resolution of light into primary colors. "Art becomes philosophical when it explores the relation between art and reality,"[23] and this is what works of virtuosity do. Mark's prime example is the set of Chopin études, and the convincingness of his argument rests heavily on his interpretation of them. One who lacks his evident deep knowledge of these études must feel hesitant about questioning that interpretation, but actually he presents very little in the way of support for the crucial claim. The études "aim, obviously, at displaying skill in piano playing, and there are a number of senses in which it is true to say that the études are about skill in piano playing"[24]—though they did not necessarily require that skill to be composed nor do they display that skill. But the *performance* of a Chopin étude does satisfy all three conditions and is a work of virtuosity. Moreover, its being a work of virtuosity is a fact about it that helps to make it the masterpiece it is. And the same is true of "Ach, ich liebte," from Mozart's *Abduction from the Seraglio*, which "is partly about singing"—as we know "neither from the title nor from internal evidence," but from a letter in which Mozart remarked that he had "sacrificed Constanze's aria a bit to the flexible throat of Mlle Cavallieri."[25]

We must agree, I think, that if the (performed) Chopin étude and Mozart aria have the semantic property of referring to the artistic skills they require and display, then this reference becomes part of what the work offers for our contemplation, and remarks about it may become relevant to critical judgment. It is still not wholly clear to me why adding this reference to whatever else the artwork is about (and if artistic skill were all that it is about, its meaning would be meager) helps to make it aesthetically better—except that it may increase its complexity without interfering with other basic properties. But more fundamentally, I should like to see more reason to accept the view that these

22. Ibid., pp. 35–36.
23. Ibid., p. 38.
24. Ibid., p. 39.
25. Ibid., p. 44.

musicworks actually do refer to artistic skill. Even Mozart's letters seem to me a rather slender reed to lean on, in the absence of internal evidence; and I do not know the rules of reference in terms of which internal features *become* evidence of aboutness.

20: *Art and Its Cultural Context*

THE fundamental task of the philosophy of art in our time, it has become increasingly clear, is that of providing a coherent and judicious account of the relationships between the arts and the other components—or segments—of culture. It is to mark out the special sphere of artistic activity, duly recognizing the peculiar and precious character of its contribution to the goodness and significance of life, while understanding art as one strand of social interaction, explaining its inherent connections with other central functions, practices, and institutions that make up a society. This theoretical task has as its practical analogue that of finding ways of preserving and enlarging the capacity of the arts to play their distinctive and needed roles in promoting the quality of social life, protecting them against the enormous political and economic forces that constantly threaten to control, distort, repress, or trivialize them.

Since there are so many concepts of culture to choose from, it may be well to say briefly at the start how I conceive it. Culture is a property of a society, I suppose (so that when we speak of "a culture" we are using shorthand for "the culture of *a* society"). It consists in forms of collective competence or capability, of what the society has learned to do or make.[1] Thus we can think concretely of a culture in terms of modes of *activity* that express these competences: its ways of dancing, insulting, building, settling disputes. Or we can think of it in terms of the persistent *entities* engendered by these activities: institutions, customs, languages, systems of thought, tools, artworks. In this broad sense, culture is not contrasted with, but allowed to embrace, social sys-

---

1. See J. G. Merquior, *The Veil and the Mask: Essays on Culture and Ideology* (London, 1979), p. 46.

tems and settled practices—or, more exactly, the ability to establish and work within such systems and to follow such practices.

There are two fundamental kinds of competence, involving two kinds of act generation, in Alvin Goldman's sense. *Causal competence* consists in knowing how to bring about results by applying means–ends rules: irrigating land, making weapons, weaving fabric. *Conventional competence* consists in knowing how to give added character or meaning to actions through the establishing of conventional rules: instituting marriage, setting up games and sports, devising systems of visual symbols. A particular form of activity, such as artistic activity, may involve competences of both kinds, a society's mastery of carving and of the signification it assigns to stylized animal figures. When I speak of cultural competence as something possessed by a collective entity, a society, I mean this literally: societies have such properties, which cannot be reduced to properties of their members, though of course they are dependent on properties of their members—the skills and talents of carvers, shamans, ayatollahs, chiefs, brewers, electronics engineers.

One further clarification: shouldn't culture rather be thought of as a set of "interdicts" and "remissions from interdicts"—to use terms suggested by Philip Rieff to express a common concept?[2] But this concept falls neatly under the competence concept of culture, though by itself it is too limited and external. Take Rieff's example of his difficulty in eating horse steak at the Harvard Faculty Club: isn't it a fact of culture that in some societies horses and dogs can be eaten, in others not? But what makes this a fact of culture, I would say, is that by introducing a distinction between permitted and forbidden food, a culture gives an added significance to the former. The dietary rules or customs make an act of eating also (that is, allow it to generate conventionally) an act of conformity. In eating the permitted food we are not only satisfying hunger, enjoying the taste, and obtaining nourishment, but celebrating our belongingness by acknowledging a norm. The culture has succeeded in giving an extra meaning to the action, and that is to create new competence: we gain the capacity to do something

---

2. See "Towards a Theory of Culture, with Special Reference to the Psychoanalytic Case," in *Imagination and Precision in the Social Sciences: Essays in Memory of Peter Nettl*, ed. T. J. Nossiter, A. H. Hanson, and Stein Rokkan (London, 1972), p. 99.

more by eating beef than we would be doing if horse meat were not forbidden or frowned upon.

At some level of abstraction, we can recognize the task I have sketched as one that a number of great philosophers, from Plato to John Dewey, have set themselves. But several factors have made our task more interesting and more difficult, not least the vast growth of relevant empirical knowledge (for example, psychological and anthropological) and the advances of philosophy (especially of aesthetics and semiotics) in our time. Each new theory or discovery tempts us into overemphasis, either on the autonomy of the arts or on the subordination of art to other social processes.

My opening words may remind you of a well-known passage on the first page of Dewey's *Art as Experience*:

> When artistic objects are separated from both conditions of origin and operation in experience, a wall is built around them that renders almost opaque their general significance, with which esthetic theory deals. Art is remitted to a separate realm, where it is cut off from that association with the materials and aims of every other form of human effort, undergoing, and achievement. A primary task is thus imposed upon one who undertakes to write upon the philosophy of the fine arts. This task is to restore continuity between the refined and intensified forms of experience that are works of art and the everyday events, doings, and sufferings that are universally recognized to constitute experience.[3]

As an admirer and sympathetic reader of Dewey's great book, I feel I can take the liberty of pointing out how this passage—which vigorously expresses his central theme—claims to restore a balance, but at the same time tips the scale in the other direction. It is plain that as Dewey perceived the aesthetic scene on which he was entering, it was dominated by theories that treated the aesthetic as something radically different from everything else in culture and as something that could not be explained in terms of a naturalistic metaphysics. So part of what he is contending for in his plea for a restoration of continuity is that artistic activities, experiences, and values can be accounted for as emergent from natural processes and from other, more basic forms of social activity. But Dewey, obsessed as usual with the dangers of dualism, tends to talk about "separations" in a strange and misleading way. The *theoretical* emphasis on the differences between, say,

---

3. *Art as Experience* (New York, 1958; first published 1934), p. 3.

aesthetic experience and other kinds of experience is associated in his mind with the *practices* of hanging paintings and playing music in special buildings, as though this practice must somehow implicitly deny the continuity he argues for. (Strangely enough, though, he did not protest the sequestering of all those paintings in the Barnes Foundation, which was almost impenetrable by art historians and aestheticians, as well as the general public, for many years.) Now there are, to be sure, some interesting and important controversies about the social role of the art museum and the concert hall, and I do not wish to beg questions here. But of course when we hang the Picasso in the Museum of Modern Art we are not really separating it from the rest of the culture, since those who go to see it bring their culture with them—though we may be separating it from classes of people who have not learned to go to art museums or cannot afford the admission fee. Dewey's figure of speech—"a wall is built around them"—is like the famous wall of separation of church and state in American constitutional law; the idea, however, is not that either church or state is to be denigrated, but that each must be free to go its own way, and that (to quote Robert Frost) "good fences make good neighbors." Separations are not at issue here, but rather distinctions and differences. We can say art is continuous with other segments of culture, if we don't overstress the term, for we don't want to deny emergence of genuine novelty, and that is, strictly speaking, *discontinuity*—in both nature and culture. We must allow for the possibility that art has distinctive functions and purposes and cultural roles; indeed, Dewey has provided some fine statements in support of this point. And if it turns out that string quartets make their cultural contribution best when performed at some remove from construction sites, this does not "render almost opaque their general significance," but on the contrary makes it most lucid.

However veridical or illusory the aesthetic landscape that appeared to John Dewey almost fifty years ago, it was very different from what we see—or at least what *I* see—today. A number of important lines of thought and inquiry have combined to give us a very strong sense of the internality of art in culture. We know much better the enormous variety of interconnections, causal and semantic, the many fundamental ways in which our artistic activities, as makers and as takers of artworks, participate in patterns of act and thought that are found in other forms of cultural activity: in other social relations, cognitive enterprises, language games, institutions, and so on. Of course we still have very much to learn. Meanwhile, I believe there is point in developing my theme, which is that we may be in danger of losing sight of the specialness of art amidst the piling up of knowledge and theory about its manifold dependencies. The search for a balanced view led Dewey to stress the continuity of art with the rest of culture; the same search, as I think, leads me to stress the ways in which art is independent, relatively self-sufficient, autonomous to a degree—though these expressions are all inadequate and misleading, and the judicious statement remains elusive. The best I can do here is to take note of some tendencies in present thought that seem to me to lead to a sadly diminished view of art in culture, and to suggest reasons for questioning and resisting them.

Unwillingness to accord to the arts their distinctive cultural role, and to give them room to do their own work, turns up in the thinking of some of the best contemporary Marxist theorists. Consider, for example, a passage from Terry Eagleton's little book *Marxism and Literary Criticism*:

> The notorious question which some Marxist criticism has addressed to literary works to assess their value—is its political tendency correct, does it further the cause of the proletariat?—entails the shelving of other questions about the work as 'merely' aesthetic. An instance of this dichotomy between the 'ideological' and the 'aesthetic' occurs in Lukács's *The Historical Novel*. 'It does not matter,' Lukács declares, 'whether Scott or Manzoni were aesthetically superior to, say, Heinrich Mann, or at least this is not the main point. What is important is that Scott and Manzoni, Pushkin and Tolstoy, were able to grasp and portray popular life in a more profound, authentic, human and concretely historical fashion than even the most outstanding writers of our day. . . .' But what does 'aesthetically superior' *mean*, if not such things as 'more profound, authentic, human and concretely historical'?[4]

Here is an interesting example of a question that purports to be rhetorical, or self-answering. But the suggested answer is so question-begging in the context that the rhetorical question itself goes begging—especially when Eagleton immediately adds: "Lukács, like several Marxist critics, is unconsciously surrendering to one *bourgeois* notion of the 'aesthetic'—the aesthetic as a mere sec-

---

4. *Marxism and Literary Criticism* (Berkeley, 1976), pp. 56–57. See also his more complicated (and obscure) discussion in *Criticism and Ideology* (London, 1978), chap. 5.

ondary matter of style and technique." Apparently one way of proving the intimate relationship between literature and political processes is simply to adopt the bold persuasive definition of "aesthetically better" as (in effect) more historically concrete and politically progressive. And the way to make this maneuver palatable is to claim that anyone who refuses to accept this absurd definition is guilty of reducing aesthetic value to a matter of "style and technique."

It appears, moreover, that Eagleton is not confining his thought here to works of literature—though the generalization of his view is, again, couched in oddly dogmatic and slippery terms: "Moreover, it *is* true that all major art is 'progressive,' in the limited sense that any art sealed from the significant movements of its epoch, divorced from some sense of the historically central, relegates itself to minor status."[5] Note that he does not refer to individual artworks, but to "art"—and yet we cannot be sure what this term encompasses. What if we reply that the art of classical chamber music and the art of classical ballet do not seem to have had much to do with "significant" political movements, but they include many masterpieces, and are by no means relegated to "minor status"? Would we be correcting Eagleton? The figurative language typical of these discussions—such words as "sealed" and "divorced"—are quite inadequate to the requirements of formulating a clear thesis. But the general thrust is evident: nothing important is to be found in a distinctive sphere of the arts; they count as significant cultural objects only insofar as they serve political purposes.

Consider one more example of the kind of one-sided view of the arts that still flourishes among Marxists and others. Umberto Barbaro begins his essay "The Marxist Redefinition of Art" with these words:

> In Marxist thought, art is an aspect of the intellectual production of a given period, part of the corresponding ideology at a given time. As such, art is conditioned by the structure, by the base, that is, by the relations of production.
>
> Marxist aesthetics opposes and denies the whole series of previous aesthetic theories which are marred from the start by their more or less direct derivation from Idealist thought, and which consider the forms and products of intellectual activity, above all, art and works of art, as *autonomous* and subjective facts; almost as

5. Ibid., p. 57.

phenomena in their own right, out of time, out of space, out of absolutely all the conditions of their genesis, of their birth. The work of art, to this way of thinking, is truly a windowless monad, closed off in its "insularity."[6]

Barbaro goes on to list a string of genetic questions that can be asked about artworks, and ends in disgust because they were of no interest to Croce or Croceans. But it should not be necessary to point out that one who believes that artworks are distinct entities with special value need not deny that they have causes and effects, which are open to empirical investigation, and is not committed to such silly ideas as that artworks are merely "subjective," or that they are "out of time, out of space," or that they can make no references to the world about them. The term "formalism," though not invented by Marxists, has certainly served them well as a way of imputing nonsensical views to those who have argued (1) that artworks are not *solely* conditioned by the "relations of production" present at their creation and (2) that the value of artworks is not *wholly* accounted for by their position in political history.

Other able Marxist philosophers of art, notably Stefan Morawski, have defended rather more balanced views about art in culture. Morawski, for example, in his essay "Art and Society," as in other essays, has made it clear that Marxism, in his complex, humanistic, and sensitive version, includes the theses

> (1) that art is not dependent on any single factor, but on a number of elements . . . among which the crucial one usually is the contemporary historical situation . . . (2) that investigation of these interdependencies will include not only the elements of so-called content but also those of *form* . . . (3) that art not only is influenced by society, but also and conversely that art has an *active* part in molding the social consciousness . . . (4) that these interrelations between art and society . . . are *mediated* above all by the creator-personality.[7]

There is probably less threat now than there was a few decades ago from rigidly holistic anthropological systems that can see in the arts only what they can see in other segments of a culture. Though not wedded to economic or technological determinism, such systems can be no less intellectually repressive than so-

---

6. From *Marxism and Art: Writings in Aesthetics and Criticism,* ed. Berel Lang and Forrest Williams (New York, 1972), p. 161.
7. *Inquiries into the Fundamentals of Aesthetics* (Cambridge, Mass., 1974), pp. 303–4. See also "Historicism and the Philosophy of Art," *Praxis* 4 (1978):71–85.

called scientific Marxism, and no less inimical to an understanding of what is special and important about the arts. In his brilliant review of various concepts of culture that have dominated the scene in recent decades, J. G. Merquior offers some pointed criticisms of extreme forms of configurationism, "superorganicism," and Talcott Parsons' functionalism. Merquior remarks that "however necessarily incomplete, competent field-work in manageable culture areas could [once] support the illusion of grasping cultural wholes," but the belief that cultures are necessarily unified in all their aspects—are all of a piece—could not survive fieldwork in more complex nonliterate societies, as in Africa, and less isolated societies, as among American Indians. Merquior stresses "what Freud never forgot—yet what Dennis Wrong had to remind structural-functionalists of: that man is a *social animal, but not an altogether socialized one.*"[8] His emphasis is on the individual person, who may in an indirect way be reflecting significant features of his culture even when he rebels against it or deliberately deviates from it, but whose rebellion or deviation cannot be completely explained by his acculturation. What I want to emphasize is rather the deviations or divergences between distinguishable components of the culture, or forms of competence: between art and the political process, between religion and economics, between myth and philosophy.

There is, first, the internal impulse to change, however slowly when the pressures of stability are strong, which can be discerned in an art, as in other kinds of institution or practice. Thus close students of the arts in nonliterate societies have frequently detected a greater range of variation, a wider room for experimentation and innovation, than used to be evident to the determined configurationist. For example, M. a M. Ngal, writing on "Literary Creation in Oral Civilizations," particularly in Africa, has remarked: "Beneath stereotyped formulas jealously retained by the conservatism and conformism of each generation, there occurs a true labor of creativity that is not the work of an anonymous community or of associations due to pure chance but rather the product of the active dynamism of the individual genius."[9] Of course it is a characteristic of the culture that it permits or encourages such

---

8. See "Remarks on the Theory of Culture," in Merquior, *Veil and the Mask*, pp. 49, 51, 53–55.

9. See the issue of *New Literary History* titled "Oral Cultures and Oral Performances," 8 (1977):336.

creativity, to a specific extent, and of course it is individual artists who shape the variations on their spoken stories or poems—but what is noteworthy is that significant changes in the realm of (oral) literary art are generated by demands or needs that arise within that art itself.

And it should not be surprising if it is in the very nature of art, at least as much as other components of culture, that it carries the seed of creative change—and even of resistance to all the other main forms of activity that impinge upon it. There is art versus political power, versus religion, versus commercial forces, versus philosophy. Of course, in many societies art is kept in thrall, or on a short leash, rigidly guarded against serious change (or at least certain kinds of change), watched and tended by political or religious or economic authorities. And this is most true, and most to be expected, when the objects that constitute the artworks are the product of mixed or mingled motives, so it is deeply feared that changes may render them incapable of fulfilling properly their religious or magical or political functions. It is easy enough to explain why, in a given culture, artistic creativity is discouraged or severely restricted; my point is that it does have to be explained, and wherever cultural conditions permit the arts, or some arts, to develop along their own lines in their own way, significant changes in style and form and quality occur. On the other hand, the kind of hectic seeking for novelty we find in Western societies today seems only partly explainable by internal impulses; we have to see it also as the result of forced effort to meet the demands of the market.

Forms of cultural competence differ significantly in their mixture of causal and conventional elements, and this must affect their liability to change, and hence development, as well as their relative rate of change. Generalization is risky here, of course, because so many factors may be involved—and it is especially risky for someone as ignorant of ethnological data as I am. Thus, for example, we might hazard the hypothesis that segments of culture in which causal competence is dominant—say, in agriculture—are likely to change faster than others because there is direct interaction with the physical world, so that people will acquire relevant empirical knowledge that will lead them to correct their causal beliefs and hence modify their practice. And no doubt under certain other cultural conditions—as in parts of medieval Europe—this hypothesis fits the facts. But even agriculture, as we well know, can be so dominated by convention—by religious and customary requirements—that empirical facts (as, for example, the fact that existing practices frequently lead to poor crops) have little or no effect. And anyway, useful empirical knowledge is not necessarily self-generating; there has to be a general acceptance of the idea of learning from experience, of induction, of experimentation in a broad sense, and this is a matter of conventional competence.

Nevertheless, some cautious general remarks can perhaps be made about the features that tend to make one cultural segment somewhat independent of another, and particularly of the arts from others—though this is only a tendency, often blocked. The arts include (or have included until recently) a large element of causal competence, of craft, and despite dogmatic teachers, where conditions permit, this must work toward change whose direction is set by what is happening within the art itself. But historians of art have always emphasized the large role in art played by conventional competence—and the work of major theorists in recent decades (notably Nelson Goodman and E. H. Gombrich) has opened up the vision of a still wider range of artistic activity that is guided by convention.

Now the very fact that artistic competence involves learned sets, even systems, of rules tends to make the artistic segment of culture go its own way, in some measure of self-directedness, independently of other cultural influences. And this can happen in two ways. First, rules of any kind, even trivial rules of etiquette, have a tendency to take on an ethical or even religious sanction ("Cleanliness is next to godliness"), and this engenders pride in following them and in teaching them to the young—to the child or the apprentice in the shop: this is the proper way to bring up the next generation, and reflects credit on the parent or master who follows the old ways. Here is a strongly conservative force within art institutions, holding them comparatively still in periods when other cultural components may be changing. This force works toward independence. But second, on the other hand, when people achieve awareness that certain of their activities are essentially a fabric of rules, and when some rules may be freed from supernatural sanction or may come to matter less to the society, then there is a chance for them to be questioned and deliberately reconsidered. Questions or doubts may arise about their point, and about their inevitability, tempting experimentation to discover better ways of doing or making, and leading to more interesting, more satisfying, or just more exciting results. Here is an internal drive within the art institution, not needing to wait upon external pressures; and it may lead to significant changes in the arts even when other components of culture are in a comparatively steady state.

A current concept of culture—and one that seems to be gaining adherents along with the growth of semiotics as a field of study—offers another possible way of subsuming the arts under a general scheme that threatens to lose sight of their special character. Its chief proponent, the Russian semioticist Jurij Lotman, has described culture as a "semiotic mechanism for the output and storage of information" and "a historically evolved bundle of semiotic systems."[10] In another essay he writes:

> If the culture is viewed as a single semiotic mechanism then one may see in it an object of the same type as an intellect. Culture, taken as a whole, not only has a special apparatus for collective memory but also has procedures for producing messages that are in principle new in languages that are in principle new, i.e. it can create *new ideas*. The combination of these qualities makes it possible to regard culture as a *collective intellect*.[11]

True, Lotman also says that "culture arises as a system of supplementary constraints imposed on physically possible actions"—which seems an echo of an older, negative notion of culture much less adequate than that which takes competence as central. But the word "arises" is to be taken seriously here. For he continues:

> The combination of complex systems of marriage constraints and structurally significant violations of them turns the addresser and the addressee of the marriage communication into personalities. The 'man and woman' given by *Nature* is replaced by the 'only him and only her' given by *Culture*.[12]

If culture consists of a semiotic system or systems, and if art is a segment of culture (as it plainly is), then art is a semiotic system, or set of systems: thus the semiotic theory of art is deductively established. But in fact culture must be something more than a

---

10. Quoted by Irene Portis Winner, "Cultural Semiotics and Anthropology," in *The Sign: Semiotics around the World*, ed. R. W. Bailey, L. Matejka, and P. Steiner (Ann Arbor, 1978), p. 342.

11. "Culture as Collective Intellect and Problems of Artificial Intelligence," in *Russian Poetics in Translation*, vol. 6: *Dramatic Structure: Poetic & Cognitive Semantics* (Wivenhoe Park, Eng., 1979), p. 84.

12. Ibid., p. 89.

semiotic system or systems, even though it certainly includes such systems among its forms of competence. I want to show this.

An initial obstacle is a certain tendency of those who are most enthusiastic about the growth of semiotics as a field of study to broaden their use of the term "sign" in what seems to me an unconscionable way. Thus the editors of a good recent collection of essays on semiotics announce in their preface:

> Semiotics derives its energy and power from the study of semiosis, the process by which things and events come to be recognized as signs by a sentient organism. Semiosis is involved in the mutual "recognition" and matching of a pair of strands of DNA, of an antibody and a particular bacterium, of parasite and host in a biosystem, of a pollen grain and an embryo in a flower, in the social and sexual behavior of animals.[13]

But the concept of sign is trivialized if it is reduced to that of a causal relationship, or even to that of causal inference; semiosis ought to be a process in which something is *used* as a sign, not just reacted to and not just "taken as" a sign. It is disconcerting to find that even Roman Jakobson has succumbed to this loose talk. After remarking, judiciously, that "the spectacular discoveries in molecular genetics of the last few years are presented by the explorers themselves in terms borrowed from linguistics and communication theory," which is true, he adds that the title of George and Muriel Beadle's book *The Language of Life* "is not a mere figurative expression, and the extraordinary degree of analogy between the systems of genetic and verbal information fully justifies the guiding statement of this volume"—to the effect that the DNA code is a "language much older than hieroglyphics."[14] Jakobson's detailed comparison of the genetic code with languages is most interesting, and shows how far either could be used as a model of the other, but it does not convince me that such terms as "code," "information," and "syntax" apply univocally to both.

A considerably narrower, but still probably too broad, concept of semiosis takes advantage of the term "communication," which can be widely stretched. Thus we have the famous statement of Lévi-Strauss, in his *Structural Anthropology*, proposing to treat all social interactions as forms of communication, on three different

---

13. *The Sign*, ed. Bailey, Matejka, and Steiner, p. vii. See also Thomas A. Sebeok, *Studies in Semiotics: Contributions to the Doctrine of Signs* (Bloomington, Ind., 1976), pp. x, 1, 69.
14. Jakobson, *Main Trends in the Science of Language* (London, 1973), p. 49.

levels: exchange of messages, exchange of commodities (namely goods and services), and exchange of women—that's what he wrote, though those who take the proposal seriously are likely to suggest that the third category should be "exchange of mates."[15] The concept of *communication*, it seems to be agreed, is intimately connected with that of *message*; but those who extend the former seem willing to extend the latter. Thus Ferruccio Rossi-Landi says commodities are messages and economics is the study of "commodity messages."[16] But this strikes me as unacceptable playfulness. We can of course send messages by exchanging commodities: for example, in getting you to trade me a healthy cow for a broken-down horse, I may be performing the para-illocutionary action of saying something like "Caveat emptor." But messages, it seems to me, should be restricted to such performances—either of illocutionary actions or of actions that do not have a locutionary base but would be illocutionary actions if they did (i.e., they are para-illocutionary). I do not of course wish to imply that such messages can always be satisfactorily paraphrased in words, though I think *some* of their content, at some level of abstraction, can always be verbalized. Nor do I hold that such "sayings," as I call them, are necessarily intentional, though they probably must be capable of being intentional.

My argument against the semiotic concept of culture requires an example, which I take from a well-known essay by Clifford Geertz, "Deep Play: Notes on the Balinese Cockfight." In this marvelously rich and penetrating essay a central social institution is considered from various points of view, but it is the semiotic interpretation that I am interested in here. I shall not pause to debate Geertz's claim that the Balinese cockfight is an "art form"[17] —not because it is beautiful, as he says,[18] but for two other reasons: (1) It has a fictive or playful character, in that though it is concerned with social status (in a way to be explained shortly), it does not *change* the social status of those who participate.[19] (2) More important, it shares with acknowledged arts the social function of generating and regenerating "the very subjectivity they pretend

---

15. See Winner, *Cultural Semiotics and Anthropology*, p. 348; Jakobson, *Main Trends*, p. 33.
16. See Jakobson, *Main Trends*, p. 36.
17. "Deep Play: Notes on the Balinese Cockfight," *Daedalus* (Winter 1972):23.
18. Ibid., p. 9.
19. Ibid., p. 23.

only to display . . . they are positive agents in the creation and maintenance" of the sensibility they represent.[20]

The primary activity of the cockfight is betting, and this is divided into two sharply different forms, governed by different rules. There is the main bet, in the center of the ring, between the cock owners and their coalitions of bettors, always for even money and comparatively high stakes. There are the numerous side bets, for small stakes, always at varying odds, freely accepted by pairs of bettors. All the main complex features of the Balinese status hierarchy are mirrored and dramatized in these arrangements, in the making of matches, the sizes of bets, the lining up of coalitions. Geertz remarks that "no one's status is actually altered by the outcome of a cockfight; it is only, and that momentarily, affirmed or insulted" by victory or defeat.[21] The financial risks in a given fight can be great, but those who can afford to take them, to engage in this "deep play," will come out fairly even in the long run. The essential thrill lies in the hope of asserting superiority in a way that is not permitted in ordinary life, and in the risk of equal humiliation if chance goes the other way (and every effort is made to make the fights fair and the outcome unpredictable). What makes the cockfight a semiotic system, then, is that it provides ways of performing cherished para-illocutionary actions (such as "affirming" or "insulting" status)—or, as Geertz says, "saying something of something."[22]

> What . . . the cockfight talks most forcibly about is status relationships, and what it says about them is that they are matters of life and death. . . .
> . . . What the cockfight says it says in a vocabulary of sentiment—the thrill of risk, the despair of loss, the pleasure of triumph. Yet what it says is not merely that risk is exciting, loss depressing, or triumph gratifying, banal tautologies of affect, but that it is of these emotions, thus exampled, that society is built and individuals put together.[23]

In this essay we have a brilliant example of what the semiotic approach to culture, especially to social institutions, can accomplish in the discovery of manifold ways in which messages are communicated by actions—as by betting in certain ways rather

20. Ibid., p. 28.
21. Ibid., p. 16; see also p. 18.
22. Ibid., p. 26.
23. Ibid., pp. 25, 27.

than others. There are Austinian conditions under which acting in a certain way will also be (or conventionally generate) a saying. But what is also very important to note, I think, is that the use of the cockfight as a semiotic system is dependent on its being regulated by another set of conventional rules, which are not themselves semiotic rules; that is, they are rules about how bets may be placed, who may bet, how payoffs are to be made, and so on, but not rules about what it *means* to bet in a certain way, what one is *saying* in so doing. A large and important part of the semiotics of culture presupposes that *some* of the rules or conventions that constitute cultural competences are *not* semiotic. So culture cannot be equated with semiotic systems. Thus I think Jonathan Culler is seriously misleading when he writes of recent developments in semiotics:

> If everything which is meaningful within human cultures can be treated as a sign, then . . . semiotics embraces a vast domain: it moves in, imperialistically, on the territory of most disciplines of the humanities and social sciences. Any sphere of human activity, from music to cooking, to politics, can be an object of semiotic study. . . . If the study of music as a sign system is assimilated to semiotics, the other aspects of musicology will form a discipline which must define itself in a new way.[24]

The limits of such imperialism are fixed. Certainly any cultural phenomenon may be investigated to discover the ways in which it is used as a semiotic system, but to be so used it must already be governed by more basic nonsemiotic conventions. Unless there is something of a *practice* of cooking, in which certain culinary combinations are prescribed or customary, how could we convey a message in serving this food instead of that?

What is evident here is the way in which distinguishable and to some degree self-determining components of culture will use each other for their own ends. Politics will make use of religion when it can, as religion will make use of politics. Religion will make use of art when that possibility conforms to its own codes (if the religion is not iconoclastic, let's say); and art will make use of religion as a source of representational subject and thematic material and human qualities for its own good purposes. Of course we have to understand these interconnections, but we have to recognize the diversity of human needs and forms of individual and social self-

---

24. "In Pursuit of Signs," *Daedalus* 2 (Fall 1977):104–5.

fulfillment. It is not aestheticism, in some evil sense, or a wicked formalism, or a bourgeois provincialism, to acknowledge that a society will seek to enlarge its semiotic competence by using its artistic competence, as well as all others, to find ways of widening its range of illocutionary action—or to acknowledge, conversely, that the arts, when free to develop, will build formal structures out of illocutionary actions, or representations of illocutionary actions, as out of anything else that comes their way, in a striving to provide experience with marked aesthetic character.

Of course we want to understand the connections between artistic activities and the other forms of life that go to make up the complexity of culture, but we cannot do so rightly unless we first form a comparatively distinct conception of what artistic activities are, in themselves, and what is their point. Perhaps no one has seen this problem more clearly or wrestled with it more persistently than Jan Mukařovský—as English-reading aestheticians have been able to learn for themselves only in recent years. In a bold and thoughtful essay of 1942, "The Place of the Aesthetic Function among the Other Functions,"[25] Mukařovský attempted a fundamental categorization of what he called "functions," defined as "modes of a subject's self-realization vis-à-vis the external world."[26] Of the four basic types, two ("practical functions" and "the theoretical functions") are "semiotic." What distinguishes the aesthetic function, according to Mukařovský, is that it "foregrounds the subject," but this means that

> An aesthetic sign does not affect any particular reality as does a symbolic sign, but instead it reflects in itself reality as a whole (hence the so-called *typicality* of the work of art, a notion which means no more than that the work of art, the purest aesthetic sign, demonstrates on the basis of a particular all other particulars as well as their set-reality).[27]

I quote this proposal not to endorse it, since I think it is clearly not endorsable—and not to denigrate it, either, since it is an interesting suggestion. But I think it shows the effect of not keeping a variety of arts in mind when talking about "the work of art," and it owes less to an open-minded survey of actual artworks than to a yearning after a simple system. How can such a partic-

25. In *Structure, Sign, and Function: Selected Essays by Jan Mukařovský*, trans. John Burbank and Peter Steiner (New Haven, 1978).
26. Ibid., p. 40.
27. Ibid., p. 42.

ular as a Bartók string quartet be a sign of all other particulars in the world, as well as of their set? If it has semiotic significance at all—which is still much disputed—that significance can hardly be interesting or important if it is shared exactly and completely not only with all other string quartets but with all other artworks of any kind.

If we are looking for distinctive roles for art to play in human life, it may turn out that they are in some broad sense semiotic, either as signifying special objects or features of objects or as signifying in a special way (perhaps as being characters in certain kinds of sign systems). But when either of these distinctions has been drawn, and if it holds up, there will still be the question of the point of art: what do artworks in general, or typically, or at their best, have to contribute to human welfare? And at least part of the answer, I believe, is one that makes no reference to signs at all, and does not require that artworks belong to semiotic systems in order to fulfill their function. Just briefly, by way of conclusion, I will sketch one such possible line of thought.

Consider first that artworks are typically particulars that are deliberately added to the world, displacing something already there through natural causes, as the sculpture replaces the uncut or even unquarried stone, yet not having the air of replacing anything. The property of being something added they share with machines and tools, for which the term "technical object" seems the handiest, if not the gracefulest—though technical objects do appear as replacements for what served a similar function. Technical objects serve a double purpose, one that is individual and obvious, the other universal but less noticed. They are designed to make the world more subservient to human wishes, more convenient for the realization of future intentions. But at a deeper level they also inject something of ourselves into our environment and help to make us at home in it, as we recognize about us human handiwork and the promise of fittingness. Thus we are assuaged of deep-rooted fears of nature independent of our will, and can live with the knowledge that earthquakes and volcanoes, storms and floods make our home a place of peril.

But by themselves technical objects cannot come close to filling this primal need for making the world friendly as well as habitable, even with the help of nature in its benign moods. Especially, indeed, as the multiplication and monstrous enlargement of technical objects—including our buildings and roads and dams and power plants—which come with the development of civilization tend to drive nature in its friendliest and loveliest aspects farther and farther from our doorsteps. By themselves, technical objects also divide and narrow our interests, serving the contrary purposes of others, go dangerously wrong—as with nuclear energy—and end by increasing the danger of our surroundings. Even objects with the best intentions—enormous parking lots and huge apartment houses—become inimical to the spirit, sources of tension, producing a sense of vacancy and dullness. When they are built without concern for aesthetic needs, they only increase the hostility of the world about us, as expressive embodiments of the unconcern or fear or contempt that so many of us feel for our neighbors.

Now enter artworks. A remarkable feature of all artworks (or, to be a bit more circumspect, *practically* all artworks) is what I call, in a broad sense, their *fictive* character. The fictive character consists in a false seeming (a playfully false seeming, not a deception), in purporting to be something it isn't, in putting on an act or show. The exemplary case is verbal fiction, in which illocutionary actions are represented but not actually performed. This case is easily generalized to all representation: the landscape painting that, in a way, claims to show you what you might see or have seen, looking from a hill or through a window, but does not demand that you believe it. I include the cheerful melody that trips along as though it had not a care in the world, somewhat like a person, though not really one—moving in a time that is not the time of the physical world. I include the abstract expressionist painting that sets its hues and rhythms in violent opposition or in subtle harmony, as though seeking a resolution or a conciliation —which is of course only a pretense. I include the gleaming and fastidious office building, technical object though it is, which is also a work of art whose expressiveness claims for its program an ideal of order, efficiency, and purity of motive that we know cannot be matched by what goes on inside it. I think Susanne Langer was on to an important truth when she developed her idea of "virtual" aspects of artworks—the dance as embodying virtual powers, visual art as embodying virtual space, and so on.[28]

The fictive character of artworks distinguishes them from the works of nature and objects that are merely tools or machines:

---

28. *Feeling and Form* (New York, 1953), chap. 4 and pt. II, *passim*.

and this enables them to feature, to flaunt, the expressive or aesthetic qualities that are in a *special* way our mark on the world around us—for they are the human regional qualities we give to things. In creating works of art we humanize the earth as we can in no other way, we warm it for ourselves, make it a place where we belong, far more fully and significantly than technical objects can do (unless, of course, they are shaped or decorated to become artworks themselves). But individual artworks cannot carry out this function, cannot serve us in this unifying, reconciling way, unless we grant them a measure of independence and autonomy, a sphere of influence all their own, in which they can be respected as individuals. We have to approach them in something like a suppliant mood, setting aside for the moment concerns about their cultural connections, their causes and effects—though not, of course, their semiotic aspects, their meanings and references, when such they have—if they are to realize their potentialities and serve us well in their fashion.

In Essay 18 I tried to identify a circumscribed mode of criticism that I labeled "aesthetic criticism." We see now that there is a point of much wider view from which a critic can consider artworks in relation to other segments of culture: mutual influences and cooperations, their explicit or hidden ideologies, their contribution to the health or decline of socially important activities, and so forth. This may be called "cultural criticism"; and much of what is now being written about artworks, especially by literary critics, belongs under this heading, it seems to me. The task is vitally important, even if it does not appear to be one whose conclusions reach to a very high degree of reliability, and the inevitable intemperate disputes are often resistant to rational resolution. It is a task for the social critic, if anyone can claim the right to such a title. Literary critics, who seem to produce most of the cultural criticism, have some of the qualifications, but seldom all the important ones. What I want most to emphasize is that cultural criticism, to be done well, must be deeply aware of the differences and divergences among cultural strands in order to do justice to each and to analyze their interactions judiciously. Thus cultural criticism does not eliminate or replace aesthetic criticism, but embraces and builds upon it; its own enterprise must acknowledge, make room for, and preserve the distinctively aesthetic point of view.

Bibliography of Writings in Aesthetics by Monroe C. Beardsley

Books and Papers

"Dostoyevsky's Metaphor of the 'Underground.'" *Journal of the History of Ideas* 3 (1942):265–90.

About twenty-five articles for the *Dictionary of World Literature*, ed. J. T. Shipley (New York: Philosophical Library, 1943). Most of the articles are short; the longer ones are: "Intention" (with W. K. Wimsatt), "Determinism," "Naturalism," "Materialism," "Idealism," "Realism." In the revised edition (1952) the articles "Naturalism" and "Realism" were rewritten in collaboration with George Becker. Further revisions were made for the third edition, renamed *The Dictionary of World Literary Terms*, published by The Writer (New York, 1970).

"The Intentional Fallacy" (with W. K. Wimsatt). *The Sewanee Review* 54 (1946):3–23. Reprinted in *Essays in Modern Literary Criticism*, ed. R. B. West, Jr. (New York: Rinehart, 1952); in W. K. Wimsatt, Jr., *The Verbal Icon* (Lexington: University of Kentucky Press, 1954, and New York: Noonday Press, 1958); in *The Study of Literature*, ed. S. Barnet, M. Berman, and W. Burto (Boston: Little, Brown, 1960); in *Problems in Aesthetics*, ed. Morris Weitz (New York: Macmillan, 1959, 1970); translated in part as "La falacia intencional," in *Papeles de Son Armadans*, no. 8, November 1956 (Madrid); in *An Introduction to Literary Criticism*, ed. M. K. Danziger and W. S. Johnson (Boston: Heath, 1961); in *Philosophy Looks at the Arts*, ed. Joseph Margolis (New York: Scribner's, 1962); in *Modern Criticism: Theory and Practice*, ed. W. Sutton and R. Foster (New York: Odyssey, 1963); translated into Polish in *Tematy* 5 (1966); in *Philosophy of Art and Aesthetics*, ed. F. A. Tillman and S. Cahn (New York: Harper & Row, 1969); in *Moderne Englishe und Amerikanische Literaturkritik*, ed. Willi Erzgräber (Darmstadt: Wissenschaftliche Buchgesellschaft, 1970); in *Critical Theory since Plato*, ed. Hazard Adams (New York: Harcourt Brace Jovanovich, 1971); translated into Finnish as "Intentionharha" in *Nykyestetiikan Ongelmia*, ed. Irma Rantavaara (Helsinki, 1971); in *Twentieth-Century Literary Criticism: A Reader*, ed. David Lodge (London: Longman, 1972); in *Issues in Contemporary Literary Criticism*, ed. Gregory T. Polletta (Boston: Little, Brown, 1973); in *On Literary Intention: Critical Essays*, ed. David Newton–De Molina (Edinburgh University Press, 1976); in *Philosophy Looks at the arts*, ed.

Joseph Margolis, 2d ed. rev. (Philadelphia: Temple University Press, 1978).

"The Affective Fallacy" (with W. K. Wimsatt). *Sewanee Review* 57 (1949): 3–27. Reprinted in W. K. Wimsatt, *The Verbal Icon* (Lexington: University of Kentucky Press, 1954, and New York: Noonday Press, 1958); with some omissions in *Critiques and Essays in Criticism*, ed. R. W. Stallman (New York: Ronald Press, 1949); in *Critical Theory since Plato*, ed. Hazard Adams (New York: Harcourt Brace Jovanovich, 1971); in *Twentieth-Century Literary Criticism: A Reader*, ed. David Lodge (London: Longman, 1972).

"Logic in Composition." *Journal of General Education* 5 (1951):254–62.

"Reading Takes a Whole Man" (with Robert W. Daniel). *College English* 17 (1955):28–32.

"The Concept of Economy in Art." *Journal of Aesthetics and Art Criticism* 14 (1956):370–75.

Theme and Form: An Introduction to Literature. Ed. M. C. Beardsley, G. L. Leggett, and R. W. Daniel. Englewood Cliffs, N.J.: Prentice-Hall, 1956; 2d ed. rev., 1962; 3d ed. rev., 1969; 4th ed. rev., 1975. *Aids to Study for "Theme and Form,"* with R. W. Daniel, 1956, 1962, 1969, 1975.

"Can We Dispute about Tastes?" *Swarthmore College Bulletin*, October 1958. Reprinted in *Introductory Readings in Philosophy*, ed. M. Singer and R. Ammerman (New York: Scribner's, 1960); in *The Challenge of Philosophy*, ed. P. F. Fink (San Francisco: Chandler, 1965); in *Classic Philosophical Questions*, ed. James A. Gould, 3d ed. (Columbus: Charles E. Merrill, 1979).

Aesthetics: Problems in the Philosophy of Criticism. New York: Harcourt Brace & World, 1958. Reprinted Indianpolis: Hackett Press, 1981. Excerpts are reprinted in *A Rhetoric Case Book*, ed. F. Connolly, 2d ed. (New York: Harcourt Brace & World, 1959); in *Basic Problems of Philosophy*, ed. D. Bronstein, Y. Krikorian, and P. Wiener, 3d ed. (Englewood Cliffs, N.J.: Prentice-Hall, 1964); in *Aesthetics and Criticism in Art Education*, ed. R. Smith (Chicago: Rand McNally, 1966); in *Essays on the Language of Literature*, ed. S. Chatman and S. R. Levin (Boston: Houghton Mifflin, 1967); in *Philosophy of Art and Aesthetics*, ed. F. A. Tillman and S. Cahn (New York: Harper & Row, 1969); in *Introductory Readings in Aesthetics*, ed. John Hospers (New York: Free Press, 1969); in *Artistic Expression*, ed. John Hospers (New York: Appleton-Century-Crofts, 1971).

"The Concept of Meter: An Exercise in Abstraction" (with W. K. Wimsatt). *Publications of the Modern Language Association* 74 (1959):585–98. Abstract in *Style in Language*, ed. T. A. Sebeok (Cambridge: MIT Technology Press and New York: John Wiley, 1960), pp. 193–96. Reprinted in W. K. Wimsatt, *Hateful Contraries* (Lexington: University of Kentucky Press, 1965); in *Approaches to the Poem*, ed. J. O. Perry (San Francisco: Chandler, 1965); in *Essays on the Language of Literature*, ed. S. Chatman and S. R. Levin (Boston: Houghton Mifflin, 1967).

"Misunderstanding Poetry: Notes on some Readings of Dylan Thomas" (with Samuel Hynes). *College English* 21 (1960):315–22.

"The Definitions of the Arts." *Journal of Aesthetics and Art Criticism* 20 (1961):175–87.
"Representation and Presentation: A Reply to Professor Dickie." *Journal of Philosophy* 58 (1961):238–41.
"A Word for Meter: Reply to Professor Hendron" (with W. K. Wimsatt). *Publications of the Modern Language Association* 76 (1961):305–8.
"The Metaphorical Twist." *Philosophy and Phenomenological Research* 22 (1962):293–307. Reprinted in *Essays on Metaphor*, ed. W. Shibles (Whitewater, Wis.: Language Press, 1972); translated in Greek as "τὸ μετα-φορικὸ στρήψιμο," ΔΕΥΚΑΛΙΩΝ (*Deucalion*) 8 (1980):135–55, and in Polish as "Odksztaleenie Metaforyczne," *Archiwum Tlumaczen z terii literatury* (Lublin, 1980).
"On the Generality of Critical Reasons." *Journal of Philosophy* 59 (1962): 477–86. Reprinted in the Bobbs-Merrill Philosophy Reprint series; in *A Modern Book of Aesthetics*, ed. M. Rader, 4th ed. (New York: Holt, Rinehart & Winston, 1973).
"Art and the Arts." In *World Book Encyclopedia*, 1962.
"Beauty and Aesthetic Value." *Journal of Philosophy* 59 (1962):617–28.
"Rhythm and 'Exercises in Abstraction'" (with W. K. Wimsatt). *Publications of the Modern Language Association* 77 (1962):670–71, 674.
"Two Theorists of Literature." Discussion review. *Yale Review* 52 (1963): 294–301.
"The Discrimination of Aesthetic Enjoyment." *British Journal of Aesthetics* 3 (1963):291–300. Reprinted in the Bobbs-Merrill Philosophy Reprint Series.
"The New Criticism Revisited: An Affirmative View." Symposium with Samuel Hynes. *Four Quarters* 13 (1964):11–19.
"Art and Accident." *The Activist* 4 (1964):116–23. Reprinted in *Literature and Aesthetics*, ed. M. Beardsley (Indianapolis: Bobbs-Merrill, 1968).
"The Creation of Art." *Journal of Aesthetics and Art Criticism* 23 (1965): 291–304. Reprinted in *Aesthetics and Criticism in Art Education*, ed. R. Smith (Chicago: Rand McNally, 1966); in *Aesthetic Inquiry*, ed. M. C. Beardsley and H. Schueller (Belmont, Calif.: Dickenson, 1967); in *75 Prose Pieces*, ed. R. C. Rathburn and M. Steinmann (New York: Scribner's, 1967); in *Aesthetics and the Arts*, ed. L. A. Jacobus (New York: McGraw-Hill, 1968); in *Problems in Aesthetics*, ed. Morris Weitz, 2d ed. (New York: Macmillan, 1970); in *Contemporary Aesthetics*, ed. M. Lipman (Boston: Allyn & Bacon, 1973); partly in *The Creativity Question*, ed. Albert Rothenberg and Carl R. Hausman (Durham, N.C.: Duke University Press, 1976); in *Readings in the Fine Arts*, ed. Jessica Haigney-Timmis (Dubuque: Kendall/Hunt, 1978); in *Art and Philosophy*, ed. W. E. Kennick, 2d ed. (New York: St. Martin's Press, 1979).
"Intrinsic Value." *Philosophy and Phenomenological Research* 26 (1965):1–17. Reprinted in *Readings in Ethical Theory*, ed. W. Sellars and J. Hospers, 2d ed. (New York: Appleton-Century-Crofts, 1970).
Aesthetics from Classical Greece to the Present: A Short History. New York: Macmillan, 1966. Reprinted University: University of Alabama Press, 1975 (paperback).

"The Limits of Critical Interpretation." In *Art and Philosophy*, ed. Sidney Hook (New York: New York University Press, 1966), pp. 61–87.

"Style and Good Style." In *Reflections on High School English*, NDEA Institute lectures, 1965, ed. Gary Tate (Tulsa: University of Tulsa, 1966), pp. 91–105. Reprinted in *New Rhetorics*, ed. M. Steinmann (New York: Scribner's, 1967); in *Maryland English Journal*, no. 5 (Fall 1966); in *Contemporary Essays on Style*, ed. G. A. Love and M. Payne (Glenview, Ill.: Scott, Foresman, 1969); in *Teaching High School Composition*, ed. Gary Tate and Edward P. J. Corbett (New York: Oxford University Press, 1970); in *Teacher's Resource Book to Accompany "Exploring Life through Literature,"* ed. Edmund J. Farrell et al. (Glenview, Ill.: Scott Foresman, 1973), pp. 89–94; in *Subject and Structure: An Anthology for Writers*, ed. John M. Wasson, 5th ed. (Boston: Little, Brown, 1975).

"The Humanities and Human Understanding." In *The Humanities and the Understanding of Reality*, ed. T. B. Stroup (Lexington: University of Kentucky Press, 1966), pp. 1–31.

"The Aesthetic Problem of Justification." *Journal of Aesthetic Education* 1 (1966):29–39.

Aesthetic Inquiry: Essays on Art Criticism and the Philosophy of Art (from *Journal of Aesthetics and Art Criticism*), ed. M. C. Beardsley and H. Schueller. Belmont, Calif.: Dickenson, 1967.

"The Classification of Critical Reasons." *Art Education* 20 (1967):17–20. Reprinted in *Journal of Aesthetic Education* 2 (1968):55–63; in *Aesthetics and Problems of Education*, ed. R. Smith (Urbana: University of Illinois Press, 1971); in *A Modern Book of Aesthetics*, ed. Melvin Rader, 5th ed. (New York: Holt, Reinhart & Winston, 1979).

"History of Aesthetics" (I.18–35) and "Metaphor" (V. 284–89). In *The Encyclopedia of Philosophy*, 8 vols., New York: Free Press, 1967. Excerpt from "History of Aesthetics" reprinted in *Contemporary Aesthetics*, ed. Matthew Lipman (Boston: Allyn & Bacon, 1973).

"Aesthetics." In *The New Catholic Encyclopedia*. New York: Catholic University of America and McGraw-Hill, 1967.

"Comments" (in a symposium at the 1965 Oberlin Colloquium). In *Art, Mind, and Religion*, ed. W. H. Capitan and D. D. Merrill (Pittsburgh: University of Pittsburgh Press, 1967), pp. 103–9.

Literature and Aesthetics. Ed. M. C. Beardsley. Indianapolis: Bobbs-Merrill, 1968.

"Textual Meaning and Authorial Meaning." *Genre* 1 (1968):169–81.

"Order and Disorder in Art." In *The Concept of Order*, ed. Paul G. Kuntz (Seattle: University of Washington Press, 1968), pp. 191–218.

"Aesthetic Experience Regained." *Journal of Aesthetics and Art Criticism* 28 (1969):3–11. Translated (in a somewhat different version) into Polish in *Studia estetyczne* (*Aesthetic Studies*) 6 (1969), and into Finnish as "Jalleen loydetty esteettinen elämys," in *Nykyestetiiken Ongelmia*, ed. Irma Rantavaara (Helsinki, 1971). Reprinted in *Art and Philosophy*, ed. W. E. Kennick, 2d ed. (New York: St. Martin's Press, 1979).

The Possibility of Criticism. Detroit: Wayne State University Press, 1970. Chap. 2 reprinted in *Philosophy Looks at the Arts,* ed. Joseph Margolis, 2d ed. rev. (Philadelphia: Temple University Press, 1978).

"The Aesthetic Point of View," with reply to comments by H. W. Janson. *Metaphilosophy* 1 (1970):39–58, 63–65. Also in *Perspectives in Education, Religion, and the Arts,* vol. 3 of *Contemporary Philosophic Thought: The International Philosophy Year Conference at Brockport, New York,* 4 vols. (Albany: SUNY Press, 1970); in *Philosophy Looks at the Arts,* ed. Joseph Margolis, 2d ed. rev. (Philadelphia: Temple University Press, 1978).

"Aesthetic Welfare." *Journal of Aesthetic Education* 4 (1970):9–20. Also in *Proceedings of the VI International Congress of Aesthetics, Upsala, Sweden, 1968,* in *Acta Universitatis Upsaliensis* 10 (1972).

"Form." In *Encyclopedia Americana,* 1970, vol. 11, p. 601.

"Aesthetic Theory and Educational Theory." In *Aesthetic Concepts and Education,* ed. Ralph Smith (Urbana: University of Illinois Press, 1970), pp. 3–20.

"On [Henry] Aiken's Defense of the Humanities." *Journal of Aesthetic Education* 5 (1971):72–76.

"Modes of Interpretation." Discussion review. *Journal of the History of Ideas* 32 (1971):143–48.

"Comments" (on essays by Vincent Tomas and Douglas Morgan). In *Artistic Expression,* ed. J. Hospers (New York: Appleton-Century-Crofts, 1971), pp. 284–87.

"Verse and Music." In *Versification: Major Language Types,* ed. W. K. Wimsatt (New York: Modern Language Association and New York University Press, 1972), pp. 238–52.

"Semiotic Aesthetics and Aesthetic Education." *Philosophic Exchange,* Annual Proceedings of the Center for Philosophic Exchange, SUNY Brockport, 1 (1973):155–71. Reprinted in *Journal of Aesthetic Education* 9 (1975):5–26.

"What Is an Aesthetic Quality?" *Theoria* 39 (1973):50–70.

"The Concept of Literature." In *Literary Theory and Structure: Essays in Honor of William K. Wimsatt,* ed. F. Brady, J. Palmer, and M. Price (New Haven: Yale University Press, 1973), pp. 23–40.

"Beauty" (1850 to the present). In *Dictionary of the History of Ideas,* ed. Philip Wiener (New York: Scribner's, 1973), vol. 1, pp. 207–14.

"Aesthetic Welfare, Aesthetic Justice, and Educational Policy." *Journal of Aesthetic Education* 7 (1973):49–61.

"Putting Down Words: Some Vicissitudes of Language." *College English* 35 (1974):740–49. Reprinted in *Guide to College Writing,* ed. James Cordier.

"Metacriticism." In *Princeton Encyclopedia of Poetry and Poetics,* ed. Alex Preminger, enl. ed. (Princeton: Princeton University Press, 1974), pp. 951–55.

Foreword to Stefan Morawski, *Inquiries into the Fundamentals of Aesthetics* (Cambridge: MIT Press, 1974), pp. ix–xvi.

"The Descriptivist Account of Aesthetic Attributions." *Revue Internationale de Philosophie* 28 (1974):336–52.

"What Is a Literary Theory?" *Centrum* 3 (1975):23–33.

"Is Art Essentially Institutional?" In *Culture and Art: An Anthology*, ed. Lars Aagaard-Mogensen (Nyborg: F. Lokkes Forlag, and Atlantic Highlands, N.J.: Humanities Press, 1976), pp. 194–209.

"The Status of Aesthetic Qualities." In *Proceedings of the VIIth International Congress of Aesthetics* (Bucharest 1972) (Bucharest: Editura Academie: 1976), vol. 2, pp. 183–85.

Essay-review of Peter Jones, *Philosophy and the Novel*. *Philosophy and Literature* 1 (1976):101–6.

"The Philosophy of Literature." In *Aesthetics: A Critical Anthology*, ed. George Dickie and Richard J. Sclafani (New York: St. Martin's Press, 1977), pp. 317–33.

"Metaphor and Falsity." *Journal of Aesthetics and Art Criticism* 35 (1977): 218–22.

"Aspects of Orality: A Short Commentary." *New Literary History* 8 (1976–77):521–30.

"*Languages of Art* and Art Criticism." *Erkenntnis* 12 (1978):95–118.

"Metaphorical Senses." *Noûs* 12 (1978):3–16.

"Some Problems of Critical Interpretation: A Commentary." *Journal of Aesthetics and Art Criticism* 36 (1978):351–60.

"Intending." In *Values and Morals: Essays in Honor of William Frankena, Charles Stevenson, and Richard Brandt*, ed. Alvin I. Goldman and Jaegwon Kim (Dordrecht: D. Reidel, 1978), pp. 163–84.

"What Are Critics For?" *Susquehanna University Studies* 10 (1978): 239–53.

"Aesthetic Intentions and Fictive Illocutions." In *What Is Literature?*, ed. Paul Hernadi (Bloomington: Indiana University Press, 1978), pp. 161–77.

"The Relevance of History to Art Criticism." In *History as a Tool in Critical Interpretation*, ed. Thomas F. Rugh and Erin R. Silva (Provo: Brigham Young University Press, 1978), pp. 1–18.

Essay-review of E. D. Hirsch, *The Philosophy of Composition*. *Rhetoric Society Quarterly* 8 (1978):109–13.

"Who Needs Critics?" *Arts Exchange* 2 (1978):6–9, 40.

"Verbal Style and Illocutionary Action." In *The Concept of Style*, ed. Berel Lang (Philadelphia: University of Pennsylvania Press, 1979), pp. 149–68.

"In Defense of Aesthetic Value." Presidential Address to Eastern Division, American Philosophical Association. In *Proceedings and Addresses of the American Philosophical Association* 52 (1979): 723–49.

"Demystifying Metaphor." Essay-review of Paul Ricoeur's *Rule of Metaaphor*. *University of Toronto Quarterly* 49 (1979):79–83.

"Reader Meets Text." Essay-review of three books. *Sewanee Review* 87 (1979):639–46.

"The Role of Psychological Explanation in Aesthetics." In *Perceiving Artworks*, ed. John Fisher (Philadelphia: Temple University Press, 1980), pp. 185–212.

"Right Readings and Good Readings." *Literature in Performance* 1 (1980): 10–22.

"Motives and Intentions." In *Action and Responsibility*, ed. Michael Bradie and Myles Brand (Bowling Green, O.: Bowling Green State University Press, 1980), pp. 71–79.

"Contemporary Issues and Values in Humanistic Perspective." *Yearbook of Comparative and General Literature* 29 (1980):28–32.

"Understanding Music." In *On Criticizing Music: Five Philosophical Perspectives*, ed. Kingsley Price (Baltimore: Johns Hopkins Press, 1981), pp. 55–73.

"Fiction as Representation." *Synthese* 46 (1981):291–314.

"Aesthetic Value in Literature." *Comparative Literature Studies* 18 (1981): 238–47.

"Logic and Rhetoric." *Teaching Philosophy* 4 (1981):249–60.

"The Name and Nature of Criticism." In *What Is Criticism?*, ed. Paul Hernadi (Bloomington: Indiana University Press, 1982), pp. 151–61.

"An Aesthetic Definition of Art." In *What Is Art?*, ed. Hugh Curtler (forthcoming).

"Notes on Forgery." In *The Forger's Art: Forgery and the Philosophy of Art*, ed. Denis Dutton (forthcoming).

Selected Book Reviews

Iredell Jenkins, *Art and the Human Enterprise*. *Journal of Philosophy* 57 (1960): 163–67.

Jerome Stolnitz, *Aesthetics and Philosophy of Art Criticism*. *Journal of Philosophy* 57 (1960):623–25.

William Righter, *Logic and Criticism*. *Foundations of Language* 3 (1967): 112–14.

Cyril Barrett, S.J., ed., *Collected Papers on Aesthetics*. *Journal of Aesthetics and Art Criticism* 26 (1967):144–46.

Etienne Gilson, *The Arts of the Beautiful*. *Philosophical Review* 77 (1968): 114–16.

Matthew Lipman, *What Happens in Art? Journal of Aesthetics and Art Criticism* 26 (1968):410–12.

Susanne Langer, *Mind: An Essay on Human Feeling*, I. *Harvard Educational Review* 38 (1968):353–57.

Ludwig Wittgenstein, *Lectures and Conversations on Aesthetics, Psychology and Religious Belief*, ed. Cyril Barrett, S.J. *Journal of Aesthetics and Art Criticism* 26 (1968):554–57.

Robert E. Mueller, *Art: The Cybernetics of Creative Communicatin*. *The Activist* 9 (1968):28–31.

Allan C. Purves, *Elements of Writing about a Literary Work*. *Journal of Aesthetic Education* 3 (1969):165–67.

Nelson Goodman, *Languages of Art*. *Philosophy of Science* 37 (1970):458–63.

Edgar De Bruyne, *The Esthetics of the Middle Ages*. *Journal of Aesthetic Education* 4 (1970):153–55.

Rudolf Arnheim, *Visual Thinking*. *Journal of Aesthetic Education* 5 (1971): 181–85.

Allan Rodway, *The Truths of Fiction. College English* 33 (1972):597–99.

Morton W. Bloomfield, ed., *In Search of Literary Theory. Centrum* 1 (1973): 77–81.

Robert Venturi et al., *Learning from Las Vegas. Journal of Aesthetics and Art Criticism* 33 (1974):245–46.

Norman Mailer, *The Faith of Graffiti. Journal of Aesthetics and Art Criticism* 33 (1975):373–74.

Karl Aschenbrenner, *The Concepts of Criticism. Journal of Aesthetics and Art Criticism* 34 (1975):199–202.

Daniel Bell, *The Cultural Contradictions of Capitalism. Journal of Aesthetics and Art Criticism* 35 (1976):229–31.

Wladislaw Tatarkiewicz, *History of Aesthetics. Journal of the History of Ideas* 37 (1976):549–55.

John M. Ellis, *The Theory of Literary Criticism. Comparative Literature* 28 (1976):177–80.

Lehman Engel, *The Critics. Journal of Aesthetics and Art Criticism* 35 (1977): 499–500.

William O. Hendricks, *Grammars of Style and Styles of Grammar. Journal of Aesthetics and Art Criticism* 36 (1977):106–7.

Robert Nisbet, *Sociology as an Art Form. Journal of Aesthetics and Art Criticism* 36 (1977):240–41.

Lewis P. Simpson, ed., *The Possibilities of Order: Cleanth Brooks and His Work. Journal of Modern Literature* 6 (1977):577–78.

Richard H. Brown, *A Poetic for Sociology. Journal of Aesthetics and Art Criticism* 36 (1978):380–81.

Douglas Davis and Allison Simmons, *The New Television: A Public/Private Art. Journal of Aesthetics and Art Criticism* 36 (1978):515–16.

Teun A. van Dijk, ed., *Pragmatics of Language and Literature. Journal of Aesthetics and Criticism* 27 (1978):96–97.

Morroe Berger, *Real and Imagined Worlds: The Novel and Social Science. Journal of Aesthetics and Art Criticism* 37 (1979):509–10.

Trevor Eaton, ed., *Essays in Literary Semantics. Journal of Aesthetics and Art Criticism* 38 (1979):215–17.

R. W. Bailey et al., *The Sign: Semiotics around the World. Journal of Aesthetics and Art Criticism* 38 (1980):337–38.

Edward A. Lippman, *A Humanistic Philosophy of Music. Musical Quarterly* 66 (1980):305–8.

Wayne Booth, *Critical Understanding: The Powers and Limits of Pluralism. Philosophy and Literature* 4 (1980):257–65.

Geoffrey Hartman et al., *Deconstruction and Criticism. Journal of Aesthetics and Art Criticism* 39 (1980):219–21.

John R. Searle, *Expression and Meaning: Studies in the Theory of Speech Acts. International Studies in Philosophy* 13 (1981):116–18.

Index

Abduction from the Seraglio (Mozart), 350–51
Ackerman, James, 225
Adler, Renata, 32–33
Aenead (Virgil), 345–46
Aesthetic, 312–15; marks of, 23, 28, 338–39. *See also* Aesthetic enjoyment; Aesthetic experience; Aesthetic value
Aesthetic auxiliaries, 120
Aesthetic capability, 119, 121–24
Aesthetic concepts, 103–5. *See also* Aesthetic qualities
Aesthetic education, 119–24, 318; dilemma of, 30–32
Aesthetic emotion, 35–36
Aesthetic enjoyment, 22, 24–45, 68–69, 255, 287–88; defined, 41–42; value of, 59–60. *See also* Aesthetic gratification; Aesthetic satisfaction; Pleasure
Aesthetic experience, 22, 77–92, 240–41, 285–97, 321, 337–39; changing concept of, 91–92; criteria of, 288–89; defined, 81; emotion in, 82, 84–85, 294–95; value of, 68–71. *See also* Aesthetic enjoyment; Aesthetic perception; Aesthetic value; Coherence; Completeness; Unity
Aesthetic gratification, 22–23; defined, 22. *See also* Aesthetic enjoyment
Aesthetic judgment, 103–6, 316–31; as aid to apprehension, 328; vs. judgment of tendency, 327; vs. personal endorsement, 328–30; vs. prediction, 326–27; and truth value, 330; vs. verdict, 327. *See also* Aesthetic value; Art criticism; Critical evaluation
Aesthetic justice, 115–19
Aesthetic opportunity, 119–21
Aesthetic perception, 96–100. *See also* Aesthetic experience; Taste
Aesthetic point of view, 15–34, 77–78, 106, 110, 284, 320, 335, 370; defined, 19–21. *See also* Aesthetic enjoyment; Aesthetic experience; Aesthetic value; Art for art's sake
Aesthetic qualities, 93–110, 142, 227–33, 370; defined, 105–6; as grounds of aesthetic judgment, 103, 110; as regional qualities, 106; semantic view of, 100–103, 107; types of, 107–110; value of, 110. *See also* Expressiveness in art
Aesthetic relevance, 28–30, 332–51
Aesthetic satisfaction, 36. *See also* Aesthetic enjoyment
Aesthetic theory, 77–78, 298–300, 302–4; and aesthetic education, 318; and anthropology, 306–12; and art criticism, 316–18; and art history, 304–6
Aesthetic value, 19–27, 66–71, 103–6, 112–13, 119, 185–87, 210, 320–21, 326–31; defined, 21, 23, 320; and originality, 342–47; primary and secondary criteria of, 42–45, 208–18; and skill, 347–51. *See also* Aesthetic judgment; Art criticism; Artistic goodness; Coherence;

Aesthetic value (*continued*)
  Completeness; Critical evaluation;
  Regional qualities; Unity
Aesthetic wealth, 113–14, 119
Aesthetic welfare, 111–13
Aldrich, Virgil, 99–100, 105
Allusiveness, 200, 234. *See also* Intentionalism
Anderson, Richard, 308–9
Anscombe, Elizabeth, 128, 131
Anthropology, 306–12
Antonioni, Michelangelo, 33
Appassionata (Beethoven), 16, 20
Architecture, 17–18, 161, 292
Artistotle, 38, 40, 45, 71, 78, 268, 317
Arnheim, Rudolph, 234–35, 243, 256, 292
Arnstine, Donald, 72–76
Arrow, Kenneth, 116
Art and Illusion (Gombrich), 227–33
Art as Experience (Dewey), 78, 354–56
Art creation, 127–28, 138, 141, 239–62; as expression, 244–46; finalistic theory of, 244, 246–49, 251, 254; inspiration for, 256–57; phases of, 256–57; propulsive theory of, 244–46, 251, 254. *See also* Incept
Art critic, 147–64, 210, 224; primary task of, 160
Art criticism, 147–218; and art history, 158; cultural, 370; defined, 320; failures of, 161–64; inevitability of, 148–49; relevance of history to, 219–35, 272–76. *See also* Aesthetic judgment; Aesthetic value; Critical evaluation; Cultural criticism of art; Interpretation of art
Art for art's sake, 32–34, 69–71. *See also* Autonomy of art
Art history, 304–6, 346–47. *See also* Aesthetic theory
Artifact, 311–12
Artistic freedom, 118, 127–28, 167, 173–74
Artistic goodness, 79–80, 87–90. *See also* Aesthetic value
Artkind instance, 285, 306
Artwork, 80, 128–30, 151, 337–38; as ascriptive concept, 137–38; changing concept of, 91–92; definition of, 19, 299; fictive character of, 369–70; immanence theory of, 170–76, 179–80, 185–87; institutional theory of, 125–43; issuing of, 158; ontology of, 139; perceptual and semantic properties of, 337–38; significance theory of, 166–70, 172–76, 179–80, 183–87; as symbol, 102–3, 107, 166–70, 362, 368; uniqueness of, 213–14
Artworld, 120, 133–35, 143, 310–11. *See also* Artwork
Asch, Solomon E., 275n
Ashley, Robert, 323–24
At Rest (Kandinsky), 230–31
Auden, W. H., 33n
Austin, John L., 191, 195
Author, defined, 189–90
Autonomy of art, 352–70. *See also* Art criticism, relevance of history to; Art for art's sake; Inherent value of art; Intentional fallacy
Avant garde, 89–92, 153–54, 312–15, 321–24, 342, 345

Baensch, Otto, 95–96
Balinese cockfight, 364–65
Balzac, Honoré de, 24–25
Barbaro, Umberto, 357–58
Barber, Samuel, 346
Baylis, Charles, 55–58
Beauty, 35–36, 39, 62, 77
Beethoven, Ludwig von, 16, 20, 25–26, 29, 252–53, 260
Bell, Clive, 35–36, 39
Bernard, Saint, 29–30, 32
Binkley, Timothy, 312–15
Blow-up (Antonioni), 12
Bohannon, Laura, 126
Bosanquet, Bernard, 186
Bradford, Curtis, 254n
Bradley, Francis Herbert, 63
Brandt, Richard, 57, 59–60
Brillo Box (Warhol), 137, 141
Broad, C. D., 48n
Broadway Boogie-Woogie (Mondrian), 142, 227–29
Brooks, Cleanth, 209, 215
Burke, Edmund, 38–40, 89

Burke, Kenneth, 277n
Burroughs, Edgar Rice, 24, 26–27
Butler, Samuel, 204–5
Byron, George Gordon, Lord, 173

Cage, John, 153–54, 156, 160
Callen, Donald, 334–35
Camp sensibility, 31–32
Canaday, John, 332
Carter, Elliott, 121
Catharsis, 86. *See also* Completeness
Cavell, Stanley, 19n
Cervantes, Miguel de, 199
Chopin, Frédéric, 350
Close, A. J., 198–99
Cohen, Marshall, 79n, 87–89
Coherence, 84, 214, 293–95. *See also* Aesthetic experience; Completeness; Unity
Coleridge, Samuel Taylor, 45
Collingwood, Robin G., 245–46, 251
Completeness, 82–86, 293, 296. *See also* Aesthetic experience; Coherence; Unity
Conceptual art, 19, 154, 313–15
Creativity. *See* Art creation
Critical criterion, 42–45, 210, 213, 217
Critical defection, 162
Critical diversion, 161–62
Critical dogmatism, 162–63
Critical evaluation, 147–64, 226, 316–51; autonomy of, 188–207, 219–35; and judgment of aesthetic value, 23–24; primacy of, 160. *See also* Aesthetic value; Art criticism
Critical interpretation. *See* Interpretation of art
Critical reasons, 208–18, 319, 321, 332–51; authoritative, 333–35; circumstantial, 333–35; explanatory, 333–34; justificatory, 333; moral considerations as, 335–37; relevance of, 337, 339–40. *See also* Aesthetic relevance; Aesthetic value; Art criticism; Critical criterion; Critical evaluation
Criticism, 318–19. *See also* Art Criticism; Critical evaluation
Crumb, George, 153

Culler, Jonathan, 206, 366
Cultural competence, 353, 360–61
Cultural criticism of art, 370
Cultural services, 122–23
Culture, 352–53; autonomy of art in, 361–62, 366–67; continuity of art with, 352–70; semiotic theory of, 362–66. *See also* Marxist art theory

Dada, 167, 173
Danto, Arthur, 120, 135–38, 141, 283, 308
Dean, Suzanne, 202
Defoe, Daniel, 204–5
DeLio, Thomas, 321–23
DeMott, Benjamin, 151–52
Depiction, 178–79, 181, 222–23
Detached affect, 288, 290–92
Dewey, John, 46, 53, 62–64, 75–76, 78–84, 87, 148, 186, 240, 246, 248–49, 286–87, 354–56
Dickie, George, 81–87, 94n, 99, 131, 133–35, 283, 293–95, 310–12
Diffey, T. J., 131–32, 134–35
Dissanayake, Ellen, 309–10
Donnellan, Keith, 202–3
Don Quixote (Cervantes), 198–99
Dostoyevsky, Fyodor, 253
Drabble, Margaret, 191
Dryden, John, 254n
Ducasse, Curt J., 35n
Duchamp, Marcel, 161
Duncan-Jones, Austin, 34n, 51n, 55n
Dürer, Albrecht, 219–20
Dutton, Denis, 309n–10n
Dvořák, Antonin, 182

Eagleton, Terry, 356–57
East Coker (Eliot), 264–65
Ecker, David, 246–49
Eichner, Hans, 326–27
Eisenstein, Sergei, 89, 291
Elegy, 129–30
Elgar, Edward, 332
Eliot, T. S., 200, 264–65
Ellis, A. J., 206n
Emerson, Ralph Waldo, 65–69
Ends in themselves, 63
Engel, Lehman, 154–55

Eroica (Beethoven), 25–26
Evaluation of art. *See* Aesthetic judgment; Aesthetic value; Art criticism; Critical evaluation
Exemplification. *See* Expressiveness in art
Exodus (Uris), 15–16, 20
Experience, 78–84. *See also* Aesthetic experience
Expressiveness in art, 101–3, 107–10, 227–33. *See also* Aesthetic qualities

Fangor, Wojciech, 296
Feldman, Anita, 322
Fiction, 173–75, 191, 369–70. *See also* Representation
Firth, Roderick, 57
Forgery, 28, 344
Forte, Allen, 252–53
Francesco, Piero della, 221–22
Fraser, G. S., 167n
Freedman, Marcia, 103–4

Gál, Hans, 255–56
Gas Masks (Tretiakov), 291
Geertz, Clifford, 364–66
Genre, 129–30
Gerard, David, 31
Gestalt, 86, 95, 257. *See also* Aesthetic qualities; Completeness; Unity
Getlein, Frank, 233–34
Gill, Brendan, 16n
Glass, Philip, 321–22
Goldberger, Paul, 158–59
Goldman, Alvin, 190, 353
Gombrich, E. H., 142, 227–33, 283, 292, 303–4, 361
Goodman, Nelson, 101–3, 107, 123, 127, 191, 228, 283, 292, 344, 361
Good of a kind, 18–19
Gorky, Maxim, 16

Haezrahi, Pepita, 88n
Haggin, B. H., 346
Hamlet (Shakespeare), 294–95
Hampshire, Stuart, 212n, 347
Hark, I. R., 204n
Henahan, Donald, 153
Henle, Paul, 267–69, 271n, 274

Hermerén, Göran, 205–6
Herrick, Robert, 201
Hirsch, E. D., 200–201, 204–5
Hitch, Stewart, 322
Hochmuth, Rolf, 32
Homer, 335–37
Hook, Sidney, 53n
Hopi drama, 307
Hough, Graham, 197–98
Housman, A. E., 173, 206–7
Hume, David, 52n, 100
Hungerland, Isabel, 94, 103, 269–70
Hutcheson, Francis, 97
Huxley, Aldous, 71–72

Ibsen, Henrik, 33
Idiot, The (Dostoyevsky), 253
Iliad (Homer), 335–37
Illocutionary act, 190–92, 194–97, 364, 366–67
Immanence theory, 170–76, 179–80, 185–87
Incept, 239, 247, 250–53. *See also* Art creation
Inherent value of art, 65–76; and catharsis, 71; defined, 70; and emotions, 72–75; vs. incidental value, 70; and perceptual awareness, 74–76. *See also* Value
Institutional facts, 128–29. *See also* Artworld; Social institution; Social practice
Institutional theory of art, 125–43, 310–12
Intentional fallacy, 161–62, 164, 188–207, 258–59, 269; vs. intentional definition of art, 306
Intentionalism, 188–207; defined, 193
Interpretation of art, 152, 155, 157, 165–87, 188; defined, 165; and artist's intentions, 188–207; and history, 219–35; rule-guided, 176–78; validity of, 176–77. *See also* Meaning
Intrinsic value, 46–64, 66–69
Intuition, 80; of intrinsic value, 59–60, 62
Irony, 203–7, 269. *See also* Intentionalism

Jakobson, Roman, 363
James, Henry, 33, 242
James, William, 61
Janson, H. W., 346–47
Johnson, Samuel, 36–37, 44–45, 266, 335–36
Judd, Donald, 313

Kandinsky, Vasili, 230–31
Kant, Immanuel, 52, 89, 290, 345
Keane, Walter, 332–33
Keats, John, 267
Kennick, W. E., 79, 166, 211–12, 214–16
Khatchadourian, Haig, 300–301, 342–43
Kierkegaard, Sören, 206
King Lear (Shakespeare), 37–38, 335–36
Klee, Paul, 231
Knights, L. C., 260–61
Kohlberg, Lawrence, 123
Kozloff, Max, 164
Krenek, Ernst, 253n
Kupperman, Joel, 296

Lang, Olga, 16n
Langer, Susanne, 101, 369
Lee, Dorothy, 307
Leibniz, Gottfried Wilhelm, 63
Lenin, V. I., 16, 29, 32
Lesser Hippias (Plato?), 335
Levinson, Jerrold, 301–2
Lévi-Strauss, Claude, 363–64
Levitine, George, 234
Lewis, C. I., 48, 54–58
Literary criticism. *See* Art criticism; Critical evaluation; Interpretation of art; Literature; Metaphor
Literature, 73–76, 167–68, 173–75; institutional practices of, 129–30; symbols in, 102
Lowenberg, Ina, 141
Lotman, Jurij, 362
Lowes, J. L., 242

Macbeth (Shakespeare), 266
McCarthy, Mary, 332–34
Mahler, Gustav, 182

Malraux, André, 303–4
Mandelbaum, Maurice, 306
Margolis, Joseph, 139–41, 330–31
Maritain, Jacques, 28
Mark, T. C., 349–51
Marxist art theory, 356–59
Maslow, Abraham, 85–86, 88
Mathers, Robert, 94n
Matisse, Henri, 255
Meager, Ruby, 213
Meaning: and aesthetic value, 185–86; linguistic, 176–77; musical, 182–87; pictorial, 178–79; symbolic, 180–82, 184–87. *See also* Metaphor; Significance theory
Meiss, Millard, 221–22
Merquior, J. G., 359
Metaphor, 180, 263–80; appropriateness of, 266–68; as irony, 269; novelty of, 272–76; object-comparison theory of, 263–69, 273; and oxymoron, 268–69, 278; verbal-opposition theory of, 264, 268, 270–80. *See also* Expressiveness in art
Meyer, Leonard, 86, 321
Mill, John Stuart, 91, 179
Mills, George, 307–8
Milton, John, 198
Mitchells, K., 94, 98–99, 103
Moby Dick (Melville), 181–82
Mondrian, Piet, 142, 227–29
Moore, George Edward, 47–51, 59–61, 63
Moore, Henry, 246–47
Moore, Marianne, 258–59
Morawski, Stefan, 358
Morris, Charles, 101
Mothersill, Mary, 211n, 213
Mozart, Wolfgang Amadeus, 246, 256n, 350–51
Mukařovský, Jan, 367–68
Music, 74–75, 83–86, 101–3, 169–71, 182–87, 260, 348–51

Nabokov, Vladimir, 332
Navajo sand painting, 307, 309
Nemetz, Anthony, 269n
Nervi, Pier Luigi, 20n
Ngal, M. a M., 359

Nietzsche, Friedrich, 148
Night Fishing at Antibes (Picasso), 233–35
Night of the Iguana, The (Williams), 163
Noland, Kenneth, 164
Normative explanation, 319, 321; and critical jusitification, 332–33, 339–40. *See also* Art criticism

Odyssey (Homer), 335–37, 345–46
Oldenburg, Claes, 19
Op art, 141
Open concept, 91–92
Originality, 90, 342–47. *See also* Aesthetic value
Oxymoron. *See* Metaphor

Painting, 75–76, 178–79, 224–33. *See also* Depiction; Portrayal; Representation
Pale Fire (Nabokov), 332–34
Panofsky, Erwin, 219, 226, 304–5
Pap, Arthur, 279–80
Parr, A. E., 113
Parsons, Michael, 123
Patrick, Catherine, 243
"Peak-experiences," 85–86, 88
Percy, Walker, 270n
Phaedo (Plato), 42–43
Philosophical Enquiry into the Origin of Our Ideas of the Sublime and Beautiful (Burke), 38–40
Piaget, Jean, 123
Picasso, Pablo, 233–35, 241, 252, 256
Pietà (Michelangelo), 140
Plato, 78, 125, 147, 335
Pleasure, 36–37; aesthetic, 36–37, 88–90, 287–88. *See also* Aesthetic enjoyment; Aesthetic gratification; Aesthetic satisfaction
Poetics (Aristotle), 38
Poetry, 129–30, 167–68, 173–75, 193, 197–98, 258–60; allusiveness in, 200; computer, 195; indeterminacy of, 200–201. *See also* Metaphor
Point of view, 318–19. *See also* Aesthetic point of view
Pop art, 180–81
Portrayal, 179–80, 222. *See also* Depiction; Representation

Potemkin (Eisenstein), 89
Powell, Anthony, 151–52
Pratt, Carroll C., 74
Principia Ethica (Moore), 47–48

Ransom, John Crowe, 263–65, 267
Read, Herbert, 309n
Reference, 179, 192–93, 195; and allusion, 200; of pictures, 179
Regan, Thomas, 26n
Regional qualities, 94–95, 106, 111, 175, 247–49, 338, 370; affirmative, 340; perception of, 99–100. *See also* Aesthetic qualities; Gestalt
Reichert, John, 198n
Representation, 179–80, 191–93, 195, 197, 369. *See also* Depiction; Illocutionary act
Rich, Alan, 163
Richards, I. A., 265–66
Rieff, Philip, 353
Rilke, Rainer Maria, 129
Rosenbaum, S. P., 242
Rosenberg, Jakob, 224–25, 227–29
Ross, Harold, 235
Rossi-Landi, Ferruccio, 364
Rudner, Richard, 347
Rukeyser, Muriel, 251

Sargeant, Winthrop, 182
Schapiro, Meyer, 29–30
Schiller, J. C. F. von, 290
Shoenberg, Harold, C., 332
Schongauer, Martin, 224, 227, 230
Schopenhauer, Arthur, 89
Schubert, Franz, 255–56
Scott, Geoffrey, 17, 20
Scriven, Michael, 278–80
Sculpture, 168–69, 172–73
Semiotic. *See* Artwork; Culture
Sense of pictures, 179
Severini, Gino, 227–28
Shakespeare, William, 37–38, 44–45, 208, 265–66, 278, 294–95, 335
Shirley, D. L., 296–97
Sibley, Frank, 93–98, 109, 142, 283
Significance theory, 166–70, 172–73, 175–76, 179–80, 183–87
Significant form, 35–36, 77
Simon, John, 163–64

Sircello, Guy, 329
Sirridge, Mary, 198n
Skill, 347–51
Skinner, Quentin, 194–95
Slote, Michael, 327
Smetana, Frederick, 182
Smith, Ralph, 122
Social institution, 126, 134, 137, 158. *See also* Artworld
Social practice, 126, 134. *See also* Artworld
Socrates, 147, 157, 335
Sontag, Susan, 31–33
Spender, Stephen, 251
Spenser, Edmund, 200
Spoils of Poynton, The (James), 33, 242
Srzednicki, J., 276n
Stallman, R. W., 200
Stauffer, Donal, 258–59
Stevens, Wallace, 276n
Stevenson, C. L., 165–66, 186–87
Stolnitz, Jerome, 39n, 326–27, 348–49
Strawson, P. F., 137
String Quartet in E-flat, Op. 127 (Beethoven). 252–53, 260
Style, 225
Sublimity, 39–40, 89
Symbolism, 180–82, 184–87
Swift, Jonathan, 204

Taste, 97–100; changes of, 117. *See also* Aesthetic qualities
Tate, Allen, 251
Tate, Nahum, 37–38
Taylor, Jeremy, 274
Taylor, Paul, 21, 58
Taylor, Roger, 341
Thomas, Dylan, 208
Thurber, James, 179
Tischler, Hans, 28
Tiv, 126
Tolhurst, William, 199–200
Tomas, Vincent, 249, 253
Tormey, Alan, 108–9, 329–30
Tovey, Donald Francis, 183

Unfinished Symphony (Schubert), 255–56
Uniqueness of art, 213–14

Unity, 293–95, 341–42; of aesthetic experience, 82–87; of an artwork, 82–83; as ground of aesthetic judgment, 103–5. *See also* Aesthetic experience; Aesthetic value; Coherence; Completeness
Urmson, J. O., 36, 41, 80

Valéry, Paul, 250–51, 253–55
Value, 19–20, 46, 49, 63–64; consummatory judgment of, 62–63; and criticism, 318–20; ideal observer theories of, 57; incidental, 70; inherent, 48, 54; instrumental, 50–54; intrinsic, 46–64, 66–69. *See also* Aesthetic value
Value judgment, 104–5
Van Meegeren, Hans, 344
Vermeer, Jan, 344
Villemain, Francis, 115
Virtuosity, 349–51
Vitruvius, 17

Wallas, Graham, 243
Walsh, Dorothy, 43–44, 93, 103
Walton, Kendall, 142, 299–300
Waste Land, The (Eliot), 200
Weitz, Morris, 44–45
Wheeler, Michael, 200
When We Dead Awaken (Ibsen), 33
Whitman, Walt, 208
Wholeness, 289, 293–95. *See also* Coherence; Completeness; Unity
Williams, Tennessee, 163
Wimsatt, W. K., 259, 266
Wisdom, John, 210, 217–18
Wittgenstein, Ludwig, 143, 284
Wordsworth, William, 102–3, 193–94, 208–9, 260–61
Work of art. *See* Artwork
Wotton, Sir Henry, 17
Wreen, Michael, 324

Yeats, William Butler, 201–2, 254n

Zenzen, M. J., 291–92
Ziff, Paul, 178, 217
Zuckerkandl, Victor, 252
Zumbo, Gaetano, 287–88, 291

The Aesthetic Point of View

Designed by G. T. Whipple, Jr.
Composed by Eastern Graphics
in 10 point Palatino (Linotron 202), 2 points leaded,
with display lines in Palatino.
Printed offset by Thomson-Shore, Inc.
on Warren's Number 66 text, 50 pound basis.

Library of Congress Cataloging in Publication Data
BEARDSLEY, MONROE C.
    The aesthetic point of view.
    Bibliography: p.
    Includes index.
    1. Aesthetics.   2. Art criticism.   I. Title.
BH39.B37   1982   701'.1'7   82-71601
ISBN 0-8014-1250-1

DATE DUE

MAY 0 5 2019			

84-1710

701.17
B38a

Beardsley, Monroe C.
The aesthetic point of view.

The Patrick and Beatrice Haggerty
Library
Mount Mary College
Milwaukee, Wisconsin 53222